FIFTY YEARS OF PAKISTAN'S ECONOMY

Traditional Topics and Contemporary Concerns

FIFTY YEARS OF PAKISTAN'S ECONOMY

Traditional Topics and Contemporary Concerns

Edited by

Shahrukh Rafi Khan

OXFORD
UNIVERSITY PRESS

OXFORD
UNIVERSITY PRESS

Great Clarendon Street, Oxford OX2 6DP

Oxford University Press is a department of the University of Oxford.
It furthers the University's objective of excellence in research, scholarship,
and education by publishing worldwide in

Oxford New York

Athens Auckland Bangkok Bogotá Buenos Aires Calcutta
Cape Town Chennai Dar es Salaam Delhi Florence Hong Kong Istanbul
Karachi Kuala Lumpur Madrid Melbourne Mexico City Mumbai
Nairobi Paris São Paulo Singapore Taipei Tokyo Toronto Warsaw
with associated companies in Berlin Ibadan

Oxford is a registered trade mark of Oxford University Press
in the UK and in certain other countries

HC
440.5
.F5
1999

ISBN 0 19 577826 X

Printed in Pakistan at
Al-Rehman Paper Craft, Karachi.
Published by
Ameena Saiyid, Oxford University Press
5-Bangalore Town, Sharae Faisal
PO Box 13033, Karachi-75350, Pakistan.

Contents

Part I. Introduction

Part II. Traditional Topics

A: The Macro Debate

B: Sectoral Issues

PART ONE

INTRODUCTION

1

Traditional Topics and Contemporary Concerns: An Overview and Summary of Findings

*Shahrukh Rafi Khan**

1. INTRODUCTION

Fifty years of Pakistan's economic experience represents the case history of a country as a laboratory where currently fashionable economic ideas are being tried out. This is one of the main themes of this book. A related theme is the transition, also a response to imported ideas, from the more traditional macro and sectoral concerns to a new set of concerns. These ideas include a concern for human development in a broad sense and, more specifically, with poverty, women and development, and a concern for the environmental impact of economic development.

That these ideas were imported does not necessarily make them less relevant. Also, from the early 1980s onwards, the ground was ripe, at least in the NGO sector, for such ideas and often they were spontaneously adopted, internalized, and brought into the public sphere. The ostensible acceptance of these ideas by the government and lip service to such ideas in government documents can, however, be viewed as the outcome of a donor agenda. How broadly these ideas will be accepted by the general public will depend on the outcome of the public debate that has already begun at various levels. It seems safe to say that environmental consciousness has begun to set in quite widely.

* Executive Director, Sustainable Development Policy Institute, Islamabad.

In section 2 of this introductory chapter, the notion of economic experimentation will be demonstrated by associating economic growth rates to periods in which different economic philosophies were applied. In sections 3 to 5, the same theme will be demonstrated by reviewing the findings of the book's authors. Also identified is what the authors indicate to be the main economic problems faced by the country, in the past and currently, and what they view to be some of the important solutions. Section 3 focuses on the macro debate, section 4 on traditional sectoral issues, and section 5 on 'contemporary concerns'. The reader will note that all chapters are very rich in findings, and the interpretive summary of findings in sections 3 to 5 is expected to whet the appetite for the main course.

2. FIFTY YEARS OF EXPERIMENTATION

Table 1 presents a summary of Pakistan's key economic growth rates and assists in telling the story of economic experimentation in Pakistan's economic history.

Table 1
Key (annual average) economic growth rates

	GDP	Agriculture	Manufacturing
1950s	3.1	1.6	7.7
1960s	6.8	5.1	9.9
1970s	4.8	2.4	5.5
1980s	6.5	5.4	8.2
1990s	5.0	4.4	5.5

Source: Banuri, Khan, and Mahmood, (1997, Table 2.1) for the growth rates for 1950s, Government of Pakistan, *Economic Survey 1996–97*, Statistical Appendix (1997, pp. 2-3), for the 1960s, 1970s, 1980s, and 1990s growth rates.
Note: Growth rates for the 1990s (based on 1990–91 to 1995–6 data) are straight averages since when computing annual averages, we found the co-efficients to be insignificant and the fit of the regressions very poor.

The 1950s was a period of the 'big push' theory which came with the birth of development economics in the late 1940s and early 1950s (Rosenstein-Rodan, 1943; Nurkse, 1953). In a nutshell, the big push theory was based on the idea that if there could be enough capital investment, growth would take off. The source for this capital accumulation could either be domestic saving or foreign aid. Aid was tied to planning which was then in vogue. Soviet inter-war progress had made a big impression on economists and Third World decision-makers. Following its independence, Pakistan clocked up a fairly reasonable growth rate considering it had to confront all the adjustment problems normally faced by a newly born country, and also the hostility from a neighbour due to the acrimonious nature of its birth.

Notwithstanding planning as exercises in constructing elaborate wish lists, Pakistani policy makers, from the country's inception, were warm to the trickle down market-based economic philosophy. With the coming to power of the first military regime of Ayub Khan (1958–68) in the late 1950s, enterprise was lauded even if highly regulated. Trickle down was expected to occur in the form of jobs and eventually higher wages because of expanding enterprise.

The 1960s represented a boom decade particularly for manufacturing which had a 10 per cent growth rate. One should keep in mind the small base in this period and that sustaining such high growth rates becomes progressively more difficult. Free market economics did not prevail. While aid and market oriented policies gave the economy an impetus, the nature of the crony capitalism practised sowed the seeds of its own destruction and also the seeds of a protected and non-competitive weak economy in the future. Rent seeking was rampant and the favoured accumulated huge economic power via external and internal protection. This concentration of economic power and the perceived injustice brought about a backlash in the form of rioting that put an end to the Ayub Khan period.

The populist response to these crony capitalist driven inequalities was nationalization and the basic needs approach. Leaving social development to the outcome of the market process was found to be too harsh a social prescription. Scholars felt that the market failed in various ways and/or worked too slowly in ameliorating the condition of the poor. Persistent unemployment was one such problem and so the answer was to target the really poor and make sure that at least their basic needs were met (Haq and Baqai, 1976). On a more radical level, the market approach was being completely rejected and less developed countries were viewed to be underdeveloped because they continued to be subjected to neo-colonial forms of exploitation with foreign trade, aid, and investments as vehicles for such exploitation (Baran, 1957; Frank, 1967).

The radical ideas of the 1960s found expression in Zulfikar Ali Bhutto's (1970–77) nationalizations. Bhutto's motivations have been questioned, and it has been suggested that his populist ideology was a convenient excuse to break the economic stronghold of political forces opposed to him, including the industrialists. Nationalizations, the civil war and the subsequent division of the country, and the oil price hike adversely affected growth rates in the early 1970s. The revival in the late 1970s could probably be partly accounted for by an increase in remittances that came in the wake of the migration to the Middle East to service the needs of the booming oil economies. Even so, the Zulfikar Ali Bhutto regime left behind a growth crisis as well as a fiscal and payments crises. The successor military regime of Ziaul Haq (1977–88) called in the IMF for assistance in 1978–9.

The failure of a direct interventionist approach via planning, controls, regulations, and nationalizations brought the market approach back in the ascendancy in the 1980s and this change in economic philosophy was mirrored in Pakistan. These specific policy changes included privatization and deregulation and market determination of key macro prices such as interest rates and the exchange rates. External competition was to be encouraged by liberalizing foreign trade. Such economic liberalization is central to the IMF/World Bank initiated policies of structural adjustment (SA). Zia was sympathetic to this economic philosophy and his successors, Benazir Bhutto and Nawaz Sharif, have also endorsed it.[1]

Part Two of the book is concerned with the debate on macro issues, including reform and structural adjustment, and with traditional sectoral issues. However, the debate on structural adjustment and reform has also led to new concerns. Internationally, the economic philosophy underpinning structural adjustment met with several criticisms which have also had a policy impact in Pakistan. Two of the most prominent critiques have been based on the social and environmental insensitivity of the neo-liberal economic philosophy. A prominent social critique emerged from the UNICEF-sponsored book titled *Adjustment with a Human Face* (Cornia, Jolly, and Stewart, 1987). This and the follow-up criticism of structural adjustment and its regressive impact resulted in an attempt to give SA a human face. This is based on the concept of human development. It differs from basic needs by concentrating not directly on the basic needs of the poor and delivering supplements but more on making the poor better market players by ensuring investment in their education and health.

Evidence indicated that between 1987–8 and the early 1990s, the period coinciding with the intensification of structural adjustment in Pakistan, poverty increased and income distribution worsened. This happened as food prices rose by more than the general price level, unemployment increased due to public sector employment retrenchments and employment freezes, and real wages of skilled and unskilled labour declined (Khan and Aftab, 1996). In Pakistan, the critique of structural adjustment was responsible for a Social Action Programme accompanying the structural adjustment programmes in order to given it a human face. Pakistan committed about $ 7.7 for SAP-I (1991–2/1995–6) and over $10 billion for SAP-II (1997–8 to 2001–2).[2]

The main focus of SAP is to improve social sector attainment and reduce gender and regional gaps in the process. SAP I has made some progress in closing these gaps. However, SAP I has been less successful in reducing political interference, changing the focus of social sector interventions from the old 'bricks and mortar approach' and inducing the incorporation of a participatory approach into social sector development. It is unlikely that the latter objective will be attained by SAP II either, given past experience and the existing capacity in the public or NGO sectors. Issues of human development are addressed in the first two chapters of Part Three of the book.

One problem with an aggregate Social Action Programme type of approach is that while the concern is with human development, the delivery of relief is via a depersonalized strategy of improving health, schooling, and water supply. There is of course a hope that the poorest too will benefit from these social sector investments. Such an aggregate approach very easily misses its mark if the concern is with the poorest. Statistics show that those most in need of the benefits of social investments are least likely to be the beneficiaries.[3] The third chapter of Part Three of the book takes up the issue of poverty since the social critique of structural adjustment does not adequately account for the poverty critique.

Another prominent critique emerged with the publication of the World Commission Report, *Our Common Future*, which was also published in 1987. It became evident that the capacity of the eco-system to provide inputs for human activity and absorb the waste from this activity had been stretched to the limit. Furthermore, there was not an adequate realization that this had happened and that therefore the rights of future generations to the contributions of the eco-system and to a reasonable quality of life were being jeopardized by current generations. In Pakistan, such environmental problems are experienced in the form of deforestation, waterlogging and salinity, excessive and improper urban waste management, natural resource depletion, desertification, and industrial and auto emissions pollution of the air, water, and soil. While the environmental critique has less of a policy impact in Pakistan compared to the social critique, the environment has none the less become part of the policy agenda. The last chapter of the book addresses this critical and forward looking issue.

3. TRADITIONAL TOPICS: THE MACRO DEBATE

Chapters 2 and 3 in Part Two of the book highlight the macro debate. In Chapter 2, Nadeem ul Haque views the neglect of education as the principal cause of a feeble indigenous intellectual base for the development of reform ideas. Consequently, he argues, the country has been susceptible to the intellectual fashions of the time promoted by donor funding. Haque addresses the fundamental question of why reform has not been successful in Pakistan. He shows that Pakistan has been successful in generating economic growth and containing inflation but not in containing the fiscal and trade deficit. In order to attain the latter goals, reform has been needed and various reform attempts have been made reflecting the ideological inclinations of the regime in question and the economic philosophy in ascendancy at the time.

Several causes, other than the neglect of education, are prominent in explaining why reform has failed to date. First, all earlier attempts at reform were interventionist. Second, there has been a lack of serious conviction and promulgating reforms was merely a means for forestalling crises. Thus, once the crisis was over, the reforms were abandoned. Haque's explanation for such policy behaviour is that the State itself, or poor governance, is the problem. A weak administrative and incentive structure results in an exodus of talent and in corruption and hence, an inability to formulate and execute reform.

As though to belie Haque's assertion that there are no indigenous intellectual reform ideas, Javed Akbar Ansari, also writing on macro-stabilization issues in Chapter 3, presents an uncompromising Islamist perspective on reform, or indeed, revolution. Ansari is also concerned with the agency that implements reform, and starts his chapter with the nature of the Pakistani state. He then ventures into a detailed periodized account of Pakistan's economic history.

Ansari's categorization of policy experimentation is different from those conventionally used; none the less, his thorough and detailed account of Pakistan's economic history once again shows varying economic influences accompanying changing political regimes. The *Second Five Year Plan 1960–65* (1960) embodied the pro-private sector economic ideology of the Harvard Advisory Group. Ayub's fall is attributed to a loss of imperial support and this ushered in the populist Bhutto era (1970–77). However, this period was characterized by waste, inefficiency, and *ad-hoc*ism and the economic legacy was that of deficits, inflation and, despite the socialist reforms, a worsening of the income distribution.

The Zia era is viewed as a modified version of Ayub's market-oriented dispensation, with an overlay of Islamic symbolism. These market-oriented policies led to a real growth rate of 6.3 per cent per annum between 1978–88. Fiscal and trade deficits, however, continued to be problems as pointed out by Haque. The various PML and PPP governments that followed Zia are viewed as all having endorsed the liberal cause he initiated but now under the tutelage of the Bretton Woods institutions. The results have been drastic compared to the 1981–8 period. GDP growth has halved, de-industrialization has occurred, investment and saving have stagnated, inflation has reached double digits, the trade deficit has increased, and reserves have fluctuated unpredictably in response to capital flows. In short, structural adjustment is viewed as having brought no benefit and much harm to Pakistan's economy.

While Haque and Ansari do not differ in identifying the economic maladies, they differ with regard to their recommendations. Haque supports economic liberalization and emphasizes the importance of full rather than half-hearted implementation as in the past. He also expresses the importance of accountable and good government and of rolling back the state. Ansari propounds the need for an Islamic revolution which rejects the liberal economic agenda and instead results in the pursuit of an independent national agenda.

4. TRADITIONAL TOPICS: THE SECTORS

Part 3 of the book focuses on the sectors that have traditionally received the most attention. While the economic significance of the agricultural sector has been declining, Mahmood Hasan Khan points out in Chapter 4 that it still engages almost half the country's labour force, accounts for about a third of exports, and contributes about a fifth of GDP. In over-viewing the sector, he points out that since 1950, the value-added contributed by major crops has declined in importance while the contribution of the minor crops has steadily increased. An important problem highlighted is that food grains per capita have decreased from 185 kgs in 1980–85 to 173 kgs in 1990–95. Thus, to ensure food security, wheat, dry milk, and edible oils have had to be imported. Wheat imports increased from 4 per cent of total output in 1980–85 to 14 per cent in 1990–95. Although crop output per unit of land (a crude measure of productivity) has increased quite dramatically across the board since 1947, among the major producers of the crops in question, Pakistan stands in the lowest 20 per cent. Also, in current yield levels for the major crops, Pakistan ranks lower than the world average. An important part of the problem has been the under-funding and management of research and extension.

Inter-regional disparities have resulted from agriculture due to the inadequacy of water in several parts of Balochistan and the south and south-eastern parts of Sindh. This has made it difficult to extend the biological and mechanical technological packages to these zones. Simultaneously, in the canal zones, waterlogging and salinity have resulted from water losses, inadequate drainage, and poor on-farm water management. Inter-farm or income inequalities have also resulted from agriculture because of unequal access to extension service, agricultural inputs like fertilizer, and credit and output markets. Unequal access has made it difficult for small and medium farmers to catch up by adopting the new technologies used by the larger farmers. Small and medium farmers were already at a disadvantage due to the lumpiness of agricultural investments such as tractors and tube-wells.

Land concentration results in unequal access to land which reinforces income inequalities. In Pakistan, technological compulsions have partly offset the reduction in land concentration resulting from population growth and Islamic inheritance laws. Thus, while in the late 1960s land ownership became less concentrated, this trend has reversed since the 1980s, and so while the average size of small farms has decreased, the average size of large farms has increased.

Land reform and agricultural income taxes could moderate agricultural inequalities. Khan has carefully documented attempts at bringing out land reform and imposing agricultural income tax in Pakistan. He concludes that the land reforms have made no significant contribution to altering land concentration and agricultural income taxes have generated very modest revenues. He points out that the argument against agricultural income tax rests on the false premise that agriculture is already highly taxed implicitly by the state via restraints on output prices. While this may have been true in the past, policy changes since the late 1980s have aligned agricultural output prices to world market prices. Also, even if this were not the case, all income should be treated equally no matter what the source, and taxing agricultural income should not be confused with taxing agriculture as a sector. Khan's recommendation therefore is that provincial governments must revise outdated PIUs (produce index units) to conform to existing productive capacity of the land, reduce the high exemption, and raise the current flat rate per PIU.

Agriculture can be a source of generating more revenues for the state to close fiscal deficits and also a means for closing trade deficits by boosting production of crops such as wheat and edible oils, importing which take up sizable chunks of hard-earned foreign exchange. Promoting exports is a neo-liberal 'mantra' but also viewed to be essential by others, given Pakistan's dire need to service its debt and import raw materials and intermediate goods for its industry. Ijaz Nabi, in Chapter 5 on trade, reviews the export competitiveness of the Pakistani economy. He reports that exports as a percentage of GDP declined in the early 1990s from 9.5 per cent to 8.8 per cent at a time when they rose significantly for Sri Lanka and dramatically for Bangladesh. Assessing Pakistani exports from 1970 to 1993, Nabi notes an encouraging trend. This is the shift from 57 per cent manufactured goods as a percentage of the total in 1970 to 85 per cent in 1993.

Nabi also notes the vulnerability of the Pakistani export sector for various reasons. First, textiles represent the bulk of manufactured exports (78 per cent) and cotton based exports represent two-thirds of the total. Since cotton output is subject to great variations due to pest attacks and floods, the economy is subject to extended shocks as foreign exchange earnings shrink. Second, another source of vulnerability is the country concentration of Pakistan's trading whereby a handful of countries account for the bulk of our trading. Finally, almost all of Pakistan's exports are low skill based (98 per cent) and labour intensive (99.5 per cent—compared to 77 per cent for India). This also makes the export sector vulnerable due to the ease of entry into such markets.

Exchange rate management has represented another problem for Pakistan's economy. In the 1960s and 1970s, a fixed over-valued exchange rate supported import substitution industrialization. A move to the managed float in the 1980s represented a period of rational currency management. Fiscal imbalances in the 1990s have made currency management problematic. The fiscal deficits feed into inflation which require currency depreciations which further feed the inflationary cycle.

With regard to trade policy reform, the New Economic Measures announced by the government in March 1997 are viewed as representing a significant move in the right direction. However, Nabi feels additional reforms with regards to trade liberalization, rationalizing export incentives, and the streamlining of exemptions are still needed. Furthermore, despite low wages, Pakistani exports are not competitive since labour productivity is low. Thus investment in education and targeted skill training programmes as well as technology upgrading programmes are called for.

Successful export promotion of high value products, at this stage in Pakistan's development, ultimately hinges on developing a successful industrial base. In Chapter 6 on industry, A.R. Kemal traces the history of industrial policy. He identifies the 1950s as the period of import substitutions industrialization (ISI) based on import restrictions and an over-valued exchange rate. The 1960s was a period of import liberalization, market decontrol, and export encouragement. The early 1970s were marked by devaluation and tariff rationalization and were followed by import restrictions and export subsidies in the late 1970s. Liberalization began again in the early 1980s and has continued since. Policies include a reduction and a rationalization of the tariff structure and a liberalization of imports.

Despite a lack of privatization and inefficiencies induced by industrial and trade policies, Kemal views Pakistan as having attained the status of a semi-industrial country with 18.2 per cent of GDP accounted for by manufacturing. Based on the data reported, there was a big dip in private investment in manufacturing (from 88.6 per cent of the total in 1969–70 to 34.7 per cent of the total in 1979–80). Subsequent market friendly policies reversed this trend and in 1994–5, private investment in manufacturing accounted for 96 per cent of the total. Despite some negative developments in the 1970s, small scale units, which effectively had a tax exempt status, started performing well in the 1970s due to equal access to imported inputs.

The contribution of large scale manufacturing units according to Kemal has been overstated. He shows that if value added in the large scale manufacturing sector is evaluated at world prices, its contribution to GDP declines dramatically. He estimated the social cost of protection to have been about 10 per cent of GDP even as late as 1980–81, though this declined to 3.9 per cent of GDP by 1990–91 and it may have fallen further since.

Thus Kemal identifies inefficiency as the major problem of Pakistan's industrial sector. He makes a number of recommendations for the goals of establishing an efficient industrial sector, accelerating the pace of industrial investment, easing the balance of payment constraint, promoting foreign private investment, maximizing employment and reducing regional disparities. Prominent among these recommendations is re-orienting the deletion programmme to incentives rather than penalties, removing regional disparities in infrastructure, investments in training rather than providing tax holidays, and removing the bias against the small scale industry with regard to import duties. Encouraging small scale industry would be the way of attaining labour-intensive, export-oriented growth. One way of doing this would be to level the playing field between large and small sectors, particularly with regard to credit policy.

Finance is the life-blood of an economic system and its smooth and efficient flow vital for macro stability and the economic health of the country. In Chapter 7, Ahmad points to a lack of coherence in Pakistan's financial policy over the last fifty years. In the early economic history of the country, credit guidelines and control were used to provide cheap credit to the corporate sector to encourage import-substitution-industrialization. Several negative outcomes resulted from this policy. First, capital intensive techniques of production were adopted. Second, the development of a market in corporate debt was discouraged. Third, credit policy was operationalized in a manner which encouraged concentration of ownership in the industrial and financial sectors and hence, also a concentration and high risk in the loan portfolio. The high risk was not compensated for by higher returns and hence, the financial system showed signs of fragility prior to nationalization.

One outcome of the nationalization was the increase in government *ad hoc* borrowing. To service its borrowing needs, the government required the commercial banks to maintain high reserves and imposed interest rate ceilings. In order to maintain spreads for covering administrative costs, the banks in turn were allowed to suppress the interest rates they offered to borrowers. As a consequence, between 1973 and 1982, real interest rates were negative. The policy of supporting 'sick units' discouraged saving and the ratio of deposits to GDP declined. The average return on assets declined by 35 per cent since 1973. The performance of the five main nationalized commercial banks declined substantially by 1990, despite the opening of a large network of bank branches across the country.

Development Finance Institutions (DFI) were set up in the early 1960s to provide long term finance. However, these also made politically dictated loans to a narrow enclave of borrowers. Since their own funding was subsidized by donor credit lines, they were under no pressure until these credit lines dried up. DFIs were also indiscriminately set up without any proper streamlined policy of needs assessment and so there was much overlapping of the targeted niches they were set up to serve.

Liberalization and denationalization was initiated in 1991. By 1995, seventeen private local banks and twenty-two foreign banks were operating in the country. The resulting competition contained the initial rise in the profit rates. While reserve requirements and interest ceilings were relaxed, commercial banks were still under pressure to service the government borrowing needs. However, responding to donor pressure, the government increasingly borrowed from non-bank sources at high interest rates and this set the stage for the future debt crisis and as interest payments grew, the continuing struggle to contain the deficit.

Another critical component for an economy's stability and growth is how well it manages its public finances or its revenue and expenditure policies. In this regard, Pakistan's performance has been found wanting. Hafiz Pasha and Mahnaz Fatima bring some important revenue and expenditure trends to the reader's notice in Chapter 8. Pakistan started out with a very low tax ratio (tax revenue/GDP) of less than 4 per cent due to a small industrial base and scarcity of foreign exchange which restrained imports. Between 1949–50 and 1969–70, this ratio rose to 6 per cent with the bulk of the increase due to excise taxes resulting from industrial growth. To encourage industrialization, many tax exemptions were granted and hence the revenue resulting from income taxes and wealth taxes (direct taxes) were less than 1 per cent of GDP.

In the 1970s, there was a big jump in the tax ratio (10.5 per cent by 1979–80) due to an increase in custom duties which yielded an additional 2 per cent to the tax ratio. This was mainly a consequence of a large devaluation in the early 1970s. In addition, income taxes rose due to a reduction in the tax holidays, excise taxes rose due to higher rates, and tax evasion declined due to nationalization. However, the tax ratio has stagnated after reaching about 14 per cent at the end of the 1980s. The significant trend in the 1990s has been the increase in yield from income and wealth taxes which contributed an additional 1.4 per cent to the tax ratio. However, there has been a corresponding decline in the custom revenues due to the onset of tariff reforms in the 1990s, a trend which will continue. Thus, Pakistan will have to be creative in finding other ways of enhancing its very modest tax effort. This is particularly the case since it is locked into expenditure patterns that produce continued deficits and a continued weakening of the productive forces of the economy.

On the expenditure side, the big jumps are in military expenditure which increased from 3.2 per cent of GDP in 1949–50 to 7.7 per cent in 1989–90. It has declined since to 6.0 per cent of GDP in 1994–5. The other big jump has been in debt service which increased from 0.2 per cent of GDP in 1949–50 to 8.9 per cent in 1989–90. Once again, debt service has declined in the 1990s to a still sizable 8.3 per cent of GDP in 1994–5. Military expenditures and debt service together accounted for 81 per cent of total central government expenditures in 1994–5.

The rapid increase in these two components of the budget has meant a crowding out of the supportive and nurturing role of the state. Expenditures on social, economic, and community service declined from 9.3 per cent of the total expenditure in 1959–60 to 3.4 per cent in 1989–90. It has increased a little since to 5.1 per cent in 1994–5. Subsidies and the 'other' category also sharply declined from a peak of 13.9 per cent in 1984–5 to 8.7 per cent in 1994–5. In keeping with these declines, expenditures on general administration declined from a peak of 24.5 per cent in 1954–5 to 5.2 per cent in 1994–5. The authors point out that these structural changes are in keeping with the ideology of Pakistan's international financiers. Pakistan needs to get its public finances in order to get on to a sustainable growth path and to generating the revenues for engendering human development. This is an issue we turn to in the next section.

5. CONTEMPORARY CONCERNS

The most fundamental of relatively new concerns has been that pertaining to alleviating poverty. Haris Gazdar presents a comprehensive account of issues, debates, and empirical work done in this area. In addition, he adds to the empirical findings of his own prior co-authored research which is methodologically very careful and transparent. This research, based on household data, indicates that poverty fell quite sharply between 1984–5 and 1987–8 and continued to fall, though less sharply, between 1987–8 and 1990–91.

Gazdar's regional analysis of poverty, done for this volume, is rich in surprising findings. Punjab and Sindh, which account for 75 per cent of the rural population, were the subject of analysis. In terms of mean income and expenditure, middle Punjab was unambiguously the wealthiest region in 1987–8. In 1991, it had the highest mean income, but upper Punjab had the highest mean consumption. Sindh, which had the lowest mean income for both years, had higher mean consumption than lower Punjab. Middle and lower Punjab had greater inequality than upper Punjab and Sindh. Gazdar demonstrated that the finding about lower Punjab being the worst off and upper Punjab being the most well off in terms of head count ratios of poverty was robust, since it held up irrespective of the choice of poverty line, welfare indicator (income or consumption), assumptions about household size and consumption effects (scale economies in consumption). Even so, another interesting finding is that the poverty ranking is sensitive to the above methodological choices, and this is demonstrated by the ranking switches between Sindh and middle Punjab.

A critical role here seems to be played by distributional and institutional factors. Thus remittances are an important reason for income equality in upper Punjab. Similarly, a higher level of literacy enabled upper Punjab residents to avail labour market opportunities abroad, in the military and in urban areas. While Sindh has the highest land inequality, the poor had the highest land access via tenancy. This, and access to loans via the feudal patron-client relationship, enabled a higher measure of income and consumption equality in Sindh than in middle Punjab under certain assumptions.

Gazdar points out early in his chapter that concern with income and consumption poverty is inherently limiting and that a greater concern with wider issues in poverty (such as with demography, health, and education) and with the agency of women is necessary. Chapter 10 and 11 focus on these issues.

New ideas in development economics very quickly seem old and jaded. Having arrived on the scene in the late 1980s, the concept of human development now appears taken for granted as part of mainstream thinking. The focus on human development came about in the late 1980s from the very effective packaging and quantification of the early 1970s concept of basic human needs into UNDP's Human Development Index. Haq and Baqai (1986) were among the main proponents of the basic human needs approach, which came as an antidote to poverty not being addressed by an exclusive focus on market economics. Haq is also the originator of UNDP's *Human Development Index*. One of the major disparities shown by the Human Development Index is that several countries have had a very robust rate of economic growth, but they do very poorly on human development indicators such as infant mortality, life expectancy, literacy, and mean educational attainment, all of which enhance the range of human choices. Many authors have since pointed out that Pakistan represents one of the countries whose economic history reveals a stark contrast between high economic growth and poor human development.

Sohail Malik and Hina Nazli repeat this message, that has now been heard several times, by carefully documenting the state of the social sectors. Repetition, however, does not make the message less important. The message is that Pakistan is performing very poorly overall because of its lack of investment in the social sectors. This also pulls down its ranking with regard to UNDP's human development index, since educational achievements are low in Pakistan and education has an important weight in the construction of the index. However, they point out that education and health improve well-being, raise equity, reduce population growth, and raise productivity and so the lack of investment in the social sectors does not bode well for future growth in per capita GDP. One problem for Pakistan has been that despite the low investment in the social sectors, per capita income more than doubled over the past three decades due to certain favourable factors, like the Afghan war-related aid inflow and overseas remittances, which cannot be expected to recur. Thus, the full impact of the neglect of the social sectors has not yet been registered on the economy or in the minds of policy makers.

Apart from the neglect of the social sectors, and related to that, the high population growth rate acts as a constraint on the growth in per capita GDP. At the time of the last Population Census, the population growth rate was estimated to have been 3.1 per cent during the inter-census period, one of the highest in the world. Overlaid with the high population growth rate is the urban bias. Crude birth rates are much higher in the rural areas and yet the urban population growth rate of 4.4 per cent was much higher than the rural population growth rate. The neglect of the rural sector extends to the large scale deprivation of basic services and amenities such as potable water (44 per cent in 1989) and sanitation (19 per cent in 1989). This in turn results in the high rate of migration to urban areas. The urban population was five million in 1947 and increased almost ten-fold to forty-nine million in 1995. Also, there is a great deal of population concentration with half the urban population living in just eight cities, a fifth in Karachi alone.

The high population growth rate has been associated with a high unemployment rate which has steadily risen from about 1 per cent in 1963–4 to a peak of 6.3 per cent in 1990–91. The official under-employment rate was reported to be 11 per cent in 1990–91. Thus, the rapid labour force growth associated with the high population growth rate has out-stripped the capacity of the economy to create livelihoods. Employment growth rate in agriculture has been low, another reason for out-migration, and it has been negative in the manufacturing sector in the 1986/87–1990/91 period. Overall, due to high capital intensity, employment growth in the manufacturing sector has been 0.1 of 1 per cent in the 1974/75–1991/92 period. It is not surprising then that the informal sector absorbed as much as 73 per cent of the labour force in 1985–6. Difficulties in access to materials and credit limit this sector's capacity for further labour absorption.

Pakistan's low performance in human development has already been mentioned. None the less, some findings reported by Malik and Nazli bear mentioning here. One of the major bottlenecks in basic education is teachers. At existing rates of school expansion, 40,000 teachers are needed annually while only 15,000 are produced. Other discrepancies include the mismatch between the products of technical vocational education and market demand. A survey showed that only 37 per cent of the graduates of these institutions found employment and even those not in the area they had acquired training in. There continues to be a robust demand for *shagirds* (apprentices) and this indigenous institution of on-the-job training could, with appropriate regulation, address youth employment needs.

Like education, the health and nutrition sector has suffered from neglect. There has been a dramatic drop in health allocations in the *Eighth Five Year Plan 1993–98* (1993) which at .86 of 1 per cent of total expenditures compares unfavourably with 4.1 per cent of total expenditures during the *Seventh Five Year Plan 1988–93* (1988). There is little evidence that health statistics have improved across the board which would justify such a reduction. For example, 65 per cent of children less than five, 45 per cent of women of childbearing age, and 90 per cent of lactating mothers suffer from anaemia.

Apart from the low performance in the Human Development Index, Pakistan also does poorly with regard to UNDP's Gender Development Index. Using 1994 data, Pakistan was ranked 139th out of 175 countries in the *Human Development Report 1997* (1997, p. 151). Shahnaz Kazi's rich paper gathers together numerous findings that elaborate on various aspects of the neglect of women. She points out that the continued prevalence of high fertility is a major cause of the poor health of women. Frequent births, followed by an average breast-feeding period of nineteen months, result in high morbidity, prevalence of anaemia, and high maternal mortality. This is particularly the case for poor rural women who have low access to health, water, and sanitation facilities.

Even though infant mortality rate for girls is lower due to a biological advantage, female child mortality rates (age 1–5) were 66 per cent greater than that of boys in 1991. These mortality rates vary inversely with income and for the upper income groups, girl survival rates exceed those of boys. On average, girls' survival rates are also lower if they are born after boys. This finding in likely to be based on discrimination in food intake and health care. In general, girls have a higher probability than boys of suffering from nutritional deficiencies and are less likely to be taken for a consultation for ailments such as diarrhoea.

There are some positive signs regarding the social condition of women. Life expectancy for women has finally overtaken that of men, although the difference is much smaller than that prevailing in the materially richer countries. Again, among the younger generations, the male-female literacy gap is lower. Still, girls comprise a third of all students at the primary level and only a fourth at the secondary level. The large gender gap in schooling has been partly attributed to unequal access to schools. Segregated schools with female teachers are an important prerequisite to making female education more acceptable. The gender gap among the poor, particularly in rural areas, is much higher where the opportunity cost of girl education is high and female educated related income earning opportunities lower.

However, the evidence shows that where such opportunities become available, culture is not an impediment for parents in seeking out education for their daughters. Research shows that the mother's education has a significant positive impact on the probability of girls getting enrolled. In rural areas, the likelihood of girls enrolling is twice as high if the mothers have attained some education. Educated women are also less likely to discriminate against daughters and more likely to improve child health. Kazi cites a simulation study which showed that a rise in the mother's education to the primary level would reduce child wasting by 8 per cent while a 20 per cent increase in per capita income would reduce child wasting by only 2 per cent.

Earlier research suggested that fertility was higher among women who worked. Based on a survey in Karachi city, Kazi contradicted these findings and argued that the causality is reversed. Thus poor women with many children are forced into the job market. One consequence of this is a significant reduction of child survival in such families. Again, findings are reported to indicate that the proportion of female headed households at 10 per cent are much higher than normally believed. Of this group, the categories of divorcees and widows and wives of non-earning husbands are particularly disadvantaged. The age-dependency ratio in these categories is twice that for the rest of the population and earnings very limited due to low assets and education. Thus Kazi has identified a target population most in need of assistance from targeted programmes.

In the last section of the paper, Kazi shows how the legal system, financial institutions, and the development establishment has consistently discriminated against women and that matters have not improved over time. Thus, despite a number of schemes that were floated, women have virtually no access to credit. The development establishment has consistently maintained a welfare oriented approach. The Ministry of Women and Development (MWD) was given a mandate to change this by influencing policies and programmes across the entire government machinery. While MWD has been constrained by very low allocations, its approach does not indicate any change. Kazi points out that, for example, a large majority of working women are actively involved in agriculture and livestock production, and yet they are almost entirely excluded from training and extension programmes.

The last chapter of the book by Shaheen Rafi Khan and Shahrukh Rafi Khan is devoted to the most recent of current concerns (i.e. the environment) and this topic is likely to be the one that will assume increasing importance in the future. This chapter is different from other chapters in the book in two respects. First, it is forward rather than backward looking. Second, it adopts a controversial position on key environmental debates as opposed to providing a general review, since several good ones exist. Thus, environmental standards such as the ISO 14,000 series are viewed as a challenge and an opportunity rather than as a Northern dictated non-tariff barrier. Green-revolution chemical agricultural inputs such as pesticides and fertilizers are viewed as environmentally and hence socially and economically disastrous and alternative options are identified that minimize the use of such destructive inputs without forgoing output. One the one hand, while waterlogging and salinity are viewed as serious environmental problems, the authors argue that mitigating factors exist that suggest that these environmental concerns may be exaggerated. On the other hand, the bio-diversity costs of inland water eco-systems resulting from a network of large dams, barrages, canals, and waterways have been neglected. The situation is complex since dealing with the impact of climate change and changing socio-economic conditions may require such large-scale water management. In the final sub-section of the chapter, they argue that the impact of climate change resulting from Northern over-consumption may easily be overstated since changes in socio-economic conditions result in similar environmental impacts such as flooding and sea-water rise. By the same token, mitigation strategies, such as afforestation and enhancing agricultural yields, address the negative environmental impacts resulting from both sources.

REFERENCES

Banuri, T., Khan, S. R., and Mahmood, M. (eds.) (1997), *Just Development: Beyond Adjustment with a Human Face*, Oxford University Press, Karachi.

Baran, P. A. (1952), *The Political Economy of Backwardness*, Monthly Review Press, New York.

Cornia, G. A., Jolly, R., and Stewart, F. (1987), *Adjustment with a Human Face: Protecting the Vulnerable and Promoting Growth*, Clarendon Press, Oxford.

Frank, A. G. (1966), 'The development of underdevelopment', *Monthly Review*, 18, pp. 17–31.

Government of Pakistan. (1960), *Second Five Year Plan, 1960–65*, Planning Commission, Islamabad.

————. (1988), *Seventh Five Year Plan, 1988–93*, Planning Commission, Islamabad.

————. (1994), *Eighth Five Year Plan, 1993–98*, Planning Commission, Islamabad.

————. (n.d.), *Pakistan Household Integrated Survey, Round 2: 1996–97*, Federal Bureau of Statistics, Islamabad.

————. *Economic Survey 1996–97*, Finance Division, Islamabad.

Haq, M. ul, and Baqai, M. (1986), *Employment, Distribution and Basic Needs in Pakistan*, Progressive Press, Lahore.

Khan, S. R., and Aftab, S. (1996), 'Structural adjustment, labour and the poor in Pakistan', *Lahore Journal of Economics*, 2, pp. 1–18.

Nurkse, R. (1953), *Problems of Capital Formation in Underdeveloped Countries*, Oxford University Press, New York.

Rosenstein-Rodan, P.N. (1943), 'Problems of industrialization in Eastern and South Eastern Europe', *Economic Journal*, 53, pp. 202–11.

Social Policy and Development Centre, (1998), *Social Development in Pakistan: Annual Review 1998*, SPDC, Karachi.

UNDP. (1997), *Human Development Report 1997*, Oxford, New York.

World Commission on Environment and Development. (1987), *Our Common Future*, Earthscan Publications Ltd., London.

NOTES

1. In Chapter 2, Ansari gives a more detail historical overview of the periods referred to above from a macroeconomic perspective while Gazdar does this in Chapter 9 from a poverty and inequality perspective.
2. SPDC (1998, p. 44).
3. This is quite clearly evident from the data reported in Government of Pakistan, FBS, PIHS 1996–7. For example, the section on education quite clearly shows that educational attainment varies inversely with the level of income (pp. 22, 32–4, 36, 41–3).

PART TWO

TRADITIONAL TOPICS

A: THE MACRO DEBATE

2

Reform Efforts in Pakistan: Limited Success and Possibilities for the Future*

*Nadeem ul Haque***

The ideas of economists and political philosophers, both when they are right and when they are wrong, are more powerful than is commonly understood. Indeed the world is ruled by little else. Practical men, who believe themselves to be quite exempt from any intellectual discipline are slaves of some defunct economist. Madmen in authority, who hear voices in the air, are distilling their frenzy from some academic scribbler of a few years back. I am sure that the power of vested interests is vastly exaggerated compared with the gradual encroachment of ideas.

John Maynard Keynes (1936:383)

1. PAKISTAN'S ECONOMIC PERFORMANCE

Pakistan's economic performance over its fifty year history has certainly been quite remarkable in its consistency. Growth has averaged about 5.5 per cent and inflation less than 10 per cent.[1] Table 1 compares average annual growth and inflation rates, as well as the ratios of the fiscal and the current account deficit to GDP for Pakistan with several groups of developing countries. As can be seen, relative to most groups of developing countries,

---

* The views expressed in this paper are those of the author and should not in any way be taken to represent those of the International Monetary Fund.
** International Monetary Fund.

other than East Asia, Pakistan has grown faster and experienced a lower rate of inflation. However, Pakistan's fiscal performance, and that of its current account, appear to have done worse. The fiscal problem in particular has been a key policy challenge for many years. Indeed, it is fortunate that this twin failure has not precipitated a deep crisis in the form of higher inflation and/or a situation of current account unsustainablity.

Table 1
Comparison of macroeconomics performance:
Pakistan and other developing countries

| | Average Annual Rates | | | |
	1970–79	1980–89	1990–96	1970–96
Real GDP growth				
Developing countries	5.93	4.49	5.82	5.37
Western Hemisphere	6.06	2.25	2.72	3.78
Middle East	6.99	2.11	3.89	4.38
Asia	5.86	7.13	8.01	6.89
Africa	4.35	2.49	2.31	3.13
Pakistan	3.74	6.15	4.83	4.91
Inflation				
Developing countries	15.86	34.72	36.22	28.12
Western Hemisphere	30.66	129.53	170.76	103.60
Middle East	12.89	22.16	26.63	19.88
Asia	7.52	8.50	9.00	8.27
Africa	13.41	15.66	27.37	17.86
Pakistan	11.97	6.74	10.76	9.72
Central govt. balance/nominal GDP				
Developing countries	–	-4.83	-2.67	-3.94
Western Hemisphere	-2.07	-3.99	-0.52	-2.38
Middle East	-0.29	-9.97	-6.82	-5.57
Asia	-2.27	-3.62	-2.24	-2.76
Africa	–	-5.14	-5.14	-5.14
Pakistan	-7.19	-7.04	-6.71	-7.01
Current account balance/nominal GDP				
Developing countries	–	-1.03	-1.57	-0.61
Western Hemisphere	-2.37	-1.97	-2.16	-2.17
Middle East	9.26	0.37	-3.06	2.77
Asia	-0.74	-0.51	-0.43	-0.57
Africa	-1.01	-2.82	-2.63	-2.10
Pakistan	-5.12	-2.67	-4.42	-4.03

Source: International Financial Statistics and Country Sources.
Note: 1 = 1980–96 average.

Despite achieving a growth rate that has been higher than the average of many other developing countries, Pakistan remains among the category of low income countries. The laudable objective of attempting to break out of this category of poverty has led to considerable thinking about the performance of Pakistan's economy. In addition, much effort has gone into the development of plans, policies, and reforms by the government as well as by external experts. These efforts have been supported by considerable external and internal financing and considerable technical analysis. Yet, as we will examine in greater detail below, results have not been forthcoming. In this paper, I examine the issue of why some of these initiatives have not yielded the expected results.

2. THE PROMISE OF REFORM

The analysis of reform: its design, analysis, implementation, and evaluation, is an extremely difficult subject to analyse. Reform can have many different dimensions and varied objectives and can seek to affect any and all aspects of society, its politics, culture, and economics. As a result, it is often neither understood nor undertaken. However, recently it has started receiving attention as many developing countries found that progress was impossible without dismantling the extensive state intervention apparatus that had been put in place in an earlier era when markets were distrusted and state-led development was in vogue. Despite this recent interest in the subject internationally, in Pakistan, the analysis of reform has received even less attention that in other parts of the world. For that reason, I am making it the subject of this paper. I will treat the subject with relatively broad brush strokes primarily to promote several hypotheses which, I hope, will be the subject of further debate and research.

In a low income country like Pakistan, It is almost natural that any discussion of reform or policy will suggest a sequencing of objectives that places economic growth and eradication of poverty before social and political issues. The writings and debate on reform in the country have tended to reflect this sequencing with all governments. Despite their ideological differences, these governments have sought a mandate for reform in order to deliver improved economic well-being. Reform and the promise of rapid economic growth has been claimed by virtually every government since independence. The nature and the ideological basis of the proposed reform may have differed, but the promise of delivering economic prosperity is common to all past administrations.[2] As evidence of this continued interest in delivering economic progress, almost all governments continued the process of developing five year plans despite their differences in ideology. In this effort, all governments were aided substantially by donor financing and technical support—for accelerating growth and eradicating poverty.

3. THE ECONOMIC IMPACT OF ANNOUNCED REFORM

Without going into a detailed examination of each government and plan document, let us look at the longer term trends in the economy to see if there are any sharp changes as a result of the interventions that are suggested in plans and government pronouncements.[3] An analysis of key macroeconomic variables for the period 1970–95 suggests the following five inferences/ hypotheses.

- The promise of acceleration of growth has been quite illusory; apart from the end-points, growth has fluctuated around 5 per cent per annum.
- Inflation has been fairly stable, averaging about 7 per cent through the 1980s.
- This has been achieved despite an apparent policy problem—the inability to contain fiscal deficits. Through most of this period, the fiscal deficit has been relatively high averaging about between 6 and 7 per cent for the period as a whole. This fiscal indiscipline no doubt leads to balance

of payments pressures which are exhibited in the continuing current account deficits and the declining trend in reserve holdings over the period.[4]

- Through the 1980s, the economy and poverty may have benefitted from the sharp increase in workers' remittances over the period. That may be the most important factor in the sharp reduction of poverty in the early 1980s.

- The gains of opening out, deregulation, and market-oriented policies are still not evident in the data. The earlier reform efforts—of Ayub Khan, Zulfikar Ali Bhutto, and Ziaul Haq—have been clouded by 'state-led' and interventionist ideologies of the past. Thus, it is understandable that the economic promise did not bear fruit in those periods. During the post-Zia period, however, administrations have been more accepting of the 'market-oriented' and the 'openness' philosophies which are now considered to be more appropriate for producing desirable economic results. During this period, economic performance should show improvement because of the reform that has been implemented.

We can conclude from even this simple exercise that the promised economic gains have not been realized. In terms of economic outcomes, growth gains have not set in, inflation remains at a stable moderate level, and the current account has not shown any significant improvement over the period. In terms of policies, the fiscal problem continues to repeatedly threaten stabilization efforts. As a result, reserves have remained at a very low level so that small losses have often threatened possible balance of payments crises. This has been a major preoccupation of various governments, so attention is continually distracted from more important and fundamental structural issues.

An important indicator of promised policy reform is the government's undertaking of structural adjustment programmes which are promises of reform negotiated with international agencies. The years during which the government announced a structural adjustment programme that is supposed to put in place efficiency increasing economic reform can be juxtaposed with the economic data. Despite numerous such programmes, we see little improvement in the economic data. The five inferences/ hypotheses made above continue to hold. In addition, none of the economic variables seem to respond to the reform intervention that the programme seems to endorse, even with a time lag.

The important question that needs to be considered is 'why has the reform process not borne any fruit?' It seems to me that there are two answers that suggest themselves:

- that the objective of the policy packages that were put in place in the name of reform were in reality intended only to forestall crises and not to generate the efficiency gains for the acceleration in growth as we assumed earlier.
- the envisaged reform was never fully implemented. To avert a possible crisis, the government promised a reform and obtained financing. When the crisis abated they reneged on the reform.[5]

Both these hypotheses suggest the same underlying motivation: the purpose of the announced reform packages was not the acceleration of growth but the preservation of the *status quo*. The success of the policy changes and their financing during this period may have served to prevent the crises which might have occurred in their absence.[6]

In the rest of this paper, I will examine the following two issues. First, the important question, 'why is it that the forces that sought merely to prevent crises won out over those seeking genuine reform and long-lasting change?' In providing this answer, I shall come to the second and more prescriptive part of the paper, that of identifying strategies for the design and implementation of successful reform i.e., one that may yield genuine improvement in the economic well-being of the population.

4. THE OVERBURDENED PUBLIC SECTOR

Two lines of argument are usually used for attempting to explain why Pakistan has resisted change. One of these uses the Marxist approach to argue that it is in the interests of the ruling classes to preserve the *status quo*. The entrenched feudal nature of the ruling classes makes them more retrogressive than otherwise [see Noman (1988)]. Since it is hard to verify the feudal nature of the state or the class structure, this argument is virtually tautological and uninteresting. The second, and perhaps equally uninteresting, argument identifies weakness in the cultural or religious heritage. Malaysia and Turkey, two countries that are quite similar to Pakistan in these terms, refute such argumentation. Moreover, this line of reasoning also relies on some notion of irrationality in the average Pakistani. Empirical observation that Pakistanis from almost all classes and locations respond very well to the incentive of migration, even to and from far-away lands, provides evidence against such hypotheses. For these reasons, and since these arguments have been extensively discussed, I will not dwell on them.

Because other countries are able to develop, starting with initial conditions similar to Pakistan, the answer may lie in factors other than cultural backwardness and feudalism. I subscribe more to the arguments based on institutional retardation and inadequate human capital development that have been raised by Samad (1993), and therefore, shall try to develop them more fully here.[7]

A. THE DOMINANT STATE
The administrative system Pakistan inherited was quite efficient in pre-independence days not only for the colonial objectives but also for developing perhaps the largest infrastructural development in the history of the subcontinent.[8] Early in the country's history, encouraged by the thinking of the time and by the availability of donor funding, the state took on the mandate for defining the national spirit, the economic direction, and the spiritual well-being. The state adopted central planning

and widespread controls that sought to centralize resources as well as initiatives. Increasingly, private sector initiatives were relegated to grey, or black, or informal markets. These trends culminated during the tenure of the Z. A. Bhutto government. The rapid expansion of the government followed the large scale nationalizations and the intensification of private sector controls. At this stage, via capital flight, some in the private sector moved out of the country.

The hands of the growing state were encouraged by the intellectual trends of the time. Strong intellectual foundation for state intervention existed in the post-colonial days of Keynesian activism which later were combined with the liberal-left argument of the 1960s in the USA. In Pakistan, this even led to the government attempting to actually set up '*roti*' (food), '*kapra*' (clothing), and '*makan*' (housing) corporations to provide the basic necessities to the people, since the private sector was not to be trusted for the purpose.

Times and the definition of sovereignty were such that all donor efforts were directed towards devising new ways of strengthening the government's hands and finances. No questions were raised on the efficiency of government expenditures while considerable emphasis was laid on resource mobilization. All flows, official as well as private, were provided solely to the government.[9]

B. THE QUALITY OF ADMINISTRATION

While the state was acquiring all this power, the colonially-inherited administrative system had been rocked to its foundations. The most common conjecture in Pakistan today is that the state has become overdeveloped and inefficient over time. It has been also been hypothesized that the inability of the reform, that has been implemented thus far, to accelerate growth may be due to the inefficient administrative machinery. After all, the policy and reform initiatives that are contemplated do need to be implemented by the government. Hence the administrative machinery may be operating like a distorting filter.

It is said that the colonial system had relied on a strong central but effective system of administration that, because of its detachment from the system, remained impartial *vis-à-vis* the natives. Certain norms of professionalism were laid out and rewarded by financial means (such as land grants), and prestige and power. The system somehow respected the colonial objectives and was efficient in achieving those objectives. Mason (1985) notes that:

> Independence and detachment of outlook were then distinguishing qualities of the company's civil servants. Independence of outlook does not usually occur without some material security; by now the company's civil servants were reasonably well paid for... 'three hundred a year alive or dead'...his widow being entitled to the celebrated three hundred.[10]

In the independent state, the detachment disappeared, and the official and the community became intertwined, and no mechanisms were found by which some form of independence could be maintained. The new political pressures saw the politician and the army each seeking to co-opt the civil servant and usurp the public sector. The first casualty of this new politicization of the civil service was the incentive structure that honoured and rewarded public service and developed professionalism in public service. The incentive structure in the new system increasingly rewarded expediency rather than professionalism. This message of the new incentive system was finally delivered with considerable clarity in the purges of the civil service that were carried out in the late sixties and early seventies. This was an important milestone on the road to administrative decline. The result was that professionalism was dispensed with as were reporting requirements such as the district gazetteer. The more difficult aspects of the job, which might require such physical hardship as information-gathering in remote areas, were no longer as rewarding as staying close to the centre of power from where all benefits accrued.

Early on, the government found that promises of economic development could be sold to get a mandate from a public hungry for improved welfare. The vision of the time was that the government was to deliver on this economic promise. A rapid growth of government resulted, which also developed substantial rent-seeking mechanisms. One important source of the distribution of public sector benefits was via the expansion of government employment. The government has come to be viewed as an employment and rent-seeking entity. It is also viewed as least concerned with productivity or quality of service.

As employment expansion and other expenditure commitments increased budgetary pressures, the government felt it convenient to employ nominal wage freezes for curtailing expenditures. This also coincided with the egalitarian thinking that had taken root. This policy of real wage declines had the following five adverse effects on government and its productivity.

- It led to an implicit acceptance of corruption and the growth of extra-legal activities.
- Increasingly, those who offered themselves for government employment were the ones who were more prone towards activities of this nature[11] and perhaps less productive.[12]
- Productivity in government declined as those in government employment were involved in other activities for earning their living and hence not concentrating on their jobs.
- As the real take-home pay declined, the proportion of perks rose and corruption increased as is suggested by standard economic theory. As a result, there was further pressure on the fiscal situation and the economy, since there is neither efficiency of use nor efficiency of provision in perks and because of efficiency losses due to corruption.[13]
- Finally and perhaps as a result of all these phenomena, the quality of human capital in the government began to decline and the civil service, from being a preferred service for the best educated, became a sorry last, after the multinationals and immigration. The brain drain from the public sector and from the country strengthened. There was little domestic thinking on the policy agenda and policy began to rely

almost completely on donor consultants. The ramifications of this change in the availability price of human capital in the domestic economy has not even begun to be fully appreciated.[14]

C. Public Sector Output

Meanwhile, through the last two decades, the weaknesses in policy making and administration are increasingly becoming evident. Table 2 presents some evidence of the declining quality of public administration as noted by several sources. In almost all areas—enforcement of law and order, market regulation, extending and improving education, and the provision of basic infrastructure—the prevailing view now is that the public sector may be operating very inefficiently.[15]

Table 2
Summary of opinion and evidence of public sector efficiency in Pakistan

Function	Evidence on quality of output of government
Maintenance of law and order	Deteriorating law and order in cities is evidenced in many newspapers and columnists' writings: murders, dacoities, kidnapping, and terrorist attacks. The most recent evidence of this was the murder of Benazir Bhutto's own brother. *See* major columnists such a Cowasjee and Amir Sethi in *Dawn*, *The Nation*, and *The Friday Times* among others.
Effectiveness of courts	Legislation is oppressive and the procedures tedious and time-consuming. Delays caused by defects in procedural regulations, an overworked and understaffed judicial machinery, reluctance of courts to compel compliance with statutory time limits, archaic office management systems used by court registries, liberal appeal procedures, and inadequate penalties against frivolous legislation—getting decree is slow, but enforcing it even more difficult (Khan et al. 1992).
Regulation and supervision of markets	Financial markets: inadequate enforcement of financial regulation, insufficient penalties in the enforcement of banking regulations, solvency of banks questionable; NCB's administrative costs significantly higher than foreign banks affecting their profitability, large spreads between lending and deposit rates to repair bank balance sheets and for domestic fiscal purposes act as

	a tax on depositors; banking payments and transactions technology inadequately developed; regulation of stock market not sufficiently autonomous or developed; secondary markets in government debt instruments not developed due to government intervention; inadequate instrument development or in sufficient financial intermediation due to government intervention; weak credit reporting infrastructure. (Haque and Carder, 1995).
Policy formulation	Continuing fiscal deficits, problems with politically motivated credit and general increase in rent-seeking and corruption leaves the government weak in this area. Hence exemptions abound in the tax code leaving the government helpless in its revenue collection. Moeen Qureshi's efforts to publicize these issues did not yield any results. Most political leaders do not pay taxes (*Newsline*, November 1995).
Education	Literacy and enrolment rates lowest in Asia. [World Bank (1995, p. 83)]. 'Universities and colleges are poorly equipped and maintained', (p. 85). Punjab university syllabi outdated, relying on books and recommending no reading from journals. The average age of books that are recommended is about thirty years from the date of publication. No funding for research. Large number of student years lost due to examination delays. [Hayes (1993)].
Health	'Previous studies indicate Pakistan's weaknesses in health care stem from high administrative costs, inappropriate training of medical personnel and poor distribution of resources. These three factors have led to very poor primary and preventive care especially in Pakistan's rural areas.' [World Bank (1995, p. 89)].
Water and sewers	'Even in areas that have water systems, water is supplied sporadically and is frequently contaminated' [World Bank, (1995, p. 89)].
Roads	'Pakistan has one of the poorest road systems in the world. The road infrastructure consists of aging and obsolete roads that have neither the geometric capacity nor the structural strength to carry the increasing traffic and vehicle loads.' [Faiz (1992)] Stone (1995) found in a survey of 200 firms that businesses are constrained by poor quality of roads.

Structural reform is undertaken but not systematically enough for the efficiency gains to kick in and fiscal policy is corrected only in a stop-go fashion. As a result, policy remains involved with crisis management rather than long-run growth acceleration. Basic law and order have become more and more difficult to maintain which has larger economic and political ramifications.

Financial crises have already imposed a tax on depositors. In three different episodes, finance companies and co-operatives were closed, since the government, as the guarantor of the financial system, refused to regulate them. Depositors lost money while there were no indictments (*see* Samad, 1993).

D. THE NEGLECT OF HUMAN CAPITAL

Economic investigation—both theoretical and empirical—have quite clearly established by now that human capital accumulation is an important variable for achieving high levels of economic growth. In order to assess Pakistan's efforts to accelerate its economic growth, we must assess what the country has done for the accumulation of human capital. Pakistan's lack of achievement in improving the educational attainment of its populations is well documented in many sources and will not be repeated here.[16] To repeat the findings of many other authors, the literacy rate in the country remains very low.

Three additional points need be made on the issue of human capital development in Pakistan:

- Perhaps the biggest decline in human capital and productivity was in the education sector. The signal that success did not depend on education permeated. Students only needed a university degree, without regard to quality, to obtain credentials to get into government jobs where rents could be easily acquired. Course contents and the value of degrees became secondary. Teaching was the least attractive profession of all, since there was hardly any dispensation of officialdom or favour.[17] All plans for educational development were based on underpaid teachers. In the thrust for numbers, substandard institutions proliferated.
- The depreciation of human capital at all levels and especially in the academic institutions has led to weakening capacity for analyzing important issues and generating the ideas so necessary for reform within Pakistan. Simultaneously, with the growth of state power and weakening of administration, the intellectual foundations of reform and construction were also weakened.

- As the educational and public sector institutions weakened, a flight of human capital from educational establishments and the country took place and, over time, led to a sharp decline in the quality of the university and research sector as well as other policy making institutions and fora.[18] In this manner, even the manpower and the institutional framework that might have laid the foundations of a domestic information and policy agenda, or provided an alternative role for the government, was withdrawn. The brain drain strengthened with the departure of intellectual merit from the country through the 1970s and 1980s.[19]

An important reason why the education and the human capital sector remains little developed, and even shows a deterioration during the half century of independence, is the general lack of respect that the country and especially the government, has had for human capital. As early as 1968, Braibanti (1968, p. 88) notes, 'the greatest handicap of the university is that it does not command the respect of the bureaucracy'. The powerful bureaucracy has especially not held the more technical aspects of academics in high regard. 'A key problem in the development of Pakistan has been the attitude of the disdain toward technical and scientific training which has characterized a bureaucracy long dominated by a classical generalist tradition' (Braibanti, 1968, p. 321). Commentators such as Hayes (1987), Kardar (1987), and Samad (1993) have all noted a continuing deterioration in the indicators of education as well as the continuing neglect of the sector as a whole. The attitude still remains dismissive of human capital at all levels of administration.

5. THE NATURE OF REFORM AND IT'S OWNERSHIP

Whatever lobbies exist for reform remain extremely weak and fragmented.[20] Because of the monopoly of the government on all academic institutions and on the electronic media, and its monopsonistic position with regard to the print media, there has historically been little domestic debate on the issue of reform and policy.

Though expression of thought and opinion is unencumbered, the decline in quality of academic institutions has effectively stifled domestic intellectual thought, debates, or the development of alternative viewpoints. The academic institutions are owned by the government and appointments are not based on merit. Journals, where they exist, are owned and operated by the government. Publishing businesses do not survive other than through government purchases since libraries and academic institutions are owned by the government, and syllabi are prescribed by the government. Newspapers and magazines have to rely on government largesse for advertising and patronage. In any case, their circulation in a limited population is too small to be meaningful.[21] Radio and television remain a monopoly of the government.

Given the lack of domestically-generated policy and reform ideas, the initiatives now come from donors. Policy ideas are a result of either direct donor work, such as that originating from the staff of multilateral financial institutions, or the result of donor initiated consulting work. Whatever policy research is done within the country is done as consulting reports for donors. Since the donors interface easily with the government and because they operate with the consent of the government, they also adopt the viewpoint that the government should lead development, paying little attention to the efficiency of government. Alternative viewpoints, even when they surface, such as Aziz (1993), Hoodbhoy (1991), and Samad (1993), are virtually ignored given the lack of institutions for debate and the concentration of research funding in the hands of donors.[22]

The symbiotic relationship between donors and the government, the control of government on thought-generating institutions, and the limited resources for the development and publication of ideas, all limit independent thought.[23] It is not surprising then that most intellectual effort goes into broad historical sweeps and journalistic efforts and there is little gathering of hard evidence or scientific research that could become the basis of generating ideas for change.[24] Responding to the incentives of state and donor patronage, most intellectuals and economists have taken on the role of defining a government role for the delivery of basic needs, social sector development, and environmental preservation.[25] Repeated exhortations to plan, and for the government to lead development, have led to a multiplication of state institutions without any evaluation of the ability of the state to deliver. The paucity of domestic idea generation has resulted in a growing dependency on the donors and external experts for ideas for reform and policy. There are at least three reasons why this dependence may be slowing down the process of change:

- First, external experts rely on a quick visit to analyse policy and recommend reform. An issue which needs to be examined further is whether these experts can develop reasonable ideas for change, that are fully cognizant of the existing institutions and their inter-linkages, based only on short visits and their international experience.

- Second, given that all reform ideas are generated by donor-financed international experts, with domestic human capital providing a minor input, these ideas are regarded with suspicion by the domestic populace. It is widely argued nowadays that for reform to be successful, it should be owned by the domestic population and the government.[26] It is hard to see how the transplanting of ideas, that may not be firmly rooted in the domestic environment, can be sold to the local population merely by means of donor-financed seminars and group discussions.

- Donor funding initiatives have also been subjected to the interests of their home-country lobbying groups and have, on occasion, pushed an agenda that may be of greater interest to those groups. For example, while there is a need to include items such as the strengthening of the administrative and judicial system in the domestic research agenda in Pakistan, funding for such work is not available.

CONCLUSION

With the collapse of communism, the government has to limit itself to the traditional role of providing social contract services such as law and order and regulation. The free market is to be the basis of the economy. Given the intellectual tradition that is in place, and the incentives of funding and positions, economists in Pakistan remain suspicious of the market and are quietly muttering their skepticism. They argue that the government needs to spend more money, even if borrowed, on the social sectors. This is despite Mustapha's (1992) finding that six education policies in the past three decades have been announced with the promise of universal adult literacy despite which literacy remains virtually unchanged at around the 30 per cent mark.

In this paper, I have argued that the government cannot act as an agent of change either in the capacity of formulator of the change or that of implementing the change. This may be an important reason why change has not taken any root in Pakistan. The quality of public institutions, including the human capital in government and administration, has deteriorated quite sharply. Moreover, the incentive mechanisms in the public sector have given rise to corruption and rent-seeking, compounding the inefficiency and institutional decline. Consequently, a necessary condition for successful design and implementation of reform may be the reform of government itself.

Another important reason why reform efforts may not have paid off is the possibility that groups that have an interest in reform have successfully been marginalized by the strong and powerful state. This suggests that an assessment of the roles and achievements of intellectuals and government, as well as donors, be made to see what sort of roles these groups have played in the formulation of policy. Unfortunately, because of the preoccupation with government plans and priorities, which are driven by donor considerations and funding, the need to direct some effort towards studying the efficiency of government expenditures has been overlooked. Plans and policy designs need to be underpinned with an adequate assessment of the efficacy of the delivery system.

There must be more domestically generated work on establishing policy and reform priorities. Such work must be more widely debated and discussed at home. It is only through such a process that better ideas and greater ownership of reform will be developed.

In terms of designing future reform, the following sequencing approach is recommended:

- first, drastically reduce the role of the government by physically reducing the size of the government and its involvement in the market place and this perhaps should be done with a big bang;
- second, an improvement in the efficiency of the government—administrative and judicial—bearing in mind human capital requirements; and
- finally the development of regulation that is needed for curbing market excesses.

Somewhere in the second stage, an effort must be made to re-invigorate academia. The lack of honest indigenous intellectual endeavour means that there really is not even a domestic agenda for research or of policy issues. The decline of universities and research, the brain drain and its possible stemming or reversal, are all issues that squarely need to be placed on such a research or policy agenda. Without adequate attention to the quality of the domestic human capital, and its ability to regenerate itself, the desirable objectives of looking after the environment, providing basic needs, reducing population growth, etc., will not be achievable.

Romer (1994, p. 36), a pioneer of the recent literature on endogenous economic growth, states that 'it takes a new theory (or at least a new point of view) to beat an old one'. The old approach of attempting to design policy exogenously and relying on the existing institutions is clearly not working. Repeated administration of that dose based on sector-specific and economy-wide prescriptions that seek to set the prices right and create competitive conditions may not work unless the core issues of governance are addressed. Moreover, purely exogenously designed reform efforts may not be either appropriately targeted or designed. The thesis presented here and by authors such as Samad (1993) and Husain and Hussain (1993) may be that such 'new points of view' need to be discussed widely. Perhaps, such a discussion will lead to the rejection of the earlier approaches and the development of the newer institutions that may result in more appropriate and workable reform prescriptions. But where will it be discussed in the absence of fora in the country?

REFERENCES

Aziz, K. K. (1993), *The Murder of History*, Vanguard Books, Lahore.

Braibanti, R. (1968), *Research on the Bureaucracy of Pakistan*, Duke University Press, Durham, NC.

Duncan, E. (1989), *Breaking the Curfew: A Political Journey Through Pakistan*, M. Joseph, London.

Haque, N. (1992), 'Economists and the role of government', *Pakistan and Gulf Economist*, Pakistan.

Haque, N., and Kim, Se-jik. (1995), 'Human capital flight: impact of migration on income and growth', *IMF Staff Papers,* September, pp. 577–606.

Haque, N., and Sahay, R. (1996), 'Do public sector wage cuts close budget deficits?—The costs of corruption', *IMF Staff Papers*, forthcoming.

Haque, N., and Sheikh, A. (1994), 'Newspapers and the concerns of society: evidence from a content analysis', *Economic and Political Weekly* , July.

Hayes, L. D. (1987), *The Crisis of Education in Pakistan*, Vanguard Books, Lahore.

Hoodbhoy, P. (1991), *Islam and Science*, Vanguard Books, Lahore.

Hussain, M., and Hussain, A. (1993), *Pakistan: Problems of Governance*, Vanguard Books, Lahore.

Johnson and Wasty. (1993), 'Borrower ownership of adjustment programmes and the political economy of reform', World Bank Discussion Papers No. 199, Washington, D. C.

Kardar, S. (1987), *Political Economy of Pakistan*, Progressive Publishers, Lahore.

Keynes, J. M. (1936), *The General Theory of Employment Interest and Money*, Macmillan, New York.

Kydland, F., and Prescott, E. C. (1977), 'Rules rather than discretion: the inconsistency of optimal plans', *Journal of Political Economy*, 85, pp. 473–92.

Lamb, C. (1990), 'Karachi squatters build' 'parallel state' 'where government never goes', *Financial Times* (UK), 12 January p. 4.

Mason, P. (1985), *The Men who Ruled India*, Rupa and Co., Calcutta.

Mustapha. (1992), 'Pakistan's education policy', *Herald*, (Pakistan), November.

Noman, O. (1988), *The Political Economy of Pakistan 1947–85*, Routledge and Kegan Paul, New York.

Romer, P. (1994), 'New goods, old theory, and the welfare costs of trade restrictions', *Journal of Development Economics*, 43, pp. 5–38.

Samad, A. (1993), *Governance, Economic Policy and Reform in Pakistan*, Vanguard Books, Lahore.

Vegh. (1992), 'Stopping high inflation', *International Monetary Fund Staff Papers*, 39, pp. 626–95.

World Bank. (1992), 'Higher education and scientific research: strategy for development and reform', World Bank Report No. 10884-PAK, Washington.

———. (1995), *Supporting Fiscal Decentralization in Pakistan*, Washington.

NOTES

1. This growth performance is difficult to explain given the country's relatively low investment and savings rates.

2. The Ayub government introduced development planning in the late 1950s, the Zulfikar Ali Bhutto government based its reform attempts on socialistic notions, the Zia administration committed itself to Islamization, while the post-Zia governments are more accepting of the more recent post-communist, market-oriented prescriptions.

3. Most of the economic work in Pakistan has been period analysis which is avoided here [*see* Noman (1988) and Chapter 3 of this book].

4. This has been achieved by allowing the exchange rate to adjust to accommodate domestic demand.

5. This is a well known time inconsistency argument in the economics literature [*see* Kydland and Prescott (1979)]. The behaviour of announcing a reform and then reneging on it once the immediate benefits of the announcement effect have been reaped by the incumbent government is not merely fanciful economic theory but has been documented to have taken place in many different economies [*see* Vegh (1992)].

6. Donors funding of policy has also been preoccupied with the prevention of crises. This may have strengthened the current system and precluded reform. Reform that allows growth-generating forces to be unleashed often occurs in the wake of a crisis. Consequently, consistent crisis prevention may have had the unintended consequence of preventing longer-term reform to be put in place.

7. *See also* Haque (1992 and 1994).

8. A large and modern communication network was established with road, rail, telecommunications, and a postal system. An education and legal system was quite efficiently developed by this administration and perhaps one of the largest irrigation networks. Perhaps the period that comes close to this is the interlude of Sher Shah Suri who had displaced the Mughal emperor Humayun.

9. In 1976, the government even tried to take over all direct scholarship and financial aid offers to students by US universities.

10. That is £ 300 in the early nineteenth century.

11. Stories of how the service of choice in the CSS (Central Superior Services) exam has changed from the District Management Group (DMG) to Customs are frequently told.

12. Human capital theory suggests that individual educational and job-experience attainments should be matched with the requirements of a job. Moreover, the emoluments associated with a job and the methods of attaining them will also determine the kind of individual who will apply for a job. Thus if the bulk of the expected earnings of a job are from some form of influence peddling and extra-legal means, individuals who are more prone to such activities will find these jobs more attractive. Since the government is a largely self-policing organization, the risks associated with extra-legal activities are low.

13. *See* Haque and Sahay (1996) for an analysis of the relationship between how wage incentives may be important both for the quality of public sector output and the curtailment of corruption.

14. The adverse consequences of the brain drain for economic growth have been analysed recently by Haque and Kim (1995).

15. Ample evidence exists on this issue and this is a subject of frequent discussion in the country [*see* Noman (1988), Husain and Husain (1993) and Samad (1993)].

16. *See* the numerous World Bank education sector reports and the documents pertaining to the Social Action Program which amply substantiate this point.

17. Hayes (1987) shows that 'primary school teachers receive...less than an unskilled day labourer', and that most teachers make more money if they sought work outside education', (page 140).

18. Hayes (1987) notes that 'it is impossible to prevent flight of good faculty from the school system', and the most capable personnel move out of teaching and into administration where there are greater possibilities for higher rank and better pay,' (page 141). Braibanti (1968) also notes the exodus from education and from the country.

19. *See* Haque and Kim (1995) for an analysis of the impact of migration of talent on economic growth.

20. This is not to say that there are no groups that are discussing and developing reform ideas. Organizations such as the Human Rights Commission of Pakistan have done some important work on constitutional and judicial reform. For the reasons mentioned in the text, these groups find themselves virtually marginalized.

21. The print media is dependent on government advertisements and newsprint import quotas that work in the government's favour. The major part of their revenues derive from such government favours. This dependence and the lack of literacy, makes the circulation of the print media very limited.

22. Interestingly enough, most donor sponsored studies and the work of the foreign academics does not draw upon domestic writings such as these. The hypotheses regarding Pakistan seldom seem to conform to what the residents are talking and writing about but to observations by visitors. Even journalistic endeavours such as Duncan (1989) and Lamb (1970) are more seriously treated than the Pakistani writers.

23. *See* World Bank (1992) which shows how fragmented and resource dried an activity research and academics is.

24. *See* Haque and Sheikh (1994) for an analysis of the print media and how it reflects the concerns of the intellectuals in society.

25. *See* Hayes (1987).

26. Studies have shown that the ownership of reform is an important issue for its success [*see* Johnson and Wasty (1993)]. The issue of whether reform can be owned in the absence of institutions for the development and dissemination of ideas has not been analysed carefully.

3

Macroeconomic Management: An Alternative Perspective[*]

*Javed Akbar Ansari***

The *Umran Hadri*,[1] to which the tastes of the townspeople lead, is characterized only by the growth of consumption. This rise in consumption is both artificial and fragile: artificial because it does not result from an increase in productivity and represents only the squandering of wealth extorted from the population as a whole, fragile in that it depends upon the vicissitudes of the political and economic powers that dominate the Muslims.

Islam alone is the indispensable ideal form of any major political movement to create and sustain *asbiya*[2] among a Muslim people.

Imam Abd Al Rahman Ibn Muhammad Ibn Khaldun (may Allah bless him).[3]

---

* Unless otherwise specified, referenced figures have been taken from the annual *Economic Survey* of the Ministry of Finance. Some data has also been obtained from the unpublished research of a study group based at the Islamic Research Academy, Karachi. All translations from Urdu texts are by Javed Akbar Ansari.
** An activist since 1962, Javed Ansari has served the Islamic movements of Pakistan, Britain, Malaysia, and Austria. He is also an economic policy analyst with interests in industry and finance. He is currently studying the World Bank's strategy in Pakistan.

1. THE NATURE OF THE PAKISTANI STATE

At stake is Riffat's being; is she to be a citizen or a mother?

To understand macroeconomic management, it is necessary to begin with the theory of the state in a broad sense and in the particular context for which the macroeconomic management strategy is being investigated. Thus we begin with the theory of the state in general and as relevant to the Pakistani context.

The purpose of macroeconomic management is to sustain the reproduction of a manageable individuality. As Foucault (1978) recognized, a liberal social order is necessarily 'a disciplinary society that stretches from the enclosed disciplines to an indefinite generalizable mechanism of "panopticism" able to bring the effects of power to the most minute and distant elements' (p. 74). Discipline is exercised to create and sustain an individuality which accepts the maximization of freedom as a universal self-evident *raison d'être* and which is capable of exercising self-discipline in this pursuit of freedom.

Macroeconomic management involves the use of liberal state institutions and processes for nurturing this particular individuality.[4] It is therefore appropriate to begin by outlining some characteristics of the liberal state.

The liberal state is comprised of an ensemble of relationships which seek to reproduce a particular social order by enforcing collectively binding decisions on the basis of a specific conception of the general will. Sustaining a particular conception of the general will is the essential and distinguishing function of the liberal state. The state must structure and facilitate ideological discourses which legitimize the particular conception of the general will which it seeks to sustain. Structuring this discourse involves intervention in society. Macroeconomic policy provides instruments for such intervention. It is one means among many through which the liberal state seeks to structure interpersonal relationships in order to universalize particular values. Political legitimacy requires both that Riffat accept certain values as consensual and the processes through which their dominance is secured as natural.

The state may be said to exist only when it possesses an administrative staff which is empowered to maintain ideological domination over the people. This administrative staff shares power with other key elements within the liberal state system, particularly its representational strata. Policy conception, articulation, and reformulation are necessarily a multi-faceted process riddled with contradictions. State policies usually emerge from shifting, unstable alliances among groups with differing perceptions and strategies. For policy initiatives to be coherent and sustainable, there must be a stable core of support representing the perceptions of a dominant coalition partner. This dominant force must strengthen the internal unity of the state ensemble through hegemonic state projects which provide the moral and ideological guidelines for the conception and conduct of state policy. The purpose of the hegemonic state project and its associated policies is Riffat's subjection. This involves both her subjection to the state apparatus and her self-subjection to a set of particular ideas whose consensuality is sustained by the state—these ideas provide a criterion for the evaluation of the behaviour of both the dominated and the dominant elements within the state system. According to Skinner (1989, p. 51), the state 'is therefore doubly impersonal, equated neither with the ruler nor with the ruled.' It is in this sense that the liberal state is conceived as 'sovereign'.

The nature of particular states depends on the particular hegemonic projects undertaken at particular points in time. Luhmann (1989) notes that new forms of organization and administration are required for state formation. State projects form particular types of states—Poleizestat, Reichstat, Sozialstat. These different forms are not mutually exclusive. An authoritarian Poleizestat may pursue liberal economic projects as a means for augmenting state power. Liberal projects necessarily qualify democratic practice by placing certain so-called 'fundamental rights' outside the framework of democratic decision-making; as Dworkin (1978) argues, the basic liberal commitment is to individualism, the 'right' of every individual to equal concern and respect, irrespective of his self-determined life plan, and not to democracy.

Similarly, liberal states need not necessarily be concerned with securing the conditions of capital accumulation in a given situation. Even Marxists like Jessop (1990, p. 119) recognize that:

> there is no single unambiguous logic of capital—unless it be the autopetic logic of continually reproducing the circuit of capital regardless of the specific form in which this occurs. It follows that there can be no single unambiguous reference point for state managers (determining) how the state must serve the needs and interests of capital.

Capital accumulation can occur under the most divergent state forms. There is little that can be said in favour of the view that a particular state form is 'required' by capital in general.

Nevertheless, the performance of certain functions by the liberal state apparatus facilitates capital accumulation. The circuit of capital can be socialized through the state. But the state's capacities to facilitate capital accumulation are necessarily limited. This is reflected in macroeconomic policy failures such as fiscal crises, inflation, unemployment, and debt overhang. Endorsement of the state's claim to represent the popular general will against private capitalist interests necessitates its exclusion from the heart of the production process. There are inherent limitations in using law and money as steering mechanisms. The World Bank literature on 'good governance' has noted these limitations at great length.

The state is thus an imperfect ensemble of institutions and instruments for determining individual consciousness. Moreover, the state is a terrain of struggle with different ideological groups seeking control and dominance. Its domination over society is therefore never complete. The functioning of both state and societal processes are characterized by a relative autonomy: relative in the sense that these processes influence but cannot determine each other. They are not self-sufficient and their strategic capacities are always limited, relative to the tasks which confront them. In other words, although state policy possesses a logic of its own, it remains part of society and its capacity to determine Riffat's being is contested both within and beyond its boundaries. The liberal state's formal responsibility of sustaining a particular interpretation of the general will requires it to manage the relative autonomy and functional interdependence of the major sub-systems (cultural, political, economic) of a particular social order. The success of a state project is measured by its ability to integrate these systems into a non-necessary, socially constituted, and sustainable relative unity.

Political practices—including macroeconomic policies—are means for sustaining this relative unity of the major sub-systems of a desired social order so as to achieve a particular subjection of Riffat. Assessing the effectiveness of macroeconomic policies requires a specification of the desired social order and the desired subjectivity that the forces which dominate the Pakistani state seek to create and sustain.

Pakistan's state managers are mainly drawn from the elite, recruited by British imperialism, after the 1857 jihad to crush Islam as a political force and to secularize Muslim society. Maulana Maududi (1989, p. 136) pointed out that 'crushing Islam as a political force has been British policy since the beginning of its imperialist dominance in India.' The main instrument for creating the new elite was the imperialist education policy symbolized by Aligarh.[5] As Maulana Maududi (1979, p. 74) stated, this new elite was 'proud of its modernity, willing to sacrifice its all to ape the West. They reject the teachings of religion and have adopted Western culture'. Political leadership passed into the hands of this elite gradually over a fifty-year period (roughly 1880 to 1930). By the time of the *shahadat* of Maulana Muhammad Ali (may Allah bless him), the *ulema* had effectively been displaced from the centre stage of Indian Muslim politics. The Quaid-i-Azam's rebuilding of the Muslim League in the 1934–7 period constitutes a definitive historical watershed. The 1937 legislative elections showed that the westernized Muslim elite and its political party, the Muslim League, was rapidly emerging as the legitimate representative of Muslim India.

The Quaid-i-Azam was a liberal Muslim. He sought to reshape the Muslim League into a mass liberal nationalist party which would legitimize liberal practice through the use of Islamic symbols. Maulana Maududi (1979, p.153) predicted that:

> (The Muslim League) consists of people whose intellectual training has been entirely along Western lines. Their political thought is based entirely on Western sources. They have however inherited a consciousness of belonging to a Muslim nation. Therefore they seek to serve the Muslim community. Their thought and practice represent a strange blend of Western thought and Islamic terminology. The proclamation of the leaders (of the Muslim League) and their party resolutions clearly illustrate the essentially nationalist character of their ideology. They are concerned not with the achievements of Islamic objectives but with the defence of their material, worldly rights and advantages against the Hindus. Islam has become merely a source of national pride in the ideology (of the Muslim League). Muslim League resolutions and the statements of their national leadership have never committed the party to the establishment of Islamic government in Pakistan. As against this, they have repeatedly stated that they seek to establish a liberal democratic government. The system of government in Pakistan will be similar to the system of government in India.

The accuracy of this prediction, made several years before the establishment of Pakistan, is reflected in the Quaid-i-Azam's inaugural address to the Constituent Assembly of Pakistan as reported by Allana (n.d., p. 573). The Quaid-i-Azam said:

> If you work in co-operation, forgetting the past... if you change your past... (accepting that) every one... no matter what his creed is first, second, and last a citizen of this state with equal rights, there will be... progress.
>
> I cannot emphasize it too much... All these angularities of the Hindu community and the Muslim community have been the biggest hindrance in the way of India to attain freedom. We must learn a lesson from this.
>
> You are free...you may belong to any religion, that has nothing to do with the business of the state... In England, conditions some

time ago were much worse... The Roman Catholics and the Protestants persecuted each other... Today you may say that there, Roman Catholics and Protestants do not exist; what exists is that everyone...is an equal citizen of the state of Great Britain.

We should keep this in front of us as our ideal and in course of time, Hindus will cease to be Hindus and Muslims will cease to Muslims, not in the religious sense, because that is the personal faith of each individual, but in the political sense, as citizens of the state.

But the Quaid-i-Azam's commitment to Islam as a personal faith was as strong as his commitment to political liberalism, as documented by Qusuri (1987, p. 141). Writing in response to Hazrat Amir-i-Millat Pir Jamaat Ali Shah (may Allah bless him) in 1943, the Quaid-i-Azam stated:

You have sent me a gift of the Holy Quran because I am a leader of the Muslims. Without a knowledge of the Quran how can the Muslims be led? I promise that I will regularly read the Quran and seek guidance from the *ulema*... you have given me a prayer carpet so that I learn to obey Allah; unless I learn to obey Him how can I expect the Muslims to obey me? I promise that I will pray regularly. You have sent me a rosary so that I can regularly invoke Allah's blessings on the Prophet.[6]

Such a leader was eminently suited to guide a party which sought to promote liberal nationalism among the Muslims. From the earliest days, the Muslim League was a broad church—it was never dominated by feudal interests as the Indian communist Ashraf (1963) claimed. It brought together commercial and feudal interests and the new Muslim intelligentsia from Aligarh.[7] The only group which stood aloof was that of the *ulema*.[8] Indeed, the League's mission was to displace the *ulema* from the centre stage of Muslim politics as it was they who had led all anti-imperialist struggles after the 1857 jihad till the *shahadat* of Hazrat Sheikh-al-Hind (may Allah bless him) in 1920.

The section of the *ulema* which had stood aloof from these struggles[9] developed contacts with the League during the 1935–

7 period, when the Quaid-i-Azam sought to develop it into a mass party. The impact of these *ulema* was restricted to the increased adoption by the League of an Islamic diction. These *ulema* did not challenge the League's commitment to liberal nationalism.

The League's political objectives on the eve of independence were as follows:

a) Maintaining a broad-based coalition of landlords, industrialists, traders, and lower middle income groups on the basis of liberal nationalist theory and practice, justified by the use of Islamic references and symbols.

b) Achievement of rapid economic and military advancement through policies which balanced the need to encourage private sector initiative with the need to promote social justice in the context of a market society.

c) Obtaining imperialist support for Pakistan's policies—it is significant that the Quaid-i-Azam ended his inaugural address to the Constituent Assembly by reading out loud the full text of the telegram sent by the American Secretary of State.

The economic policy framework was not spelt out in a systematic and coherent form.[10] However, in this regard, the League had no major differences with the Congress on economic issues. This is illustrated by Mr Liaquat Ali Khan's famous 'poor man's budget' presented to the central Indian legislature in February 1947.[11] The Budget contained proposals for the following:

1. Nationalization of the Reserve Bank of India.
2. Regulation of commodity and share markets to control speculation.
3. Establishment of a commission to investigate tax evasion and fraud.
4. Raising of the income tax exemption limits.
5. Abolition of the salt tax.
6. Imposition of special income tax at the rate of 25 per cent on high commercial earnings.
7. Imposition of a capital gains tax.[12]

Several Congress leaders described this as 'India's first national budget' and, despite vehement opposition by the business lobby, the Finance Bill was approved on 25 March 1947 with minor modification. As Sajid (1987) points out, at about the same time, the Punjab Muslim League committed itself to abolishing the zemindari system.

The economic reforms mentioned in the 1946 election manifesto and those contained in the poor man's budget were overshadowed by the need to come to grips with problems created by the withdrawal of capital, the confrontation with India, and the influx of refugees during the first phase of Pakistan's independent existence.[13] Nevertheless, the basic commitment to a high growth, liberal economy, guided by a strong state, and supported by imperialism, remained intact during 1947–88.

The new colonial period following 1988 is characterized by a softening of the state and the emergence of a consensus among the different elite segments to submit to colonialist hegemony. As Iqbal (1994) shows, the economic manifestos of the PPP and the PML are very similar. However, the Islamic parties have distanced themselves from this consensus and established the Milli Yakjahti Council (MYC) on an explicitly anti-imperialist platform. Ansari (1996) indicates that resistance to imperialist hegemony is growing at the mass level and can develop into a national threat to the liberal elite which has dominated the Pakistan state since 1947.

The state project of the Quaid-i-Azam was to construct a Muslim nationalist liberal state in the subcontinent. This project cannot succeed because Muslim nationalism is a contradiction in terms: in order to survive, Pakistan must become a front line Islamic state against imperialism. The history of the first fifty years shows that the Pakistani state processes did not have the capacity to nurture liberal individuality. While the elite has remained committed to liberalism at the level of state discourse, this commitment has not been sufficiently dominant to override particularistic perceptions of interest or to iron out the contradictions in policy conception and articulation. The state has therefore weakened and the private sector is in no position to take up the slack. The liberal subjection of Riffat requires that discipline be exercised by an external 'archangel' agency without particularistic commitments. Pakistani society does not have space for the 'self-interested' representation of freedom (or 'capital in general'). If left to itself, there is a natural tendency for the 'politics of might' to dominate 'the politics of rights'.

Since the elite cannot rule itself,[14] the state is naturally collapsing into its pre-independence form. Riffat—and the domestic elite—must be ruled by the direct representatives of the liberal imperialist order.[15] This direct imperialist subjection has been made possible by the erosion of the effectiveness of state policy as made clear in the sections that follow.

2. MACRO POLICIES: A PERIOD ANALYSIS

The central purpose of macroeconomic management in Pakistan is the creation and sustaining of liberal individuation; but do Pakistani state institutions and processes have the capacity to nurture liberal individuation? Does the state possess sufficient autonomy to preserve a broad coalition of groups with varying ideological perceptions and strategies? Is the administrative apparatus capable of circumventing the contradictions which riddle the policy conception and implementation processes? Is there an effectively dominant partner in the social coalition which provides core support for the Pakistani state? How effectively have the major state projects been undertaken, and what has been the impact of these projects on the form of the Pakistani state? And did changes in form—transition from a Reichstat (1947–58) to a Poleizestat (1959–72) to a Sozial-Poleizestat (1972–7)[16] to a Poleizestat (1977–88) to a Reichstat (1988–)—lead to a modification in purpose?

A. REICHSTAT 1947–58

We address these questions by describing the major macroeconomic state projects in different periods of Pakistan's history. We periodize this history with reference to changes in the form of the Pakistan state.

The areas which constituted Pakistan were among the most underdeveloped regions of British India. With the exception of a few cities, these areas produced raw material which was transported to industrial and trade centres in India for manufacture or export. Delhi, Bombay, Madras, and Calcutta housed the central offices of all major finance and business concerns. The East Pakistan economy was crippled by the separation of Calcutta and the refusal of the Indian authorities to accept Pakistan's proposals to jointly levy trade taxes and excise duties.

India began an economic war against Pakistan from the first day of independence. The trade and communication network linking the two countries collapsed following unabated Muslim genocide in East Punjab, Delhi, Bihar, and West Bengal. India refused to transfer Pakistan's share of currency reserves (which amounted to Rs 1 billion).[17] Other problems which were left unresolved, included the assessment of assets of the Government of British India, double taxation, regulation of currency in circulation, separation of foreign exchange accounts, and provision of temporary loan facilitates to Pakistan by the Reserve Bank of India.

Economic warfare was accompanied by military confrontation. The jihad in Kashmir began in September 1947. During 1947–8, over a million Muslims attained martyrdom in India and in the next four years, five million refugees crossed into East and West Pakistan.[18]

Papanek (1970, p. 24) wrote that 'at independence Pakistan was widely considered an economic monstrosity.' There was literally no alternative to state interventionism. According to Maulana Maududi (1979), the political leadership proved ineffective and directionless; there were many instances of Muslim League leaders participating in the looting of refugee camps and in usurping evacuee property. The civil and military leadership was more disciplined. It was dominated by graduates from Aligarh—Ayub Khan the top-ranking Pakistani in the military was an Aligarh graduate—and by Muslim émigrés. This group had a strong commitment to liberal nationalism and to the development of a strong and modern economy.

The leadership's first bold policy initiative was the decision not to devalue the rupee in the wake of the sterling devaluation of 1949. India, which did devalue, intensified its economic warfare by suspending all trade with Pakistan. Pakistan had to impose import controls during 1949–50, but these were lifted following the impact of the Korean boom on commodity prices. Pakistan had a substantial trade surplus during 1950 to 1953. But agriculture's sectoral terms of trade deteriorated, and manufacturing industry grew at an annual average rate of well over 25 per cent during this period.

Raw material prices collapsed in 1953–4 and import controls were re-imposed. These remained in place for over a decade and an incentive system was thus created for the rapid expansion of manufacturing investment. Papanek (1970) pointed out that rates of return in industry were so high that investors were able to recover the full value of their investment, sometimes on an annual basis. Pakistan's commitment to import substitution dates from 1953–4. The sectoral terms of trade continued to move against agriculture as the government imposed controls on commodity prices.

The modernizing commitments of the government were thus clear as was its commitment to liberalism. It saw the private sector as the main agent of development. The foreign reserves that had been accumulated during the Korean boom were used to finance private sector machinery imports and the Pakistan Industrial Development and Investment Corporation (PICIC) and the Pakistan Industrial Financing Corporation (PIFCO) were set up to establish public industrial units which were then transferred to the private sector—PIDC played a crucial role in the development of the East Pakistan jute industry dominated by the Ispahani group, a major Muslim League financier since the early 1940s.

High rates of output and investment growth were maintained during 1949–54 and GDP grew at the annual average rate of over 5 per cent per annum. But this growth proved unsustainable due to stagnant agricultural productivity. As Haq (1961) shows, foreign exchange reserves fell and increased amounts had to be committed to import grain: this increased imperialist leverage over the economy. The US played a key role in the ouster of Khwaja Nazimuddin's government in 1953 by withholding wheat shipments. This in turn paved the way for Pakistan's incorporation within the global military alliance centred on the Baghdad Pact, SEATO, and NATO.

Agricultural stagnation led to a fall in the demand for manufacturing goods and the devaluation of 1956 proved ineffective. The government initiatives in 1955–6 to revive agricultural production (through subsidization of fertilizers and expansion of irrigation facilities) was principally concerned with relieving the constraint on manufacturing growth. Ahmad and Amjad (1986) point out that the pro-urban industrial bias of government policy was not reduced. This is reflected in the government's rigorous control of prices and the rationing of grain. Khan (1967) shows that while manufacturing profits soared, real wages remained stagnant during the 1950s.[19]

The government pursued a mildly expansionary fiscal policy during the 1950s. Revenue receipts rose slowly in real terms and capital receipts were small. The overall deficit to GNP ratio fell from 2.6 per cent in 1949–50 to 2.0 per cent in 1957–8. The share of external resources in capital receipts rose from less than 5 per cent in 1949–50 to 14.6 per cent in 1957–8. Capital expenditure of the government doubled during this period. Revenue expenditure rose from Rs 1.2 billion to Rs 2.4 billion. Andrus and Mohammad (1966) show that the income elasticity of taxation remained low, but indirect taxes were marginally more elastic than direct taxes. Estimates of deficit financing vary widely, but it is generally accepted that it was the main source of development expenditure during the 1950s. According to Haq (1961), its inflationary impact was modest.

Monetary policy was conservative. Its main objective was offsetting the balance of payment trends. In 1948, the State Bank fixed a bank rate of 5 per cent and low cash reserve requirements. From 1950, the State Bank became concerned principally with protecting the value of the rupee—it banned the forward booking of foreign exchange and imposed a high deposit requirement for opening letters of credit. These restrictions were eliminated after the building up of external reserves during the Korean boom. The impact of the rise in reserves on the growth of money supply was reduced by the imposition of export duties. In 1952, following a dramatic decline in reserves, the open general licence under which most importing occurred, was suspended. During 1953–5, the money supply rose rapidly but price stability was maintained due to a decline in the private sector's demand for credit. During 1955–8, monetary assets rose sharply while production remained stagnant. Inflationary pressure increased due to increased deficit financing and monetary policy was ineffective. The State Bank could not influence government expenditure levels and the excess liquidity position of the banks rendered variations in reserve requirements and in the bank rate ineffective. The State Bank restricted its initiatives to influencing the composition (rather than the size) of bank credit.

Overall, the first decade of independence saw the consolidation of liberal, modernizing policies. There was no effective opposition to this policy orientation. The Islamic parties suffered serious political set-backs and, following the expulsion of Pir Saheb Manki Sharif and the humiliation of Maulana Sulaiman Nadvi (may Allah bless them), the Muslim League become a totally secularist party. The stage seemed set for building a modernized, secular Pakistan.

B. POLEIZESTAT 1959–72
The elite administrative and military services became disillusioned with the Reichestat which, in their view, hindered progress. The effective execution of the liberal modernizing state project required the form of a developmentalist Poleizestat.

Papanek (1970, p. 117) calls the 1958–68 period 'the era of good economic management.' Throughout his book, he stresses the continuity of policy perspectives from the 1950s. Ayub represented an acceleration of the pace of implementation of the state project aimed at the liberal modernization of Pakistan. Ayub was a more consistent and more resourceful liberalizer, than his predecessors. His downfall was therefore more dramatic.

The period began with the imposition of strict controls on prices and attempts at eliminating black marketing. But by June 1960, prices were decontrolled, the trade regime was liberalized and private sector investment was officially recognized as 'the engine of growth'. There were large increases in the inflow of foreign loans.

But as in the 1950s, the Ayub boom was a short-lived phenomenon. After the 1965 jihad, foreign loans dried up, food shortages re-emerged, industrial growth slowed, and controls on imports had to be re-imposed.[20] The country was torn apart by major political upheavals during 1968–71 which prevented the economy from reaping the full benefits of the improvement in grain yields during 1968 and 1969.[21] According to Qayyum (1980), land reforms envisaging unification of conditions of tenancy throughout West Pakistan, abolition of jagirs (with compensation), and the imposition of ownership ceilings were generally regarded as ineffective and not particularly injurious to feudal interests.[22]

The Second Five Year Plan (1960–65) committed the government to an economic ideology approved by the Harvard Development Advisory Group.[23] As mentioned by Papanek (1970), this approach celebrates the 'social utility of greed' and assumes that pro-private sector policy orientation will ensure the availability of substantial foreign resources for filling both the domestic savings and the foreign exchange gaps.[24] The Perspective Plan of the Government of Pakistan (1965) envisages that the need for foreign concessional assistance would decline significantly over a twenty year period.

Pro-private sector policies entailed import liberalization through easier accessibility to import licences and an expansion of investment and trade businesses in which government sanction was not required. The industrial bias of the 1950s was maintained through over-valuation of the rupee and the maintenance of control on agricultural prices.[25] Tax holidays, accelerated depreciation, and interest subsidization also facilitated industrial sector growth which averaged 17.6 per cent per annum during 1959–65. Wages of urban workers were also kept low.

Output growth was accompanied by price stability. The wholesale price index increased at a rate of less than two per cent per year during 1960–65. Export earnings were enhanced by the introduction of the export bonus scheme. This increased the earnings of exporters by almost 40 per cent in a typical year.[26] Other export incentives were also instituted. Lewis (1969) noted that the effectiveness of the scheme was constrained by the increased pace of import liberalization after 1963.

The system started to be strained in the fiscal year 1965–6. There were a series of bad harvests and a gradual drying up of foreign loan inflows. This led to a slowing down of manufacturing sector growth and a re-imposition of import controls. Macroeconomic planning was effectively abandoned in 1967 and the proposed shift from 'easy' import substitution— the transition from a consumer to a capital goods dominated industrial structure—could not be achieved. Inter-regional and inter-personal disparities of income and wealth increased. Baqai (1976) argues that there is little hard evidence to substantiate the claims of net transfer of resources from West to East Pakistan, since both regions were deficit areas in terms of inflow of foreign resources. However, in East Pakistan the economy grew more slowly and private investment was less responsive to the growth in public development spending. Also, Guisinger and Irfan (1974) show that the stagnation in real wage growth was more pronounced in East Pakistan.

Throughout the Ayub era, the government maintained tight control on expenditure. Revenue receipts rose from Rs 2.45 billion in 1957–8 to Rs 8.2 billion in 1967–8. Capital receipts rose even faster, from Rs 1.67 billion to Rs 5.1 billion in 1967–8.[27] There was a substantial surplus on the consolidated budget in a typical year. But by 1967–8, this had turned into a small deficit. External resources usually amounted to 50 per cent of capital receipts. Public sector investment exceeded private sector investment but the former was concentrated in the agricultural, water and power, and transport sectors. Heavily subsidized institutional credit was made available to the private sector.

Despite relative price stability, money supply growth was high during 1959–65. Private sector demand was the prime cause of monetary expansion. Bank credit grew rapidly and remained cheap despite an increase in the bank rate. Reserve requirements were raised in 1963 and a credit quota system was introduced. In 1965, the quota system was abolished and the bank rate raised to 5 per cent. The liquidity ratio was raised to 25 per cent and credit ceilings were imposed. Annual credit budgeting was introduced in 1968. In January 1971, the credit quota system was re-introduced and margin requirements against imported consumer goods were raised. Meenai (1977) notes that margin requirements were also imposed on advances for opening letters of credit and on advances against deposits and real estate.

The fiscal stance and monetary policy remained conservative throughout the period. Ayub Khan fell because his macroeconomic strategy was premised on the continued availability of imperialist support. However, imperialist support was withdrawn after the 1965 jihad. Moreover, political resources were not available to the regime to counter the initiatives of its major rival—the Awami League—which also enjoyed imperialist support. The Basic Democracy system was not designed as an instrument for political mobilization. Ayub did not possess domestic political resources to withstand imperialist betrayal. His was a typical client regime.

Ayub's opposition in West Pakistan was secular but not committed to liberalism. It swept to power on a tide of rising expectations and economic grievances. The Islamic parties endorsed the economic agenda of the secularists although they rejected the political content of secularist manifestos.[28] The

Islamic parties had become part of the democracy movement since the Mohtarama Fatima Jinnah campaign. As Islam is essentially an anti-democratic world view, apologetics aimed at Islamizing democratic practices necessarily lack coherence. The political defeat of the Islamic parties at the end of the Ayub era was a consequence of their endorsement of democratic programmes.

C. SOZIAL-POLEIZESTAT 1972–7

The second failure of the liberal state project led to its temporary abandonment in West Pakistan. Supporters of the Zia regime, like Burki and La Porte (1984, p. 16), later accused Bhutto 'of the total destruction of the institutions which contributed to the economic growth in the sixties.' But the destruction was sporadic, half-hearted, unintentional, and incomplete.

Lodhi (1979) has shown that the Pakistan's People's Party (PPP) contained two major disparate elements. The feudal lords dominated the parliamentary party and the provincial leadership. Communist activists and intellectuals, with a strong hatred of Islam, led the labour wings and were well represented in the central leadership. Policy making had to be *ad hoc* and sporadic because these forces pushed in opposite directions. Moreover, as Burki (1981, p. 74) points out,

> one result of the anti-Ayub agitation was Bhutto's assessment that economics alone could not build and sustain political constituencies (and hence) Bhutto's commitment to economic development was weakened.

Consequently, so was economic performance. Ahmad and Amjad (1986) show that the land reforms undertaken in 1972 and 1977 were ineffective. Nationalization within the industrial sector was initially restricted to heavy industries. Hussaini (1974) argues that the benefits granted to labour and the peasantry were merely symbolic. As early as 1972, the Bhutto administration used strong repressive measures to crush the trade union movement. GDP growth averaged only 4 per cent during the Bhutto era.

The influence of the feudal lords was reflected in the 1972 massive devaluation of the rupee (which fell from Rs 4.9 to Rs 11 per dollar) and the 100 per cent increase in agricultural procurement prices. Both the devaluation and the rise in procurement prices had favourable economic consequences initially. Due to the rise in procurement prices, agriculture grew at an annual average rate of over 4 per cent and due to the positive impact of devaluation on exports, large-scale manufacturing grew at the rate of 6 per cent during 1972–4. However, the increase in exports led to a substantial increase in monetary expansion and inflation reached 30 per cent in 1973–4. The increase in the price of crude led to a doubling of the import bill. There was a sequence of floods and droughts. Commodity sector growth fell and private sector dis-investment accelerated during 1974–7. To counter this trend, the government embarked on a course of large-scale public sector investment in 1974. Capital expenditure rose from Rs 5.1 billion in 1972–3 to Rs 16.5 billion in 1976–7. In a typical year, expansionary financing accounted for 25 per cent of public capital expenditure. The projects financed had long gestation periods and generated little employment due to high capital intensity.

The public sector's share of total fixed investment rose from 52.7 per cent in 1972–3 to 79.5 per cent in 1976–7. Public sector saving was negligible: negative in 1972–3 to 1974–5 and 1.3 per cent of GDP in 1975–6 to 1976–7. Foreign resource inflow increased, as did remittance inflows, but gross domestic saving was lower in 1976–7 than it had been in 1972–3.

The period was characterized by waste, inefficiency, and *ad hoc*ism. There were large increases in current expenditure. This meant that banks (which had been nationalized in 1974) and public sector industries became the property of the PPP men and their associates in the bureaucracy. Policy implementation was so ineffective that agriculture's sectoral terms of trade were lower in 1976–7 than in 1964–5 (the heyday of the urban bias policy). Similarly, Burki (1981) contends there is considerable evidence to show that despite the PPP's loudly trumpeted socialism, income distribution actually worsened during 1972–7.

The ineptness of state initiatives was most graphically evident in the field of monetary management. Monetary assets grew at an annual average rate of over 16 per cent during 1972–7. GDP real growth was however only 4 per cent per annum. The price indices soared. The banks faced an acute liquidity shortage. Interest rates rose and margin requirements were imposed against imports. Janjua (1988) contends that credit planning proved ineffective since medium-term national planning was abandoned and the annual development plans became victims of *ad hoc*ism. The State Bank found it impossible to contain government borrowings. Public sector borrowings from the banking system also skyrocketed after 1974–5.

The Bhutto era was characterized by a high level of victimization of political opponents within and outside the PPP. Nepotism, corruption, and sycophancy typified the political culture of the PPP. Amir (1981) views the PPP as an anti-Islamic party and in the mid-1970s it openly flouted Islamic norms and values, encouraging the growth of obscene literature and the erosion of Islamic morality. It was not surprising that the mass movement launched in the wake of the heavily-rigged 1977 elections soon assumed an Islamic character. The revolutionary potential of the Nizam-i-Mustafa movement was considerable. It represented a coming together of the Islamic parties and a brief demonstration of the capacity of the mosque as a revolutionary base. However, the Islamic orientation of the movement was overshadowed by its commitment to the restoration of a constitutional order and to democracy. It did not succeed in conceptualizing the process of transcending the secular and liberal political order. Bhutto's downfall remained its only major achievement.

D. POLEIZESTAT 1977–88

Bhutto's successor saw the need to assimilate this movement and dissipate its revolutionary potential. Hence the emphasis on Islamic symbolism and the concern to accommodate an Islamic element within the power elite. The political system the new regime sought to create was a modified version of the Ayub dispensation and care was taken to re-name existing practices—interest was rechristened 'mark-up', land tax 'ushr' etc.—to gain Islamic support for Zia's economic policies.[29]

In the opinion of the World Bank (1989, p. 7), 'with continuously improving policies in the 1980s, Pakistan's economic performance has been strong relative to (most) developing countries.' Real GDP growth averaged 6.3 per cent per annum during 1978–88. Strong growth occurred in large-scale manufacturing (almost 8 per cent per annum). Fixed investment growth was usually lower than the growth in GDP.[30] Gross domestic saving fluctuated widely but remittances soared, averaging about $ 2.3 billion in the early 1980s when they were the most important source of foreign exchange earnings. Despite this, the current account deficit was usually large, averaging over $ 1.4 billion or about 5 per cent of GDP. Long-term public capital inflows grew rapidly in addition to massive military aid for the support of the Afghan jihad. Despite this, debt service ratios remained modest—typically, 15 per cent of exports.

From its inception, the Zia regime espoused a pro-private sector ideology but it moved cautiously in dismantling the initiatives of the Bhutto era. Banks and DFIs were not denationalized and within the public sector, the capital and intermediate goods public industries continued to operate much as before, serving as channels for the dispensation of favours by the government. Economic planning was revived and the Sixth Five Year Plan (1983–8) was applauded by the World Bank (1987, pp. 17–8) for its success in:

> the liberalization of investment sanctioning, de-regulation of cement, edible oil, and fertilizer prices, (encouragement) of private sector marketing of rice, edible oil, and fertilizer, (increase) of gas prices (and) more flexible management of the exchanges rate.

Zaidi (1995) indicates that after 1982, when an IMF standby facility was acquired on the basis of the commitment to institute Pakistan's first structural adjustment programme, pressure started to mount for reducing the budget deficit which averaged

8 per cent of GDP during 1978–88.[31] The fiscal deficit rose after 1981–2 despite the curtailment of the public investment programme—the main explanatory factor here was a rapid increase in interest payments on government debt. This reflected a conscious switch in the deficit financing strategy of the government. According to Haque and Montiel (1991), under instruction from the Bank and the Fund, the government substituted non-bank borrowing for both falling short-term external credit and domestic borrowing from the banking sector. Interest rates rose also on approval from the World Bank (1987). By 1987–8, public sector interest payments were accounting for over 70 per cent of the increase in the debt-GDP ratio. The external debt to GDP ratio rose from about 35 per cent to almost 43 per cent during 1982–8.

Inflation remained low during most of the 1980s. Credit planning became more effective. As Janjua (1988, p. vi) notes, 'Credit budgeting at least at the macro level has proved an effective method of containing monetary growth and in restraining price pressure.' Whatever monetary indiscipline existed was a consequence of the need to accommodate the fiscal and balance of payments deficits. Private sector credit expansion also tended to exceed targeted levels, but this was mainly offset by the decline in borrowings by public corporations.

Unlike his predecessors, Zia did not experience an economic downturn. He outflanked his political rivals. There was massive popular approval for his bold support of the Afghan jihad. He encouraged the growth of ethnic movements in Sindh to reduce the influence of the Jama'at-i-Islami. Ahmed (1986) suggests that his administration also fostered the anti-Islamic women's movement as a means for countering demands for the implementation of Islamic laws. Despite this, he retained the support of influential segments of the Tablighi Jama'at and the Jama'at-i-Islami and the policy-liberalizing process he initiated was brought to fruition by his successors—Benazir and Nawaz Sharif.[32]

E. REICHSTAT 1988–

At the time of General Zia's *shahadat*, both major political parties espoused the liberal cause.[33] The Islamic parties were fragmented, marginalized, and factionalized. They were easily incorporated within the alliances led by the liberal parties.

In its first month of office, the Benazir administration ratified an agreement with the IMF which committed it to a medium-term macroeconomic and structural adjustment programme for 1989–91. Pakistan thus embarked on a never ending adjustment process in which the first IMF agreement has been followed by SAF/ESAF/EFF and several sectoral agreements in 1991, 1993, and 1995.

These agreements commit the government to meeting quarterly macroeconomic targets set by the IMF. Economic sovereignty has been surrendered and Pakistan is well on its way to becoming an American colony. The key features of the successive SAF/ESAF/EFF agreements are as follows:

1. Reduction in the level of military expenditure.
2. Competitive devaluation.
3. Privatization and de-regulation of the economy.
4. Liberalization of foreign trade and elimination of controls on capital flows.
5. Reduction in the consolidated budget deficit.
6. Curtailment of the growth of high-powered money and of domestic credit and linking domestic interest rates to international money markets.[34]

Fiscal and monetary policies are constrained by these commitments and economic planning has been abandoned.[35] There were deviations from the course chartered by the IMF in 1991–2, 1995, and 1996, but the imperialists now have the political resources within Pakistan to dispossess the segment of the liberal governing elite which falls out of line. This is the lesson to be learnt from Nawaz Sharif's replacement by the US client regimes of Moeen Qureishi and Benazir and the subsequent dismissal of Benazir.

Singh (1994) argues that in Pakistan, as in most developing countries, Fund/Bank sponsored adjustment programmes have failed in their stated objectives of achieving sustainable improvements in fiscal and payments balance. They have led to a significant deceleration of output growth which has been halved during 1988–95 in comparison to 1981–8 and de-industrialization has occurred—the share of large-scale manufacturing in GDP has fallen from 12.9 per cent in 1987–8 to 12.6 per cent in 1994–5.[36] Investment and saving rates have stagnated. The current account deficit remains large. External reserves have fluctuated widely in response to uncontrollable inflows and outflows of capital. Inflation has reached double digit proportions and is fuelled by accelerated currency depreciation. Government bank borrowing is high and the budget deficit has averaged over 6 per cent during 1988–95.

The IMF (1996, p. iii), the major sponsor of the colonial economic strategy, has recognized 'the emergence of large macroeconomic imbalances in Pakistan' and has drawn up 'a medium-term programme of adjustment and structural reform for a three year period at the start of (fiscal) 1996–7 (with the) support of multi-years fund arrangements.'[37]

Fiscal policy during the new colonial period (1988–) has concentrated on a switch from trade to withholding and domestic sales taxes, a reduction in public capital expenditure, and an increase in user prices of utilities. Khalid et al. (1993, 1994, 1995) show that interest payments on public debt typically absorbed 37 per cent of total resources available to the government. The share of defence expenditure has fallen since 1990. Privatization proceeds have not been used for debt retirement.

Monetary policy during the new colonial period has been restrictive. Prudential regulations have been introduced. This has led to a severe curtailment of long-term financing.[38] The State Bank has become the main instrument for the implementation of colonialist macroeconomic policy. Interest rates have been jacked up and concessional credit schemes have been reduced; credit planning has been abandoned (in 1995); open market operations and control over the growth of reserve money and the net domestic assets of the banking system have become the major policy instruments. However, the SBP has been relatively powerless to check the growth of government bank borrowings which have generally exceeded targets negotiated with the IMF.

3. IMPACT

A. GROWTH AND STRUCTURAL CHANGE

The deceleration of GDP growth during the 1990s has been widely noted. A recent careful evaluation of growth trends by Iqbal (1995, p. 2) shows that 'since 1975, Pakistan's economy has been operating below capacity'. Iqbal finds that foreign exchange is the binding constraint on the potential growth rate of Pakistan's economy, but paradoxically, 'the growth rate of the potential output of Pakistan's economy is quite low (i.e., 2.3 per cent) when foreign exchange is the dominant binding constraint' (p. 11). Iqbal shows that 'increased capacity utilization reduces potential output when foreign exchange is the binding constraint' (p. 11).[39] Pakistan is a typical colonized economy dependent on foreign resource inflows characterized by a low elasticity of substitution between domestic and foreign resources.

Structural deformities in Pakistan's economy emphasizing its colonized status have been noted by most comprehensive analyses. The revised PIDE model prepared in the mid-1980s indicates that decreasing customs duties reduced imports through the negative impact on public investment and consumption. Using this model, Naqvi (1986, p. 64) illustrates 'the extreme sensitivity of the macroeconomy to even a small reduction in foreign capital inflows'. He notes in addition, that there is a structural tendency for a relative secular fall in public and private investment growth and an increase in the trade gap and in private consumption. Manufacturing value-added (MVA) and export growth rates also have a tendency to decelerate. The high growth experienced in some years is due to exogenous shocks and low capital output ratios.

Structural deformities are also apparent in the commodity producing sector. Agricultural sector growth has been low and mainly confined to exportables. Nabi et al. (1986) contend that land reforms have been ineffective (as earlier indicated also) and that the tenure system constrains growth. Doros and Valdes (1990) claim that effective protection rates have remained highly negative for non-exportable food crops since 1972, although they have improved for agricultural exportables.

As earlier indicated, Pakistan is experiencing de-industrialization. Large-scale manufacturing industry's share in gross fixed capital formation has stagnated at an average of 19 per cent during 1988–95, and its employment share has now fallen to a little over 5 per cent.[40] Moreover, Griffin and Khan (1972), among many others, assert that industrial growth has been highly inefficient in the 1950s and 1960s. Naqvi and Kemal (1991) confirm that inefficiency and variations in protection levels did not improve during the 1970s and the drastic fall in manufacturing sector growth in the 1990s illustrates that policy liberalization has had a negative impact on manufacturing efficiency.

Structural change within the manufacturing sector has been perverse in that the share of the capital goods sector in total production (ISIC 381, 382, 383, 384, and 385) has declined from 13.1 per cent in 1977–8 to about 8.3 per cent in 1993–4.[41] Their share in manufacturing value-added is now also about 8 per cent, reflecting the backwardness of the technology employed. Pakistan's technological underdevelopment has been noted by authors such as Thomas (1992) as well as several others.

The underdevelopment of the capital goods sector is directly related to the drastic reduction in defence spending. This has fallen dramatically from an average of over 40 per cent of government current expenditure during 1982–8 to about 26 per cent in 1996. Empirical research has shown that there is a strong positive association between defence spending and growth of output per capita for developing countries as a group (Benoit, 1978; Fredricksen and Looney, 1982) and for Pakistan (La

Citivita and Fredriksen, 1991; Tahir, 1995). But defence spending cannot be locally sourced in a colonized economy and, since 1988, its growth is seen as a threat to imperialist hegemony. Multilateral agencies and their local quislings are therefore campaigning vigorously against growth in defence expenditure despite the growth of the threat from American forces in the Gulf and the rising tide of Indian atrocities in held Kashmir.

B. INVESTMENT AND SAVING

The stagnation of investment and saving rates has been a consequence of the growing ineffectiveness of monetary and fiscal policies. It is widely noted by many researchers (such as Singer, 1994; Carbo, 1992) that an unavoidable consequence of the implementation of the IMF/Bank-sponsored colonialist reintegration programme is a fall in the investment/GDP and domestic saving to GDP ratios. Moreover, outward orientation usually contributes to a deterioration in the terms of trade. Structural adjustment failed in achieving its stated objectives in Pakistan's case. In the new colonial period, as Iqbal (1994, pp. 13–14) states, 'our relatively robust regression results show that real output growth declined, the inflation rate increased, and (the growth of) exports remained insignificant while imports and government consumption increased.'

The inability to control the fiscal deficit reflects both the income inelasticity of the taxation structure and the domestic debtfuelled expansion of current public expenditure. Pasha (1995) contends that the tax and tariff structural changes envisaged in the SAF/ESAF programmes have been widely resisted and their implementation has been sporadic and halting. These changes have been resisted by powerful outsider groups— specially national industry—which stand to lose from de-industrialization and from the increased regressivity of the taxation structure. This opposition can prove effective in the long run only if it challenges the legitimacy of the process of state policy recolonization.

The ineffectiveness of monetary and fiscal policies is illustrated by Naqvi (1989, p. 23): examining the inflationary process during the 1970s and 1980s, he shows that 'three-fourths of inflationary expansion is caused by factors which are not manipulatable by domestic policy action... An adverse movement in import prices may suddenly upset the apple cart rather unceremoniously'. For the 1990s, however, it has been found that 'contrary to popular perception, the contribution of supply shocks and monetary expansion to the increase in the rate of the wholesale price index in 1994–5 is somewhat limited'. The principle factors contributing to inflation appear to be the rise in procurement prices (wheat), administered prices (energy), and the increase in indirect taxes (GST). Many of these actions have been taken as part of the agreement with the IMF as documented by Hassan et al. (1995, p. 15). Fiscal policy is becoming effective but in the perverse sense that it is stifling growth and subordinating domestic price structures to the price formation processes in imperialist markets. The effectiveness of monetary policy is declining. Aslam (1995, p. 21) points out: 'Money supply is not exogenous. It depends heavily upon the position of international reserves.'

The recolonization of the economy is also evident in the gradual build-up of a major financial crisis in Pakistan. This has been achieved by the implementation of World Bank (1994) sponsored financial sector restructuring.[42] The costs of public borrowing have increased astronomically since 1987–8; interest payments on domestic debt have tripled and in 1994–5 this constituted 31 per cent of total government current expenditure. Treasury bill rates have more than doubled since auctioning started in 1991.

The recovery position of the banks and DFIs has deteriorated. The total uncollectible debt now exceeds Rs 200 billion according to State Bank estimates. According to the World Bank (1994, p. 14), 'The DFIs have virtually used up all of their foreign origin funds and will have to phase out of term lending.' It is this rapid deterioration in asset quality which has made privatization in the financial sector little more than a farce.[43]

The increase in interest rates and the application of prudential regulations are contributing to an increase in the concentration of credit. However, according to the World Bank, (1994, p. 15), 'credit demand is greater at the level of medium and small enterprises which usually have no access to commercial bank or DFI funds.' While several new domestic and foreign banks have appeared since the advent of financial liberalization, none of them focus on the small and the medium segment of the market.

The private manufacturing sector's share of bank credit has fallen dramatically during the financial liberalization period. In 1988, private manufacturing received 5.1 per cent of total scheduled bank advances. In 1994, its share had fallen to 1.8 per cent. In absolute terms, credit advanced to private manufacturing by banks amounted to Rs 8.5 billion in 1988. In 1994, this had fallen to Rs 7.3 billion—a 15 per cent decline in absolute terms. This is de-industrialization with a vengeance. The capital goods industries are virtually totally starved of long-term credit now.

There is no systemic evidence to show that the liberalization of financial policy has contributed to an increase in financial intermediation. The financial intermediation ratio continues to remain in the 40 to 42 per cent range. During 1994–5, the growth in currency in circulation was by far the single most important cause of M2 growth, accounting for about 46 per cent of the latter. Financial deepening has occurred at the top of the market with the development of sophisticated instruments, but the financial base itself remains narrow. This amounts to a strategy for turning the financial sector into an enclave of foreign capital.

C. Colonial Re-integration

The Financial Sector Deepening and Intermediation Project (FSDIP) 1995–2000 is explicitly designed to subordinate Pakistan's financial system to imperialist money markets. The bank inspection and supervision system of the State Bank is to be redesigned to maximize imperialist penetration. An Information Systems Strategy Plan (ISSP) is being implemented to facilitate transmission of information to Washington. The Corporate Law Authority is to be similarly restructured to facilitate financial sector sabotage by metropolitan capital. All public financial institutions are to be sold to international consortia.[44] Foreign domination of the insurance industries is also envisaged.

Metropolitan capital has already established a stranglehold over Pakistani money and capital markets. In 1994 and 1995, almost fifty per cent of banking sector profits were made by foreign banks. Citibank—a family bank of the Rothschild group—is now the fifth largest bank in Pakistan and the leading market maker.[45] Foreign firms almost totally dominate the brokerage business in association with local underdogs. Capital market activity is influenced by the international fund managers and foreign company scrips make up the bulk of the 'blue chips' listed at our stock exchange. Within the manufacturing sector, multinationals dominate the intermediate branches—chemicals, pharmaceuticals, energy, and petrochemicals—which now produce about a quarter of total manufacturing value-added. Food manufacturing, which is one of Pakistan's largest manufacturing branches, also has a very high proportion of multinational investment.[46]

Foreign domination of the Pakistan economy has been facilitated by devaluation. Since the beginning of the new colonial period (1988), the Pakistani rupee has depreciated by about 70 per cent in terms of the US dollar, the Deutschmark, and the Japanese yen. This has had very little impact on the balance of trade. As Khan and Aftab (1995) show in an incisive study, the sum of import and export demand elasticities is only slightly greater than one—indeed, if the assumption of initial trade balance is discarded, the sum of demand elasticities is below unity. During the new colonial period (1988–96), the official and free market exchange rates have been close and only one-third of Pakistan's major exports are likely to respond positively to devaluation.[47]

Devaluation is necessitated by the colonial policy commitment to achieve a rapid cheapening of Pakistani assets, thus opening up Pakistan's economy to imperialist penetration. This penetration is reflected less by an increase in the trade/ GNP ratio—which has risen slowly from about 27 per cent at the beginning of the new colonial period to about 29 per cent in 1995[48]—and more in the growth of external indebtedness which is now almost 40 per cent of GDP. External debt servicing absorbs more than a quarter of the total export earnings. External debt is likely to grow rapidly since the IMF is encouraging the substitution of foreign loans for domestic borrowings.

An important channel for the transmission of imperialist control is the growth of the 'underground' economy. The share of the black economy is estimated at between 22 to 37 per cent (Shabsheigh, 1996; Ahmad and Ahmad, 1995) and its share now accounts for almost half of the value-added generated in the import sector (Shabsheigh, 1996). After the implementation of the new colonial policy package, according to Shabsheigh (1996), the 'underground GDP (is) dominated by the rise of underground economic activities in the external sectors'.

D. MORAL DECAY

The growth of the black economy is one aspect of the moral decay that is fostered by the state's commitment to liberalism. Liberalism is a quest for freedom and therefore inherently evil. Liberalism is a humanism seeking deification of the individual and announcing a fictional death of God.[49] Its rejection of the need for *fana* and for worship necessarily makes love impossible. This leads to the inexorable destruction of the family in liberal society through the univerzalization of female employment.

Defeminization—the commodification of female labour—is the central index measuring moral decay. Voluntary commodification of her labour power reflects Riffat's perception of herself as an antecedently individuated being incapable of surrender (Islam): she chooses citizenship, rejects motherhood. She rejects her role as a creator, thus distancing herself from her own Creator and Sustainer.

Commodified female labour exists mainly in the urban centres.[50] Here female labour participation rates have grown modestly from 11.8 per cent in 1978–9 to 14 per cent in 1991–2.[51] Moreover, the most rapid growth has been in the 35–44, 45–54, 55–59 and 60+ age groups. These are the post-childbearing age groups. Female labour participation rates have grown much more slowly in the 15–19 and 20–24 age groups. Female labour participation in these age groups is still less than 15 per cent.[52] By Allah's grace, the World Bank (1995) reports that Pakistan's fertility rate is still 6.1 as against 3.2 for India. It thus appears that the growth of female employment is mainly non-voluntary and occasioned by economic hardship. The Islamic virtues of *haya*, *ghairat,* and *iffat* retain legitimacy in Pakistani society. Defeminization is mainly confined to the social strata which are the local clients of imperialism.

The state has sought to promote defeminization through an extensive family planning programme. Success is however somewhat limited as, according to World Bank estimates, currently only about 14 per cent of ladies of childbearing age use contraceptives in Pakistan (World Bank, 1995), as against 40 per cent in Bangladesh, 43 per cent in India and 83 per cent in China. Mahmood and Zahid's (1993) finding that married ladies do not want more children is based on a survey which does not include a representative sample of Muslim women whose commitment to *haya* makes it impossible to respond to such surveys. Mahmood and Zahid (1993) show that contraceptive use has declined in rural areas (during 1983–91).

Some researchers have argued that there has been an increase in contraceptive use since 1993, but there is little evidence of association between contraception use and desired number of children. Mahmood and Zahid (p. 7) themselves find that 'the number of desired children do not explain variations in contraception use.' This is because prostitutes are the main users of contraceptive and family planning services in Pakistan. It is widely recognized that 'inflated service statistics' produced by the de-population industry in Pakistan represent a massive diversion of services to prostitutes and their clients. This cannot of course be revealed in official statistics.

Systematic evidence on prostitution is not available. The *Pakistan Household Integrated Survey 1990–91* has shown that marriages are being delayed, specially in urban areas. Other pilot studies conducted by the Islamic Research Academy, Karachi, have found an increase in casual prostitution only in lower middle class localities in Karachi and in rural northern Punjab. There is no nationwide trend towards a decline in the observance of *purdah* and the state-sponsored media campaign for the promotion of obscenity and pornography has had relatively limited impact.[53] The lifestyle of the liberal elite, specially of its youth, is widely condemned and the social isolation of the liberal elite is becoming increasingly apparent.

4. CONCLUDING REMARKS: THE JIHAD AGAINST LIBERALISM

The vibrancy of the Islamic spirit in Pakistan is evident from various indicators. There are 110,000 mosques and *madrasahs* in Pakistan and roughly 17,000 new mosques are built every year. *Madrasah* enrollment is growing at the rate of 13 per cent per annum; primary school enrollment is growing at the rate of 11 per cent. About 11 per cent of the male population regularly participates in daily congregational prayers and the proportion of female devotees is marginally higher. Three popular Islamic movements—the Tablighi Jama'at, the Ithna Ashari and the Dawat-e-Islami—have strong roots among the masses.

Islamic forces have immense political potential and strength in Pakistan. Their relative ineffectiveness since 1947 is explained by their inability to challenge liberal political practice. The theoretical basis for such a challenge was explicated by Hazrat Thanvi (may Allah bless him) in several tracts.[54] In the 1930s, Maulana Maududi (1937, 1953) also formulated a social theory which challenged attempts to legitimize Western civilization on Islamic grounds.[55] But the anti-democratic orientation of these theories was overwhelmed by the endorsement of liberal politics by Maulana Maududi[56] and by the followers of Hazrat Thanvi.[57]

The Islamic political parties became parts of democratic alliances in 1970, 1977, 1988, 1990, and 1993. Islamic mass movements remained ostensibly aloof from the political process.

The legitimization of democratic practice led to the emergence of an Islamic liberal elite which became influential in the policy making processes of parties such as the Tablighi Jama'at and the Jama'at-i-Islami. Islamic liberals sought to construct a national consensus on the basis of the Islamic provisions of Pakistan's constitution and to demonstrate the compatibility of Islamic and liberal economic policies. For this, the sub-discipline of Islamic economics enjoyed a brief popularity during the first half of the Zia decade when it had the support of the Gulf states, the World Bank, and the IMF.[58]

But Islamic liberalism—despite Binder's hopes—has failed in Pakistan. Islamic parties have suffered several electoral defeats. Liberal Islamic economic policies have been brushed aside by even sympathetic leaders such as Nawaz Sharif.[59] Islamic liberals have adopted a lifestyle which has distanced them from the ordinary members of the Islamic parties and from the Muslim masses. Moreover, Pakistan's subordination within the international financial system makes the piecemeal reforms proposed by the Islamic liberals impossible to implement.[60]

Meanwhile, there is tremendous pressure on Islamic parties to adopt a revolutionary stance. The nationalist claims of the liberal Muslims have proved false and the state they created in the name of Muslim nationalism is collapsing into the imperialist order. The Islamic groups have a glorious tradition of anti-imperialist struggle dating back to the jihad of 1857. They cannot accept a reduction in Pakistan's defence expenditure to less than 5 per cent of GDP while Indian defence expenditure has doubled during 1992–97 and US forces in the Gulf continue to pose a regional threat. Islamic groups are attracted to policies which reject liberal premises and IMF surveillance and make possible the creation of a jihadi economy in Pakistan capable of de-linking from the liberal imperialist order. Pakistan can and must develop as a front line Islamic state against liberal imperialism.

The vulnerability of liberalism has been heightened in recent years. Post-modernist authors have demonstrated the emptiness of the fundamental liberal categories of freedom and transcendental subjectivity. Western thought has come to be divided into two hostile camps with regard to its own self-image. This has engendered a legitimization crisis, exposing the false nature of the modernist's claim that ultimate justification can be provided on the basis of reason. Liberalism as a modernism has no future, for as Wittgenstein writes:

> The sense of the world must lie outside the world. In the world, everything is as it is and happens as it does happen. In it there is no value and if there were, it would be of no value. If there is a value which is of value, it must lie outside all happening and being so. For all happening and being so is accidental. What makes it non-accidental cannot lie in the world, for otherwise it would be accidental. It must lie outside the world. (1961).

The jihad against liberalism is based on the pre-Augustinian commitment 'Thy kingdom come, on earth as it is in heaven' and on a rejection of the possibility of the coexistence of the city of God and the city of Man. Christian and Islamic fundamentalism offer powerful alternative visions for they seek Riffat's eternal salvation and not her material well-being.[61] They remind her of her commitment to creation (motherhood) and to her Creator; how long can she prefer the fleeting pleasures of this illusory world to His and my eternal love? It is this remembrance which makes possible the transcendence of liberal autonomy, for Allah commands:

> Hold fast all together to the bond with Allah and do not separate...

REFERENCES

Ahmad, V., and Amjad, R. (1984), *The Management of the Pakistan Economy, 1947–1982*, Oxford University Press, Karachi.

Ahmad. (1986), 'Idarya', *Meesaq*, March, Lahore, pp. 1–11.

Ahmad, M., and Ahmad, Q. (1995), *Estimates of the Black Economy*, PIDE Eleventh Annual Conference, Islamabad.

Alavi, H. (1966), 'The army and the bureaucracy in Pakistan', *International Socialist Journal*, April, pp. 74–103.

———. (1972), 'The state in post colonial societies', *New Left Review*, July, pp. 15–47.

Ali, M. C. (1967), *Zahoor-i-Pakistan*, Karvan Press, Lahore.

Allana, G. (n.d.), *Pakistan Movement: Historic Documents*, Paradise Subscription Agency, Karachi.

Amir, I. (1981), *Bhutto ki Amriyat*, Maktaba-i-Tulaba, Karachi.

Andrus, F., and Mohammad, A. (1966), *Trade, Finance and Development in Pakistan*, Oxford University Press, London.

Ansari, J. A. (1966), 'Milli Yakjahti Council ka ayinda lai-e-amal', *Jassarat*, Karachi, February 26–9.

Ashraf, M. (1967), *Muslim Siyasat*, Vohra, New Delhi.

Aslam, M. (1995), 'Money supply, deficit and inflation in Pakistan', PIDE Eleventh Annual Meeting, Islamabad.

Avramovic, D. (1988), *Conditionality, Facts, Theory and Policy; Contribution to the Reconstruction of the International Financial System*, WIDER, Helsinki.

Azad, A. K. (1991), *Hamari Azadi*, Orient, New Delhi.

Banuri, T. (1995), 'Why sustainable development is neither', PIDE Eleventh Annual Meeting, Islamabad.

Banuri, T. and Marglin, A. (1992), *Who Will Save the Forests?* London, Zed Press.

Baqai, M. (1970), 'Disparity in per capita income', *Pakistan Economic and Social Review*, (Special Issue), 66–87.

Benoit, E. (1978), 'Growth and defence in developing countries', *Economic Development and Cultural Change*, 26, pp. 64–91.

Bhutto, B. (1989), 'Democratic nations must unite', Harvard, 8 June.

———. (1989), 'Moral as well as political partners', address to the Joint Session of US Congress, Washington, 7 June.

Burki, S. J. (1981), *Pakistan under Bhutto*, Oxford University Press, London.

Burki, S. J., and Laporte, R. (1984), *Pakistan's Development Priorities*, Oxford University Press, Karachi.

Chenery, H. (1979), *Structural Change and Development Policy*, John Hopkins Press, Baltimore.

Corbo, V. et al. (1992), *Adjustment Lending Revisited*, World Bank, Washington.

Denffer, A. (1992), *A Day with the Prophet*, Islamic Foundation, Leicester.

Doros, P., and Valdes, A. (1990), *Effects of Exchange Rate and Trade Policies on Agriculture in Pakistan*, IFPRI, Rome.

Dworkin, R. (1978), '"Liberalism" in S. Hampshire', *Public and Private Morality*, Cambridge University Press, Cambridge, pp. 113–64.

Foucault, M. (1978), *Discipline and Punish*, Pantheon, New York.

Fredericksen, P. and Looney, R. (1982), 'Defence expenditure and economic growth', *Journal of Development Economics*, pp. 143–64.

Government of Pakistan. (1965), *Pakistan's Perspective Plan*, Planning Ministry, Islamabad.

———. (1966), Budget speech 1966–7, Ministry of Finance, Islamabad.

———. *Pakistan Economic Survey*, Economic Advisors Wing, Finance Ministry, Islamabad (annual).

Guisinger, S., and Irfan, M. (1974), 'Real wages of industrial workers of Pakistan', *Pakistan Development Review*, pp. 348–77.

Haq, A. (Maulana). (1956), *Ist'imar ki Chalain*, Jama'at-i-Islami, Balochistan, Quetta.

Haq, M. (1961), *Deficit Financing in Pakistan*, PIDE, Karachi.

Haque, N. U., and Monteel. P. (1991), 'The macroeconomics of public sector deficits: the case of Pakistan', Working Paper Series No. 673, World Bank, Washington.

Hare, R. M. (1970), *Freedom and Reason*, Cambridge University Press, Cambridge.

Hasan, A., Khan, A. H., Pasha, H., Rashid, A. (1995), 'What explains the current high rate of inflation in Pakistan', PIDE, Eleventh Annual Meeting, Islamabad.

Hayee, A. (Maulana). (n.d.), *Ma'arif' Hakim al Ummat*, Darul Ulum, Karachi.

Huda, N. (1993), *Hamara Dehi Ma'ashrati Nizam*, IRA, Karachi.

Hussaini, A. (1974), *Mazdur Tahrik par Bhutto key Mazalim*, NLF, Karachi.

Ibn Khaldun. *Muqadama*, (1937), Translated into Urdu by Maulana Hifz-ur-Rahman, Idara Nur, Delhi.

Ihsan, S. M. (1972), *Unees Sau Suttar key Intikhabat*, Ravi, Lahore.

IMF. (1995), *Memorandum on Economic Policies in Pakistan*, Washington, November.

———. (1995), *Staff Report: Article IV Consultation*, SM/92/298, Washington, November.

Iqbal, J. (ed.). (1994), *Siyasi Jamaton key Manshoor*, Islamic Era Publications, Lahore.

Iqbal, Muhammad, Allama. (1934), *Reconstruction of Religious Thought in Islam*, New Era Publishers, Lahore.

Iqbal, Z. (1994), 'Macroeconomic effects of adjustment lending', PIDE, Tenth Annual Meeting, Islamabad.

———. (1995), 'Constraints on the economic growth of Pakistan: a three gap approach', PIDE, Eleventh Annual Meeting Proceedings, Islamabad.

Janjua, A. (1985), *Monetary and Credit Control in Pakistan: Regulatory Approach*, SENEZA, Sydney.

Jessop, B. (1990), *State Theory*, Pennsylvania State University Press, Pennsylvania.

Kalecki, M. (1970), 'Observations on the social and economic aspects of intermediate regimes', in *Essays on Developing Economies*, (ed. M. Kalecki), Brighton, Harvester, pp. 87–101.

Khalid Majid Husain Rahman. *Tax Memorandum: Finance Bill*, Karachi (annual).

Khan, A. H., and Siddiqui, A. N. (1990), 'Money prices and economic activity in Pakistan: a test of causal relation', *Pakistan Economic and Social Review*, 127, pp. 121–36.

Khan, A. R. (1967), 'What has been happening to real wages in Pakistan', *Pakistan Development Review*, Autumn.

Khan, A. R., and Griffen, K. (eds.). (1977), *Growth and Inequality in Pakistan*, Macmillan, London.

Khan, S. R., and Aftab, S. (1995), 'Devaluation and the balance of trade in Pakistan', PIDE, Eleventh Annual Meeting Proceedings, Islamabad.

La, Citivita, C. and P. Fredrikren, (1991), 'Defence spending and economic growth', *Journal of Development Economics*, pp. 247–71.

Lacoste, Y. (1966), *Ibn Khaldun: Naissance de l'Historie Passe du*, Teirs Monde Libraire Francois, Maspero.

Lewis, S. R. (1970), *Pakistan Industrialisation and Trade Policies*, Oxford University Press, London.

Lodhi, M. (1979), 'The Pakistan People's Party', London School of Economics, unpublished Ph.D. thesis.

Luhmann, N. (1989), 'Staat und statraeson im ubergang von traditioneller. Herrschaft zu moderner politick', *Gesellschaft und Semantic*, Vol. 3. Frankfort, Subrkamp, pp. 65–148.

Mahdi, M. (1957), *Ibn Khaldun's Philosophy of History*, Brill, London.

Mahmood, N., and Zahid, G. (1993), 'The demand for fertility control in Pakistan', PIDE, Ninth Annual Conference, Islamabad.

Maududi, A. (1937), 'Islami Tahzeeb aur uske Usul-o-Mabadi', *Tarjumanul Quran.*

———. (1953), *Tanqeehat*, Islamic Publications, Lahore.

———. (1979), *Tahrik-i-Azadi-Hind aur Musalman*, pp. 1, 11, Lahore Islamic Publications Limited.

Meenai, S. A. (1977), *Money and Banking in Pakistan*, Royal Book Company, Karachi.

Muhammad, Ali. (1956), *My Life: A Fragment*, Orient, Karachi.

Nabi, I., Naveed, H., Zahid, S. (1986), *The Agrarian Economy of Pakistan*, Oxford University Press, Karachi.

Naqvi, S. N. H., and Ahmad, A. (1986), 'PIDE macroeconometric model for the Pakistan Economy', PIDE, Islamabad.

Naqvi, S. N. H., and Kemal, A. R. (1991), *Protectionism and Efficiency in Manufacturing: Pakistan*, ICEG / PIDE, San Fransisco.

Naqvi, S. N. H., and Khan, A. H. (1989), 'Inflation and growth: an analysis of recent trends in Pakistan', PIDE, Islamabad.

Papanek, G. (1970), *Pakistan's Development*, Oxford University Press, Karachi.

Pasha, H. (1995), *The Political Economy of Tax Reform: the Pakistan Experience*, AERC, Karachi.

Qayyum, A. (ed.). (1982), 'Policies and implementation of land reform in Pakistan', in Innayatullah, *Land Reform: Some Asian Experiences*, APDAC, Kuala Lumpur, pp. 18–44.

Qusuri, M. S. (ed.). (1987), 'Amir-i-millat aur tahrik-i-Pakistan', *Pakistan*, 2, Karachi.

Sajid, Z. (ed.). (1987),'Quaid-e-Azam ki qiadat ka awaleen jauhar jamhooriat', *Pakistan*, 2, pp. 134–47.

Shabshigh, G. (1996), 'Pakistan's underground economy', *Financial Post*, Karachi, March.

Singer, H. W. (1994), 'Structural adjustment programmes: evaluating success', in Gunning, J.W. et al. (eds.) *Trade, Aid and Development*, Macmillan, London, pp. 107–24.

Singh, A. (1994), *Policy Lending Approach*, AERC, Karachi.

Skinner, Q. (1989), State, in (ed. Ball, T.), *Political Innovation and Conceptual Change*, Cambridge University Press, Cambridge, pp. 90–131.

Tahir, R. (1995), *Defence Spending and Economic Growth: India and Pakistan*, PIDE, Islamabad.

Thomas, H. (1992), *Small is Beautiful*, NMC, Karachi.

Tumbly, E. W. R. (1954), *The Transfer of Power in India*, Allen and Unwin, London.

Usmani, Taqi, Maulana. (1990), 'Hakim al ummat kay siyasi afkar, *Al Balagh*, Karachi, 24, pp. 73–94.

Wittgenstein, L. (1961), *Tractcus logico-philosophicus*, (trans. Pears, D. S. and Guiness, B.F.), Routledge and Kegan Paul, London.

Wizarat, S. (1993), 'On profitability and industrial concentration in Pakistan', *Journal of Economic Behaviour and Organization,* 17, pp. 343–69.

World Bank. (1987), *Sixth Plan Progress and Future Prospects*, Report No. 6533 (Pak), Washington, February.

———. (1989), *Pakistan Medium-Term Policy Adjustments,* Report No. 7951 (Pak), Washington, March.

———. (1991), *World Development Report 1991*, Washington.

———. (1994), *Pakistan Financial Sector Deepening and Intermediation Project*, Report No. 12733-Pak, Washington.

———. (1995), *World Development Report 1995*, World Bank, Washington.

Zaidi, A. (1995), 'Locating the Budget Deficit in Context: The Case of Pakistan', *Pakistan Journal of Applied Economics*, 11, 1 and 2, pp. 113–28.

NOTES

1. Translated by Muhsin Mahdi as 'civilization' (Mahdi, 1957). More frequently rendered as 'life of the townspeople'.
2. Translated by Lacoste as 'the motor of the development of the state' (Lacoste, 1966).
3. Ibn Khaldun (1937). This is an Urdu translation. I have rendered this passage into English from Urdu.
4. Microeconomic policy is concerned with the management of civil society as a means for disciplining this individuality.
5. The Mohammadan Anglo Oriental College established by Sir Syed Ahmad Khan in the early 1870s to promote Western education among the Muslims.
6. Upon whom be peace and Allah's eternal blessings.
7. The inaugural session of the Muslim League was attended by the Aga Khan III (representing the commercial interests), Nawab Viqar-ul-Mulk (the feudal interest) and Maulana Muhammad Ali and Major Bilgrami (Aligarh).
8. Although maverick *ulema* such as Azad were involved as early as 1906. Azad himself attended the 1906 Dhaka session. *See* Azad (1991, pp. 148–52).
9. The two leading figures here being Ala Hazrat Ahmad Raza Khan Fazil Barelvi and Hazrat Hakim-ul-Ummat Ashraf Ali Thanvi (may Allah bless them).
10. Most pronouncements on economic issues by the League and its leaders during the 1940s were of a general, all-inclusive, and rhetorical nature.
11. Liaquat Ali Khan was the Minister of Finance in a coalition government, including both the League and Congress members, established after the 1946 elections.
12. The budget is evaluated in detail in Ali (1967). Chaudhry Mohammad Ali was the main author of this budget.
13. These reform commitments were extremely vague.
14. In Hare's (1970) terms, the elite possesses a consciousness of 'selfishness' and not 'self-interestedness'. It cannot accept self-discipline on the basis of the liberal rationality which it endorses at the level of discourse.
15. This conception of the purpose of policy is at apparent variance with Alavi's (1972) class centric discussion of the relative autonomy of the bureaucratic and military oligarchies of the 'overdeveloped' post colonial state. As a *zindiq*, Alavi pre-supposes that individuals are committed to the maximization of their welfare/power. Classes-for-themselves represent these 'interests'. The bureaucracy can be autonomous only if it seeks the universalization of liberal/capitalist rationality (aggregate welfare maximization), otherwise it is merely a 'caste' which cannot stand above society. As a Muslim, I reject the pre-supposition about the necessary

commitment of individuals or groups to welfare/power maximization. Such a commitment may be a consequence of the preference for freedom over *ibadat* (worship), for this world over the hereafter.

16. A hybrid state form combining elements of the Poleizestat and the Sozialstat, characteristic of many third world countries and aptly described by Kaleki (1976) as an 'intermediate regime'.

17. The total Indian reserves amounted to Rs 5 billion at the end of June 1947. The Congress offered to transfer Rs 200 million to Pakistan. The Muslim League demanded Rs 1 billion (one-fifth of the total). In January 1948, Rs 750 million were transferred to Pakistan.

18. These are conservative estimates.

19. The urban-industrial bias is reflected in the fact that the share of the manufacturing sector in total monetary investment rose from 30.4 per cent in 1949–50 to 35.1 per cent in 1959–60. The private sector accounted for more than 85 per cent of this investment (Papanek, 1970).

20. During 1966 and 1967.

21. This was due to the impact of the green revolution and also a consequence of the investments in the irrigation system undertaken during the second half of the 1950s.

22. *Jagirs* represented the transfer of rights of revenue collection and ownership of government-owned land by the British authorities to those traitor families who had supported the imperialists during the several jihads of the nineteenth and early twentieth centuries.

23. This group had been increasingly influential since the setting up of the Pakistan Institute of Development Economics (PIDE) under the directorship of Emille Despres. In the 1960s, its most influential members included Papanek, Lewis, Power, Waterston, Mahbubul Haq, and Nurul Islam.

24. Elasticity of substitution between domestic savings and foreign exchange is generally assumed to be low in the two gap models.

25. The rupee over-valuation was estimated at between 40 per cent to over 80 per cent in different years of the Ayub era.

26. To compensate for currency over-valuation, exporters were issued import permits to the value of up to 4 per cent of their export. These 'bonus vouchers' could then be sold at a premium of 130 per cent due to the existence of import shortages. Bonus rates varied in the 1960–66 period but were unified in 1967.

27. They had peaked at Rs 6.5 billion in the previous year.

28. Ihsan (1971) compares the economic elements of the PPP and the Jama'at-i-Islami election manifestos for 1970 and shows little major differences on key issues.

29. Local bodies were constituted broadly on the basic democracies pattern. Advisory councils were nominated and partyless elections and referenda were held on several occasions.

30. Except in 1987–8, when fixed investment grew by over 12 per cent in constant prices.

31. During 1972–7, the budget deficit to GDP ratio averaged well over 10 per cent but there were no warnings of impending doom from the World Bank or the IMF.

32. The Jama'at-i-Islami was the only Islamic party to support General Zia in the 1985 referendum.

33. The Muslim League was resurrected by General Zia as a liberal nationalist party. Benazir's return to Pakistan in 1986 was made possible by US pressure on General Zia. Benazir reciprocated by abandoning anti-imperialist socialist ideology and adopting economic and political liberalism as her party's platform in the 1988 and all subsequent elections. *See* Bhutto (1989).

34. These represent a combination of demand and supply conditionalities. The former include cutting deficit, raising interest, trade liberalization, and devaluation while the latter include investment restructuring and price de-control; cross conditionality—the linking of the conditionality of different sectors—has also been built into the most recent programmes. (*see* Avramovic, 1988).

35. The Eighth Five Year Plan (1993–8) was stillborn. As of March 1996, the Planning Ministry had not initiated the mid-term review rituals.

36. There are no reliable statistics for the small-scale sector which is presumed to have grown at the annual average rate of 8.4 per cent every year since 1980–81.

37. The Eighth Five Year Plan 1993–8 has thus been aborted by the ESAF/EFF of 1993–6, the Eighteen Month Programme of 1996–7 and the Medium Term programme planned for starting in July 1996.

38. Most term lending institutions referred to as the Development Finance Institutions (DFIs) are facing a terminal crisis. They have exhausted multilateral credit lines and resources raised in the domestic market are of a short-term nature. To avoid a mismatch in structure of assets and liabilities, DFIs have become merchant banks.

39. Data used to generate these results are for the period 1972–92.

40. Reliable statistics are not available, but the *Economy Survey 1994–95* shows that the mining and the manufacturing sectors account for about 12 per cent of the employed labour force of which roughly 75 per cent is in small industry.

41. The last year for which data are available in the UNIDO industrial statistics database.

42. Financial Sector Adjustment Loan (FSAL) implemented during 1989–91 and Financial Sector Deepening and Intermediation Project (FSDIP) under active consideration since 1995.

43. In March 1996, the share price of Pakistan's second largest bank, UBL, was Rs 15.6. Four years earlier, MCB had fetched Rs 56 and ABL Rs 74 per share.

44. The World Bank (1994) report mentions ICP, NIT, NDFC, Habib Bank, UBL, BEL, and PICIC.
45. Its deposits at the end of 1995 exceeded Rs 33 billion.
46. The estimates from UNIDO database are for 1993–4 and are therefore on the low side.
47. As expected, Khan and Aftab (1995) show that demand elasticity is high for primary products (raw cotton, leather, carpets). Colonies are suppliers of raw material to mother countries.
48. This reflects both the sluggishness of exports and the inability to finance import growth.
49. I seek the refuge and forgiveness of Allah for expressing this blasphemy.
50. Female labour in the agricultural sector is usually not commodified as remuneration is retained by the family. It is thus a form of household labour and has not led to family disintegration despite significant migration. Due to the preservation of joint family traditions, an elder male relative has usually taken the place of the migrant husband as the head of the household (*See* Huda, 1993).
51. More recent data are not available.
52. As against 18 per cent in the post-childbearing age groups.
53. The IRA study finds however a weakening of the *biradari* system in the small towns of the Punjab, a significant decline in *purdah* in the MQM-dominated localities of central Karachi, and an increased expenditure on hiring of video films to total earnings ratio in Northern Punjab (also in Lahore, Multan, Peshawar, and Khuzdar).
54. For example, *Fadail al ilm wal Khashia* and *Zum-al-Nisian* reproduced in part in Abdul Haye (n.d).
55. The view that some Western intellectual traditions were in conformity with the spirit of Islamic civilization was forcefully presented by Allama Iqbal (1934) and Maulana Muhammad Ali (1956).
56. Maulana Maududi (may Allah bless him) launched a movement for legitimizing the liberal state through the adoption of Islamic clauses in a democratic constitution in 1948.
57. Hazrat Thanvi's supporters, Maulana Shabbir Ahmad Usmani and Maulana Zafar Ahmad Ansari (may Allah bless them), joined the Muslim League and endorsed its policies. Maulana Shabbir Ahmad Usmani was present in the Constituent Assembly on 11 August 1947 when the Quaid-i-Azam gave his notorious 'you are free to go to your temples' speech and did not protest; Maulana Zafar Ahmad Ansari became the Joint Secretary of the Muslim League.
58. Islamic economics represents an attempt at legitimizing the ethics and institutions of capitalism. Islamic economists work within the neo-classical paradigm. The 'Islamic' consumer/producer/public policy maker is a utility maximizer (like his neo-classical compatriot) and the definition of his utility function is regarded as unproblematic. Although the

constraints within which utility maximization is sought by the Islamic economists are claimed to be uniquely Islamic, this is of little significance. For the Islamic economists also claim that in the long run, the elimination of interest, the introduction of Zakat etc., are necessary for the maximization of efficient production. The Islamic constraints thus appear in the guise of procedures which constrain short-term utility maximization so that long-term utility may be maximized. The Islamic economists are rule utilitarians and short-term constraints turn out to be no constraints at all in the long run.

This methodological similarity necessitates that the ethics of capitalism—acquisitiveness, competition, primacy of material well-being, freedom, liberal equality—are all endorsed by Islamic economics. Islam is seen not as a distinct civilization but as a means for reforming capitalism. Capitalism is criticized not for the ends it sets itself but for failing to achieve a 'balance' in the attainment of legitimately conflicting ends. Liberalism's history is littered with such apologetics. For a defence of liberal public order and its objectives (he calls it 'affluence'), *see* Banuri (1995, 1992).

59. He shelved the Khurshid Ahmad Report on Self-Reliance, refused to implement the anti-interest recommendations of the Islamic Ideology Council, and rejected the Draft Outline of the Eighth Five Year Plan. This last document is the swansong of the Islamic liberals and reflects the extraordinary political simplicity and intellectual naiveté characteristic of this group.

60. The Islamic liberals do not reject international financial integration. The Khurshid Report on self-reliance, for example, recommends privatization and a weakening of the state sector as the main means for Islamization of the financial system. In this perception, Islamization of the financial system requires a substitution of foreign public debt flows by foreign private equity. The capitalist property form is not considered illegitimate.

61. Hasan bin Ali bin Abi Talib said that when Allah sent Muhammad (PBUH), He said, 'This is My Prophet, this is My Prophet, this is My chosen one, love him and adopt his path. Doors are not locked up after him, nor do doorkeepers stand for him and trays of food are not served to him but he sits on the ground and eats his food from the ground. He wears coarse clothes and rides on a donkey with others sitting behind him and he licks his fingers after taking food. He says, "he who does not like my *sunna* does not belong to me". *Tabqat ibn Sa'ad*, quoted in Denffer (1992, p. 3).

PART TWO

TRADITIONAL TOPICS

B: SECTORAL ISSUES

4

Agricultural Development and Changes in the Land Tenure and Land Revenue Systems in Pakistan

*Mahmood Hasan Khan**

1. INTRODUCTION

The agricultural sector, including its structure of production, resource utilization, and technology, has undergone significant changes which have affected the national economy since Pakistan came into being in 1947. However, the agrarian structure and the system of land tax have changed little. Such changes could affect the structure of rural society, growth and distribution of agricultural income, and the state revenues for investment in building the social and physical infrastructure for the rural areas. Despite the much greater growth of industrial and urban economy, there is a disproportionately large influence of the rural elite on the social, political, and administrative structure of Pakistan. Its effects are visible in different and disturbing forms throughout the society. The process of agricultural transformation has been greatly distorted by the influence of the landed elite and the wrong policies of successive governments with regard to the land tenure system, agricultural taxation, price support and subsidies, and excessive regulation and control of the agricultural marketing system and processing industries.

This chapter focuses on some explanations of the process of agricultural transformation in Pakistan since its inception in

* Professor of Economics, Simon Frazer University, Canada

1947. More specifically, it analyses three major aspects of the transformation process: (1) changes in agricultural production, productivity, and their underlying sources, including inputs, technology, and public policy; (2) changes in the agrarian structure and land reforms; and (3) problems associated with the land tax (revenue) system.

2. CHANGES IN AGRICULTURAL PRODUCTION AND PRODUCTIVITY

In 1947, about 85 per cent of Pakistanis lived in rural areas and over one-half of the GDP was contributed by the agriculture sector. Notwithstanding the fact that non-agricultural sources have become quite important contributors to the national income, agriculture remains the key sector in terms of its backward and forward linkages affecting the living standards of rural and urban households. The transition referred to above has been brought about by several factors, including (i) growth of output and diversification of agriculture, (ii) employment of labour in non-farm activities and migration of rural labour to urban areas, (iii) growth of population, and (iv) changes in the pattern of landownership, tenurial relations, and parcelization of landholdings due to the growth of population and laws of inheritance.

The issues of rural poverty and development cannot be fully appreciated without examining several interrelated aspects of changes in the agriculture sector. Rural areas are the major reservoir of poverty in Pakistan and agriculture is the main activity on which most rural people depend for their livelihood. To understand the impact of agricultural growth on poverty in rural areas, it is particularly important to examine first the nature of agricultural growth in the last fifty years. The transformation of Pakistan's economy and the importance of agriculture are reflected in Table 1.[1]

Table 1
Importance of agriculture in Pakistan's ecomomy, 1950–1995

Year	Per cent share of agriculture in:			Per cent rural	
	GDP	Exports	Imports	Labour	Population
1950	53	80	21	68	85
1960	45	70	26	59	78
1970	38	63	19	57	74
1980	29	59	15	52	71
1990	23	25	19	47	69
1995	22	30	17	45	65

Source: *See* endnote 1.

Though the importance of agriculture has been declining in the overall process of economic growth in the country, its contribution is still significant: it engages 45 per cent of the country's labour force; creates over one-fifth of the Gross Domestic Product (GDP); absorbs nearly one-fifth of the imports; and contributes about one-third of the value of exports. Its real contribution to the GDP and exports is perhaps larger if allowance is made for price distortions and if the agro-based raw materials and goods are taken into account. A vast majority of the rural population—which is about 65 per cent of the country's population—depends on agriculture for its income.

Pakistan's economic record has not been too bad, considering the average annual GDP growth rate of 5 per cent since 1950 as evident from Table 2.

Table 2
Growth of gross domestic product agriculture value–added and population 1950–1995

Period	Annual average rate of growth of		
	Gross domestic product (GDP)	Agriculture value–added	Population
1950–55	3.4	1.4	2.0
1955–60	3.1	2.1	2.1
1950–60	3.2	1.7	2.0

1960–65	6.8	3.8	2.4
1965–70	6.8	6.4	3.0
1960–70	6.8	5.1	2.7
1970–75	4.5	0.8	3.2
1975–80	6.6	3.9	3.1
1970–80	5.5	2.4	3.1
1980–85	6.6	3.5	3.1
1985–90	4.6	4.4	3.0
1980–90	5.6	4.0	3.0
1990–95	4.1	3.4	2.9

Source: As in Table 1.

It seems that changes in the growth of GDP have been affected by the growth in agricultural output. Agricultural growth has, however, been modest and quite uneven: agricultural output has grown annually at just over 3 per cent in the face of a rising annual rate of population growth from 1.9 to nearly 3.0 per cent. The most impressive record of agricultural growth was in the 1960s, followed by the decade of the 1980s; the rate of agricultural growth was less than the population growth rate in the 1950s and 1970s. In the first half of the 1990s, the annual average growth rate has fallen to 3.4 per cent from 4 per cent in the 1980s. The lower rate of growth of agriculture and the relatively slow growth in industrial output have kept the annual average growth rate of GDP at just over 4 per cent in the first five years of the 1990s.

The highly aggregate growth rates of agricultural output do not reveal several important aspects of growth and distribution. For one, thing, not all sub-sectors in agriculture have experienced sustained growth, which is amply demonstrated by serious commodity imbalances within one crop year and over time. Second, not all growth in output, even in those activities in which it has been experienced in any significant way, has come from increased efficiency or at lower cost. Third, the growth experience has been highly uneven between various regions even within one province, particularly between regions with or without irrigation. Of course, provinces with limited irrigation facilities and infrastructure have been seriously handicapped. Finally, farm groups have also been affected unequally, depending upon their access to land and other related income-earning opportunities within agriculture or outside. All of these generalizations cannot be demonstrated with precision mainly because of insufficient data, but they are supported by a substantial body of evidence from studies based on the scattered primary (farm-level) and secondary (aggregate) data.

Agricultural output consists mainly of crops and livestock products, with fishing and forestry accounting for less than 6 per cent of the agricultural value-added. Major crops include all cereals (foodgrains), gram, cotton, sugarcane, tobacco, rapeseed, mustard, and sesamum. Minor crops include pulses (lentils), vegetables, and fruits. Livestock products (meat, milk, hides, wool, and eggs) are contributed by cattle, sheep, goats, and poultry. The growth in agriculture has come mainly from the major crops as shown in Table 3.

Table 3
Distribution of agriculture value-added
1950–1995

Period	Per cent share in agriculture value-added			
	Major crops	Minor crops	Livestock	Forestry & Fishing
1950–55	49.0	13.1	36.8	1.1
1955–60	50.3	11.9	36.7	1.1
1960–65	51.8	11.6	35.2	1.4
1965–70	55.4	12.4	30.5	1.7
1970–75	58.0	12.0	28.5	1.5
1975–80	56.8	13.5	28.5	1.2
1980–85	56.5	13.0	29.1	1.4
1985–90	48.7	17.5	28.8	5.0
1990–95	46.2	17.4	31.5	5.7

Source: As in Table 1.

The major crop sub-sector has dominated the agriculture sector and the national economy, with wheat, rice, cotton, and sugarcane playing the dominant role in providing food security and foreign exchange earnings. Minor crops have shown a more significant and sustained process of growth than that experienced by major crops. They have escaped the government's procurement policies and have responded well to the relatively sharper price increases in the open and unregulated markets. The increasing demand for fruits and vegetables in the domestic and Middle East markets has led to significant production increases and an expansion of the area used for orchards and vegetables.

Livestock products account for nearly one-third of the value-added in agriculture. Their annual growth rate increased from about 2 to 3 per cent in the period from the early 1950s to the early 1970s to around 5 per cent in the early 1980s and has been around 6 per cent since the mid-1980s. Sharp price increases of livestock products and the increased area for fodder crops have been the two main sources of development in this sub-sector. Favourable changes in public policy and the increased private investment since the early 1980s have shifted the emphasis from small-scale (fragmented) production to the development of large-scale cattle farms. The dairy and meat industries are apparently now responding to the rapid growth of demand for these products. A relatively well-organized and efficient poultry industry has already emerged in the urban areas of the country since the late 1970s.

Aggregate agricultural production, both in terms of value-added and physical output, has increased quite unevenly in the past fifty years as shown in Table 4.

Table 4
Changes in agricultural production
1950–1995

Year	Index of value-added in agriculture	Index of crop production		Index of value-added in agriculture per capita	Index of foodgrain output per capita
		All crops	Food crops		
1947–48	na	74	81	na	na
1949–50	86	87	97	110	125
1954–55	90	88	86	102	96
1959–60	100	100	100	100	100
1964–65	120	128	120	105	106

1969–70	163	186	177	124	138
1974–75	170	187	183	110	122
1979–80	205	239	145	115	143
1984–85	241	275	265	115	131
1989–90	304	334	302	136	130
1994–95	357	374	343	126	127

Source: As in Table 1.
Note: The value of the index for all variables is 100 in 1959–60. The indices are based on real value.
na=not available.

The most impressive increase in the agricultural valued-added was in the 1960s (63 per cent) followed by the 1980s (48 per cent). The increase in the decade of the 1950s was very slight (16 per cent), resulting in a fall of agriculture value-added in per capita terms. In the 1970s, while there was a modest increase (26 per cent) in the overall value-added, there was again a decline in the value-added per capita. The value-added per capita rose significantly only in the second half of the 1980s, but has fallen in the first half of the 1990s. There has been a similar instability in the growth of crop output, particularly of food crops. In per capita terms, food output fell significantly in the 1950s, followed by an impressive increase in the 1960s. It fell again in the first half of the 1970s and rose in the second half of the 1970s. The important point is that the growth in foodgrains since the early 1980s has been quite slow, resulting in a falling trend of foodgrain production per person.

In the last fifty years, the aggregate output of major crops has increased by very different proportions.

Table 5
Output of major crops
1947–1995

Period	Foodgrains	Wheat	Rice	Maize	Sugarcane	Cotton	Foodgrains
	(............ in million metric tons............)						kilograms
1947–50	5.63	3.77	0.75	0.38	6.78	1.10	162
1950–55	5.16	3.24	0.84	0.39	7.19	1.52	136
1955–60	5.73	3.68	0.91	0.46	10.32	1.68	134
1960–65	6.57	4.15	1.18	0.49	15.85	2.10	134

1965–70	8.81	5.72	1.72	0.75	22.26	2.81	156
1970–75	11.02	7.22	2.31	0.73	21.65	3.82	168
1975–80	13.87	9.35	2.94	0.81	27.99	3.21	181
1980–85	16.51	11.56	3.33	0.99	33.58	4.46	185
1985–90	18.54	13.47	3.21	1.13	32.64	8.10	178
1990–95	20.85	15.66	3.40	1.22	40.60	9.65	173

Source: As in Table 1.

The annual output of foodgrains has nearly quadrupled as has been the case for wheat and rice separately. However, the output of foodgrains in per capita terms declined from 162 kg in the late 1940s to 134 kg in the mid-1960s, then rose to 185 kg in the first half of the 1980s, but has fallen to 173 kg in the mid-1990s. The output of cotton and sugarcane has increased by nearly nine and six times, respectively, since the inception of Pakistan. The data on milk, meat, and fish production are available only since 1971 and are perhaps less reliable. They show that milk output per capita was declining throughout the 1970s (from 123 kg in 1971 to 112 kg in 1980), but has increased significantly since the mid-1980s, rising from 115 kg to 151 kg until the mid-1980s. On the other hand, there has been an almost consistent increase in the level of meat output per capita, rising from 9 kg in 1971 to 11 kg in 1985 and 18 kg in 1995.

Successive governments have imported various food commodities in substantial quantities to provide 'food security' in Pakistan. The most striking increase has been in the import of edible (soybean and palm) oils to meet the rapidly growing demand for vegetable oil and *ghee* in the face of very slow growth of the output of non-traditional oil crops in the country. Wheat has been imported in different quantities, ranging from about 4 per cent (1981–5) to 14 per cent (1970–75 and 1990–95) of the domestic output. Similarly, refined sugar has been imported at a level of about 4 per cent to 20 per cent (1986–90) of local production. Its import has fallen to less than 5 per cent of domestic output since 1990, which is a reflection of the growth of sugarcane and sugar in Pakistan mainly because of the generous protection given to the sugar industry. The import of dry milk has increased since the late 1970s because of the rapid increase in urban demand

and inadequate increase in local production. Governments have also imported variable quantities of lentils and onions to meet the seasonal (periodic) shortages in urban markets.

Among the crude indicators of agricultural productivity, crop output per unit of land has been used quite widely. The current yield levels of major crops, except seed cotton, in Pakistan are lower than the world average. The yield gaps are very large for corn, soybean, sugarcane, and rice. Among the major producers of each of these crops, Pakistan stands in the lowest 20 per cent. The estimated trend rates of yield levels show some interesting changes. In the last fifty years, cotton yield has increased at nearly 13 per cent, followed by wheat (10 per cent), rice (7.7 per cent), corn (4.1 per cent), and sugarcane (3.2 per cent). In the first eight years after 1947, the crop yields were either stagnant or fell (wheat, rice, and sugarcane), except for cotton. In the fifteen years following 1959–60, there was significant growth in the yield levels of wheat, rice, and cotton but modest growth in sugarcane. Since 1980, the cotton yield has maintained a high rate of growth (16 per cent), followed by wheat (9.3 per cent) and sugarcane (6.6 per cent); the yield level of rice has shown a slightly falling trend (0.8 per cent).

As stated above, the yield levels of major crops, with the exception of cotton, either fell or stagnated in the 1950s, followed by some increase in the 1960s.

Table 6
Output per hectare of major crops
1947/48–1994/95

Year	Foodgrains	Wheat	Rice	Maize	Sugarcane	Cotton lint
		Yield level in metric ton per hectare				
1947–48	0.74	0.85	0.88	0.99	30.51	0.157
1949–50	0.79	0.94	0.87	1.01	35.61	0.203
1954–55	0.70	0.75	0.87	1.00	29.19	0.221
1959–60	0.76	0.80	0.99	1.03	29.93	0.212
1964–65	0.83	0.87	1.00	1.09	37.11	0.258
1969–70	1.13	1.16	1.48	1.03	42.53	0.304
1974–75	1.24	1.32	1.44	1.22	31.56	0.312
1979–80	1.41	1.57	1.58	1.25	38.30	0.350

1984–85	1.48	1.61	1.66	1.27	35.55	0.450
1989–90	1.62	1.83	1.53	1.37	41.56	0.560
1994–95	1.80	2.05	1.58	1.49	45.24	0.558

Source: As in Table 1.

The yield level of foodgrains, after remaining stagnant in the 1950s, rose by about 86 per cent during the period of fifteen years from the mid-1960s, but by only 22 per cent in the last fifteen years. Most of this change has been due to changes in the yield levels of wheat and rice: nearly a 100 per cent increase for wheat and 60 per cent for rice followed by slower growth in the case of wheat and some decline in rice. Corn yield rose by little until 1970, but has increased by just under 50 per cent in the last twenty-five years. The yield level of sugarcane showed no trend during the first fifteen years, then rose for a decade in the 1960s, but fell in the 1970s. It has shown a clearly rising trend since the mid-1980s. Cotton (lint) yield has increased by about 350 per cent in the last fifty years, but it has shown a rising trend only since 1960. The yield level rose quite significantly during the 1980s, followed by a slight fall in the first half of the 1990s.[2]

A better measure of the efficiency of resources (land, capital, and labour) used in crop production is the 'total factor productivity' (TFP). TFP is the productivity that cannot be accounted for by measured increases in physical inputs. Two studies, using the same methodology, have estimated the change in TFP for the crop sub-sector during a period of forty years (1953 to 1993).[3]

In the first study, TFP grew annually at just over one per cent in the first twenty-five years (1953–78) with considerable differences in various sub-periods: the TFP rate fell in the 1950s; rose significantly in the 1960s; and there was almost no growth in the 1970s. The estimated growth rate of TFP in the second study was just over 2 per cent during the 1980–93 period, with a somewhat higher rate in the first part of the 1980s. The contributions of technological change and additional inputs to the increased agriculture value-added seem to differ significantly in the two periods: the contribution of technological change was 32 per cent in the first period (1953–78), but 62 per cent in the second period (1980–93).

3. SOURCES OF AGRICULTURAL GROWTH

Increased inputs have, of course, been an important source of the observed increases in agricultural production and productivity, including cultivated area, irrigation water, seeds, fertilizer, machinery, credit, and agricultural labour.

Table 7
Land use for agricultural production
1947/48–1994/95

Year	Reported Area	Cultivated Area	Cropped Irrigated Area	Cropping	Irrigation Area Intensity
		(......million hectares......)		(%)	(%)
1947/48	46.08	14.69	12.04	8.83	82.60
1949/50	46.56	14.99	12.75	8.98	85.60
1954/55	46.69	15.32	13.24	9.97	86.65
1959/60	48.46	16.51	14.69	10.35	89.63
1964/65	52.86	18.72	16.25	11.44	87.61
1969/70	52.93	19.23	16.77	12.49	87.65
1974/75	53.92	19.55	17.37	13.34	89.68
1979/80	53.71	20.23	19.22	14.74	95.73
1984/85	58.13	20.61	19.92	15.76	97.76
1989/90	57.97	20.94	21.46	16.89	102.81
1994/95	58.06	21.40	22.44	18.00	105.84

Source: As in Table 1.
Note: Cropping intensity=cropped area/cultivated area x 100; irrigation intensity = irrigated area/cultivated area *100.

Table 8
Changes in use of agricultural inputs
1950/1995

Year	Water avail-ability (A/F/ha)	Improved seeds (kg/ha)	Fertilizer (NPK) (Kg/ha)	Tubewells (ha/tube-well)	Tractors (ha/trac. worker)	Workers (ha/hectr.)	Credit Rs/
1950/51	3.2	–	–	–	–	2.16	0.56
1954/55	3.4	–	1.1	10,215	30,389	2.10	0.37
1959/60	3.8	–	1.3	3,066	4,088	1.88	5.88
1964/65	4.0	–	5.4	481	1,290	1.66	7.85
1969/70	4.5	1.2	18.3	196	633	1.62	9.26
1974/75	5.1	1.5	24.4	114	459	1.55	58.15
1980/81	5.1	3.8	55.8	97	202	1.50	208.38
1984/85	5.2	4.3	62.9	80	149	1.50	485.64
1989/90	5.4	2.9	86.3	66	138	1.40	634.25
1994/95	5.8	9.3	99.3	52	110	1.39	617.18

Source: As in Table 1.

Fertilizer use has quadrupled since the mid-1970s and is now around 100 kg per hectare. The density of both tubewells and tractors has increased sharply in the last twenty years. Institutional credit has increased from Rs 10 in 1970 to Rs 617 per cropped hectare in 1995. However, it should be added that improved seeds have not become a significant factor in crop production, except for cotton.

Technical progress in Pakistan's agriculture has been through two phases. The first phase was of the 'Green Revolution', starting with the development of water resources in the early to mid-1960s and use of fertilizer with the high-yielding varieties of wheat and rice in the late 1960s. The process of adoption of this technology had probably run its course by the early 1970s with the introduction of pesticides in major crops on a wide scale. The second phase has been of mechanical technology, which began in the mid-1970s and has since become a dominant feature in at least the Indus basin. In addition, there has been further diffusion of the packages of technology, containing water, quality seeds, chemical fertilizers, and pesticides with advanced cultivation practices and improved on-farm water management. In both phases, two factors have played a central role in the adoption of the new technology and in the distribution of its benefits. One consists of state policies (through price and non-price incentives) and investment in physical infrastructure (canals, roads, etc.), agricultural research, and extension services. The other factor has been the changes in the agrarian structure, including changes in the distribution of land and tenurial arrangements.

A. USE OF MAJOR INPUTS

Irrigation water from the Indus river system is the lifeline of agriculture. The rain-fed (*barani*) areas give ample evidence of the absolute constraint that water imposes on all farmers, but its consequences on small farmers are often devastating. Dependence on uncertain rainfall, as in the *barani* areas of Punjab and NWFP, and inadequate canal water and no tubewells, as in several parts of Balochistan and in the south and south-eastern parts of Sindh, have been the major barriers to the use of new seeds and fertilizers, resulting in increased inter-regional disparities. The canal irrigation system—inherited from the British administration and concentrated mainly in the plains of Punjab and Sindh—in the early 1950s was inadequate in meeting the water requirements of even the traditional cropping patterns. Further, water losses from the canal system were no less serious, partly because of inadequate drainage and partly due to poor water management at the farm level. Vast national resources were required to expand the surface irrigation system and to alleviate the increasing menace of waterlogging and salinity. A rapid expansion of water resources was initiated in the late 1950s in order to increase the cultivated area and to improve the yield levels after the stagnation of agriculture in the 1950s. Development of water resources was a major focus of public investment in the 1960s. It was also in the 1960s that the installation of private tubewells as a supplementary source of water became profitable. The development of private tubewells in the central and eastern districts of Punjab had become impressive and its results manifest by the late 1960s. Private tubewells provided additional water and, at the time, were most needed for optimum plant growth. New crops could now be grown, which required more water, and the use of fertilizers became profitable. It also facilitated the adoption of the high-yielding seeds of wheat and rice introduced in the late 1960s.[4]

An expanded water supply from the canal system has been a major source of change in the use of land. However, the· availability of water has been constrained by several factors, some at the regional and others at the village level. Water acts as a major constraint because its management at the canal and farm levels is very poor, caused by inadequate physical infrastructure and the low level of water charges. Its distribution generally discriminates against the tail-enders and small farmers because of the unequal power of the small and large landowners in the village. In view of the chronic shortage of canal water in the country, the regions at the tail-end of the system are handicapped in adopting new crop varieties and adjusting the cropping patterns. Farmers in Sindh, in particular, are adversely affected since they are at the tail-end of the canal system and they cannot make use of the groundwater. Added to these problems is the persistent shortfall in the government's irrigation revenue to cover the maintenance and operation costs of the canal system. As part of the structural adjustment support given by the International Monetary Fund (IMF) and the World Bank since the mid-1980s, the canal irrigation system is expected to be transferred from the provincial irrigation departments to the so-called autonomous (private) irrigation authorities. While this programme is consistent with the adjustment policies of the two international agencies, it has generated much genuine debate and controversy in the country with regard to its likely benefits and costs in the current social and operational environment.

Additional and assured supply of water was a major factor in raising the private profitability of fertilizers and the new seeds of wheat and rice. Farmers started using chemical (mainly nitrogenous) fertilizers in the early 1960s with around 35,000 metric tons. Fertilizer consumption rose to around 300,000 metric tons in 1970–71; over one million metric tons by 1980–

81; and around 2.2 million metric tons or about 100 kg per hectare of crop land in the mid-1990s. With the increased amount of fertilizer, farmers have also shifted from the mainly nitrogenous to more complex (compound) fertilizers containing phosphorus and potash. Several factors have contributed to the increasing use of chemical fertilizers: increased and assured supply of water; expansion of cropped and cultivated areas, especially of major crops; fertilizer-responsive varieties of grains and other crops; expansion of private sector production and marketing network; and the public sector support for distributional facilities, price subsidy, and expansion of credit.

The use of fertilizers and new seeds has been accompanied by serious inter-regional and inter-farm disparities. The regional disparities have simply been due to the relative shortage of water in some regions, particularly in the areas dependent on rain or without good quality of groundwater. The inter-farm disparities have been observed between the rich (generally owners of large landholdings) and poor (generally owners of small landholdings) farmers because of unequal access to (a) the state bureaucracy and (b) the fertilizer, credit and output markets. Small owner-operators were late in adopting the Green Revolution technology and the process of catching up has not been easy and is still far from complete. Small peasants have clearly indicated that an insufficient and uncertain supply of water, with inadequate cash or credit, militate against increasing fertilizer use and coverage of the crop area. In addition, the credit problem has been aggravated by the unequal access to the public sector research and extension services, which are supposedly the carriers of applied (and profitable) knowledge about new technology.

There has been much debate about how the size and tenure of farms can affect the level of farm productivity and the distribution of benefits resulting from new technologies (Mahmood and Haque, 1981; Chaudhry, 1982; Khan, 1983). There is, however, no dispute that land is the primary factor determining the access to other factors in agriculture. Smaller farms exhibit higher intensities of land use, labour, and animal power. The traditional superiority enjoyed by the small owner-operator was premised on his intensive use of family labour and animal resources on land. However, with the unequal spread of the Green Revolution technology—small farmers were latecomers and have faced greater constraints in getting the new inputs—the size-productivity relationship seems to have been reversed. Small farmers have not been able to compete effectively with large landowners either for public sector resources or in the marketplace. This has constrained their capacity to rapidly innovate and earn profits.

The second phase of technical progress in Pakistan's agriculture began in the mid-1970s with the rapid expansion of tractors and machines like threshers. Their impact has been controversial.[5] Most of the tractors are between 33 and 55 HP, and are owned by farmers with holdings of more than 10 hectares. The case for tractors was first made in the early 1960s. It was argued that tractors would increase crop yields, reduce the cost of farm power by replacing draft animals, increase cropping intensity by hastening the pre-sowing and post-harvest operations, and lead to more, and not less, demand for labour, so that the net employment effect would be positive. There were, however, doubts about some of these effects, particularly on the yield level and multiple cropping. Some have contended that rapid mechanization (tractorization) would result in labour displacement and tenant eviction, and expansion of holdings which were already large. Implicit in this was the notion that rich peasants and landlords would increasingly encroach upon the lands which were earlier available for cultivation to small owner-operators and landless tenants.

The government started to encourage the import of tractors in the mid- to late 1960s by following a cheap credit policy and maintaining an overvalued exchange rate. These policies did not, however, lead to a rapid expansion of the demand for tractors and related machines until the mid-1970s. One important reason for this was that the increased demand for labour that the Green Revolution technology apparently induced could be met by the existing supply of labour. In addition, labour migration to urban areas and the Middle East led to some increase in the real wage rate in several areas of the Indus basin, especially the irrigated districts of Punjab. The large landowners started to opt for increased use of tractors mainly because, with the displacement of tenants that had already begun in the late 1960s, they encountered difficulties in hiring labour and using the animal power during short periods. However, with the spread of mechanized implements like tractors, harvesters, and threshers, the displacement of labour became even more serious, as reflected in the resumption of land from the sharecropping tenants and lower demand for short-term workers. In the labour market, the response was increased migration to the cities and abroad, resulting in periodic and acute labour shortages during the peak demand periods. The overall demand for labour in rural areas increased mainly because of the remittances from the migrant workers.[6]

Farm credit can be a major source of acquiring new technology for an efficient and profitable agriculture. Farmers in Pakistan have been greatly constrained by the inadequacy of the credit market. Private debts are usually under-reported among the sharecropping tenants whose relationship with their landlords almost always involves significant borrowing and accumulated debt. Some of the under-reporting is because most households borrow in small amounts from friends and relatives and they are unwilling to reveal these sources of debt. Most of the credit acquired by small farmers comes from non-institutional sources, including friends, relatives, moneylenders, traders, commission agents, and landlords. Until the 1960s, the involvement of the institutional sources was minimal. There were limited 'taccavi' (distress) loans given by the provincial governments in case of crop failure due to natural calamities and equally limited funds were available through the Federal Agricultural Bank (FAB) and the Agricultural Development Finance Corporation (ADFC). The role of the credit co-operatives was not significant either. The private commercial banks kept their activities concentrated in the industrial (urban) sector. Farmers, particularly those with small holdings, were considered high-risk borrowers with limited collateral and low incomes.

In the early 1960s, it was realized that inadequate credit was inhibiting the progress of agriculture. The first response was to establish the Agricultural Development Bank of Pakistan (ADBP), which remained the only major source of farm credit until the early 1970s. The five private commercial banks were inducted into lending for agriculture after their nationalization by the Pakistan People's Party (PPP) government in 1972. The co-operative system was restructured under the Federal Bank of Co-operatives (FBC). The government maintained its intervention in the rural credit market by regulating the public credit institutions under the umbrella of the central bank. The growth of institutional credit has been quite impressive since the early 1970s, with the ADBP and commercial banks accounting for most of the lending. Institutional credit is given only for production-related activities, although a sizable part of it apparently gets channelled into consumer spending. There is some division of labour between the various lending institutions.

The co-operative credit system has been a massive failure in Pakistan in terms of poor farmer participation, weak administrative capacity to extend and recover loans, and inefficient management of financial affairs. The absence of multi-level societies and dominance of the provincial bureaucracy has not encouraged participation by small farmers. Consequently, the large farmers tend to dominate the apex level of co-operative organizations. The introduction of 'pass books' in 1973 and the policy of interest-free loans in the early 1980s—which were supposed to make institutional credit more accessible and cheap to small farmers—led to many rent-seeking practices by both public officials and landowners. Similarly, the practices of ADBP, which focused on development or investment loans, have not been altogether fair or efficient: three-quarters of the loans have been channelled to farmers with holdings of more than 5 hectares and about two-thirds of the value of loans has been used for purchasing tractors and machines and installation of tubewells. A substantial subsidy implied in public loans for agricultural production has been transferred to a small number of large landowners, farmers and entrepreneurs, mainly on the basis of their political influence or contacts. In fact, the financial viability of the co-operative banks and ADBP has become a major national issue since the early 1990s.

There are no estimates of the total demand for agricultural credit, based on the rate of return, level of technology, and financial conditions. Since the supply of institutional credit has been rationed and the rate of interest has been much below the equilibrium rate, there has always been excessive demand for loans. A bias in favour of large landowners and well-connected farmers is built into the credit system because of risk minimization through the collateral requirement, low administrative cost and convenience, and the influence of landlords and similar urban-based groups. These constraints militate against the landless, who must depend on the non-institutional sources. Sharecroppers have no direct access to institutional credit. Their major credit source is the landlord, who also acts as a conduit for seasonal loans when they are available. The cost of loans acquired from the landlord is difficult to measure, but it is never insignificant if account is taken of the asymmetrical relationship between the landlord and his tenants.

Non-institutional sources remain important for the small peasants. Friends and relatives cannot be always be a stable and adequate source of loans to meet the investment requirements for profitable farming. Acquiring credit from the moneylenders and merchants may be convenient, but the debt charges can easily exceed the total cost of procuring from the institutional sources. For most of the small landowners and sharecropping tenants, credit from the non-institutional sources also provides cash for consumer spending and expenses between seasons. It is often the consumer needs of the peasants which explain their dependency on moneylenders and discourage investment spending or innovation. Small farmers, who constitute three-quarters of the farming population, cannot get loans for developing or improving their land, although these investments could make a big difference in the level of production. They do not usually require large amounts of money to acquire seasonal inputs. Since the hidden cost and inconvenience of acquiring public sector loans for seasonal inputs are high, they either go to the non-institutional sources or do without the inputs required to increase their incomes and farm productivity. This, in turn, adversely affects their capacity to survive as productive farmers.

B. PUBLIC POLICIES AND INVESTMENT

Governments have played an active role in agriculture in a variety of ways, e.g., readjusting the agrarian structure, providing physical infrastructure and inputs, regulating domestic and foreign trade, adjusting the foreign exchange rate, intervening in the producer and consumer prices, and using fiscal and monetary policies. These interventions have affected the incentives for farmers, distribution of benefits between classes, terms of trade for agriculture with the rest of the economy, and the government revenue. Their exact impact is not easy to measure because of the complex interactions among them. Certain policies have not been used or followed through because of political constraints, even when the objectives were well-defined and generally regarded as desirable, e.g., radical changes in the land tenure system and land taxes. These constraints reflect the highly unequal distribution of economic and political power within agriculture and the conflict between the agricultural (rural) and industrial (urban) elites about the inter-sectoral transfer of resources in the development process. Often the policies and actions of governments have not been consistent with one another or with the expressed goals. Another major constraint has been the inadequate management capacity of the public sector institutions.

The role of price support and input subsidy, regulation of internal and external trade, and exchange rate policies of governments have been debated quite extensively in the literature both at the level of the theory and in the context of Pakistan.[7] There is, however, general agreement that the agriculture sector in Pakistan has transferred considerable surplus to the rest of the economy through these policies. While the rate of surplus transfer has varied during different periods and economic regimes, it seems to have fallen significantly in the 1990s due to favourable adjustments in prices, exchange rates, and deregulation of trade.

The terms of trade for the agriculture sector have also changed. The barter terms of trade for agriculture fell in the 1950s, rose in the early to mid-1960s, fell again in the late 1960s, improved in the 1970s, fell throughout the 1980s, and have improved significantly in the first half of the 1990s. But the income terms of trade have kept on improving since the 1950s, rising rapidly in the 1960s, slowing down in the early 1970s, followed by rapid improvement in the late 1970s and the early 1980s; the improvement slowed down considerably in the second half of the 1980s followed by a significant improvement in the 1990s. This shows that the purchasing power of farmers has gone up in most of the period since the early 1960s. The nominal protection coefficients—ratios of domestic to international prices—for the major crops have shown an implicit tax on wheat, cotton, and Basmati rice, a subsidy on sugarcane, and no tax on IRRI rice. However, since the early 1990s, there has been a clear improvement in the relative prices of wheat, Basmati and IRRI rice, and cotton. The subsidy on sugarcane price has also decreased. That the purchasing power of farmers has not deteriorated over time is also indicated by changes in the support price of major crops and retail price of fertilizers (urea) since 1959–60: one kilogram of each of the four major crops (wheat, rice, cotton, and sugarcane) now buys more or at least the same amount of urea as before.

Successive governments have given subsidies on the price of almost all of the major agricultural inputs. Some of these input subsidies are easy to measure but many are not as amenable to quantification. It is clear from the existing literature that the subsidy on inputs—fertilizers, plant protection, improved seeds, tubewells, canal water, electricity and fuels, and farm credit—was started in the 1960s from less than one per cent of the value-added in agriculture in 1961 and rose to 5 per cent in 1980. This subsidy was down to around 4 per cent in the late 1980s and has fallen further to about 3 per cent of the agriculture value-added in 1995. Financial subsidies for fertilizers, pesticides, and seeds have been almost completely eliminated and reduced quite significantly for farm credit. Devaluation of the rupee has also reduced the subsidy on imported machinery and components used in the agriculture sector. But there is still a significant subsidy on the price of canal water and electricity and some on credit.

The real problem with dependence on a price support policy for producers and consumers since 1959–60—when the government started paying serious attention to the development of agriculture—is that it has been used to meet contradictory objectives. Rather than restructure the land tax system, the government has taxed the agriculture sector through price and subsidy policies as a soft option. Several forms of indirect and hidden taxes with few, if any, positive effects, have been imposed on the agriculture sector. The dependence on a variety of indirect taxes is a reflection of the failure of successive governments to make taxes direct, flexible, and progressive. They have transferred the agricultural surplus to other sectors without, at the same time, returning to producers the benefits of investible resources for their own development and well-being. In addition, there is evidence that the government's intervention in the price system may have also affected the distribution of the tax burden and income in favour of the large and powerful landowners and farmers, at the expense of the small owner-operators and tenants.

The public sector spending on the development of water resources, agricultural research, extension, and education, and the financial subsidy on fertilizers has been an integral part of the five-year plans from 1955, but its share in the total development spending has fallen significantly since the late 1980s. The share of spending for water resources, agriculture, and fertilizer subsidy in the first plan (1955–60) was at 30 per cent, rising to around one-half in the second and third plan periods (1960–70). During the 1960s, three-quarters of the spending earmarked for these activities was on the development of water resources. Since 1970, the share of agriculture (including fertilizer subsidy) and water in the total public sector development spending has fallen: to 26 per cent in the 1970s; 20 per cent in the fifth plan period (1978–83); 17 per cent in the sixth plan period (1983–8); 13 per cent in the seventh plan period (1988–93); and is targeted at just over 8 per cent in the eighth plan period (1993–8).

It is well known that research and extension services can play a key role in the growth of agricultural productivity. In one study, it has been shown that the public investment in agricultural research and extension in Pakistan has yielded a 36 per cent real rate of return during 1955 and 1980 (Khan and Akbari, 1986). The capital and current expenditure on agricultural research and extension at the federal and provincial levels has been rising more rapidly than the growth of GDP and the value-added in agriculture: the ratio to GDP has increased from 0.12 per cent in the first plan period to 0.45 per cent in the eighth plan period (1993–8); the ratio to the value-added in agriculture has likewise increased from 0.41 to 1.40 per cent during this period. In spite of this increase in spending on agricultural research and extension, two serious problems have been clearly brought out in recent literature.[8] The first one is that Pakistan even now spends relatively far less of its resources on these services than many other underdeveloped countries. The more serious problem is that the management and quality of the national and provincial research and extension systems have not improved their effectiveness. It has been argued that their quality and adequacy may have in fact declined in the last decade, notwithstanding the introduction of the much publicized training and visit (T&V) system since the early 1980s.

4. THE LAND TENURE SYSTEM AND REFORMS

A. THE LAND TENURE SYSTEM
Pakistan inherited a variety of land tenure systems in 1947. In the 'unsettled' areas, such as almost all of Balochistan, some parts of NWFP, and the Northern Areas (Gilgit, Hunza, Baltistan, Diamer, Darel, and Tanger), the property rights were either ill-defined or a tribal ownership existed, in which the traditional tribal leaders or rulers—*sardars*, *maliks*, *mirs*, and *rajas*—enjoyed a predominant position. In the 'settled' areas, a mix of two land tenure systems existed, with regional variations in tenurial arrangements in the layers of intermediaries on land

in the degree of land concentration.[9] At that time, the *zemindari* (landlord-tenant) system was the more dominant and co-existed with the other system which comprised small owner-operators or peasant-proprietors. There were thus two basic classes involved in the cultivation of land: a small minority of landlords (*zemindars* and *jagirdars*) who did not cultivate the land but depended on rent, and a vast majority of cultivators who were either sharecropping tenants (*haris* or *muzaras*) of landlords or owned small landholdings based on family labour. Capital and wage labour were at best in rudimentary form.

Most of the agricultural population in 1947 consisted of landless tenants and small owner-operators. The majority of farms in Sindh were operated by the *haris*, while much of the cultivated area in Punjab and NWFP was operated by the *muzaras*. Landownership was highly concentrated: owners of holdings of over 40 hectares constituted less than one per cent of all landowners in Punjab and NWFP, though they owned nearly one-quarter of the area. In Sindh, 8 per cent of all landowners claimed more than 50 per cent of the land. Landowners with holdings of more than 200 hectares owned nearly 30 per cent of the area in Sindh, although they accounted for about one per cent of the landholding classes. These large landowners owned about 10 per cent of all land in Punjab and NWFP.

The rural scene in Pakistan was dominated by two factors. Power was concentrated in the hands of a few whose only contribution to agricultural output was that they owned and controlled most of the land. Most peasants were landless tenants and small owner-operators. The tenure of the landless tenant was precarious and the position of the small landowner was only marginally better. The asymmetrical relations in this quasi-feudal system were maintained and re-inforced by the monopoly power of the absentee landlords, supported by the machinery of the state. The landless tenants, as direct producers, had a largely subservient economic and social status, with a large part of their surplus passing on to the landlords (*zemindars* and *jagirdars*) as the dominant class. The small owner-operators (*ryot*) played an important role only in the newly-settled areas of Punjab and in the irrigated valleys of NWFP. However, at least in Punjab, many of them had lost their lands to moneylenders in the early period of the settlement (1880 to 1900) when no legal protection existed against land alienation through mortgage. Those who survived faced an increasing fragmentation of holdings due to the rising pressure of population on land and the operation of the customary Muslim law of inheritance. In some areas, many of these small landowners could not sustain their families by their holdings alone. Their existence, without supplementary income, was only slightly less precarious than that of the landless tenants.

The agrarian structure has undergone several changes since the early 1950s. Some changes reflect the effects of various tenancy and land reform acts, but most have been brought about by rapid population growth, laws of inheritance, new technologies and the forces of markets, rural to urban migration and flow of remittances, and government policies of support prices, inputs subsidies, and farm credit. Landownership, as shown by individual records, is still quite concentrated, although the concentration seems to have declined in every province.

Table 9
Changes in inequality in landownership
and access to land
1950/1990

Year	Landowners and owned area				Operational holdings and farm area			
	Pakistan	Punjab	Sindh	NWFP	Pakistan	Punjab	Sindh	NWFP
1950	0.64	0.62	0.66	0.49	–	–	–	–
1960	–	–	–	0.62	0.59	0.51	0.73	–
1971/72	0.57	0.53	0.59	0.41	0.52	0.49	0.43	0.64
1976	0.55	0.52	0.58	0.41	–	–	–	–
1980/81	0.53	0.49	0.55	0.38	0.53	0.51	0.47	0.57
1990	–	–	–	0.57	0.53	0.50	0.61	–

Source: The data for landownership by holding size are from the Federal/Land Commission based on individual land records. The data for operational holdings (farms) and farm size are from the Agricultural Census Reports of 1960, 1972, 1980, and 1990.
Note: The ratios are the Gini Coefficients for landownership and access to land use.

The number of owners and the area of small landholdings (less than 5 hectares) has increased somewhat; the proportion of large landowners (more than 20 hectares) has gone down from 2.7 to 2.0 per cent and their share in the total area has declined from 26 to 23 per cent. In Pakistan, about 96 per cent of the landowners have holdings of less than 10 hectares, but they own 64 per cent of the area. The highest concentration of landownership is in Sindh. Small landowners (with less than two hectares) are preponderant in NWFP (96 per cent) and Punjab (80 per cent), but they own only 55 and 36 per cent of the area in the two provinces. They comprise 40 per cent of all landowners in Sindh and own less than 10 per cent of the area. The large landowners (with more than 20 hectares) own 38 per cent of land in Sindh, 20 and 14 per cent in Punjab and NWFP, respectively.

Three major changes in landownership seem to have occurred since the late 1960s. First, the ownership and area under very small landholdings have increased mainly due to the subdivision of holdings by the law of inheritance and rapid population growth, though some of it may be the result of distribution of land to the landless following the land reforms of 1972. Second, there has been a significant fall in the number and area of very large landholdings due to the intra-family land transfers in anticipation of and in response to the land reform acts of 1959 and 1972. Finally the medium-size holdings (10 to 40 hectares) have gained, especially in Sindh, both in number and area.

Of course, not all landowners cultivate their land, either their own or anyone else's, and not all cultivators own land. There are, therefore, several tenancy arrangements for cultivation purposes, of which the sharecropping tenancy and self-cultivation by (mainly small) landowners are the major forms. The access to land for cultivation is reflected in the distribution of 'operational holdings' or farms by size and tenure. The data on changes in the distribution of farms and farm area by size and tenancy have been published in the 1960, 1972, 1980, and 1990 Agriculture Census Reports. Generally speaking, Sindh has had the least concentration of farms due mainly to the widespread sharecrop tenancy; NWFP has been at the other end because of the preponderance of self-cultivation of small holdings as evident from Table 9. Note that land concentration has declined mildly in all provinces since 1960, but with some interesting changes during the period of 1960 to 1990. Apparently, land concentration fell significantly in the 1960s, but rose marginally in Punjab and Sindh in the 1970s and substantially in all three provinces in the 1980s. These changes reflect a clear tendency towards reduced sharecropping tenancy and increased incidence of self-cultivation on all farm sizes.

The average farm size has declined from 5.3 hectares to 3.8 hectares, but the average size of large farms has increased. The number of farms has increased from about 3.75 million in the early 1970s to just over five million in the early 1990s. The share of small farms has increased slightly (from 67 to 71 per cent) in number but declined in area from 52 to 39 per cent. These changes reflect the large relative increase in the number and area of very small farms. While the share of large farms has fallen in number (from 11 to 7 per cent) their share in the area fell only slightly from 43 to 40 per cent. Tenurial arrangements seem to have changed significantly in the last thirty years. The proportion of owner-operated farms has increased significantly both in number and area. In fact, the owner-operated area has increased from just over one-half to three-quarters of the total farm area. Most of the owner-operated farms are small and located in Punjab and NWFP. Sharecropping is still the major form of tenancy, especially in Sindh and some areas of Punjab and NWFP. Sharecropped farms are in the range of 3 to 5 hectares, but they have declined sharply in both number (34 to 19 per cent) and area (from 30 to 16 per cent). A similar reduction has been observed in the case of 'owner-cum-tenant' farms, but large farms have been increasing. The tendency away from sharecropping is clearly reflected in the reduction of tenant-operated area from 46 to 26 per cent of all farm area. It seems that large landholdings dependent on tenants have also reduced their tenant-operated area.

The transition from the quasi-feudal to the capitalist mode of agrarian structure in Pakistan has made the land tenure system even more differentiated than it was before the 1960s.[10] The capitalist farmers have emerged from the ranks of landlords and rich peasants. Labour is increasingly provided by landless workers, who could be from among the poor peasants (family farmers) and displaced or evicted sharecroppers as the landlords transform into capitalist farmers by extending their self-cultivated (*khud kasht*) area. However, not all of the landless labour is absorbed in the capitalist sector of agriculture. Increasing numbers of unattached workers are either engaged in non-farm activities in the rural area or migrate from the village to towns and cities.

The gradual dissolution of the quasi-feudal and peasant systems has revealed several interesting features. In the landlord-tenant system, landlords have not entirely been in favour of evicting the sharecroppers on a large scale. This is partly to avoid legal problems which a large-scale tenant eviction could cause. The more important reasons are perhaps economic. Subsidized inputs, including tractors and other machines, since the late 1970s have raised private profits which the landlords are unwilling to share with their tenants. On the demand side, the structure of production has been changing in terms of cropping patterns in response to the growth of urban population, rising income levels, and expanded export opportunities. Some landlords have, therefore, adopted the policy of sharing the cost of all modern inputs with sharecroppers, including those which have weakened the tenants' bargaining position by making the cost of animal power high to maintain. Also, landlords have expanded their self-cultivated area, mainly by reducing the size of parcel they give to each sharecropper. These policies increase the pool of dependent and relatively cheap labour without increased dependence on seasonal wage labour, the supply of which may be uncertain and costly.

In the peasant system, increasing involvement in non-farm employment and migration of part of the household labour have become a necessity for the poor and even middle peasants since they bring additional income for survival. Non-agricultural incomes, particularly remittances from outside the rural area, have also become a source for acquiring additional land which can be leased or bought from the poor peasants (small landowners) who cannot evidently survive on their incomes from the small plots they own. Addition to one's landholding means increased chances of survival in farming, with reduced vulnerability to competition from rich farmers, or even of joining the ranks of capitalist farmers. The peasant system at the lower end has probably thus extended its life-span and remains a contending force to the rapid development of capitalist agriculture in Pakistan.

The growth of wage labour is an indicator of changes in the agrarian structure. Despite the decline in the proportion of labour working in agriculture, from 60 per cent in the early 1960s to around 45 per cent in the mid-1990s, the absolute numbers are still rising. The level of demand for labour and the conditions of employment are directly affected by the organization and performance of the agriculture sector itself. Employment in agriculture is of two types: (i) self-employment as household labour on farms cultivated by small landowners and tenants, and (ii) hiring out of labour by the households of landless non-farm workers, tenants, and small landowning peasants. Several significant changes have occurred in the composition and use of labour in the last twenty-five years. The use of family labour on small farms has not declined by much, but its use on larger farms has certainly fallen. While permanent hired labour was traditionally used mostly on large farms, fewer farms are now reporting its use. A high proportion of farmers now hire casual labour: its share in wage labour has increased from 30 to nearly 55 per cent. Pakistani farmers no longer depend entirely on family workers and most of them engage outside workers, at least for some of the time during the crop season. It is also a fact that an increasing proportion of the labour from farm households is engaged in non-farm activities on a short- or long-term basis because wage income from farming activities is insufficient to meet the growing needs of the family in a cash economy.

B. Land Tenure Reforms

At independence, the ruling Pakistan Muslim League (PML)—dominated by Muslim landlords and large landowners—created the impression that it was deeply concerned about the economic and social effects of the quasi-feudal land system and stressed the need for land tenure reforms, including the abolition of the *jagirdari* (land revenue free) estates, redistribution of land, and radical adjustments in the existing tenancy arrangements. In Sindh, attempts were made in 1943 to 1945 by some of the Muslim leaders to introduce at least tenancy reforms, but they were neutralized by the inaction of the provincial Muslim League government. The PML Agrarian Reform Committee—led by a landlord from Punjab—published its report in 1949, in which it identified several short-term and long-term measures to radically alter the land tenure system by abolishing *jagirs*, granting landownership rights to the (occupancy) tenants in Punjab, providing security to tenants-at-will, adjusting crop shares of landlord and tenant, and redistributing land by establishing a ceiling on individual landholding (60 hectares on irrigated and 180 hectares on unirrigated lands) with compensation to former owners for the resumed area. The PML Council accepted these recommendations, but the Agrarian Committee Report was then filed without action. However, this Report became an importance source of reference for future documents on land reforms and probably exerted some influence on the tenancy reform acts in Punjab, Sindh, and NWFP in the early 1950s.[11]

The demand for tenancy reforms was initiated first in Sindh soon after its separation from the Bombay Presidency as a province in 1936. As a result of the tenancy reforms in other parts of India and the increased activities of the Sind Hari Committee as a peasant organization, the Sindh provincial government appointed the Tenancy Legislation Committee in 1943; its report was published in 1945 with two strong notes of dissent, one arguing for radical changes in the existing landlord-tenant relations and the other note was against any new rights to the tenants. The government disregarded the recommendations of the Tenancy Legislation Committee and took no action. The pressure for action was, however, intensified and the government appointed the Hari Enquiry Committee in March 1947. The majority report of this committee was published in late 1948, over one year after the creation of Pakistan. Its recommendations were essentially to remove the non-statutory exactions (*haboob*) paid by tenants to landlords over and above the latter's crop share, but excluded the right of permanent tenancy to tenants-at-will (*haris*). The provincial government disallowed the publication of the Minute of Dissent by one of the three members of the Hari Enquiry Committee until 1949. Eventually, a bill was passed by the Sindh Assembly called the Sind Tenancy Act of 1950. This Act gave some security of tenancy to the *haris*, but its enforcement was thwarted by the powerful landlords who enjoyed substantial power in PML and exercised great influence on the civil and police administration. In 1955, the provincial government passed an executive order to abolish *jagirs*, but it was successfully challenged in the courts and the matter stayed until 1959.

After the creation of Pakistan, and at the behest of the PML Agrarian Committee, the Punjab government appointed a Tenancy Law Enquiry Committee in 1949. Of the three recommendations of this committee—abolition of occupancy tenancy; transfer of ownership rights to occupancy tenants; abolition of non-statutory exactions (*haboob*) paid by tenants to their landlords; and guarantee of secure tenancy to the tenants-at-will—the government only abolished the payment of *haboob* by tenants under the Punjab Tenancy Act of 1950. In 1952, the Punjab government amended the Punjab Tenancy Act of 1950 and adopted the recommendations of the Punjab Tenancy Laws Enquiry Committee. At the same time, it abolished the revenue-free estates (*jagirs*) and other such grants under the Punjab Abolition of Jagirs Act of 1952. However, in spite of these changes, landlordism remained intact, for there was no limit to the area of land one could own as long as the owner paid legal dues (land revenue and water rate) to the state.[12]

The tenancy reforms of the 1950s enacted in the three provinces had little impact on the contractual arrangements between landlords and sharecroppers. The first visible pressure on the large landlords came with the Land Reform Act of 1959 (Martial Law Regulation 64) in February 1959, enacted by the first Martial Law government in Pakistan. The 1959 Act abolished *jagirs* without compensation and imposed a ceiling on what had been unlimited individual landholdings. However, there is evidence that the 1959 Land Reform Act did not significantly alter the concentration of landownership, because the ceiling on individual holding remained quite generous— expressed in land area and the Produce Index Unit (PIU)—and there were substantial intra-family land transfers and even outright evasion of the ceiling requirement on individual holdings.[13] Consequently, the landless and the near-landless peasants received little land. A high proportion of the beneficiaries were the small and medium landowners. The Act did not introduce changes in the existing tenancy laws of what was then the province of West Pakistan.

The second land reform act was passed by the Pakistan People's Party (PPP) in 1972, soon after the separation of East Pakistan. The Land Reform Act of 1972 (Martial Law Regulation 112) was seemingly more radical than the 1959 Act. Though the impact of the 1972 Act on land redistribution was far more limited than the 1959 Act in terms of the area resumed by the state, its tenancy legislation apparently had a favourable effect on the legal position of sharecroppers. The third land reform act (Act II of 1977) was introduced by the PPP a few months before it lost power in 1977. Its major provision was to reduce the ceiling on individual holdings to 40 hectares for the irrigated (and 80 hectares for the unirrigated) lands. After the imposition of Martial Law in July 1977, little progress was made in implementing the Land Reform Act of 1977. In 1982, the military government made several important amendments to the Land Reform Act of 1977 in order to promote the development of large-scale private (mainly livestock) farms in Pakistan.

Under the three land reform acts (of 1959, 1972, and 1977), the government has distributed 1.4 million hectares to about 288,000 beneficiaries from a total area of 1.8 million hectares (about 8 per cent of the country's cultivated area) resumed from the large landowners. About two-thirds of the resumed area and three-quarters of the distributed lands were under the Act of 1959. It should be added that a substantial part of the distributed land was not of high quality. Secondly, not all beneficiaries have been sharecroppers; a high proportion of the recipients in the 1959 Act were already landowners. Less than three-quarters of the distributed area was under cultivation in any case.

It is difficult to make quantitative judgments about the impact of these land reforms because of the absence of systematic micro-level studies. However, on the basis of the available evidence, some important observations can be made (Khan, 1981).

- Resumption and distribution of land were greatly diluted by numerous exemptions and allowances included in the land reform acts, and by evasion and concealment during the implementation process. The administrative structure was seriously handicapped in countering the social and political strength of the landlords.
- There was no follow-up support system, providing protection to the new landowners from their former landlords and the access to inputs needed to increase production. On the contrary, it seems that a deliberate and systematic policy was followed against organizations or groups supporting small landowners, sharecropping tenants, and landless wage workers.
- The small parcels transferred to the new owners generally had a positive impact on employment and productivity, given the more intensive use of household labour and new inputs.
- While the Land Reform Act of 1972 provided increased security of tenure than existed previously—by expanding the occupancy rights and defining the division of produce and costs of inputs—there remain serious problems in the sharecropping system.

It is fair to say that the land reform efforts so far have made no major contribution in redirecting the process of differentiation observed in the agrarian structure of Pakistan. The existing duality of the land system—between the landlord and tenant and between the large and small landowner—affects all interactions in the marketplace and in the access to public sector services between the contending groups. Since landownership is highly concentrated, the control of land confers upon large landowners considerable economic and political power. Public policies on providing infrastructure and inputs, price support and subsidies, services of research and extension, etc. tend to exacerbate inequalities and adversely affect farm productivity. There is substantial evidence that a small proportion of the landowners exercise a disproportionately large influence on the machinery of the state in promoting their own interests. For the last twenty years, a structural reform programme of the land tenure system has not been on the national (government) and international (donor) agenda, although much lip service has been paid in the last decade to institutional reforms to make agriculture more productive and improve the well-being of people in rural areas.[14]

5. CHANGES IN THE LAND REVENUE (TAX) SYSTEM

At present there are only two forms in which the government taxes landowners (landholders) directly and includes the revenue in its budget: (i) land revenue as a tax on land that generates incomes and (ii) wealth tax on agricultural land as immovable property. The former is assessed and collected by the provincial governments and the latter by the federal government. In 1982/83 the military government introduced, as part of its policy of 'Islamizing' the national economy, the *ushr* levy on Muslim landowners in lieu of land revenue, but the *ushr* revenue was not to be part of the government's budget. The *ushr* revenue therefore acts as a substitute for land revenue for those Muslims who choose to pay the *ushr* to the Local Zakat Committees.

The revenues from the wealth tax on agricultural land are nominal, because those whose incomes are derived only from agriculture do not pay the wealth tax. The land revenue collected by the provincial governments was around Rs 48 million in 1948 and rose to Rs 135 million by 1960. In the next fifteen years, land revenue increased to Rs 194 million by 1975, but stayed at around Rs 250 million in the next decade (from 1975 to 1985). A substantial increase in land revenue started in 1985, when the provincial governments of Punjab, NWFP, and Balochistan increased their tax rates on an *ad hoc* basis, reaching Rs 693 million in 1989–90 and Rs 1,100 million in 1994–5. Much as the recent increase in land revenue appears impressive, it should be seen in relation to the growth of income from crops, provincial revenues, and provincial taxes in the last nearly five decades.

Table 10
Changes in land revenue collections
1949/49–1994/95

Year	Land revenue	Provincial revenue	Provincial taxes	Crop value-added	Cultivated area
	(............ million rupees ....)			(mill. hectares)	
1949/49	48	317	106	–	15.16
1950/51	47	383	145	–	15.15
1954/55	58	494	202	–	15.31
1960/61	135	844	248	5,011	18.12
1964/65	154	1,053	374	7,066	18.72
1969/70	172	1,325	539	11,102	19.23
1974/75	194	2,024	1,458	23,271	19.55
1979/80	257	2,368	1,809	43,993	20,23
1984/85	253	4,298	3,297	80,126	20.61
1989/90	693	6,619	5,431	115,065	20.94
1994/95	1,100	17,800	10,000	245,847	21.80

Source: As in Table 1.

The ratio of land revenue to crop income has fallen almost consistently from nearly 3 per cent in the 1950s to 0.45 per cent in 1995. Put differently, the direct tax (land revenue) paid by farmers works out to Rs 51 per hectare in 1995. Using a conservative figure of Rs 3,000 per hectare for net crop income, the average direct tax would be around 1.67 per cent of a farmer's net crop income. The contribution of land revenue to the provincial taxes and provincial revenue has fallen significantly: land revenue used to contribute from 30 to 55 per cent to the provincial taxes during the first twenty-five years of Pakistan (1947–72) but has contributed 8 to 14 per cent in the last twenty-five years; likewise its contribution to the provincial revenue has decreased from 13 to 16 per cent to 6 to 11 per cent in the two periods.

A. Land Revenue as a Tax on Land

The land revenue system in Pakistan has a very long history, but, in its present form, it was concretized by the British colonial government in the Punjab Land Revenue Act of 1887.[15] The West Pakistan Land Revenue Act of 1967 extended the Punjab land revenue system on a uniform basis to the other parts of what was then the province of West Pakistan or all four provinces of today. The land revenue, determined for each revenue 'circle' at the time of 'settlement', is a maximum of 25 per cent of the 'net assets'. The net assets are calculated as the value of gross produce minus the 'normal' cost of cultivation of crops in the case of owner-cultivators or the land rent received by landowners minus the charge of collecting the rent from tenants. The period of each revenue settlement is a minimum of ten and maximum of twenty-five years. Land revenue is paid in cash and is determined on the basis of information about the average crop area matured, crop yield, and prices. The revenue rates are classified by soil type for a village or group of villages in the revenue circle.

Since the revenue settlements in most districts of West Pakistan were completed before 1947, the government raised the basic revenue rates by 25 per cent on an *ad hoc* basis and adopted the new rates for all of West Pakistan in 1967. Even after the division of West Pakistan into four provinces in 1969, no basic change was made in the land revenue system until after the dismemberment of Pakistan in December 1971. The first change was made in the land revenue system of Sindh after the promulgation of the Land Reform Act of 1972 in Pakistan. A flat rate of land tax was introduced, based on the predetermined value of the Produce Index Unit (PIU), first used in Punjab in 1947 to settle the claims of Muslim refugees from East (Indian) Punjab and then extended to all districts of West Pakistan for implementing the Land Reform Act of 1959. The flat rate in Sindh was simply the revenue demand of the three previous years (1969–72) divided by the PIUs per unit of land in each village according to the soil type and mode of irrigation. The flat rate was fixed for five years, 1972–3 to 1977–8, after which a new rate was to be established on the basis of the revised PIUs per hectare.

The revenue rates in all provinces, including the flat rate in Sindh, were increased as multiples of the existing rates in 1975–6, with complete exemption to the owners of landholdings of up to five hectares (irrigated). This concession was part of the promises made to the 'peasants' by the PPP government in 1976. The PPP followed this up with a radical change in the land revenue system in January 1977, when the federal government replaced the tax on land with a tax on agricultural incomes (Finance Act of 1977), except for those whose landholdings were 10 hectares or less. The presumed income from agriculture would be determined on the basis of the number of PIUs per hectare, which had not been changed anywhere in Pakistan since the late 1940s. This radical change in the land revenue system was part of the agricultural reform package— including the Land Reform Act of 1977—offered by the PPP just before the national and provincial elections in March 1977.

After the *coup d'état* in July 1977, the military government (i) suspended the Finance Act of 1977, (ii) restored the tax exemption on agricultural income in the Income Tax Ordinance of 1979, and (iii) reintroduced the land revenue with new (higher) rates starting from the 1976–7 season. The land revenue exemption for owners of holdings of up to 10 hectares was allowed to stay, but the rates for all other sizes were increased as multiples of the 1975–6 rates in all provinces. Two major changes, affecting the land revenue system, were introduced in 1982–3 as a result of the Zakat and Ushr Ordinance of 1980: (i) Sunni Muslims would pay the *ushr* levy at the rate of five per cent of gross produce—to be assessed and collected by the Local Zakat Committees—in cash, subject to a basic exemption, and (ii) the Shia Muslim and non-Muslim landowners would pay the land revenue instead.[16] In addition, the land revenue rates were increased again, as multiples of the 1975–6 rates, and the exemption from land tax was restricted to landowners of up to one hectare in Punjab, NWFP, and Balochistan. At the same time, the provincial government in Sindh replaced the 1972 flat rate system—which was itself based on the unrevised number of PIUs per hectare—by the system it had followed before 1972 and was in use in other provinces, but maintained the land revenue exemption at 10 hectares. The result of these *ad hoc* changes in the system and the increased land revenue rates is that after 1983 the overall land revenue yield has increased substantially in Punjab, NWFP, and Balochistan but has fallen significantly in Sindh.

B. Wealth Tax on Agricultural Land

Wealth tax was introduced in Pakistan in 1963, following the recommendations of the Taxation Enquiry Committee of 1959. Under the Wealth Tax Act of 1963, all movable and immovable wealth is subject to tax, with a basic exemption of Rs one million. All assets on which *zakat* has been paid under the Zakat and Ushr Ordinance of 1980 are exempt from the wealth tax. Agricultural land is considered immovable wealth, subject to the basic exemption of Rs 100,000. The Wealth Tax Act of 1963 was amended in 1970 to exempt the owners of agricultural land whose agricultural income was not liable to any tax. This would exclude everyone who owned agricultural land but did not have taxable income from non-agricultural sources since agricultural income was exempt from taxation under the Income Tax Ordinance of 1979. The other problem was that the value of land for wealth tax was set at Rs 10 per PIU—and since no individual was allowed to own a land area with more than 8,000 PIUs under the Land Reform Act of 1977—the maximum value of land (Rs 80,000) would be well under the allowable exemption of Rs 100,000.

Starting in 1990, and mainly because of the pressure from the Asian Development Bank (ADB) and the World Bank, the federal government has raised the assessment value of agricultural land for wealth tax from Rs 10 to Rs 250 per PIU in two stages, although the 1990 Taxation Committee was in favour of raising this value to Rs 400 per PIU which is used on agricultural land to serve as collateral for acquiring loans from the banking system. However, these changes in the Wealth Tax Act of 1963 have made little impact on tax receipts from agricultural land because of at least three reasons: (i) low rate of assessment of the PIU (Rs 250 per PIU); (ii) unchanged number of PIUs per hectare since the late 1940s in spite of the substantial increase in the productive capacity of land due to expanded irrigation, use of modern inputs, development of roads, and urbanization; and (iii) generous deductions announced by the federal government after removing the wealth tax exemption in 1994. The federal government has not accepted the suggestion by donors that it should revise the number of PIU per hectare as a good measure of the productive capacity of agricultural land for wealth tax purposes. It is obvious that without raising the assessment value of land to Rs 400 per PIU and the upward revision of PIUs per hectare, the wealth tax receipts from agricultural land would remain inconsequential.[17]

C. Land Revenue Reform: Taxation of Agricultural Incomes

The existing land revenue system has no redeeming feature: it is a relic of the past developed under feudal, authoritarian, and colonial regimes. Even as a land tax, it has no merits now because of the *ad hoc* changes made in the rates and exemptions in the last twenty-five years. The land tax is no longer linked to the presumptive capacity of the land one owns, hence it is highly inequitable among landowners. Also, it yields very modest revenue to the provincial governments in spite of the increases in the rates in Punjab, NWFP, and Balochistan in 1983–4.

There is a long history of opposition to the idea of taxing agricultural incomes in Pakistan, going back to the times of the British rule in India. The British were ambivalent about the tax on income from agriculture for several reasons. For one thing, a tax on the incomes of those (landlords) who they had themselves created or supported in the countryside could have jeopardized their power in India. The landed interests were the bulwark of British administration. After the establishment of direct rule by the British sovereign in 1858, an income tax system based on the experience of Britain was tried in India, including the agriculture sector. However, this experiment was abandoned after nearly twenty-five years in 1886. With the passage of the Income Tax Act of 1886, agriculture was to have only the land revenue system. The Income Tax Act of 1922 granted specific tax exemption to agricultural incomes, which is still available in Pakistan under the Income Tax Ordinance of 1979. It is important to note that a national committee on taxation in 1926 argued strongly in favour of taxing all incomes in British India. The India Act of 1935 granted new powers to the provinces, including the power of taxation on agriculture (land and income).

The arguments against a tax on agricultural incomes have always been couched—both in the colonial period and since independence—in terms that sound superficially convincing. In recent years, two new arguments have been made: (i) the agriculture sector is already taxed too heavily and (ii) the federal government has no jurisdiction in this matter under the 1973 Constitution. The first argument confuses the issue of the tax burden on the agriculture sector with the issue of tax on the personal income and wealth of rich farmers. Further, as indicated earlier, the burden of implicit taxes on agriculture has decreased significantly due to major policy reforms in the 1980s and 1990s. The second argument is also tenuous because it has been rightly suggested that the National Assembly, on the advice of the federal government, can make the necessary constitutional amendments.

The first major endorsement for a tax on agricultural incomes in Pakistan was made by the Taxation Enquiry Committee of

1959. It recommended that the principle of tax on income should be applied irrespective of the source of income. It, therefore, favoured the abolition of the graduated surcharge on land revenue as had existed in Punjab since 1948. The Committee urged the federal government to replace the surcharge with a tax on all incomes and assume responsibility for the assessment and collection of these taxes in the agriculture sector as well. The latter recommendation would have changed the power given to the provincial governments to tax agriculture under the Government of India Act of 1935, which power was enshrined in the defunct Constitution of Pakistan in 1956. After the failure of the Taxation Enquiry Committee of 1959, the Taxation and Tariffs Commission of 1964 recommended strongly in its report (published in 1967) that the provincial land revenue be merged with the existing income tax levied by the federal government. The recommendation was not accepted due to the opposition of the provincial government of the then West Pakistan. A presumptive tax on agricultural income was proposed by the Agricultural Enquiry Commission (1970–74) on the basis of computing income from agriculture at Rs 2 per PIU and 'clubbing' the agricultural income with non-agricultural income for determining the rate of tax on the latter. This recommendation was, however, not implemented.

A major breakthrough on the taxation of agricultural incomes came with the enactment of the Finance (Supplementary) Act of 1977, which abolished the land revenue and replaced it with a uniform and universal income tax in the country in January 1977. Two options were allowed to the tax payers in agriculture with holdings of over 10 hectares: either assess their taxable income from agriculture by deducting from the gross income several specified expenses and pay the tax according to the existing tax slabs and conditions applicable to taxable incomes from other sources, or pay a flat rate of Rs 6 per PIU irrespective of the size of landholding or the number of PIUs held in the land revenue records. The first option was a direct tax on earned (real) income and the second was a tax on presumed income from agricultural land. The Act of 1977 was first announced under the Emergency Proclamation as the Finance (Supplementary) Ordinance by the President of Pakistan, repealing that part of the Income Tax Act of 1922 which exempted agricultural income from taxation. However, before the PPP government could initiate the implementation of the Finance Act of 1977, a *coup d'état* in July 1977 imposed Martial Law which first suspended the Act and then cancelled its implementation. The former tax exemption on agricultural income under the Income Tax Act of 1922 was restored in the Income Tax Ordinance of 1979.

During the 1980s, the question of changes in direct taxes in agriculture, including land revenue, *ushr,* and income tax, was examined by at least three 'expert' committees. The majority view was against introducing a tax on agricultural incomes. They emphasized the need to improve the assessment and collection of land revenue and *ushr*, but without specific recommendations on the methods of implementation. The National Taxation Reform Commission in 1986, the National Commission on Agriculture in 1988, and the Committee of Experts on Taxation of Agricultural Incomes in 1989 used the argument that the federal government could not legislate a tax on agricultural income because of the division of powers between the federal and provincial legislatures under the amended Constitution of 1973. It was argued that the National Assembly was not empowered to legislate on matters falling in the provincial jurisdiction, except in a state of Emergency under Article 232 of the Constitution. As stated earlier, it has been rightly suggested by one of the dissenting members of the 1989 Committee of Experts that the federal government could ask the National Assembly to amend item 47 in Part I of the Federal List contained in the Fourth Schedule, read with Article 70(6), to state 'Taxes on income' instead of 'Taxes on income other than agricultural income'. Also, there is room for the federal government in Article 260 of the Constitution to make the necessary amendment in the Income Tax Ordinance of 1979 (Clause I, Section 2).

It is well known that the tax exemption for agricultural incomes has been misused by individuals who receive income from other sources, like industry, trade, etc. Also, taxes are avoided (and evaded) on non-agricultural incomes in several ways, e.g. by purchasing agricultural land and claiming it as the source of other incomes; agriculturists claiming income generated from other businesses as agricultural income; and fictitious loans being made by agriculturists to industrialists (and traders) to help the latter class of taxpayers avoid tax on their non-agricultural incomes. A minor policy reform with respect to agricultural income was, therefore, introduced by the federal government in the Finance Ordinance of 1988 (Ordinance II of 1988). It amended the Income Tax Ordinance of 1979 (Second Schedule in Part I, Clause I) to include agricultural income (if any) in the 'chargeable income' for determining the tax rate for non-agricultural incomes. This so-called clubbing formula, introduced with the Federal Budget of 1988–9, has had no major impact on tax evasion and the income tax revenue. At the end of 1990, the PML government appointed a Taxation Committee, which was in favour of a tax on agricultural income but in its view, the federal government did not have a clear constitutional authority to introduce a tax on agricultural income. So the Committee recommended that the federal government redefine the concept of agricultural income by excluding the rental part received by landowners and incomes earned from orchards, livestock, and poultry farms. However, the government apparently took no action on this recommendation.

The persistently high fiscal deficit and the pressure of the international donor community since the early 1990s have moved up the issue of reforming the land revenue system on the government's policy agenda in Pakistan. The caretaker government—after the dismissal of the PML government in July 1993—acted on two fronts in September–October 1993. First, it amended the Wealth Tax Act of 1963 and removed the exemption for agricultural land as immovable property for wealth tax purposes. Second, it issued ordinances in all provinces to introduce a flat tax rate of Rs 2 per PIU on all landholdings above 4,000 PIUs to replace the existing land revenue. In February 1994, the newly elected PPP government enacted a somewhat watered down version of the Wealth Tax (Amendment) Ordinance in line with the recommendations of the Prime Minister's Task Force on Agriculture to justify the changes in the original legislation. All provincial legislatures have enacted revised land tax legislation, introducing a graduated scale of tax on presumptive income expressed in rupees per acre per annum, and the implementation process has begun. According to preliminary press reports, the target expected amount to be generated from these taxes is Rs 3.7 billion, which represents about 11 per cent of provincial public sector expenditure under the annual development plan.[18]

CONCLUSION

In 1947 Pakistan inherited an economy dominated by the agricultural sector. Industrial activity was limited to a few large processing and manufacturing units of sugar and cotton and a large number of small establishments processing and manufacturing a variety of consumer goods. Most of the industrial plants and economic activity were located in the areas that are now part of India. The major characteristics of the agriculture sector then included: dependence on traditional crop rotations according to the availability of water; most of the food crops—wheat, rice, corn, millet, sorghum, and barley—were produced largely for household consumption with little surplus marketed to towns and cities; cotton was the most dominant cash crop, followed by sugarcane in some areas; fruits and vegetables were produced on a small scale for both local consumption and market sales; and livestock production was similarly organized on a small scale, mainly to meet the household needs with very little surplus for sale.

The important resources (factors) used in agricultural production included land (of which a large proportion was rain-fed or inadequately irrigated); human labour (drawn mainly from the peasant household); and animal power. Capital inputs were limited to small implements and tools used by human labour and assisted by draft animals. The productivity of land and other factors was very low due to the lack of changes in the traditional technology that largely excluded improved seeds, chemical fertilizer, pest control, capital equipment, and improved cultivation methods. Land utilization was limited in both area and quality because of the unreliable and inadequate supply of water and other complementary inputs of human and physical capital. It was also adversely affected by the high concentration of landownership and a sharecropping tenancy that co-existed with the owner-operated small land parcels.

The agrarian structure—control of and access to agricultural land—was dominated by a quasi-feudal land tenure, in which a large proportion of the farm area was owned and controlled by a small proportion of the rural elite and a large proportion of the cultivators (peasants) were either small owner-operators or sharecropping tenants. In fact, a significant share of farmland was cultivated by sharecroppers with very tenuous claims or rights to tenancy and who were almost totally dependent on the considerable economic and social power of the large landowners (landlords). Tenants and small landowning peasants were in a state of almost perpetual debt to the commercial class and landlords at the village level. Landlessness and near-landlessness were the major sources of the poverty and powerlessness of a majority of the rural population. Lack of opportunities for alternative sources of employment was, therefore, a major cause of dependence on agriculture and the rural elite. The predominantly rural society of Pakistan was stratified in many areas on the basis of attachment to land, caste, tribe, and clan.

Historically, a major interest of the colonial state in British India was to extract an agricultural surplus and raise the revenue to run the administrative machinery of the colony. After the annexation of the territories from local potentates, the colonial administrators established or confirmed property rights in land according to their own need for stability in the rural society and to raise the level of agricultural output to extract a rising surplus for domestic and international trade. The land tenure system established in British India clearly reflected the political and economic priorities of the new rulers in each area. Investment in building the physical infrastructure, particularly roads, railways, ports, and canals was also accorded a high priority because of the potential contribution of the new infrastructure to the production of increased agricultural surplus. Most of the state revenues were collected through a tax on agricultural land (land revenue) since agriculture was the single most important source of production, employment, and income. The land revenue system developed by the British in India was, of course, a modified form of the land tax that had existed in one form or another for centuries before the British rule. Pakistan, therefore, inherited a highly differentiated agrarian structure and a land tax system evolved during the colonial period to meet the British imperial objectives in India.

The agricultural crisis of the 1950s has been well documented.[19] Farm productivity stagnated and the rate of growth of population started to gather momentum. The agrarian structure was highly differentiated, except that at the lower end of the peasantry, there was increasing subdivision and fragmentation of landholdings. The settlement of millions of Muslim refugees from India, at least in Punjab, added to the increasing number of middle and poor peasants. In Sindh, the cross-border movement of people and their settlement tended to aggravate the conditions of the sharecropping tenants (*haris*), as most of the settled refugees joined the ranks of absentee landowners. The political environment for land reforms, so much publicized in the early days of Pakistan, remained unfavourable and the landed elite remained intransigent. The tenancy reforms of the early 1950s in the provinces introduced some marginal changes for the occupancy and non-occupancy tenants. The increased incidence of waterlogging and salinity and the adverse government policies related to agricultural prices and provision of infrastructure also contributed to the low growth rate of agricultural output. As in many other underdeveloped countries, rapid industrial growth at the expense of agriculture was a major (and largely wrong-headed) strategy of economic development pursued by the governments in Pakistan.

The somewhat robust growth of agricultural output and productivity in the 1960s was facilitated by: (i) the development of water resources in the public sector and installation of private tubewells (mainly in Punjab), (ii) the spread of new seeds of wheat and rice, and (iii) increased incentives through price support and subsidies on inputs like fertilizers, irrigation water, and institutional credit. There may have been some effect of the land redistribution policies of the early 1960s, which favoured the development of capitalist agriculture and threatened the feudal tenancy arrangements. The bimodal strategy of agricultural growth in the 1960s included several important features which were by no means neutral to the existing agrarian structure. The availability and use of the productivity-augmenting inputs are a function of the social conditions in which they appear. There is some evidence that the distributive effects of robust agricultural growth in the 1960s were not benign, since the farming community was highly differentiated by landownership, access to land, and employment opportunities.[20]

The growth process was disturbed in the first half of the 1970s due to: (i) the weakening impact of new seeds, (ii) political turmoil following the civil war and secession of East Pakistan, (iii) drought followed by floods, (iv) a virus attack on cotton, (v) the uncertainty created by a new land distribution programme in 1972, (vi) widespread nationalization of industries, and (vii) macroeconomic imbalances reflected in high inflation, large deficits in the government budget and current account, and a permissive money supply. The agricultural growth rate increased significantly in the 1980s because of several significant policy changes with respect to agriculture, including (i) favourable adjustment in the prices of outputs, (ii) transfer of major activities from the public to the private sector, (iii) re-orientation of public investment from large-scale projects to improvement in research, extension, and infrastructure, and (iv) introduction of new cotton varieties. The rapid expansion of credit from the public sector institutions for mechanical technology and investment in large-scale private farming and processing have also been important factors in the growth process.

The lacklustre performance of the agriculture sector since 1990 has highlighted the importance of several factors: natural calamities, including floods and virus attack on cotton; rapid changes of governments and political instability since 1988; macroeconomic imbalances; reduced vigour of crop seeds; deterioration in land quality due to waterlogging and salinity; uneven supply of irrigation water; and sharp increase in the cost of production. There is also evidence that, thanks to the slow-down in overall economic growth, the distribution of income in both urban and rural areas may have deteriorated, with increased incidence of unemployment in the country. The rising unemployment in rural and urban areas may also have been contributed to by the sharply reduced migration of labour to the Middle East and that in urban Sindh, particularly in Karachi and Hyderabad, due to civil unrest.[21]

REFERENCES

Binswagner, H. (1986), 'Agricultural mechanization: a comparative historical perspective'. *World Bank Research Observer*, 1, p. 1.

Bose, S.R., and Clark, E.H. (1969), 'Some basic considerations on agricultural mechanization in Pakistan', *Pakistan Development Review*, 3, p. 9.

Chaudhary, G.M. (1982), 'Green revolution and redistribution of rural incomes: Pakistan's experience', *Pakistan Development Review*, 3, p. 21.

Cheong, K.C., and D'Silva, E. (1984), 'Prices, terms of trade, and the role of the government in Pakistan's agriculture', World Bank Staff Working Paper, No. 643, World Bank, Washington D.C.

Faruqee, R. (1995), 'Structural and policy reforms for agricultural growth: the case for Pakistan', World Bank Staff Working Paper, World Bank, Washington, D.C.

Gotsch, C.H. (1973), 'Tractor mechanization and rural development in Pakistan', *International Labour Review*, 2, p. 107.

Gotsch, C.H., and Brown, G. (1980), 'Prices, taxes and subsidies in Pakistan agriculture, 1960–76', World Bank Staff Working Paper, No. 387, World Bank, Washington, D.C.

Government of Pakistan. (1959, 1962), *Land and Crop Statistics.*

———. (1960, 1972, 1980, 1990), *Agriculture Census Reports.*

———. (1993), Report of Prime Minister's Task Force on Agriculture, Minstry of Finance, Revenue and Economic Affairs.

———. *Agriculture Statistics of Pakistan*, various issues.

———. *Economic Survey*, various issues.

———. *Report of the National Commission on Agriculture*, March 1988.

———. *Statistical Yearbook*, various issues.

Kazi, S. (1987), 'Intersectoral terms of trade for Pakistan's economy, 1970–71 to 1981–82', *Pakistan Development Review*, 1, p. 26.

Khan, M.A. et al. (1986), *Socioeconomic Impact of Tractorization in Pakistan*, Punjab Economic Research Institute, Lahore.

Khan, M.H. (1966), *The Role of Agriculture in Economic Development: A Case Study for Pakistan*, Centre for Agricultural Publications and Documentation, Wageningen.

———. (1981), *Underdevelopment and Agrarian Structure in Pakistan*, Boulder, Colorado, Westview Press.

———. (1983a), 'Classes and agrarian transition in Pakistan', *Pakistan Development Review*, 3, p. 22.

———. (1983b), 'Green revolution and redistribution of rural incomes: Pakistan's experience—a comment', *Pakistan Development Review*, 4, p. 22

———. (1994), 'The structural adjustment process and agricultural change in Pakistan in the 1980s and 1990s', *Pakistan Development Review*, 1, p. 33

Khan, M.H. and Akbari, A.H. (1986), 'Impact of agriculture research and extension on crop productivity in Pakistan: a production function approach', *World Development*, 6, p. 14.

Khan, M.H. et al. (1989), *Structural Change in Pakistan's Agriculture*, Pakistan Institute of Development Economics, Islamabad.

Mahmood, M. and Haq, N. (1981), 'Farm size and productivity revisited', *Pakistan Development Review*, 2, p. 20.

McInerney, J.P., and Donaldson, J.P. (1975), 'The consequences of farm tractors in Pakistan', World Bank Staff Working Paper, No. 210, World Bank, Washington, D.C.

Naqvi, Khan, and Chaudhary. (1987), *Land Reforms in Pakistan: A Historical Perspective*, Pakistan Institute of Development Economics, Islamabad.

Qureshi, S.K. (1987), *Agricultural Pricing and Taxation in Pakistan*, Pakistan Institute of Development Economics, Islamabad.

Qureshi, S.K. et al. (1989), 'Taxes and subsidies in agriculture as elements of intersectoral transfer of resources', *Pakistan Development Review*, 2, p. 28.

Wizarat, S. (1981), 'Technological change in Pakistan's agriculture, 1953–54 to 1978–79', *Pakistan Development Review*, 4, p. 20.

———. (1994), 'The structural adjustment process and agricultural change in Pakistan in the 1980s and 1990s', *Pakistan Development Review*, 1, p. 22.

NOTES

1. The figures and estimates used in this study, unless otherwise indicated, are based on the published data in *Pakistan Statistical Yearbook* (various issues); *Economy Survey* (various issues); *Agriculture Census Reports* (1960, 1972, 1980, and 1990); *Land and Crop Statistics* (1959 and 1962); and *Agricultural Statistics of Pakistan* (various issues).

2. Caution should be exercised in interpreting the observed changes in crop yields because of the wide seasonal fluctuations in crop area and output. Meat output per metric ton of foodgrains has increased more or less consistently since 1970, rising from 0.06 metric ton to 0.10 metric ton in 1985 and 0.17 metric ton in 1995. However, milk output per metric ton of foodgrains in the same period did not rise in the 1970s from the level of 0.84 metric ton, but then rose quite significantly in the early 1980s from 0.96 metric ton in 1985 to 1.54 metric ton in 1995.

3. Wizarat (1981), Khan (1994), and Faruqee (1995) asserted, without documented support, that agricultural (crop) productivity in Pakistan has been either stagnant or falling since the mid-1970s. This assertion seems to run counter to the documented positive rates of change in the yield levels of crops and the TFP.

4. In terms of the impact of private tubewells on the regional distribution of benefits and impact on farmers' income, there are four aspects worth noting here. First, private tubewells have been installed mainly in the plains of Punjab. They are not economical in the mountainous areas because of the depth at which water is available. Similarly, they have not spread in Sindh because of the depth and poor quality of water. This uneven development of groundwater has been an important factor in some of the inter-regional disparities observed in the country. Second, tubewells have been installed mostly by landowners with holdings of 10 hectares or more. Given the indivisible and large capacity of the diesel and electric tubewells, even the middle peasants cannot afford their fixed and variable costs. Therefore, there is a high concentration of tubewell ownership. This has two associated problems: (i) While a market for tubewell water has developed, it has not been easy for non-owners to buy water at reasonable rates and at the time when they need it most. This has created increased uncertainty, which acts against innovation. (ii) The other problem is that the apparently high concentration of tubewells has provided added incentive to large landowners to lease their neighbours' land or buy it. In addition, the inducement to invest in tubewells has been

provided by handsome public subsidies on fuels, electricity, installation, and maintenance costs. In fact, these subsidies have become an important component in transferring public tubewells—which were installed in the Indus basin to alleviate the problem of waterlogging and salinity—to private ownership since the mid-1980s. Finally, private ownership of tubewells has been encouraged by a credit policy in which loans have not only been readily available, given the collateral of land, but distributed at low rates of interest and with convenient terms of repayment.

5. A general analysis of this issue has been done by Binswanger (1986). In the context of Pakistan, *see*, for example: Bose and Clark (1969); Gotsch (1973); McInerney and Donaldson (1975); Khan, et al. (1986).

6. Some important generalizations can be made about tractors in Pakistan. Apparently they have had little or no positive effect on crop yields. Their ownership by large landowners has led to an increase in the average size of the already large landholdings, by leasing the land from marginal and small landowners and by resuming the land from sharecroppers for self-cultivation. There is thus a general increase in the size of farms at the upper end of the size distribution of operational holdings. Cropping intensity with tractors has increased only if there is additional water. Tractors do not provide incremental power, but tend to substitute for the power of draft animals. Private returns to tractor ownership are high because of the subsidies on credit and fuel costs. There is no conclusive evidence that tractors have created more employment, but there is considerable evidence that they have weakened the position of the tenant and also reduced dependence on outside labour. Tractors and other machines give greater control over the labour required in agriculture. The adoption of tractor-powered threshers and other machines and the spread of machine-hiring services are producing labour-saving effects on all types of farms.

7. A survey of this literature is contained Khan (1994). Specific studies on the terms of trade and resource transfer include: Gotsch and Brown (1980); Cheong and D'Silva (1984); Kazi (1987); Quresh (1987); *Report of the National Commission on Agriculture* (1988); Qureshi, et al. (1989); Government of Pakistan, *Report of Prime Minister's Task Force on Agriculture* (1993).

8. These issues are discussed in some detail by Faruqee (1995).

9. Most of the material in this section is from Khan (1981), Naqvi, Khan, and Chaudhry (1987 and 1989).

10. Some of these changes have been analysed by Khan (1983).

11. The *First Five-Year Plan (1955–60)* document reiterated the need for radical land reforms in Pakistan in accordance with the recommendations of the PML Agrarian Committee in 1949.

12. Tenancy reforms along the lines of Punjab were enacted in NWFP during 1950 to 1952.

13. This is well documented in Khan (1981, Chapter 5). The Produce Index Unit (PIU) was established in the 1940s as a measure of land claim—based on the equivalent 'productivity' of one unit of land in separate locations—for Muslim refugees in Pakistan. It is important to note that the values of the PIU established in the 1940s have not been changed until now in spite of the massive changes in the relative productivity of land in different areas of Pakistan. *See* Khan (1994).

14. *See*, for instance, Government of Pakistan, *Report of the National Commission on Agriculture* (1988) and Government of Pakistan, *Report of Prime Minister's Task Force on Agriculture* (1993), and Faruqee (1995).

15. A detailed study of the land revenue system, with historical background and sources, is given by the author in Khan (1981, Chapter 8).

16. The military government's declared objective of the 1980 Zakat and Ushr Ordinance was to collect the *zakat* and *ushr* levies to spend for the welfare of the 'needy' individuals or households in each community and to support those institutions directly involved in assisting these groups. Later, the PPP government made two major changes in the Zakat and Ushr Ordinance of 1980. First, in the Finance Act of 1989, the autonomy of Zakat Councils was reduced and the *zakat* and *ushr* funds could be used for other activities that might have an impact on the lives of the poor. Second, the Finance Act of 1990 placed the responsibility of assessment and collection of the *ushr* levy (as arrears of land revenue) with the provincial Land Revenue Departments. These changes were intended to increase the government's intervention and expand the *ushr* base (as a social safety net) for providing relief to the poor in rural and urban areas. In 1991, the Islami Jamhuri Ittehad (IJI) government appointed a committee to examine the means to improve the system and reverse the falling trend in the *ushr* revenues. But, so far, no practical measures have been implemented in the provinces. In the meantime, the annual *ushr* collections have fallen from Rs 260 million in 1983–4 to less than Rs 50 million in 1994–5.

17. The Central Board of Revenue (CBR) does not publish the figures of wealth tax revenue from agricultural land. However, in 1990, the CBR estimate of this revenue was Rs 15 million collected from only 2,000 individuals since those whose incomes were derived only from agriculture were not then required to pay the wealth tax on agricultural land.

18. The figures about the provincial public sector expenditure under the annual development plan have been taken from *Economic Survey 1996–97*, statistical appendix, (1997, p. 219).

19. A detailed study of agriculture in the first fifteen years of Pakistan has been done by Khan (1966).

20. These issues have been analysed in Khan (1981). There is considerable debate in the literature on the distributive impact of the Green Revolution,

including productivity differentials between farm size and tenancy arrangements. A summary of the debate is given in Khan (1983).

21. The growth performance and changes in public policy in the 1980s and 1990s are analysed in Khan (1994).

5

Patterns and Growth of Pakistan's Industrial Sector

*A.R. Kemal**

1. INTRODUCTION

Pakistan's manufacturing industries have grown at an annual average rate of 7.4 per cent since 1949–50. Pakistan has also made a successful transition from an agrarian economy, with only a handful of manufacturing units at the time of independence, to a semi-industrialized country where manufacturing accounts for 18.2 per cent of GDP. However, major structural problems, such as the lack of diversification in the industrial structure and inefficiencies in the manufacturing process suggest that in the absence of major policy initiatives, the high growth rate of the sector may not be sustained. Accordingly, Pakistan has initiated tariff rationalization to improve efficiency and ensure industrialization in accordance with its dynamic comparative advantage (*see* Chapter 3).

In its brief economic history, Pakistan has pursued an import substitution industrialization strategy, even though efforts have also been made to tilt the policies towards export orientation. Since the import substitution industrialization strategy, in general, negates a competitive market structure, it leads to gross inefficiencies. These inefficiencies and structural problems have also slowed industrial growth, and the dispersion in protection rates favoured traditional and penalized efficient industries.

* Chief Economist, Planning and Development Division.

Consequently, most investment flowed into traditional industries such as textiles and food, while industries such as chemicals and engineering lagged behind. It is, therefore, no wonder that Pakistan's manufacturing is concentrated in a few industries and its exports lack diversification.

This chapter focuses both on the major achievements as well as failures of the industrial sector in different periods of Pakistan's history. By analysing industrial policies, growth and pattern of investment, output and exports, and inefficiencies in industrial production, the paper examines the future prospects of industry in Pakistan.

The chapter outline is as follows: industrial policies are reviewed in section 2; the growth and pattern of industrial investment are examined in section 3; industrial growth has been analysed in section 4; structural change in industry in section 5; the sources of growth of manufacturing industries have been reviewed in section 6; changes in industrial efficiency and protection to manufacturing industries (including the social cost of protection) have been analysed in section 7; and concluding recommendations for the manufacturing sector are presented in section 8.

2. INDUSTRIALIZATION STRATEGIES

Pakistan has pursued an import substitution industrialization (ISI) strategy which provides protection to industries producing import competitive goods but tends to discourage exports. Along with fiscal incentives, it tends to increase capital intensity and, as such, has adverse implications for employment and distribution of income.

Even though Pakistan has pursued an ISI strategy, some important differences in the policies pursued during different time periods are evident. In the 1950s, severe import restrictions and an overvalued exchange rate penalized exports. In the 1960s, imports were considerably liberalized, the bias against exports was reduced, and markets were de-controlled. Pakistan devalued its currency and tariffs were rationalized in the early 1970s, but by the late 1970s import restrictions and selective subsidies to exports re-appeared. From 1983–4 onwards, there has been a period of considerable liberalization. The changes in policies in different periods are reviewed below.

A. INDUSTRIAL STRATEGY IN THE 1950s

The industrial policy during the 1950s was dictated by the *Statement of Industrial Policy* issued in 1948, which aimed at manufacturing products based on indigenous raw materials such as cotton, jute, hides, and skins. An assured market at home and abroad was assumed for such products. In addition, consumer goods industries were to be developed to meet the requirements of the home market since the country was heavily dependent on imports at that time. In 1953, when the Korean War boom was over, an Economic Appraisal Committee was appointed which laid down the criteria for the selection of industries and suggested measures to promote manufacturing industries. The Committee recommended that industrial growth be governed by the following considerations:

- availability of indigenous raw materials,
- reduction of imports, particularly of essential items,
- maximum productivity of capital and maximum employment, and
- net social and economic advantage to the country.

While the availability of indigenous raw materials and the reduction of imports were given priority, improving productivity and net economic advantage were relegated to the third and the fourth place. Thus the report emphasized import substitution, which played a major role in the growth of manufacturing industries of Pakistan. Unlike the *Statement of Industrial Policy*, which restricted import substitution to consumer goods only, the committee recommended it for 'essential items' such as pharmaceuticals, insecticides, disinfectants, refined petroleum and other allied products, chemical fertilizers, certain heavy chemicals, and high and medium engineering. The Committee recommended that manufacturing industries be promoted through a cascaded tariff structure but in case of severe foreign exchange shortages, the use of quantitative restrictions on imports could also be used to protect industries.

The two main characteristics of the policies pursued up to 1959 are direct controls and a bias against exports. Not only imports but investment and prices of some manufactured products were also subject to direct controls which resulted in rigidities and hampered the growth of the manufacturing industries in particular and of the economy in general.[1] During this period, too much emphasis seems to have been placed on the reduction in imports and too little effort seems to have been made to increase export earnings. Corresponding to tariffs and quotas on imports, there were no subsidies for exports, which made domestic production more profitable than export production.[2]

B. INDUSTRIAL STRATEGY IN THE 1960s

By the end of the 1950s, it was realized that direct controls had resulted in rigidities which hampered growth and that urgent reforms were needed. The Second Five Year Plan, issued in 1960, emphasized the need to remove different controls and recommended the abolition of price controls and the rationalization or removal of controls on the imports of machinery and intermediate inputs. During the 1960s, price controls were lifted from almost all products, and the foreign exchange market was liberalized to a large extent in that market forces were increasingly used to ration scarce foreign exchange.

Besides liberalizing the foreign exchange market and subsidizing exports, the government provided a number of incentives to exporters, such as the export bonus scheme, tax rebates, tax exemptions, export performance licensing, and pay-as-you-earn schemes. Moreover, tax holidays and accelerated depreciation allowances to increase post-tax profits in the production of manufactured products were also granted. Accordingly, the protection rates in the period were high and resulted in excessive profits for producers. The growth pattern in the 1960s has been extensively analysed. The major finding is that manufacturing output increased sharply, but by the end of this decade structural problems in the sector had started emerging.[3]

C. INDUSTRIAL STRATEGY IN THE 1970s

A number of important initiatives were taken during the 1970s which had a long-run bearing on industrialization. The most important initiative was the nationalization of heavy industry, and a number of sectors including cement, fertilizer, oil refining, engineering, and chemicals were exclusively reserved for the public sector. Also, the policy of disinvesting profitable public sector units was discontinued. Moreover, industrialists faced a number of restrictions, including price fixation, under the Profiteering and Hoarding Act. The nationalization of forty-two big industrial units and other forms of direct industrial intervention created considerable uncertainty, which resulted in capital flight and a sharp fall in private investment.

Another significant decision in the 1970s was the over-due devaluation of the rupee. This significantly reduced the multiplicity of exchange rates and provided a level playing field to large and small scale industries in importing inputs. Furthermore, the unification of the exchange rate encouraged small sector exports; at the overvalued exchange rate only formal sector exports were provided subsidies. Small scale production had the additional advantage of exemption from excise duties and labour laws.

Licensing procedures were significantly simplified and tariffs were rationalized following the devaluation. Incentives for manufacturing also changed. Subsidies to manufacturing were reduced significantly; export subsidies and tax holidays were withdrawn; import duties on finished goods were reduced; and anti-monopoly measures, along with price controls, were instituted. As a result, private investment and even total investment in manufacturing as a percentage of GDP fell during the period.[4]

D. INDUSTRIALIZATION POLICIES OF THE 1980s AND 1990s

During the 1980s and 1990s, direct controls have been replaced with market-oriented forces; import policy has been liberalized, tariff structure has been rationalized, par value of the rupee has been brought nearer to its equilibrium value and it has been made convertible on the capital account, investment licensing is no longer required, prices have been de-controlled and public enterprises have been divested.

Since 1983–4, import restrictions in Pakistan have taken the form of Negative and Restricted Lists.[5] Products on the negative list are banned, while those on the restricted list are imported only subject to various conditions including origin of imports, standardization, type of users, sector (public only), and the satisfaction of the safety and health standards. Along with the liberalization of import policy, tariffs have also been rationalized. In addition, the tariff rationalization initiated in the 1980s, gained momentum in the 1990s.

The maximum rate of import duty at present is 45 per cent, and it is expected to be brought down to 35 per cent. While statutory rates of import duties, on average, have exceeded 50 per cent, the average duty actually realized from imports was around 25 per cent in the early and mid-1990s. As shown in Chapter 3, the differential results from the exemptions and concessions given from payment of import duties to a large number of products. These exemptions and concessions have been withdrawn in a number of cases, but they still exist, especially in industries subject to deletion programmes.

An effort is being made to remove the anti-export bias. Export duties on raw cotton and cotton yarn have been removed, and certain other facilities are being provided to exporters. These include income tax rebates graduated with the degree of processing, drawback of custom duties, sales taxes, surcharges on imported inputs, and excise duties. In addition, there are the bonded warehouses and the export processing unit schemes to provide duty free access to imported inputs, so as to encourage exports.[6] An export development cess at a rate of 0.25 per cent of f.o.b. value has been introduced to set up institutions in the private sector to develop the requisite skills and improve quality, grading, and testing facilities.[7]

A number of fiscal incentives were provided in the form of tax holidays, tax credits, accelerated depreciation allowances, concessions in import duty on intermediate and capital goods, exemptions from sales tax on output, lower interest rates, freight subsidy, and lower fuel costs, etc. However, all types of tax holidays and other fiscal incentives, except accelerated depreciation allowance and tax credits, have been withdrawn.

Another feature of industrial policy in Pakistan was the requirement of obtaining prior permission from the government before establishing large-scale industries. Such industrial regulations as investment licensing, the import restrictions on capital and intermediate inputs, locational clearances, and constraints on payments of technical fees and royalty, slowed the pace of industrial investment. In the 1984 industrial policy, the scale limit of industries requiring these licences was raised and by 1992, all the restrictions were removed. Investment sanctions are no longer required except for arms and ammunition, high explosives, and radio-active substances.

Foreign investment restrictions have also been eased and there are now no equity restrictions on foreign investors or any compulsion for them to go public, as long as they hold at least 51 per cent of the equity. Ceilings on payment of royalties and technical fees have also been removed while work permit restrictions on expatriate managers have been withdrawn. All foreign exchange controls have been abolished; the investor can bring capital, issue shares, remit dividends or interest, and transfer capital out of Pakistan without any restriction.

In order to encourage assembly-cum-manufacturing, the government provides incentives to assembly through lower import duties on components if the producers agree to a programme of indigenization called 'deletion programme' in Pakistan. The deletion policy has met with success in that, except for motor vehicles, indigenization has exceeded 60 per cent. However, currently the indigenization policy relies on penalties for defaulters whereas an incentive-based policy would be preferable.

Public enterprises in manufacturing, banks, tele-communication, and electricity generation are being divested. As many as ninety industrial units, two banks, 12 per cent of the shares in telecommunication, 10 per cent of the shares in PIA, and one thermal power station have so far been divested. All the remaining manufacturing enterprises, all the banks except the National Bank of Pakistan, Development Finance Institutions (DFIs), thermal plants, and telecommunication are expected to be divested.[8]

The preceding discussion shows quite clearly that a number of incentives have been provided to manufacturing investment over the last fifty years. These incentives did result in high growth rates of output but behind a steep wall of protection which resulted in gross inefficiencies and a concentrated industrial structure. In recent years, industrial policy has focused on reduction in protection to foster competition. A liberal import policy, the rationalization of tariffs, and the removal of tax holidays on the one hand, and market-friendly policies on the other hand, are expected to result in efficient industrialization.

3. GROWTH AND PATTERN OF INVESTMENT

Total investment in Pakistan increased sharply from 3.5 per cent of GDP in 1949–50 to 22.8 per cent by 1964–5, but by 1969–70 it fell to 15.8 per cent. It has ranged between 16 to 19 per cent of GDP in subsequent periods. Investment in Pakistan seems to have been constrained by investible funds, because it fell as soon as foreign capital inflows dropped. A similar pattern was also observed in manufacturing investment, which declined from 5.0 per cent of GDP in 1964–5 to 3.3 per cent of GDP in 1969–70 and further to 2.3 per cent in 1974–5. While it increased to 4.3 per cent in 1979–80, it fell once again to 2.9 per cent of GDP in 1984–5. Since then it has shown an increasing trend and by 1994–5, 4.1 per cent of GDP was invested in the manufacturing sector as indicated in Table 1.

Table 1
Investment in manufacturing industries

Year	Total investment as proportion of GDP	Investment in manufacturing as proportion of GDP
1949–50	3.5	–
1959–60	13.6	4.8 *
1964–65	22.8	5.0
1969–70	15.8	3.3
1974–75	16.4	2.3
1979–80	18.5	4.3
1984–85	18.3	2.9
1989–90	18.9	3.7
1994–95	18.7	4.1

Source: *Economic Survey*, various issues.
Note: *= Data for 1963–64.

Investment in the manufacturing sector fell sharply in the post-1965 period due to three main factors. First, capital inflows fell steeply and investment in Pakistan is constrained by the availability of investible funds. Second, the manufacturing sector suffered from a lack of demand; the inefficient industrial sector that developed behind the steep wall of protection was unable to compete in the export market and domestic demand was insufficient for adequate growth of traditional industries. Third, the private sector was shy of investing in new industries and, as noted above, in the existing industries, room for expansion was rather limited. Therefore, while nationalization may have resulted in scaring away the private capital sector, the investment in the manufacturing sector had already started falling, even before the advent of nationalization policies. Also, despite various incentives, private investment in manufacturing as a percentage of GDP fell further to 2.9 per cent by 1984–5. Since then, however, private investment has gradually increased as indicated in Table 2.

Table 2
Investment in manufacturing industries during the 1980s

Year	Investment in manufacturing as percent of GDP			Share of private investment in total
	Private	Public	Total	Manufacturing
1964–64	4.6	0.2	4.8	96.6
1964–65	2.9	0.5	5.0	90.6
1969–70	2.9	0.4	3.3	88.6
1974–75	1.3	1.0	2.3	57.4
1979–80	1.5	2.8	4.3	34.7
1984–85	2.1	0.8	2.9	71.1
1980–90	3.3	0.4	3.7	93.0
1994–95	3.9	0.2	4.1	96.8

Source: *Economic Survey*, various issues.

Since Pakistan relied almost exclusively on the private sector in the 1950s and 1960s, the share of the public sector was minimal. This ocurred despite the establishment of the Pakistan Industrial Development Corporation in 1958 with the expressed purpose of setting up industries where private investment was not forthcoming. The share of the public sector was just 11.4 per cent even in 1969–70. The nationalization of forty-two industrial units and restricting heavy industries to the public sector only in the 1970s resulted in a sharp increase in public investment to 42.6 per cent in 1974–5 and further to 65.3 per cent by 1979–80. However, because of the focus on market-friendly policies in the 1980s and the 1990s, the share of private investment has increased significantly again with public investment at just 3.2 per cent of total investment in manufacturing in 1994–5.

Investment which flows into existing units for expansion, balancing, modernization, and replacement should be distinguished from investment flowing into new industrial enterprises. This is because investment in the existing industrial units (which have already accumulated useful relevant experience in the field) may result in a larger increase in output than similar investment in a new unit. However, investment flowing into existing firms may imply monopolistic market tendencies. Because of the strong bias in fiscal policies towards the establishment of new firms, about three-fourths of industrial investment has flowed into new investment companies and one-fourth into existing firms. Tax holidays and other fiscal incentives for industrial units have built-in incentives for opening new firms rather than expanding existing ones.

4. INDUSTRIAL GROWTH IN PAKISTAN

At the time of independence, Pakistan's economy was essentially agrarian and there were only a handful of manufacturing units in the country. However, the growth of manufacturing output has been quite impressive at an average annual rate of 7.4 per cent over the 1949–50 to 1994–5 period. Table 3 shows growth rates by finer period disaggregation.

Table 3
Growth rate of the manufacturing sector

Period	Small-scale manufacturing sector	Large-scale manufacturing sector	Total manufacturing sector
1950–60	2.3	15.4	7.7
1960–70	2.9	13.3	9.9
1970–80	7.9	3.9	4.8
1980–90	8.4	8.1	8.2
1990–95	8.4	4.4	5.5
1995–96	8.4	3.1	4.8
1950–95	5.4	9.4	7.4

Source: *Economic Survey*, various issues.

Starting from a low industrial base, the manufacturing output registered a growth rate of 7.7 per cent in the 1950s. The growth rate accelerated further to 9.9 per cent in the 1960s but fell to 4.8 per cent in the 1970s. The growth rate of manufacturing output, however, increased to 8.2 per cent during 1980s but has fallen to 5.5 per cent in the 1990s.

The small-scale and large-scale manufacturing sectors need to be distinguished as the two show divergent growth trends. While the divergence in the growth rates of the two sectors may also reflect their growth potential, it essentially reflects the policies of the government. The share of these two sectors in total manufacturing is shown in Table 4.

Table 4
Percentage sectoral share of manufacturing in GDP (constant prices)

Period	Small-scale manufacturing sector	Large-scale manufacturing sector	Total manufacturing sector
1949/50	5.5	2.2	7.8
1959/60	5.1	6.9	12.0
1969/70	3.5	12.5	16.0
1979/80	4.6	12.4	17.0
1989/90	4.9	12.7	17.6
1994/95	5.8	12.4	18.2

Source: *Economic Survey*, various issues.

Small-scale manufacturing in the 1950s and the 1960s grew at the rates of only 2.3 per cent and 2.9 per cent, mainly because incentives were focused on large-scale manufacturing and there was discrimination against small-scale manufacturing which had to purchase raw materials at a relatively higher cost. During these two time periods, the growth of large-scale manufacturing was 15.4 per cent and 13.3 per cent respectively.

During the 1970s, the growth rate of small-scale manufacturing increased to 7.9 per cent while that of large-scale manufacturing declined to 3.9. The small-scale manufacturing sector had better access to imported inputs and also benefited from the exemption of sales and excise taxes. It is estimated that since the 1970s, the growth rate of small-scale industries has been in excess of 8 per cent. Large-scale manufacturing industries also registered a sharp growth of 8.1 per cent in the 1980s, but this growth rate could not be sustained in the 1990s and fell to 4.4 per cent. The growth rate in the 1980s in large-scale manufacturing was essentially due to policy-induced productivity enhancement in public sector enterprises as well as the removal of restrictions on investments and imports.

Even though the growth rate of the manufacturing sector has been quite impressive, value-added in this sector is grossly overstated and highly distorted. If value-added in the manufacturing sector is evaluated at world prices, its contribution to GDP is much smaller, reflecting gross inefficiencies. Even in 1991, when some of the distortions had already been removed, more than 30 per cent of value-added could be ascribed to protection. Since 1991, a number of initiatives have been taken to reduce the level of protection further, with the 1997 'New Economic Measures' representing a continuation of such initiatives.

5. STRUCTURAL CHANGE IN INDUSTRY

Pakistan's industrial structure is highly concentrated and, even in 1990–91, more than 40 per cent of industrial value-added was contributed by food and textiles. While the share of industries, which are exclusively based on indigenous raw materials, fell over time, this still accounted for almost three-fifths of value-added. The industries based almost exclusively on indigenous raw materials accounted for 71.0, 61.5, 50.6, 64.5, 52.4, and 58.7 per cent of value-added in 1954, 1959–60, 1969–70, 1980–81, 1985–6, and 1990–91 respectively.

The removal of quantitative restrictions, lifting of import bans, and reduction in tariff rates on the import of raw materials and intermediate goods during the 1980s has led to some diversification of manufacturing output. The greater availability of intermediate inputs at lower prices enhanced the rate of capital utilization and led to higher levels of output in the import-intensive industries. Moreover, because of an increase in the profitability of import-intensive industries, more investment flowed into such industries. A comparison of the shares of various industries in the total value-added in manufacturing for 1980–81, 1987–8, and 1990–91 indicates a decline in the share of traditional and indigenous raw material-based industries in Table 5.

Table 5
Shares of different manufacturing industries in the value-added originating in the manufacturing sector

Industry	1954	1959–60	1969–70	1980–81	1985–86	1990–91
1. Food manufacturing	8.5	7.6	10.0	24.2	15.7	14.1
2. Manufacturing of beverages	0.4	0.3	0.1	0.9	1.5	1.4
3. Tobacco manufactring	5.5	5.3	6.1	3.0	2.9	6.4
4. Manufacturing of textiles	46.7	39.1	28.5	24.3	19.9	26.3
5. Manufacturing of footwear and other wearing apparel	3.5	2.4	3.8	2.7	1.9	1.4
6. Manufacturing of paper and paperboard	–	1.6	1.2	1.0	1.3	1.6
7. Printing and publishing industries	2.7	2.4	5.2	1.2	1.5	2.3
8. Manufacturing of leather and leather products except footwear	2.4	0.7	2.2	1.6	2.3	1.5
9. Rubber and rubber products	0.9	0.5	0.7	1.3	1.9	1.0
10. Chemicals and chemical products	9.5	8.3	7.9	13.2	23.5	12.3
11. Non-metallic mineral products	4.0	6.1	2.5	2.3	4.9	7.6
12. Basic metal industries	2.1	3.1	2.0	6.6	5.3	5.5
13. Manufacturing of metal products	2.1	3.9	3.7	1.3	1.1	0.9
14. Non-electrical machinery	0.9	2.1	3.9	2.6	3.3	2.5
15. Electrical machinery	0.8	2.7	2.6	4.3	4.0	4.1
16. Transport equipment	1.1	3.4	1.6	2.5	3.4	2.6
17. Other industries	8.9	10.5	18.1	7.3	5.9	8.5

Source: *Census of Manufacturing Industries*, various issues.

6. THE SOURCES OF GROWTH IN MANUFACTURING INDUSTRIES

Import substitution has played a major role in the growth of manufacturing industries in Pakistan during its earlier stages of development. This is demonstrated in Table 6.

Table 6
Sources of manufacturing growth

Period	Domestic demand	Export expansion	Import substitution
1951–51 to 1954–55	2.40	1.80	96.60
1954–55 to 1959–60	53.10	24.00	22.90
1959–60 to 1963–64	95.70	4.60	−0.30
1963–64 to 1970–71	60.00	15.00	25.00
1980–81 to 1988–89	79.70	10.20	10.10
1988–89 to 1991–92	60.40	37.90	1.70

Source: Khan (1964), Lewis (1970), Kemal (1990, 1993).

During the 1951–2 to 1954–5 period, 96.9 per cent of growth was accounted for by the import substitution and the contribution of export expansion and the increase in domestic demand was negligible. However, since 1955, it has never been a major source of manufacturing growth. Export expansion has been as important as import substitution but both were overshadowed by increase in domestic demand. In the 1988–9 to 1991–2 period, however, export expansion accounted for about two-fifths of industrial growth.

The low level of import substitution indicated in Table 6 is contrary to expectations. In a cross-section study of developed and developing countries, Chenery and Taylor (1968) found that import substitution typically accounted for about one-half of the growth of manufacturing output as per capita income grew from $100 to $600. Only one-quarter of the growth could be attributed to import substitution up until 1970–71 in Pakistan. Its contribution declined even further in later periods.

7. CHANGES IN INDUSTRIAL INEFFICIENCY AND COSTS OF PROTECTION

A number of studies have been carried out to determine effective protection rates and industrial efficiency of Pakistan's industrial sector.[9] Effective protection has declined and efficiency seems to have increased over time. The average rates of effective protection, according to Corden's definition, was as high as 271 per cent in 1963–4.[10] It fell to 125 per cent in 1968–9 and to 66 per cent in 1980–81 but increased once again to 77 per cent in 1990–91.[11] Domestic resource costs, which measure the level of inefficiency, fell from very high levels in 1963–4 to around 1.20 in 1968–9, increased to 3.33 per cent by 1980–81, and then declined sharply to 1.44 per cent during the 1980–81 to 1990–91 period.[12]

Table 7
The average implicit effective protection rates and the domestic resource costs

	IEPRs	DRCs
1968–69	125	1.20
1980–81	66	3.33
1990–91	77	1.44

Source: Kemal (1978), Naqvi and Kemal (1991, 1996).

Since the 1980–81 and 1990–91 numbers are based on similar data and methodology, these have been analysed more intensively and the results are reported in Tables 8 and 9. Out of sixty-six inefficient industries, forty-eight had a very high rate of effective protection and out of thirteen efficient industries nine were penalized. This suggests that efficiency and protection had a negative association.

Table 8
Degree of protection and level of inefficiency in the manufacturing sector: 1980–81

	Negative value	IEPR>Average	IEPR>50	0<IEPR<50	IEPR<0	Total
Negative value-added	9	–	–	–	–	9
Extremely inefficient DRC > 2.0	–	34	3	–	4	41
Highly inefficient 2.0≥DRC> 1.50	–	1	–	5	4	10
Very inefficient 1.50≥DRC> 1.25	–	2	–	1	3	6
Moderately inefficient 1.25≥DRC>1.00	–	0	–	2	1	3
DRC≤1.00	–	1	–	3	9	13
Total	9	38	3	11	21	82

Source: Naqvi and Kemal (1996).

While the number of industries suffering negative value-added rose to twelve, the number of highly protected and extremely inefficient industries fell to just six in 1990–91. In all, twenty-two out of seventy industries were inefficient. However, despite the fact that fewer industries were inefficient, protection remained high. As many as twenty-nine efficient industries got a very high rate of protection, while thirteen such industries had a less than 50 per cent effective rate of protection. In 1990–91, only three efficient industries of a total of forty-five were penalized with negative protection.

Table 9
The number of industries by efficiency and levels of protection: 1990–91

	Negative value	IEPR>Average	IEPR>50	0<IEPR<50	IEPR<0	Total
Negative value-added	12	–	–	–	–	12
Extremely inefficient DRC > 2.0	–	6	–	–	–	6
Highly inefficient 2.0≥DRC> 1.50	–	3	–	–	–	3
Quite inefficient 1.50≥DRC> 1.25	–	2	–	–	–	2
Moderately inefficient 1.25≥DRC>1.00	–	–	1	1	–	3
DRC≤1.00	–	28	1	13	3	45
Total	11	34	3	14	3	70

Source: Naqvi and Kemal (1996).

The social cost of protection may be defined in the following ways: as wasteful use of domestic resources in the activity of earning (saving) foreign exchange, i.e., total cost borne by the entire economy; as the increase in the share of the manufacturing sector in the GDP *due to protection*, measured at world market prices. Protection cost corresponding to the first definition amounted to 9.9 per cent of the GDP in 1980–81 but fell to 3.9 per cent of the GDP in 1990–91. According to the second definition, the cost of protection amounted to 5.7 per cent of the GNP in 1980–81 which fell to 5.0 per cent of GNP in 1990–91 (*see* Table 10).

Table 10
Social cost of protection

	(Percentage of GDP)	
Cost of protection	1980–81	1990–91
Higher cost of domestic resources compared to its earning of foreign exchange	9.9	3.9
Increase in the share of manufacturing in GDP due to protection	5.7	5.0

Source: Naqvi and Kemal (1991).

8. CONCLUDING RECOMMENDATIONS FOR THE MANUFACTURING SECTOR

The above analysis indicates that Pakistan's manufacturing sector has grown rapidly, but remains inefficient and lacks diversification. No doubt there have been improvements in efficiency and also, the reliance on food and textiles industries has declined. However, manufacturing in Pakistan continues to confront major problems. There is a need to prioritize policy objectives and suggest concrete measures to deal with them.

The objectives of industrialization policy in Pakistan have generally lacked coherence and consistency. For example, the Industrial Policy of 1989 sets out four objectives, viz., maximization of employment, dispersal of industries, encouragement of small-scale industries, and promotion of 'key' industries. These objectives are not necessarily mutually consistent and do not include export orientation and efficient industrialization. In practice, Pakistan's industrialization process has largely been governed by trade and tariff policies which are driven by revenue and/or balance of payments considerations rather than by a coherent industrial policy framework.

Pakistan's industrial policy should have the following objectives and priorities:

a) an efficient industrial structure based on long-range comparative advantage;
b) accelerating the pace of industrial investment;
c) export-oriented industrialization and, by making special efforts, to improve the quality and the standardization of goods;
d) promotion of foreign private investment to acquire technology, access to markets, and managerial know-how;
e) maximization of employment through promotion of labour-intensive industries and technologies; and
f) regional dispersal of industries while ensuring that the short-term costs of dispersal do not become a permanent drag on the country's resources.

A. ESTABLISHING AN EFFICIENT INDUSTRIAL STRUCTURE

An industrial structure which accords with the dynamic comparative advantage of the country maximizes the growth of industrial output over the long run. The industrial structure is determined by the structure of incentives which in turn is largely governed in Pakistan by the protection structure. The protection provided to different industries needs to be rationalized to move towards uniform effective protection rates over a specified period. Moreover, any departures from the uniform effective protection rates should be governed by the age of the industry rather than just by the stage of processing. Pakistan is trying to rationalize its tariff structure, but the pace needs to be expedited.

B. ACCELERATING THE PACE OF INDUSTRIAL INVESTMENT

Industrial investment depends upon the demand for investment, the supply of investible funds, and the speed of adjustment towards the desired level of investment. While political stability and the continuity in policies over the long run build up the confidence of investors, the demand for investment is largely determined by the incentives for industrial activities. High levels of protection, low interest rates, tax credits and accelerated depreciation allowances, and other fiscal incentives have ensured high rates of profits in manufacturing industries. It seems likely that fiscal incentives and protection can be reduced without adversely affecting the investment levels.

C. Easing the Balance of Payments Constraint

Pakistan has all along been pursuing a policy which focussed on saving foreign exchange rather than earning it, i.e., import substitution policies have been preferred over export-oriented ones. This strategy has not only led to the establishment of inefficient industries but has also constrained the growth of foreign exchange earnings. Obviously, concern for saving foreign exchange led Pakistan to restrict imports, including imports of intermediate goods. A large number of intermediate goods have been subject to high rates of import duties. That and the problems associated with refunds, bonded-warehousing, and the export processing unit scheme discouraged the establishment of export-oriented industries.

Foreign exchange earnings may be increased through diversifying the export structure which may take the form of exports of 'non-traditional' goods and, more importantly, diversifying the mix of traditional textiles. Standardization and improvement in the quality of goods can be effective in increasing foreign exchange earnings.

D. Promoting Foreign Private Investment

Pakistan needs to encourage foreign private investment both to increase foreign exchange earnings and to improve efficiency through acquisition of new technologies in production, management, and marketing. Technology transfer in many industries is typically achieved through progressive indigenization programmes. Pakistan's deletion policy, despite major reversions in 1987 and 1992, continues to rely on penalties to enforce unrealistically high levels of indigenization. While high levels of indigenization have been realized in some industries, there is a need to reform the system in such a way that instead of penalties there are incentives for indigenization and the producers decide themselves about the deletion levels.

E. Maximizing Employment

Maximizing employment is one of the primary concerns in Pakistan and the investment in labour-intensive industries and adoption of labour-intensive production techniques would enhance the labour-absorptive capacity of the economy. The labour-intensity of manufacturing industries may be enhanced by pursuing export-oriented industrialization and concentrating on the small-scale industries. An export-oriented industrialization strategy would favour labour-intensive industries which in turn would promote small-scale industries. However, it is difficult for the small producers to get up-to-date information on the changing fashions and demand in the export markets. Therefore, an information dissemination centre for the small-scale sector would be helpful in promoting foreign exchange earnings as well as employment.

At present, small-scale industries are discriminated against since they have to pay higher duties (at commercial rates) on imported inputs than are paid by large producers, who pay at the concessional rates allowed to industrial users. Accordingly, removal of the differential in the import duties for industrial users and commercial importers would help in eliminating the bias against small-scale industry and thus generate more employment opportunities.

F. Regional Dispersal of Industries

Industry in Pakistan is concentrated in and around a few urban centres giving rise to rapid migration towards the larger cities of the country. To promote regional dispersal of industry, the government in the past has focused on fiscal concessions in the form of tax holidays. Since such concessions only transform relatively lower pre-tax profits into relatively higher post-tax profitability, these policies have generally failed because the profits, if any were earned at all, of most industrial units in the underdeveloped regions were, at best, meagre. The failure of backward regions to attract investment despite tax holidays reflected a higher production cost because of poor infrastructure and non-availability of complementary inputs, including trained labour. Thus the focus in developing backward regions should be on improving infrastructure and complementary inputs such as trained labour.

Implementing this recommended policy framework should assist in achieving an efficient industrial structure and higher growth rates of output and exports.

REFERENCES

Azhar, B. A., and Sharif, S. (1974), 'The effects of tax holiday on investment decisions: an empirical analysis', *Pakistan Development Review*, 13, pp. 409–32.

Chenery, H., and Taylor, L. (1968), 'Development patterns: among countries and over time', *Review Economics and Statistics*, 4, pp. 39–416.

Government of Pakistan. Finance Division, Economic Advisor's Wing, *Economic Survey*, (various issues).

IMG Consultants. (1988), *Industrial Efficiency Improvement and Development Strategy*, prepared for Government of Pakistan, Islamabad.

Islam, N. (1967), 'Comparative cost, factor proportions and industrial efficiency in Pakistan', *Pakistan Development Review*, 7, pp. 213–46.

Kemal, A. R. (1978), 'An analysis of industrial efficiency in Pakistan: 1959–60 to 1969–70', unpublished Ph.D. thesis, University of Manchester.

———. (1987), 'Effective protection rates: A guide to tariff making', *Pakistan Development Review*, 26, pp. 775–85.

———. (1990), *Industrial sector review of Pakistan*, study prepared for the Asian Development Bank.

———. (1993), *Recent developments in the manufacuring sector*, study prepared for the Asian Development Bank.

Kemal, A. R., Burney, N. A., and Hamid, S. (1981), *Quota restrictions, tariffs and the scarcity premium on licences*, Statistical Papers Series, No. 2. Pakistan Institute of Development Economics, Islamabad.

Kemal, A. R., Mahmood, Z., and Athar, M. A. (1993), *Protection structure, efficiency and profits in Pakistan*, study being finalized for Resource Mobilization Commission.

Kemal, A., and Alvi, Z. (1975), 'Effect of 1972 devaluation on Pakistan's balance of trade', *Pakistan Development Review*, 14, pp. 1–22.

Kemal, A.R., Zafar, M., Ather, M. A. (1994), *Structure of Protection, Efficiency, and Profitability, Islamabad*, Pakistan Institute of Development Economics, Islamabad.

Khan, A. (1964), 'Import substitution, export expansion and consumption liberalization', Pakistan Development Review, 3.

Lewis, S. (1969), *Economic Policy and Industrial Growth in Pakistan,* George Allen and Unwing Ltd., London.

———. (1970), *Pakistan: Industrialization and Trade Policies,* O.E.C.D., Paris.

Lewis, S., and Guisinger, S. (1968), 'Protection in a developing country—case of Pakistan', *Journal of Political Economy,* 76, pp. 1170–98.

Lewis, S., and Soligo, R. (1965), 'Growth and structural change in Pakistan's manufacturing industries 1954–64', *Pakistan Development Review,* 5, pp. 94–139.

Little, I. M. D., Scitovsky, T., and Scott, M. (1970), *Industry and Trade in Some of the Developing Countries,* O.E.C.D., Paris.

Naqvi, S. N. H. (1965), 'The balance-of-payments problems and resource allocation in Pakistan—A linear programming approach', *The Pakistan Development Review,* 3, pp. 349–70.

———. (1971), 'On optimizing gains from Pakistan's export bonus scheme', *Journal of Political Economy,* 79, pp. 114–21.

Naqvi, S. N. H., and Kemal, A. R. (1991), *Protectionism and Efficiency in Manufacturing: A Case Study of Pakistan,* International Centre for Economic Growth and Pakistan Institute of Development Economics, ICS Press, San Francisco, California.

———. (1991), *Structure of Protection and Allocation Efficiency in Manufacturing in Pakistan,* International Growth Centre, New York.

———. (1996), *The Burden of Protectionism—A Case Study of Pakistan's Manufacturing,* Oxford University Press, Karachi, forthcoming.

Naqvi, S. N. H., and Sarmad, K. (1984), *Pakistan's Economy Through the Seventies,* Pakistan Institute of Development Economics, Islamabad.

Pal, M. (1964), 'The determinants of the domestic prices of imports', *The Pakistan Development Review,* 4, pp. 597–622.

———. (1965), 'Domestic prices of imports in Pakistan: Extension of empirical findings', *The Pakistan Development Review,* 5, pp. 547–85.

Papanek, G. (1967), *Pakistan's Development—Social Goals and Private Incentives,* Harvard University Press, Cambridge.

Soligo, R., and Stern, J. J. (1965), 'Tariff protection, imports substitution and investment efficiency', *The Pakistan Development Review,* 5, pp. 249–70.

Thomas, P. (1966), 'Import licensing and import liberalization in Pakistan', *The Pakistan Development Review,* 6, pp. 500–544.

NOTES

1. Because manufacturing industries in Pakistan were heavily dependent on imports for their capital and intermediate goods, rigid import quotas resulted in neither the optimal allocation of investment nor in the use of capital at an optimal level of intensity. Similarly, price controls resulted in fewer incentives to expand production in the most profitable branches of production.

2. For details of the policies and impact on industries, *see* Naqvi (1965), Khan (1964), Lewis and Soligo (1965), Lewis (1969), Lewis and Soligo (1969), and Papanek (1967).

3. For detailed analysis, *see* Islam (1967), Lewis (1969, 1970), Lewis and Guisinger (1968), Little, Scitovsky, and Scott (1970), Papanek (1967), Soligo and Stern (1965), Naqvi (1965, 1971), Pal (1964, 1965), Thomas (1966), and Kemal (1978).

4. For details of policy initiatives and growth in the 1970s, *see* Azhar and Sharif (1974), Kemal and Alvi (1975), Naqvi and Sarmad (1985), and Naqvi and Kemal (1991).

5. In the 1994–5 import policy, the restricted list was abolished. However, most of the products on the restricted list have been transferred on to the negative list which bans products based on health and safety criteria.

6. The bonded warehouse scheme allows an exporter to import raw materials and intermediate goods without payment of duties or taxes and to store these in a bonded warehouse located in the factory premises. In the Export Processing Unit Scheme, a firm which exports 50 per cent of its products in the first two years and 60 per cent thereafter, is allowed to import duty-free inputs.

7. F.o.b means 'free on board' or import value before adding to it the cost of insurance, freight, and handling.

8. For details of policies and their impact on manufacturing industries, *see* IMG Consultants (1988), Kemal (1990, 1993), Kemal, Mahmood, and Ahmed (1993), and Naqvi and Kemal (1996).

9. Effective protection could be thought of as the protection given to factor payments to allow domestic industry to compete. Thus, due to tariff protection, domestic industrialists could use factors such as labour and capital inefficiently and still compete internationally.

10. *See* Lewis and Guisinger (1968) and Little, Scitovsky and Scott (1970).

11. *See* Kemal (1978) and Naqvi and Kemal (1991).

12. Ibid. Domestic resource costs could be thought of as the amount required in rupee terms to earn a unit of foreign exchange in a particular activity. If an industry is efficient, this amount would be less than the official exchange rate.

6

The Competitiveness of Pakistani Exports

*Ijaz Nabi**

1. INTRODUCTION

Long-term sustained GDP growth requires strengthening the competitive foundations of the economy to capture a larger share of world markets. Currently, Pakistan's exports constitute barely 0.2 per cent of total world trade and the trade to GDP ratio has hovered at around 30 per cent. Moreover, there has been little diversification of exports, both in terms of the commodities exported and the direction of exports. This must change to enable Pakistan to join the ranks of successful developing countries. The instrument for bringing about the change is a trade policy that has a longer-term perspective.

This chapter briefly reviews the salient features of Pakistan's medium-term trade policy. Section 2 describes Pakistan's recent trade performance in the regional context. The international competitiveness of Pakistan's exports is evaluated in Section 3. This is followed by identifying the principal policy instruments through which further outward orientation of the economy is to be achieved to increase the share of trade in GDP. Section 4 focuses on the exchange rate and section 5 on tariff reform. Section 6 outlines the policy intervention needed to improve productivity for sustained export growth. Pakistan's progress in meeting the commitments made in the Uruguay round are evaluated in section 7.

* World Bank

2. PAKISTAN'S RECENT TRADE PERFORMANCE

A summary measure of the outward orientation of an economy is the share of traded goods in GDP. On this measure, Pakistan is less outward-oriented compared to the rapidly growing South-East Asian economies (*see* Table 1). Pakistan's traded goods account for about 31.3 per cent of GDP compared to Malaysia's 167.6 per cent and Thailand's 69.6 per cent. Within South Asia, Pakistan is more outward-oriented compared to India and Bangladesh, but far less so than Sri Lanka.

Table 1
The importance of trade

Countries	1983 Share of imports plus export in GDP (in %)	1994 Share of imports plus exports in GDP (in %)	Export value (million $)	Import value (million $)
Malaysia	93	167.6	58,756	59,581
Thailand	41	69.6	45,262	54,459
Indonesia	48	41.2	40,054	31,985
India	14	17.7	25,000	26,846
Pakistan	32.4	31.3	7,370	8,890
Sri Lanka	58.3	68.2	3,210	4,780
Bangladesh	21.7	28.1	2,661	4,701

Source: *World Development Report*, 1996, p. 216.

Disconcertingly, Pakistan's outward orientation has fallen in recent years. In 1983, the share of traded goods to GDP was 32.4 per cent; it came down to 31.3 per cent in the 1990s. Meanwhile the dynamic ASEAN economies (Malaysia and Thailand) substantially increased the share of international trade in GDP.

The recent decline in Pakistan's outward orientation has been due to a slowdown in export growth (Table 2). In 1990–94, exports grew, on average, by 8.8 per cent which is less than the average growth of 9.5 per cent in 1980–90. The recent export performance is discouraging not only compared to the successful

East Asian economies but also in the context of South Asia. In the first half of the 1990s, Sri Lanka and Bangladesh registered export growth of 17 per cent and 12.7 per cent respectively.

Table 2
Growth in trade (annual average growth rate)

Countries	Export Growth		Import Growth	
	1980–90	1990–94	1980–90	1990–94
Malaysia	11.5	17.8	6.0	15.7
Thailand	14.3	21.6	12.1	12.7
Indonesia	5.3	21.3	6.2	9.1
India	6.3	7.0	4.5	2.7
Pakistan	9.5	8.8	2.1	10.3
Sri Lanka	6.3	17.0	2.0	15.0
Bangladesh	7.5	12.7	1.8	5.3

Source: *World Development Report*, 1996.

A first look at the structure of Pakistan's exports suggests that this has moved in a desirable direction in recent years (Table 3). Primary commodities in 1993 accounted for 14 per cent of total exports compared to two-fifths of total exports in 1970, and manufactured goods' share increased to 85 per cent compared to 57 per cent in 1970. However, machinery and transport equipment exports (that reflect the engineering content of exports) have remained negligible compared to the impressive increases recorded by Malaysia and Thailand. Furthermore, the heavy reliance on textiles (which account for 78 per cent of total exports) continues unabated. Of the seven countries listed in Table 3, only Pakistan and Bangladesh rely so heavily on textile exports.

Table 3
Structure of merchandise exports

Countries	Fuel, minerals, metals		Other primary commodities		Machinery & transport equip.		Other manufactures		Textile (fibres, and clothing)	
	1970	1993	1970	1993	1970	1993	1970	1993	1970	1993
Malaysia	30	14	63	21	2	41	6	24	1	6
Thailand	15	2	77	26	0	28	8	45	8	15
Indonesia	44	32	54	15	0	5	1	48	0	17
India	13	7	35	18	5	7	47	68	27	30
Pakistan	2	1	41	14	0	0	57	85	75	78
Sri Lanka	1	1	98	27	0	2	1	71	3	52
Bangladesh	–	0	–	18	0	–	81	–	–	78

Source: *World Development Report*, 1995.

The narrow range of products exported from Pakistan can be seen in Tables 5 and 6.[1] In recent years, only 8 product categories have accounted for 90 per cent of total exports. The cotton-based exports in the 1990s accounted for nearly three-quarters of Pakistan's total exports. This heavy reliance is now a serious policy concern. First, the cotton crop is highly prone to pest attacks and the monsoon cycle. Heavy monsoons cause the relatively flat Indus basin to become a gigantic lake which damages the standing cotton crop. A bad cotton harvest pulls down the gross domestic product. Indeed, in the last twenty years, cotton output has perfectly cradled overall GDP growth. Second, the political economy of cotton pricing has resulted in administered prices all along the cotton chain, from the grower to the textile manufacturer. Such non-market pricing has made it difficult to ascertain Pakistan's comparative advantage in cotton exports. Third, Pakistan's textile exports have remained concentrated in the relatively low value-added segment of the market, which has retarded the realization of Pakistan's true potential in textiles exports. Thus, the need is to both diversify exports across different product categories and also to move to higher value-added textile exports. This will be discussed in greater detail in the section on textiles.

Table 4
Structure of merchandise imports

Countries	Food		Fuels		Other primary commodities		Machinery & transport equip.		Other manufactures	
	1970	1993	1970	1993	1970	1993	1970	1993	1970	1993
Malaysia	22	7	12	4	8	4	28	54	31	305
Thailand	5	5	9	8	7	7	36	45	43	36
Indonesia	9	7	3	8	4	9	40	42	45	34
India	21	4	8	30	19	10	23	14	29	42
Pakistan	21	14	7	17	7	6	31	35	35	27
Sri Lanka	47	16	3	9	4	3	18	21	29	51
Bangladesh	–	15	–	14	–	30	–	13	–	28

Source: *World Development Report*, 1995.

Table 5
The structure of Pakistan's international trade
(US$m. and $)

% Share in exports	1970–71	1990–95	1994–5
Primary commodities	33	19	11
Semi-manufactures	24	24	25
Manufactured goods	44	57	64
Total value of exports	420	2,958	8,137

% Share in imports			
Capital goods	52	33	35
Industrial raw material for capital goods	11	7	5
Industrial raw material for consumer goods	26	44	46
Consumer goods	11	16	14
Total value of imports	757	5,409	10,394
Total exports as a share of imports	55.5	54.7	78.3

Source: *Pakistan Economic Survey*, 1995–96.

Table 6
Pakistan's most important exports in 1994–95
(Million US Dollars)

Commodity description	1991–2	1994–5	Change (1994–5 over 1991–2)
Textile yarn, made up articles n.s. & related products	3,363.4 (48.7%)	4,295 (52.8%)	27.7%

Articles of apparel and clothing accessories	1,362.3	(19.7%)	1,669.9	(20.5%)	22.6%
Rice	416.2	(6.0%)	454.6	(5.6%)	9.2%
Leather, leather manufactures n.s. & dressed furskins	251.7	(3.7%)	281.2	(3.5%)	11.7%
Sugar & honey	56.0	(0.8%)	215.3	(2.7%)	284.5%
Fish fresh, frozen	114.8	(1.7%)	154.3	(1.9%)	34.4%
Cotton	581.5	(8.4%)	126.8	(1.6%)	-78.2%
Professional, scientific, and controlling instruments and apparatus n.s.	91.2	(1.3%)	114.6	(1.4%)	25.7%
Petroleum, petroleum products, and related materials	82.4	(1.2%)	80.8	(1%)	-1.9%
Vegetables & fruit	58.3	(0.8%)	56	(0.7%)	-3.4%
Footwear	40.1	(0.6%)	49.1	(0.6%)	0.4%
Total Exports	6,912.2		8,143.3		17.8%
Share of most important items in total exports	64.2% 92.1%				

Source: *Annual Report*, State Bank of Pakistan 1994–5.

A concern also is the narrow country concentration of Pakistan's trade. The major destinations for exports are the US, Japan, Germany, and the UK (in that order). These are also the major sources of Pakistan's imports. In the 1970s and the 1980s, Saudi Arabia was a major trading partner, but its position has declined in recent years. Meanwhile, Pakistan's trade share with Malaysia has doubled from 4 per cent to 9.3 per cent in 1994–5.

Table 7
Pakistan: major trade partners (Rs in million)

Countries	1974–75				1984–85				1994–95			
	Exports	as % of T.exp.	Imports	as % of T.imp.	Exports	as % of T.exp.	Imports	as % of T.imp.	Exports	as % of T.exp.	Imports	as % of T. imp.
USA	384	3.73	3097	14.80	3965	10.44	11289	12.57	40600	16.16	30111	9.38
Japan	699	6.80	2633	12.58	4573	12.04	12002	13.37	16753	6.67	30667	9.56

Germany	462	4.49	1558	7.45	2163	5.70	5163	5.75	17620	7.02	21714	6.77
UAE	476	4.63	244	1.17	1936	5.10	4608	5.13	10154	4.04	12778	3.98
Saudi Arabia	621	6.04	1559	7.45	2627	6.92	9570	10.66	7182	2.86	15871	4.95
France	195	1.90	501	2.39	978	2.58	1582	1.76	8319	3.31	7761	2.42
UK	687	6.68	1230	5.88	2538	6.68	5277	5.88	17725	7.06	16410	5.11
Malaysia	65	0.63	700	3.35	123	0.32	4677	5.21	1571	0.63	28159	8.78
Kuwait	183	1.78	1224	5.85	392	1.03	7105	7.91	742	0.30	18673	5.82
Italy	250	2.43	599	2.86	1564	4.12	2164	2.41	7375	2.94	16754	5.22
Total	10286		20925		37979		89778		251173		320892	

Source: *Pakistan Economic Survey*, 1995–96.

3. INTERNATIONAL EXPORT COMPETITIVENESS[2]

A central trade policy concern in Pakistan is to increase the share of manufactured exports in world trade. This requires strengthening the international competitiveness of exports. The competitiveness of a country's manufacturing exports may be assessed by grouping exports according to a fourfold matrix, based on whether exports are 'competitive' in world markets (whether the country's exports are gaining or losing in world market shares in those products) and whether the products themselves are 'dynamic' in trade (i.e., whether the products' shares of world trade are rising). The four possible combinations are described below and the classification presented in Table 8:

- 'Rising stars'. Exports with strong competitiveness (i.e. rising world market shares) in 'dynamic' products (which are growing faster than total trade).
- 'Lost opportunities'. Exports whose competitiveness is declining (falling market shares) in dynamic products.
- 'Falling stars'. Exports with rising market shares in non-dynamic products, which indicates competitive vulnerability.
- 'Retreats'. Exports that are losing market shares in non-dynamic products, which is desirable.

Table 8
Export dynamism classification

Share of country's export in world trade	Share of product in world trade	
	Rising	Falling
RISING	OPTIMAL 'RISING STARS'	VULNERABLE 'FALLING STARS'
FALLING	WEAKNESS 'LOST OPPORTUNITY'	RESTRUCTURING 'RETREAT'

Clearly, the most desirable category is 'rising stars' followed by 'retreats'. Ideally, a country's exports should be concentrated in these categories. Such a country would be dynamically competitive in exports because its share in products with increasing opportunities would be increasing and the share in products with decreasing opportunities would be declining. A high concentration of exports in the other two categories would suggest that the country's exports are dynamically uncompetitive.

To assess Pakistan's dynamic export competitiveness *vis-à-vis* its competitors, data on exports were collected over the period 1985–92, for eight countries: Pakistan, Sri Lanka, Bangladesh, Mauritus, Malaysia, Thailand, and Taiwan. The results are reported in Table 9. Percentages are reported both for total manufactured exports and for the values for which the classification was made; missing data are in the last column but they are relatively minor.

Table 9
Dynamism of manufactured exports
1985–92 ($ million)

Country	Rising stars	Falling stars	Lost opportunity	Retreat	Total	Missing data
Pakistan	3347.94	1400.29	554.51	235.87	5538.61	35.84
% of total	60.4%(60.1%)	25.3%(25.1%)	10.0%(9.9%)	4.3%(4.2%)	100.0%(99.4%)	(0.6%)
Sri Lanka	801.24	58.16	542.23	065	1402.28	28.28
% of total (% of overall total)	57.1%(56.0%)	4.1%(4.1%)	38.7%(37.9%)	0.0%(0.0%)	100.0%(98.0%)	(2.0%)
India	7285.95	2263.67	4078.87	311.50	13939.99	479.17
% of total	52.3%(59.5%)	16.2%(15.7%)	29.3%(28.3%)	2.2%(2.2%)	100.0%(97.7%)	(3.3%)
Bangladesh	904.13	0.00	453.31	161.36	1518.80	2.56
% of total	59.5%(59.4%)	0.0%(0.0%)	29.8%(29.8%)	10.6%(10.6%)	100.0%(99.8%)	(0.2%)
Malaysia	13409.90	2847.66	6231.82	0.00	22497.53	815.74
% of total	59.6%(57.5%)	12.7%(12.2%)	27.7%(26.8%)	0.0%(0.00)	100.0%(96.5%)	(3.5%)
Thailand	18656.46	2247.48	1827.16	0.00	22731.10	445.07
% of total	82.1%(80.5%)	9.9%(9.7%)	8.0%(7.9%)	0.0%(0.0%)	100.%(98.1%)	(1.9%)
Taiwan	38335.48	6935.35	15834.31	183.85	61288.99	1065.12
% of total	62.5%(61.5%)	11.3%(11.1%)	25.8%(25.4%)	0.3%(0.3%)	100%(98.3%)	(1.7%)
Mauritius	549.90	32.68	228.26	0.00	810.84	29.69
% of total	67.8%(65.4%)	4.0%(3.9%)	28.2%(27.2%)	0.0%(0.0%)	100%(96.5%)	(3.5%)

The evidence shows that Pakistan's export competitiveness compares well with other countries in the group. Thailand, at over 80 per cent, has the highest concentration of exports in the 'rising stars' category. Pakistan, at 60 per cent, falls in the second tier of competitive countries along with Taiwan, Mauritius, Bangladesh, and Malaysia. India and Sri Lanka lag behind. The classification reported in Table 9 says little about the prospects of continued export expansion and thus can be misleading. If exports are excessively concentrated in low technological, low skill categories, they are clearly vulnerable to new entrants. For example, if Pakistan's textile exports remain concentrated in low value-added products, they are vulnerable to competition because entry is easy. Witness the recent success of Bangladesh in the export of garments. Thus, export dynamism must be assessed in terms of technological characteristics of exports.

A first look at the skill structure of manufactured exports reported in Table 10 is disturbing. Malaysia, Thailand, and Taiwan have achieved sustained and rapid export growth and they have a high concentration of high skill products in their exports. South Asian exports, on the other hand, are highly concentrated in low skill products. Within South Asia, Pakistan at 97.7 per cent, has a much larger share of low skill exports compared to India's 76.5 per cent.

Table 10
Skill structure of manufactured exports (%)

	Pakistan			Sri Lanka			India			Bangladesh		
	1980	1985	1992	1980	1985	1992	1980	1985	1992	1980	1985	1992
Low skill products	96.5	87.9	97.7	100.0	90.8	92.7	78.8	79.8	76.5	97.8	96.8	99.8
High skill products	3.5	12.1	2.3	0.0	9.2	7.3	21.2	20.2	23.5	2.2	3..2	0.2

	Malaysia			Thailand			Taiwan			Mauritius		
	1980	1985	1992	1980	1985	1992	1980	1985	1992	1980	1985	1992
Low skill products	21.8	19.2	21.4	81.8	78.1	56.7	54.9	51.4	30.8	97.3	94.7	95.0
High skill products	78.2	80.8	78.6	18.2	21.9	43.3	45.1	48.6	69.2	2.7	5.3	5.0

A finer decompositon of the technological characteristics of exports further underscores the vulnerability of Pakistan's international competitiveness. Table 11 shows the classification of exports on the techonological basis of competitive advantage (using developed country data). Based on this classification, Table 11 shows the breakdown of rising stars in Pakistan's exports by their technological characteristics and in comparison to its competitors.

Table 11
Technological basis of competitive advantage

Activity	Major competitive factor	Product examples	OECD exports 1985
Resource–intensive	Access to natural resources.	Aluminium smelting, oil refining.	13.5%
Labour–intensive	Cost of un- or semi-skilled labour.	Garments, footwear, toys.	9.8%
Scale–intensive	Length of production runs.	Steel, automobiles, paper.	33.8%
Differentiated	Production tailored to varied demands.	Machine tools, generating equip.	27.5%
Science based	Rapid application of science to technology.	Electronics, biotechnology, medicines.	15.5%

A country's export competitiveness is more vulnerable, the more it relies on a labour-intensive basis of exports, because new entrants (e.g., Bangaldesh, China, and Vietnam) can more easily capture markets. The weak foundation of Pakistan's rising stars is underscored by the technological characteristics reported in Table 12. Virtually all of the rising stars are concentrated in labour-intensive activites compared to India's 38 per cent and Sri Lanka's 64 per cent. In contrast, the rising stars of South-East Asian economies have significantly more diverse technological characteristics compared to South Asian economies.

Table 12
Breakdown of rising stars by technological characteristics ($m and %)

	Sri Lanka	India	Bangladesh	Pakistan	Malaysia	Thailand	Taiwan	Mauritius
Resource-based	185.5	3355.3	Nil	17.5	999.8	3079.5	2135.4	41.2
% of total	22.8	44.1	Nil	0.5	7.2	16.5	5.6	7.1
Labour-intensive	520.3	2889.6	904.1	3366.3	2614.9	7123.8	8335.8	512.4
% of total	64.1	38.0	100.0	99.5	18.7	38.1	21.7	88.4
Scale-intensvie	71.8	868.0	Nil	Nil	556.4	1107.7	2662.4	Nil
% of total	8.8	11.4	Nil	Nil	4.0	5.9	6.9	Nil
Differentiated	19.0	Nil	Nil	Nil	4996.2	2910.0	9552.0	26.0
% of total	2.3	Nil	Nil	Nil	35.8	15.6	24.9	4.5
Science-based	15.3	488.4	Nil	Nil	4799.3	4483.4	15649.9	Nil
% of total	1.9	6.4	Nil	Nil	34.4	24.0	40.8	Nil
Total	812.0	7601.4	904.1	3383.8	13966.6	18704.4	38335.5	579.6

The sections that follow review the key determinants of the international competitiveness of Pakistani exports.

4. THE EXCHANGE RATE POLICY

The exchange rate has been a key instrument of Pakistan's trade policy. Up to the early 1980s, Pakistan's exchange rate policy was designed to support the country's import substitution industrialization strategy. A fixed exchange rate regime was followed whereby the rupee was over-valued *vis-à-vis* other currencies to keep imports of machinery and raw material cheap. Since the 1980s, the exchange rate has been a managed float, with international relative prices adjusting smoothly, reflecting balance of payments performance. In more recent years, the exchange rate has become more an instrument for adjusting the country's macroeconomic imbalances rather than for supporting the trade policy.

A. RECENT EXCHANGE RATE MANAGEMENT

The managed float exchange rate regime now prevalent in Pakistan has avoided the kind of distortions that existed up to the late 1980s. There is little evidence that the Pakistani rupee is seriously overvalued. This is clear from the movement in the nominal exchange rate *vis-à-vis* major trading partners (the US, Japan, Germany, UK, and France) who together account for nearly half of Pakistan's foreign trade (imports plus exports).

Table 13 gives the movement in the nominal effective exchange rate or NEER (which is simply an index of the nominal exchange rates of the five major trading partners weighted by their shares in trade) between 1980–81 and September 1995. The calculations show that NEER depreciated from 100 to 405. In other words, the same unit of major trading partners' currency now costs nearly four times as much as in 1980–81. This is a substantial nominal devaluation of the rupee.

Table 13
Nominal effective exchange rate

Countries	1980–81 R0	Sept. 1995 R1	(R1 - R0)/R0 Trade Weight		NEER
USA	9.91	31.55	2.2	35	111.4
France	2.11	6.64	2.1	8	24.5
Germany	4.92	22.29	3.5	19	86.1
UK	22.68	50.4	1.2	17	37.8
Japan	0.0463	0.32	5.9	21	145.1
				SUM	404.9

Source: Calculations by author.

But how have the relative prices moved? Table 14 traces the movement of prices in Pakistan and its five major trading partners. The last column of the table shows that the trade-weighted consumer price index of trading partners has increased from 100 to 168, while the index for Pakistan has increased from 100 to 323.

To compensate for differences in inflation. The real effective exchange rate (REER) needs to be adjusted, which is simply the NEER (calculated in Table 13) divided by relative price index (calculated in Table 14). Notice that NEER is 405 and the relative price index is 241. Thus the depreciation in the nominal exchange rate has more than compensated for the higher inflation in Pakistan relative to the major trading partners. In fact, there has been a substantial depreciation of the real effective exchange rate.

Table 14
Trade-weighted relative price index

Countries	1980-81 P0	1995 P1	(P1-P0)/P1	Trade weight	TWCPI
U.S.A.	100	172	0.72	35	60.2
France	100	204	1.04	8	16.3
Germany	100	148	0.48	19	28.1
U.K.	100	218	1.18	17	37.1
Japan	100	125	0.25	21	26.3
Pakistan	100	323	2.23		167.95
			Relative price index		241

Source: Calculations by author.

There is one cause for worry in current exchange rate management. The economy's outward orientation is taking place at a time when macroeconomics stabilization efforts are also going on. At the root of macroeconomics instability lies the failure to slash the fiscal deficit. Money supply increase during years of slow economic growth (1993–5) has resulted in double digit inflation (in the range of 12 to 14 per cent). This causes the real effective exchange rate to appreciate, leading to an adjustment in the nominal exchange rate. Frequent adjustments in the nominal exchange rate further fuel the inflationary spiral. Thus, avoiding fiscal adjustment results in instability in the exchange rate, which may adversely affect the outward orientation of the economy.

5. THE TARIFF REGIME

Perhaps the most important instrument of trade policy is the tariff regime. It influences the cost of inputs and also provides protection on the output side. Thus it determines the profitability of the traded goods sector. A rational tariff policy is therefore an important determinant of investment in the export sector. South Asian economies, including Pakistan's, have generally maintained more protectionist trade polices than East Asian economies. This is an important reason for the much higher trade to GDP ratio in the latter compared to the former.

Before reforms began in 1988, Pakistan's tariff protection was high and uneven. In the early 1980s, the average (unweighted) ad-valorum rate was about 77 per cent with a standard deviation of more than 50 per cent. The tariff structure allowed numerous tariff concessions to industries and regions. The first tariff reform, instituted in 1987–8, resulted in an average tariff reduction of about 10.3 per cent, from 77 per cent to 69 per cent. The government further reduced tariffs, particularly tariff peaks, resulting in average ad-valorum statutory import tariff of about 50 per cent in 1994–5. Other trade reforms included: (i) the reduction of the Negative List from 300 to 75 items between 1988 and 1994; (ii) a reduction in the average statutory tariff from 77 per cent to 50 per cent; (iii) the integration of 'para-tariffs' (6 per cent import fee and 5 per cent surcharge and regulatory duties) into the single tariff rate in mid-1994; (iv) further reduction followed by elimination of import licensing and the Restricted List; and (v) liberalization of the foreign investment regime and abolition of industrial licensing.

The Finance Supplementary Amendment Bill, 1997, further reduced the maximum tariff rate to 45 per cent. Other reform measures included abolishing the 10 per cent regulatory duty imposed in 1995 and suitably cascading the duties on primary raw material, secondary raw materials, intermediate goods and capital goods, and limiting SROs (Statutory Rules and Orders). Much work still remains to be done on tariff reform to strengthen the competitive foundations of the economy to achieve trade objectives. Reform needs to focus on three sorts of issues. First, the country's tax structure must be designed to support growth rather than short-term revenue targets. This requires continuing to move away from taxing trade to taxing consumption and income. Second, reform needs to ensure that the incentive element in the tariff structure avoids negative effective protection.[3] Implementing the 1997 reforms will go a long way towards avoiding this. Third, the incentive administration system, as represented by the SROs, needs to be streamlined and made more transparent.

A. THE TAX STRUCTURE

As much as one-third of the country's total tax revenue is collected by taxing trade, principally in the form of import duties on inputs and intermediary goods. This has seriously eroded the competitive foundations of several export sub-sectors. In textiles for example, raw materials constitute around 60 per cent of total costs, interest payments around 15 per cent, energy charges around 8 per cent, and wages around 5 per cent. Interest rates and energy charges are now at world prices or above. Levying duties on imported inputs raises the cost of raw material above international prices also, and makes it very hard for firms to remain internationally competitive.

An important recommendation of the medium-term trade policy would thus have to be that the tax structure rely less on import duties and more on consumption and income taxes for meeting the budget targets. Recently conducted exercises have shown that reduction in import duties that lower the maximum tariff rate would result in revenue loss but this could be compensated for by increasing other forms of taxes that are less biased against trade. Table 15 shows the anticipated revenue loss from reducing the maximum tariff rate to 35 per cent.

Table 15
Revenue impact of tariff reform

	35 per cent case terminal year (Rs in billion)
Loss in revenue due to changes in statutory tax rates	-38.6
Gain in revenue due to selective withdrawal of import duty SROs	+18.4
Gain in revenue due to broadening of sales tax at the import stage	+ 6.2
Gain in revenue due to withdrawal of concessions in income tax	+ 5.0
Overall revenue impact	- 9.0

Source: *Report of the Tariffs Reforms Committee, 1993.*

B. RATIONALIZING INCENTIVES TO EXPORT

A commonly used trade policy instrument is to levy a low duty rate on the import of raw material and equipment and a higher duty rate on the final product to give effective protection to exporters. This trade policy instrument appears to have been blunted lately, partly on account of revenue considerations, partly due to the administrative failures of the duty drawback scheme, and partly because of the extreme complexity in the effective tariff rate caused by the SRO regime (the last will be discussed below). For example, until the 1997 reforms, the capital goods sector has faced a higher statutory duty on the import of raw materials than on the import of competing capital goods (*see* Table 16). This statutory tariff regime may have retarded the growth of the engineering exports. Such remaining anomalies would need to be redressed while implementing an export-push strategy.

Table 16
The incidence of import duties on capital goods
(1983–4 to 1992–3)

	Raw material for capital goods	Capital goods	Total
1983–4	50%	49%	52%
1984–5	38%	39%	41%
1985–6	45%	42%	46%
1986–7	39%	35%	47%
1987–8	45%	38%	42%
1988–9	44%	38%	36%
1989–90	43%	39%	40%
1990–91	41%	39%	39%
1991–2	39%	34%	33%
1992–3	44%	32%	35%

Source: *CBR Year Book,* 1992–93
Note: Figures are for Customs House, Karachi only.

C. STREAMLINING EXEMPTIONS
Pakistan currently has two tariff schedules:
- a statutory schedule conforming to international norms listing the duty rate applicable to each good as described under the Harmonized Commodity Description and Coding System (HS), and
- an 'exemption' schedule defined by the SRO's (160 are currently in effect) that grant partial or full exemption from the statutory duties and make such exemptions end-user specific.

The result of these dual tariff schedules is that there can be a substantial divergence of statutory tariffs and actual effective tariffs. For example, for machinery and equipment, the unweighted average tariff rate, based on the ten bands of the statutory tariffs, is calculated as being 35 per cent. However, the implied average tariff (revenue collected divided by the value of imports) is about 12 per cent. Clearly, for machinery and equipment, the exemption schedule dominates the statutory schedule. But this is not true for other items. For example, for motor vehicles, the average implied tariff is fairly close to the statutory rates.

Moreover, since exemptions are end-user specific, there can be a substantial variation in the duty actually paid by different importers on the same item. For example, the thirty-odd SRO's regarding the import of raw materials result in eight different duty rates (ranging from 0 per cent to 35 per cent) depending on the end user. This results in loss of transparency and leads to abuse and revenue loss.

More importantly, a revised SRO can suddenly change the cost structure for firms undertaking investment or production. This uncertainty mars the investment climate and can be detrimental to the export-push strategy.

Streamlining the SRO regime involves rationalizing the exemptions. The central objective of the reform of exemptions will be to bring the statutory and the actual effective (SRO determined) schedules closer together. The final schedule would bring the two together and would also reflect the tariff rates that will prevail over the longer term (bring down the maximum tariff rate to 35 per cent and raise the lowest to 10 per cent).

A ranking of exemptions would be required based on their effect on the private sector and the extent to which changes would run counter to a formal understanding reached between firms and various levels of the government. The scaling down or cancellation of longer term investment plans already in the pipeline, following withdrawal of exemptions, also need to be considered. Exemptions that are time-bound, are part of the package of incentives announced in a government programme or they contain protective clauses that agreements would be honoured.

6. PRODUCTIVITY GROWTH

Protection via the tariff regime and input subsidies cannot sustain long-term export growth. Such price support programmes have important budgetary implications and taxpayers are unlikely to continue to bear the brunt of such policies. Long-term sustained export growth has to be anchored in productivity growth. This is what makes firms internationally competitive and allows them to expand market share. Critical determinants of productivity growth are the availability of a skilled labour force, acquisition of new technology, and the quality of exported products. A longer term trade policy must address each of these.

A. LABOUR SKILLS

A large labour force with relatively low wages, such as Pakistan possesses, is unfortunately not the crucial determinant of international competitiveness. The proper indicator of competitiveness is the unit labour costs (wage costs divided by productivity) that measures the cost of a unit of output. A comparison of the index of unit labour cost across different countries shows that unit cost of production in Pakistan is high despite low wages. The reason is the low productivity of labour which, in turn, is caused by their poor skill endowment.

Firm level evidence also supports the view that Pakistan is a high unit cost economy. For example, in the drive to diversify exports, emphasis is usually placed on the need to increase value-added products. An important constraint faced by firms engaged in high value-added exports is the shortage of skilled labour. In textiles, for example, firms find it hard to obtain designers and technicians who can quickly adapt to changing demand in import markets and produce quality products. In the engineering goods sector, the shortage of machine operators and mid-level technicians and inadequate skills training programmes result in learning on the job, which is time-consuming and expensive.

The solution, in part, lies in improving the woefully inadequate formal education system in the country. An overall literacy rate of 37 per cent, and the abysmal transition rate from primary to secondary and higher technical education, paint a grim picture. This is in stark contrast to the successful trading nations of East and South-East Asia that have achieved a 100 per cent literacy rate and are endowed with technically-skilled labour force. Formal analyses of the East Asian Experience shows that education and an open trade regime together contribute to the sustained rapid growth of exports.[4] The renewed interest in the Social Action Programme promises to redress past neglect. Exporters will do well to remember that they have a direct interest in the success of SAP and other education-related initiatives and they need to follow the programmes vigilantly.

The other part of the solution lies in implementing skills training programmes for specific export sub-sectors. An important objective of trade policy is to evaluate such skills development initiatives (such as the cess levied on the textiles exporters for setting up specialized training institutes) and suggest improvements. Experience from other countries, such as Malaysia's Skills Development Fund, should also be evaluated to improve institutional design.

B. TECHNOLOGY UPGRADING

Export diversification through higher value-added products will require firms to upgrade their technology. Moving up the technology frontier typically involves acessing three tiers: (i) tailoring existing technology and processes to specific production requirements; (ii) improving processes within the existing technology design and (iii) changing technology design. In the textile sector, technology and the process are usually embodied in the machinery and therefore are largely imported. In the engineering sector, process modification at the firm level is common; however, introducing new designs and new products is very costly and few firms undertake it.

For long-term sustained export growth, all three tiers of technology will need to be accessed. Realistically speaking, however, in the medium term, Pakistani firms are likely to continue to import basic technology design from abroad, but their ability to modify processes and tailor existing technologies to local specifications should be strengthened. This essentially involves small incremental changes focused on the skilled work force employed within the firm. In this manner, the demand for technology upgrading by firms is met by the firms themselves.

Given the nature of technology acquisition, cost-effective interventions would consist of three complementary components: (i) removing financial, intellectual property rights (patent laws etc.) and fiscal (the tax incentive regime) impediments that repress firms' demand for technology deepening; (ii) ensuring adequate supply of skilled workers to firms, and (iii) orienting public sector research and technology institutes towards supporting firms' technology needs.

The recommendations for technology deepening for export growth in the medium-term trade policy should be made after consultations with the Ministry of Science and Technology which has initiated a programme for orienting public research institutes (especially PCSIR) towards working more closely with the private sector.

C. PRODUCT QUALITY

Two determinants of the quality of exported merchandise are the skills of workers and the technology used in production. These have been discussed above. The third, and the most important, determinant is producing to international standards. These standards have been codified in the ISO 9000, 14000, and other series, that lay down product specifications and prescribe the internationally acceptable production environment. Successful exporting countries have instituted crash programmes to facilitate firms to get international standards certification. In Pakistan, despite the emphasis by the Export Promotion Bureau in its publicity campaigns and training programmes, the take-up by firms of such certification is not impressive. This is surprising, given the stress placed by importers on the need for such certification. If Pakistan is to expand its share of world trade, firms' attitude towards standardization has to change. The medium-term trade policy will seek the views of the private sector to devise programmes for rapid and cost-effective certification.

7. THE URUGUAY ROUND AND PAKISTAN[5]

The recently concluded Uruguay round has set tariff targets that will help create a liberal trading environment. However, it has important implications for the design of LDC trade policy not only with respect to the tariff structure but also for streamlining non-tariff measures (such as anti-dumping measures and countervailing duties, export subsidies, balance-of-payments provisions, import licensing, rules of origin, customs evaluation, pre-shipment inspection), Trade-Related Investment Measures (TRIMS), Trade-Related Intellectual Property Rights (TRIPS) and trade in services. Participating nationals will fully benefit from the more trade liberal WTO setting if they have moved on all these fronts. An evaluation is made below of the salient outcomes of the Uruguay Round from Pakistan's perspective.

An important objective of the Uruguay Round was to substantially improve the market access of trading nations. The results for Pakistan are that its exports to OECD countries now face an overall weighted average tariff level of 6.9 per cent. This is higher than the average weighted tariff of 4 per cent imposed on imports from other countries. Pakistani exports to non-OECD countries face a considerably higher average weighted tariff of 9.1 per cent. The Uruguay Round has also helped to bring down non-tariff measures faced by exports. Such measures on Pakistan's exports should eventually fall from about 60 per cent to 8 per cent.

The outcome of the Uruguay Round regarding the Multi-Fibre Arrangement (MFA) is of special interest to Pakistan because textiles and clothing comprise 70 per cent of its exports. The ten-year, four-stage, end-loaded programme under which MFA is to be integrated into WTO, has been disappointing (17 per cent of 1990 import volumes were integrated into GATT

1994, 34 per cent of 1990 import volumes will be integrated after a further three years, and the remaining 49 per cent at the end of the ten-year period). The schedule for quota growth rates will help in mitigating the lengthy phase-out period for quotas. The bottom line, however, is that tariffs on exports from South Asian countries will fall from 83 to 22 per cent compared to 38 per cent and 15 per cent for all participants in the MFA.

Pakistan has retained the right in the Uruguay Round of being a textile import restricting country during the MFA phase-out period. (In 1993, inputs imported for Pakistan's textile sector faced a weighted average tariff of 35 per cent while semi-finished and finished items face weighted average rates of 74 per cent and 77 per cent respectively). This is not surprising, given that Pakistan is an MFA-restricted country. However, Pakistan enjoys proven export competitiveness in textiles and, by maintaining a more open import regime, it could further strengthen its competitiveness and, moreover, could take a lead in the dismantling of MFA.

Non-tariff barriers, anti-dumping measures, and countervailing duties are likely to emerge as potential contentious issues in the future as demands on Northern governments increase for protectionist measures following the trade liberalization commitments of the Uruguay Round. Pakistan has neither been a serious victim nor a user of these measures, but this may change as Pakistan's exports increase. Pakistan should play a more active role in strengthening the WTO to monitor such protectionist tendencies in developed countries. As an importer, Pakistan should introduce clarity in measuring dumping and transparency in the legal procedures for invoking anti-dumping measures in order to minimize the use of this tool as a protectionist device.

The Uruguay Round also made progress on the thorny issue of subsidies. These have been defined as financial contributions by governments, foregone revenue that benefits enterprises and provision of goods and services (free or at less than market prices) other than infrastructure, and price supports from which the producers benefit. Export subsidies are included but not subsidies given to agriculture. However, countries with income per capita of less than US$1000 per annum may retain export subsidies on manufacturers at their 1986 levels. Pakistan has retained export subsidies to mitigate the 'anti-export' bias of past import substitution policies. These go beyond the allowed limits and will have to be progressively eliminated.

On balance-of-payments, the Uruguay Round allows developing countries to use import restrictions temporarily to deal with foreign exchange shortages. However, there is a preference for using price-based measures affecting the whole range of imports rather than quantitative restrictions limited to a few sectors. Pakistan invokes GATT balance-of-payments provisions in respect of 140 tariff lines. With a more flexible exchange rate and improved management of the float, Pakistan now has a more desirable instrument for managing balance-of-payments than the blunt instrument of import restrictions.

A summary assessment of Pakistan's progress in meeting the GATT requirements for a more liberal trade regime is that a large gap still exists between what needs to be done and what is actually being achieved. This gap is partly due to the disappointing outcomes with respect to MFA and agricultural subsidies in developed countries. The speed with which developed countries have moved on their preferred agenda items, such as TRIPS, has also contributed to a sense of disappointment. However, in order to meet the WTO deadline and to benefit from the more liberal trade regime, Pakistan needs to move more quickly on trade liberalization.

REFERENCES

Government of Pakistan. (1993), *Central Board of Revenue Yearbook*, Central Board of Revenue, Islamabad.

―――. (1993), *Report of the Tariff Reforms Committee*, Islamabad.

―――. (1995), *Annual Report 1994–5*, State Bank of Pakistan, Karachi.

―――. (1996), *Economic Survey 1995–6*, Economic Advisors Wing, Islamabad.

Low, P. (1995), 'Pakistan: The Uruguay Round and Trade Policy Reform into the Next Century', background paper for Pakistan 2010, World Bank, Washington.

World Bank. (1996), *World Development Report 1996*, Oxford University Press, New York.

NOTES

1. Although non-traditional exports grew by an impressive 18 per cent in 1994–5, tradtional exports grew by almost 20 per cent and cotton-based exports by 21 per cent. The share of non-tradtional exports in total exports has thus not increased.
2. The methodology is taken from the UN Economic Commission from Latin America, which uses it to classify the export strengths and weaknesses of countries in that region.
3. A higher tariff on intermediate goods than on the final good.
4. These human development issues are addressed in Part III of the book.
5. This discussion is based on Low (1996).

7

Fifty Years of Public Finance in Pakistan: A Trend Analysis

Hafiz A. Pasha* and Mahnaz Fatima**

1. INTRODUCTION

The public finances of Pakistan have witnessed a fundamental transformation during the last fifty years. Not only has the level and structure of taxation changed drastically but the level and composition of public expenditure has also altered dramatically. Today, while Pakistan's tax to GDP ratio is substantially higher than that at the time of partition, partly because of the increase in taxable capacity due to the cumulative increase in per capita income and partly because of modernization and diversification of the tax system through reforms, expenditure obligations are also greater because of the continued commitment to heavy defence outlays and the rapidly rising burden of debt-servicing.

The analysis of Pakistan public finances over a period of almost fifty years, from 1947–8 to 1994–5, is complicated by a number of factors. First, there is the problem that the institutional capacity for collection, analysis, and dissemination of statistics was relatively underdeveloped in the earlier years of the nation's history. For example, the estimates of Gross Domestic Product

* Hafiz A. Pasha is a former Deputy Chairman, Planning Commission and Finance Minister and currently the Chief Executive of the Social Policy and Development Center.

** Mahnaz Fatima is Associate Professor, Institute of Business Administration, Karachi. They gratefully acknowledge the assistance of Yasir Chughtai and Sameen Rafi, Research Assistants at the IBA, in the preparation of this paper.

and the relevant tax bases are available in many cases only from 1959–60 onwards. Second, the method of presentation of budget-related information has changed over the years. Soon after partition, reporting of such information was on the basis of the accounting conventions developed during the days of the British Raj. As such, there was no consolidated statement of revenues, expenditures, and overall deficit of the central government and the provincial governments (of East and West Pakistan) combined. This made it difficult to get an overall picture of public finances. Also, the demarcation between current and capital budgets was not entirely clear, with complications caused by development expenditure on the revenue account and non-development outlays on the capital account. It is only since 1975–6 onwards that the Ministry of Finance of the Government of Pakistan has been publishing annually the summary of public finance, consolidated for the federal and provincial governments, with a clear separation between tax and non-tax revenues on the one hand and between current and development expenditures on the other. Consequently, estimates have also been provided of the national budget deficit.

Third, a major problem is created by the structural break in the time series after 1971 due to the breakaway of the former East Pakistan. There is a visible once-and-for-all change in tax-to-GDP and expenditure-to-GDP ratios after 1971–2. It has not been possible to construct a consistent set of time series of key public finance magnitudes since partition for the part of the original country which now comprises Pakistan (the former West Pakistan). The Central Board of Revenue has published figures from 1947–8 onwards of collection of central taxes from the territory which presently constitutes Pakistan. However, the problem of a structural break still persists because of the change in tax bases following the breakaway of East Pakistan. For example, there was a diversion of the inter-wing trade of West Pakistan to international markets. This changed significantly the size and nature of the tax base of custom duties after 1971.

An even more serious problem is encountered in the context of expenditures by the central government prior to 1971.

Presumably, some part of these expenditures, albeit the minor share, was incurred in the former East Pakistan. Therefore, there is a structural break in the series of expenditures after 1971, which can only be removed if an allocation of these expenditures between the two wings is made. This is an extremely difficult task which has not been undertaken by government statistical agencies. Consequently, we have had to work with overall central government expenditures, and it is not surprising that given the dominant share of West Pakistan in these expenditures, there is a large once-and-for-all increase in the expenditure to GDP ratios after 1971.

The approach that we have adopted in this paper to overcome these difficulties is essentially to analyse the trends for two sub-periods, one period from partition to the breakup of the country in 1971 and the other for the period thereafter. In order to establish some correspondence with plan periods and to highlight more sharply the changing trends, tables in the text of the paper give the magnitudes from 1949–50 onwards, at five yearly intervals, up to 1994–5. The first period covers 1949–50 to 1969–70 and the second period from 1974–5 to 1994–5. The paper is organized as follows: Section 1 highlights changes in the level and structure of taxation and section 2 describes the trends in the level and composition of public expenditure. In each section there is a discussion of any assumptions made in generating the numbers and the methodology used for reconciling changes in coverage, definition, etc., of the key public finance magnitudes.

2. TRENDS IN TAXATION

The trend in the tax-to-GDP ratio of Pakistan is given in Table 1. As indicated in the table, the figures from 1949–50 to 1969–70 are for undivided Pakistan and the figures thereafter (from 1974–5 onwards) are for the present Pakistan. The table reveals that the overall tax-to-GDP ratio was very low in the initial years, at less than 4 per cent. At the time of partition, Pakistan's per capita income was extremely low at about US $80 (as compared to about $475 currently). This implied a very limited taxable capacity. Also, the areas which constituted Pakistan were industrially backward and predominantly agricultural. Despite the fact that Pakistan accounted for 70 per cent of jute production in the subcontinent, there were no jute mills. Also, despite a large cotton crop, there were only three textile mills at the time of independence. Consequently, the tax base for corporation income tax and excise duties was very small. For example, in 1949–50, these two taxes combined yielded less than 1 per cent of the GDP.

Table 1
Tax to GDP ratio
Overall and for individual taxes of the
central government

Year	Income and wealth tax	Customs duty	Excise duty	Sales tax	Surcharges	Total taxes
1949–50	0.6	2.2	0.3	–	–	3.1
1954–55	0.9	2.0	0.6	0.5	–	4.0
1959–60	1.0	1.8	0.9	0.5	–	4.2
1964–65	0.7	2.2	1.5	0.6	–	5.0
1969–70	0.6	2.3	3.0	0.5	–	6.4
1974–75	1.5	4.5	3.5	1.0	–	10.5
1979–80	2.5	5.9	4.5	1.1	–	14.0
1984–85	2.2	5.5	3.6	1.1	0.8	13.2
1989–90	2.0	6.4	2.9	2.4	1.3	15.0
1994–95	3.4	4.6	2.6	2.6	1.3	14.5

Sources: Government of Pakistan, *Economic Survey,* various years, and Government of Pakistan, *25 Years of Pakistan in Statistics* (1972).

Customs duty was the principal source of revenue, collected both on imports and exports (especially of jute and cotton). Here also, the size of the tax base was limited by the scarcity of foreign exchange and the overvalued exchange rate (Rs 3.20 per US$ up to 1955–6 and then Rs 4.70 upto 1970–71) which reduced the rupee value of imports. In the initial years, a large part of the imports consisted of basic consumer goods and capital goods for industrialization, which implied that duty rates had to be kept relatively low.

From 1949–50 to 1969–70, however, the tax-to-GDP ratio improved significantly to reach the level of over 6 per cent by the latter year. However, much of the improvement occurred in excise duties, which emerged as the largest single source of revenue by the end of the decade of the 1960s, with a tax-to-GDP ratio close to 3 per cent. This was primarily a reflection of the remarkable progress made by Pakistan in the process of industrialization. For example, during the Second Plan period (1959–60 to 1964–5), Pakistan maintained a double-digit growth rate in large-scale manufacturing. The tax base for excise duties expanded rapidly and, simultaneously, tax rates in sectors like tobacco were enhanced.

It is of some interest to note that the same buoyancy was not reflected in income tax revenues, which remained below 1 per cent of GDP. This was the consequence of the general regime of tax holidays that were in operation during the period. These were designed as fiscal incentives to promote investment by the private sector. Apparently, the strategy of the policy makers at the time was to expand the tax base through expansion in capacity and mop up incremental revenues essentially through indirect taxes. This not only explains why the share of direct taxes declined but also highlights that one of the factors responsible for the deterioration in the distribution of income in the 1960s was the failure of the tax system to act as a redistributive device.

The sales tax, which was taken over from the provincial governments by the central government in 1951, also did not show any substantial buoyancy. The major share of collection was at the import stage and the tax base remained restricted due to the overvalued exchange rate. Altogether, the salient feature of the development of the tax system of Pakistan upto the end of the decade of the 1960s, was the emergence of excise duties.

Following the breakup of the country in 1971, the tax system has evolved very differently. There was a large once-and-for-all jump in the tax-to-GDP ratios for most taxes because, prior to the dissolution of the country, the part (West Pakistan) which is now Pakistan accounted for over 75 per cent share in tax revenues. This was substantially in excess of its 60 per cent share in the GDP. Beyond this, there was a major improvement in the tax-to-GDP ratio during the decade of the 1970s. A number of factors are responsible for this improvement. First, revenues from customs duties increased from about 2 per cent of the GDP in 1969–70 to almost 6 per cent by 1979–80.

The primary factor responsible for this was the large devaluation of the Pakistani rupee (from Rs 4.76 to the dollar to Rs 10.47) in 1972–3 which substantially increased the rupee value of imports and multiplied the tax base of customs duties. Second, excise duties continued to show rapid growth, partly because of the reduction in tax evasion following the nationalization of industries and partly because of continued enhancements in tax rates. Third, revenues from income tax also showed rapid growth during the 1970s. This was a reflection of a change in fiscal policy leading to a large-scale withdrawal of generalized tax holidays and their restriction to backward areas only. It is significant that in the 1970s, contrary to the experience of the 1960s, tax revenues witnessed fast growth in a period when the overall GDP growth rate, and that of the manufacturing sector in particular, experienced a significant slowing down.

During the 1980s and the first half of the 1990s there has been a visible stagnation in the tax-to-GDP ratio which has fluctuated within the range of 13 to 15 per cent. The contribution of excise duties, in particular, has declined from 4.5 per cent of the GDP to 2.5 per cent, as demand for excisable goods like tobacco has not grown rapidly and the elasticity of the tax has been adversely affected by the specific nature of tax rates, which have not been revised frequently. The contribution of customs duties continued to increase in the 1980s when effective rates of tariffs were enhanced by imposition of import and iqra surcharges. In the 1990s, however, with the onset of tariff reforms involving reduction in the maximum tariff rates, the contribution of import duties has declined.

These declines have been compensated for by the improved performance of income and sales taxes. The income tax-to-GDP ratio has increased rapidly from 2 per cent to almost 3.5 per cent during the first five years of the present decade. This spectacular growth has occurred during a period of generally falling tax rates, both personal and corporate, largely because of the effective broad-basing of the tax through tax reforms involving the imposition of withholding and presumptive tax on various sectors and various streams of income (from interest, rent, exports, etc.). The buoyancy of the sales tax in the second half of the 1980s is also attributable to withdrawal of exemptions at the import and manufacturing stages and enhancement in the tax rate more recently.

Altogether, in broad terms, the decade of the 1960s can be described as the period of development of excise duties and the 1970s and 1980s as the period when maximum reliance was placed on customs duties. The 1990s promised to be the decade of the growing importance of income and sales taxes. This broad statement is supported by Table 2 which gives the share of tax revenues from different heads.

Table 2
Percentage distribution of tax revenues

Year	Income and wealth tax	Customs duty	Excise duty	Sales tax	Surcharges	Total taxes
1949–50	19.4	71.0	9.7	0.0	0.0	100.0
1954–55	22.5	50.0	15.0	12.5	0.0	100.0
1959–60	23.8	42.9	21.4	11.9	0.0	100.0
1964–65	14.0	44.0	30.0	12.0	0.0	100.0
1969–70	9.4	35.9	46.9	7.8	0.0	100.0
1974–75	14.3	42.9	33.3	9.5	0.0	100.0
1979–80	17.9	42.1	32.1	7.9	0.0	100.0
1984–85	16.7	41.7	27.3	8.3	6.1	100.0
1989–90	13.3	42.7	19.3	16.0	8.7	100.0
1994–95	23.4	31.7	17.9	17.9	9.0	100.0

Sources: As in Table 1.
Note: Row totals may not add up to 100 because of rounding.

In the initial period of Pakistan's history, customs duties were the predominant source of revenue, with a share in excess of 70 per cent. This share declined continuously during the 1950s and 1960s, with a corresponding rise in the share of excise duties so that by 1969–70, the latter had become the principal revenue source. Thereafter, we see a reversal of trends, with the share of excise duties falling rapidly and that of customs duties rising once again. During the mid-1980s and 1990s, there has been a diversification of revenues, with increasing shares of income and sales taxes and the introduction of surcharges on POL and gas. The latter, however, remains a relatively small source of revenue.

The questions which arise from the above description of the development of the tax system of Pakistan are as follows: has the tax system become more or less equitable over the last fifty years or so? Has the tax system become more efficient over time in terms of mobilizing resources while creating fewer distortions in the economy? Has the tax system become more or less elastic with respect to the growth of the GDP with the passage of time? Answers to these questions will, of course, have to await more formal and careful analysis. We discuss now the long-term trends in public expenditure since Independence.

3. TRENDS IN EXPENDITURE

The trend in the expenditure-to-GDP ratio is given in Table 3. As indicated previously, the figures for the period 1949–50 to 1969–70 are for undivided Pakistan and those after 1974–75 are for the present Pakistan.

Table 3
Central government expenditure
heads-to-GDP ratios

Year	Defence	Debt-servicing	General admn.	Social, economic, & community services	Subsidies & others	Total expenditure
1949–50	3.2	0.2	0.8	0.2	0.1	4.4
1954–55	3.0	0.4	1.3	0.4	0.3	5.4
1959–60	3.3	0.7	1.2	0.5	0.1	5.8
1964–65	2.7	0.9	1.1	0.4	0.1	5.2
1969–70	3.8	1.3	1.0	0.5	0.1	6.6
1974–75	6.7	2.2	1.8	0.5	0.7	11.8
1979–80	6.0	5.0	1.2	0.5	1.3	14.0
1984–85	7.5	6.0	1.0	0.6	2.4	17.5
1989–90	7.7	8.9	0.9	0.7	1.9	20.0
1994–95	6.0	8.3	0.9	0.9	1.5	17.7

Sources: As in Table 1.

Total expenditure as a percentage of GDP increased from 4.4 per cent in 1949–50 to 17.7 per cent in 1994–5. This significant increase has primarily been due to a sizeable jump in the defence and debt-servicing expenditures. Defence expenditure as a percentage of GDP increased from 3.2 per cent in 1949–50 to 6 per cent in 1994–5 and debt-servicing increased from 0.2 per cent of GDP in 1949–50 to 8.3 per cent in 1994–5.

The share of various expenditure heads as a percentage of total expenditure is reported in Table 4.

Table 4
Percentage distribution of various expenditure heads
in total expenditure

Year	Defence	Debt-servicing	General admn.	Social, economic, & community services	Subsidies & others	Total expenditure
1949–50	73.1	3.6	17.2	4.2	1.9	100
1954–55	55.5	8.2	24.5	6.8	5.0	100
1959–60	57.0	11.3	20.1	9.3	2.3	100

1964–65	52.6	18.0	20.9	7.0	1.5	100
1969–70	58.1	19.6	14.4	7.0	0.9	100
1974–75	56.5	18.4	15.3	3.9	5.9	100
1979–80	42.9	35.5	8.3	3.8	9.5	100
1984–85	42.8	34.4	5.5	3.4	13.9	100
1989–90	38.6	44.6	4.3	3.4	9.2	100
1994–95	34.2	46.9	5.2	5.1	8.7	100

Sources: As in Table 1.
Note: Row totals may not add upto 100 because of rounding.

Defence expenditure as a percentage of total expenditure declined from 73.1 percent in 1949–50 to 34.2 per cent in 1994–5, mainly because of the enormous increase in debt-servicing that came to occupy a share of 46.9 per cent of total expenditure in 1994–5. This was a sharp jump from its level of 3.6 per cent in 1949–50. These two expenditure heads are largely responsible for the increase in total expenditures which show that the increased size of the government could not really contribute to general public welfare as had been the case in the more developed countries of the West. The expenditure on social, economic, and community services did not register a noticeable increase during the above period and remained below 1 per cent of GDP for the period studied. As a percentage of total expenditures, this expenditure actually declined from 9.3 per cent in 1959–60 to 5.1 per cent in 1994–5.

Contrary to popular belief of government over-spending, the expenditure on general administration remained below 1 per cent of GDP in 1994–5 as it was in 1949–50. Its share in total expenditure actually declined from 17.2 per cent in 1949–50 to 5.2 per cent in 1994–5. However, because of its high visibility, it invites criticism. Unfortunately, this shifts the focus of the debate away from more important core issues that need to be dealt with, such as debt and deficits. There is, therefore, a need for the government to utilize this head of expenditure judiciously and wisely and to make a concerted effort to display frugality in utilizing its allocated expenditures.

Further, the above also shatters the myth of 'big government' in Pakistan, which is a slogan imported from the West, where the size of the government has contributed significantly to the welfare of nations. They are perhaps now in a position to opt for 'less government'. Given the above trend, we in Pakistan should actually be advocating a case for 'right-sizing' the government instead of 'down-sizing' it. The slogan of 'less government' in Pakistan only leads to a curtailment or restriction on appropriate increases in those essential expenditures that the government needs to continue to incur/increase in the interest of the nation's welfare.

As is also evident from Table 4, the share of expenditure on social, economic, and community (SEC) services exhibited a declining trend from 1959–60 to 1989–90 as the slogan of 'less government' gained popularity in the decade of the 1980s. In the decade of the 1990s, however, the SEC expenditure actually picked up to a level of 5.1 per cent of the total in 1994–5. This was perhaps due to a renewed emphasis on social sector development in less developed countries. However, the fact that it remained less than 1 per cent of GDP, even in 1994–5, shows the interaction of renewed social sector emphasis with the emphasis on reducing the size of the government. The latter line of reasoning seems to have prevailed also due to the resource mobilization constraints that Pakistan continued to experience, despite tax reforms, and the continued pressure of defence and debt-servicing expenditures.

Our government's inability to contribute to the nation's welfare, as depicted by the abysmally low levels of SEC expenditures, keeps labour productivity low, which in turn depresses their contribution to national income and further leads to difficulty in servicing the debt. The share of debt-servicing in total expenditure increased from 3.6 per cent in 1949–50 to 19.6 per cent in 1969–70. It decreased to 18.4 per cent in 1974–5 and then rose sharply to 35.5 per cent in 1979–80, 44.6 per cent in 1989–90, and 46.9 per cent in 1994–5.

The popular belief is that the government's high public sector investments have been largely responsible for the increased debt-servicing burden. A major portion of public sector investments have been in physical infrastructure projects which should actually have contributed to the improved efficiency of the industrial sector. Had this happened, there would have been a consequent ability of the economy to service the debt and to eventually reduce dependence on heavy borrowings. The enormous increase in the debt-servicing burden shows our economy's inability to turn the borrowed fund over into increased national income which could, in turn, have eased our debt burden over this period of time. The fact that public sector investments failed to increase the national product and internal revenue generation capability in a commensurate manner is a very strong reflection on the institutional, organizational, and management capability of our enterprises, whether they were in the public or in the private sectors. Further, this trend was maintained in the decades of the 1960s, 1970s, and the 1980s. It seems to be continuing in the 1990s, regardless of which sector, public or private, is pronounced as the engine of growth.

So, based on the above trends, one can only view very skeptically the current emphasis on the economic policies of privatization and deregulation, as these will also reduce the contribution that the privatized units were making to the federal government revenues when they were in the public sector. Their contribution amounted to a third of federal government revenues during the decade of the 1980s. With the above reduction in the sources of federal government revenues and the economy's continued limited ability to mobilize compensatory revenues, it is worrisome as to how the need for enhanced SEC expenditures, heavy debt-servicing, and defence expenditures will be satisfied.

A study of the trends in defence expenditures reveals interesting findings. While defence expenditure-to-GDP ratio increased from 3.2 per cent in 1949–50 to 6 per cent in 1994–5, its share in total expenditure declined from 73.1 per cent in 1949–50 to 34.2 per cent in 1994–5. Table 5 shows defence expenditure-to-GDP ratio and the share of defence expenditure to total expenditures for some additional years between the period 1947–8 to 1994–5.

Table 5
Defence expenditure trends

Years	Defence expenditure to GDP ratio	Defence expenditure as percentage of total expenditure
1947–48	0.9	65.3
1948–49	2.5	71.4
1949–50	3.2	73.1
1954–55	3.0	55.5
1957–58	3.0	59.7
1958–59	3.6	57.1
1959–60	3.3	57.0
1964–65	2.7	52.6
1965–66	5.6	69.3
1969–70	3.8	58.1
1970–71	4.3	56.0
1971–72	7.5	56.3
1974–75	6.7	56.5
1979–80	6.0	42.9
1984–85	7.5	42.8
1987–88	7.8	39.8
1988–89	7.5	36.0
1989–90	7.7	38.6
1990–91	7.1	36.8
1991–92	7.0	35.8
1992–93	7.3	35.7
1993–94	6.7	33.0
1994–95	6.0	34.2

Sources: As in Table 1.

Table 5 shows the pronounced increase in the defence expenditure-to-GDP ratio from 0.9 per cent in 1947–8 to 2.5 per cent in 1948–9, that is immediately after the Indo-Pakistan war of 1948. The share of defence expenditure in total expenditures also increased from 65.3 per cent in 1947–8 to 71.4 per cent in 1948–9. During the period 1949–50 to 1957–8, defence expenditure-to-GDP ratio did not fall below 3 per cent, indicating the commitment of the civilian government to defence prior to the 1958 martial law. During the Ayub Khan regime, however, the defence expenditure-to-GDP ratio declined from

3.6 per cent in 1958–9 to 2.7 per cent in 1964–5. The reduction in this ratio is surprising given that tension was brewing on the Kashmir border in 1964–5. However, after the 1965 war, this ratio shot up to 5.6 per cent in 1965–6 and was then brought down to 3.8 per cent in 1969–70. After the 1971 war with India, defence expenditure-to-GDP ratio shot up again from 4.3 per cent in 1970–71 to 7.5 per cent in 1971–2. This also depicts the structural break in the series resulting from the division of Pakistan. This ratio was brought down to 6.7 per cent in 1974–5 and 6.0 per cent in 1979–80. However, after the Soviet invasion of Afghanistan, this ratio again experienced a noticeable increase to 7.5 per cent in 1984–5 and 7.7 per cent in 1989–90. The ratio has, however, been brought down to 6.0 per cent in 1994–5, showing a tendency on the part of the democratic governments to reduce defence expenditure. This is perhaps also in line with the requirements of international financiers.

However, interestingly enough, since the take-over by democratic governments in 1988, the defence expenditure-to-GDP ratio shows some revealing shifts in the democratic government's policy towards defence expenditures. During the first Benazir government, this ratio increased from 7.5 per cent in 1988–9 to 7.7 per cent in 1989–90, which also proved to be the last year of the first Benazir government. At the end of the first year of the Nawaz Sharif government in 1990–91, this ratio decreased again to 7.1 per cent. It further decreased to 7.0 per cent in 1991–2 and was then raised to 7.3 per cent in 1992–3, which proved to be the last year of the then Nawaz Sharif government. The above trend shows that during the initial first or two years in office, democratic governments tend to reduce this ratio as they perhaps feel sufficiently secure. It is when they begin to experience intensified political opposition that they tend to increase the defence expenditure-to-GDP ratio, as the first Benazir government did in 1989–90 and the Nawaz Sharif government did in 1992–3. Despite this increase, these governments could not continue in office. This leads to the question whether the defence forces' support of a civilian government is related to a civilian government's decision *vis-à-*

vis defence outlay. The popular belief regarding a relationship between defence expenditure and the stability/continuity of a civilian government, needs, therefore, to be tested further.

During the second Benazir government, defence expenditure-to-GDP ratio had declined steadily in its first two years to a level of 6.0 per cent in 1994–5. This could have been due to the influence of international financiers who require a reduction in defence outlay and who are a force that can prevail over the influence of the military in determining defence expenditures in the country. The above analysis, therefore, points to the need for a further study of the determinants of defence expenditure, the influence of the military in providing continuity to civilian governments, and consideration of economic approaches to regional security enhancement that could perhaps divert scarce resources towards areas that would contribute both to economic development and regional security enhancement.

Another noticeable feature in expenditure trends has been the withdrawal of subsidies after a period of continuing rise from the 1970s when the state began to provide maximum support. This ratio has been declining since 1984–5 and dropped to 1.5 per cent of GDP in 1994–5 as a part once again, of the influence of international financiers in withdrawing state support, reducing the size of the government, and market reform. This has resulted in increased cost of inputs and thereby cost-push inflation. This has, in turn, depressed profitability and the contribution to national income and government revenues, as it has served to restrict the expansion of some crucial tax bases. There is, therefore, a need to do a cost-benefit analysis of the withdrawal of subsidies and an impact evaluation of this measure on the country's economy.

The total expenditure-to-GDP ratio, after reaching a high level of 20 per cent in 1989–90, has dropped to 17.7 per cent in 1994–5. It actually declined after reaching an all-time high of 20.4 per cent in 1992–3, which was the last year of the Nawaz Sharif government. The peak also depicts the culmination of a rising tendency in this ratio since the division of Pakistan in 1971. The break in the series in 1971 shows that the bulk of expenditure was on the territory that currently comprises Pakistan while the former East Pakistan perhaps contributed comparably to the GDP. This serves to support a point raised earlier regarding the adoption of economic approaches to the country's security enhancement.

CONCLUSION

Currently, debt-servicing and military expenditure more than absorb the total revenue generated. There is little scope for further cuts in government development and recurring expenditures. Cuts in social expenditures and subsidies are worsening the quality of life of the poor. Alternative approaches to regional security, as well as revenue generation, need to be actively sought so as to invest in human development and hence in the enhancement of total factor productivity in the country. This is central to dealing with the debt and related deficits. Without this, it will not be possible to make a visible impact on the lives of the people, despite rising total expenditure-to-GDP ratios.

REFERENCES

Government of Pakistan. (1972), *25 Years of Pakistan in Statistics 1947–72*, CSO, Economic Affairs Division, Ministry of Finance and Planning and Development, Karachi.

————. *Economic Survey*, Finance Division, Economic Advisor's Wing (various issues).

8

Financial Markets and Economic Development in Pakistan: 1947–1995

Bashir Ahmad Khan*

1. INTRODUCTION

The role played by financial markets in economic development has been at the centre of a debate for some time. The debate has focused on three main issues: the link between the financial sector and economic development; the emergence of financial institutions to support economic growth and development; and, the role of government policy in encouraging or discouraging this process. This chapter explores the inter-relationships between these three aspects of financial and economic development and government policy in Pakistan.

2. FINANCE AND ECONOMIC DEVELOPMENT

Financial market reforms in Asia, Africa, the Middle East, and Latin America during the 1980s and 1990s are testimony to the growing recognition that suitable financial structure development is complementary to economic development. An increase in financial savings, unlike physical capital accumulation, contributes to both investment and growth. Simple measures of financial asset growth, such as the ratio of monetary assets to

* The author is Assistant Professor, Department of Finance, Lahore University of Management Sciences, Graduate School of Business Administration.

GDP, are used to define growing financial systems. In general, such ratios indicate that more developed nations exhibit larger financial systems. For example, they often have ratios near or greater than one while most developing countries have ratios closer to 0.5. Pakistan's ratio in 1991 was only 36. This illustrates a need for greater financial depth resulting from more sophisticated banking systems and operationally more efficient capital markets.

To raise the rate of financial savings, two critical factors must co-exist: people must be willing to save, and they must have opportunities to invest. The latter requires suitable financial institutions and instruments, such that the public is rewarded for deferring consumption and the savings thus mobilized can be channelled into their most productive use. This role of 'intermediation' is the primary purpose for the existence and development of financial markets in developing countries. The acceptance of the primacy of the intermedial function, reflected in the growth of suitable financial institutions and instruments, risk diversification, aggregation of funds, lower transactions costs, and value-enhancing information flows leads to the following policy conclusions: First, the government has various policy options *vis-à-vis* the development of the financial sector. Second, when the government is unclear on whether the financial system is to help the development process, or to act as 'side-show', the result is inefficiency, market segmentation, and disintermediation. These issues are examined next.

3. PAKISTAN: FINANCIAL POLICY BRIEF

In the decade and a half after independence (1947), successive Pakistani governments adopted a policy of 'supply-leading' finance (*see* Wai and Patrick, 1973). This policy entailed the creation of financial market intermediation in anticipation of the demand for it. During the 1950s and 1960s, this policy was illustrated by the rapid expansion of the commercial bank branch network and the foundation of specialized banks. Such a policy was a corollary of the import-substitution type development model being pursued by the country and required the mobilization and allocation of large amounts of term finance for the long-gestation projects associated with industrialization.

The success of such a policy was predicated upon a number of factors. First, it was necessary that the intermediation created in the formal financial sector should provide sufficiently attractive terms to investors so that there was a positive impact on deposit mobilization, otherwise there would be a reversion to traditional savings forms in the informal sector. Second, it was necessary that any gap between capital mobilization and requirements would be filled through corporate borrowing (internal and external). Third, if the government intervened to create bridge finance, then its own borrowing (deficit financing) should not 'crowd out' the private sector. These factors were important because they determined whether government policy towards the financial sector would be active or passive in terms of its intervention. In Pakistan, this dilemma has been visible in a historical conflict between the public and private sector, regulator and intermediaries, nationalized and de-nationalized, and reflected in very mixed signals and policy shifts being sent to the financial market. This has resulted from the discrepency created such that the government's primary policy motives is at odds with its secondary and perhaps more important motives. The best example of this discrepency is the emphasis on the stock market (symbolic of reform) while the more critical component of financial structure, the banking system, remains underdeveloped.

4. BANKS AND ECONOMIC DEVELOPMENT IN PAKISTAN

In Pakistan, the problem of inadequate financial intermediation during the early years was overcome by the creation of a nation-wide system of commercial bank branches. Banks were encouraged to mobilize deposits and lend to the corporate sector.

Historically, prudent banking guidelines followed maturity matching between assets and liabilities, but industrial loans were of longer tenor, and this led to several imperatives for financial institutions. First, to ensure a positive response from the banking system, credit guidelines (eventually to become quantitative credit controls) were established. Second, to ensure a positive response from the corporate sector, funds were provided at rates below those that would have prevailed in a competitive market in a capital-constrained economy.

These policies had major repercussions. Credit guidelines and controls and disequilibrium pricing created signalling distortions in the capital market. With term finance available cheaply from the banking system, there was an incentive to adopt capital-intensive techniques in production. In the financial markets, cheap capital was a direct hindrance to the development of a market for corporate debt. Pricing anomalies also affected banks' balance sheets and their profitability. Over time, this restricted the ability of the banking system to mobilize and allocate funds efficiently and contributed to disintermediation and the over-abundance of financial institutions in the country.

A. TRENDS IN COMMERCIAL BANK INTERMEDIATION IN PAKISTAN

The country's policy of relying on bank credit for different maturities of funds continues to this day. The policy made commercial banks in Pakistan into universal banks, although the institutional and structural side of the market was unable to keep pace with the changes in the banking system, especially in the 1990s. Government policy has been the key determinant of the growth of commercial banking. By 1995, there were over forty commercial banks in the country, together with investment banks, brokerage houses, mutual funds, and life insurance companies. It is possible to identify three time periods which illustrate the changes in this sector since 1947.

1. Pre-Nationalization

In the formative years of the development of banking in Pakistan (1947–72), governments intervened in the banking system in three ways. First, a central bank, the State Bank of Pakistan (SBP), was established and given a multiplicity of functions: regulating the monetary and credit systems, fostering economic growth, undertaking money market operations, and supporting the development of the capital market. Second, low cost financing was made available both through the commercial banks and through newly emerging specialized banks. For the former, this was made possible by the fact that almost 50 per cent of the deposits mobilized during this period paid no interest to the holders. For the latter, concessional lines of credit allowed low interest rates on loans. Third, the increase in the number of bank branches allowed a phenomenal increase in bank credit, based on the increase in commercial bank deposits, from 29 per cent of total deposits to 75 per cent by the mid-1960s. However, there were also negative aspects to these trends. Economic policy supported lending to specific industrial enclaves, and the growth in the volume of assets was accompanied by a concentration of ownership of assets in the industrial and financial sectors as well as in the loan portfolios. Second, the growth in the loan portfolios placed a premium on liquidity with banks frequently reverting to the SBP for additional credit. Also, since a substantial component of this credit was being directed towards the public sector, a considerable proportion of bank investments was also directed towards government debt securities.

As a result, commercial bank performance eventually suffered. By 1971, six of the fourteen scheduled commercial banks had run into financial problems. Data compiled for the period reveal that of the fourteen commercial banks, none had a return on assets greater than 0.75 per cent in 1971–2. By 1972, two of these banks had ceased to function and several others were in serious financial trouble.[1] Ten of the banks had leverage multipliers exceeding fifty times, reflecting aggressive lending policies.[2] Similarly, the banks had above average credit risk, ranging from 30 to 50 per cent. Technically, a high credit risk should be associated with higher returns: however, given the low return on assets, it appears that asset growth was far greater than any commensurate trend in profitability. Finally, since only one private bank had a capital-to-asset ratio greater than 5 per cent, and eight had ratios of less than 2 per cent, this suggested a high degree of capital risk or inadequate capitalization for the existing level of lending.

This had three implications. First, lending rates probably did not adequately reflect the prevailing risk premiums in the market place and affected the spreads between lending and borrowing rates. Second, loan recovery was poor and the rate of default high with a corresponding write-off of losses and lower earnings. Third, volume growth did not adequately compensate for the reduced spreads over the long run. Hence, by 1971–2, the banking system was showing signs of fragility; however, the government's response to this situation appeared to be dictated by motives other than an improvement in performance.

2. Nationalization

In 1973, the government nationalized and consolidated the Pakistani financial system, ostensibly on the grounds of reversing socio-economic inequity and for improving the direction of economic development. Nationalization had both structural and portfolio implications for the banks.[3] The Pakistani private banks were consolidated into the 'big five' nationalized commercial banks (NCBs): Habib, National, Muslim Commercial, United, and Allied, whose 7,500 branches dominated the financial services industry until the early 1990s. They contributed to a phenomenal growth of banking liabilities and assets during the 1970s and 1980s: between June 1975–90, the average annual growth in demand and time liabilities for the NCBs was 55.5 per cent and asset growth was higher still. By the end of 1990, the NCBs had mobilized over Rs 275 billion in deposits, and had Rs 548 billion in assets.

The impact of the expansion of the balance sheets of the NCBs was strongly affected by the regulatory and the administrative framework in which credit expansion took place.

In 1972, the National Credit Consultative Council (NCCC) was created to take charge of the annual credit plan. Credit was allocated to the commercial banks based on their past performance in mobilizing deposits. These allocations then became the new credit ceilings for each bank. Since the onus was on historic performance, the policy was not only uncompetitive for banks but accommodated established borrowers at the expense of newer ones (Mohammad, 1992). In 1974, the Government of Pakistan created the Pakistan Banking Council (PBC), which took over administrative authority for the NCBs. The PBC co-existed with the SBP, which remained the primary regulatory authority for the banking system. The main purpose served by the PBC was that by acting as the link between the Ministry of Finance and the overall banking system, it allowed the government to increase its borrowing through *ad hoc* means.

The system of credit ceilings, quotas, and controls was complemented by high mandatory reserve requirements, which reached 35 per cent of demand and time liabilities during the 1980s. But the 'moral suasion' exerted by the government in terms of its borrowing needs encouraged the NCBs to maintain reserve ratios well in excess of the requirements.[4] Since a substantial part of their investments was maintained in low-yield government securities, given interest rate ceilings, banks controlled deposit rates to maintain spreads. Thus, between 1973–7, real interest rates were estimated to be –10.5 per cent, with some improvement to –2.9 per cent during the 1978–82 period (Klein, 1992).

These trends affected the ability of the financial system to generate resources for economic development. Negative real interest rates encouraged disintermediation from the formal to the informal financial sector, where nominal rates of return were substantially higher. The term structure of (nominal) interest rates was made abnormal, due to the absence of competitive long-term rates, which militated against term finance. Even the impact of partial deregulation of interest rates, realized by the introduction of profit-and-loss sharing in the mid-1980s, was lost as a result of the competition reducing withdrawal of conventional interest-based deposit. Indeed, the main impact of the 'Islamization' of the financial sector in Pakistan was that it encouraged new types of financial intermediation (positive), and also exposed the inefficacy of the loan recovery system (negative) and the inability to price term capital (negative).

By 1990, the financial performance of the five NCBs had declined substantially since nationalization. The average return on assets had declined by 35 per cent since 1973, and the gains in productivity, achieved through improved asset utilization, were at the expense of higher liquidity and capital risk. Additionally, government borrowing requirements increased throughout this period with major negative investment portfolio effects for the NCBs. The official policy of supporting 'sick units' reduced loan quality and raised concerns over insolvency. Investors reacted negatively: the ratio of deposits to GDP began to decline in the late 1980s, and time deposits with the banking system declined in absolute terms in 1988–9. The only plus points were the improvements in interest rate and credit risk, which were largely the result of greater prudence forced upon the NCBs by the competition of the foreign banks in Pakistan. State Bank statistics reveal that the NCBs had over 85 per cent of deposits and contributed an equal share in profits in 1973. However by 1990, with a more or less similar market share, foreign banks were contributing over 35 per cent of the profits. The entry of the Pakistani private banks also contributed to this trend.

3. Post-Nationalization

The five years following 1991 have seen more substantive changes in the Pakistani banking system than at any other time in the country's history. A liberalization policy, involving disinvestment of state-owned commercial banks and deregulation of financial and monetary controls initiated in 1991, had far-reaching effects on the banking system. Two NCBs were privatized: Muslim Commercial Bank and Allied Bank, while licenses were given to ten private banks during 1991. The growth of the financial sector as a whole also attracted a number of new foreign banks, and encouraged existing banks to expand their branch networks. By 1995, there were twenty-two foreign banks operating in the country, complementing the seventeen private and six government-owned banks.

The changing financial structure was accompanied by reforms which had an impact on the inter-linkage between financial and money markets, such as the introduction of a competitive auction market for government debt, an across-the-board increase in yields on government debt, an increase in rupee deposit rates to make them more attractive to investors, permission for banks to raise foreign currency deposits to attract funds from the informal sector, and revised prudential ratios on both credit expansion and maximum lending and deposit rates to allow for an expansion in assets and make the loan market more competitive.

On the surface, these changes were positive. To some extent, since 1991, the market for government issue and the rates prevailing in it have been market-determined. The competition among financial intermediaries to raise deposits has resulted in improved service quality and higher yields, with the expectation that the disintermediation away from the banking system in the late 1980s is in the process of being reversed. This will improve the system's ability to mobilize and allocate funds. However, the extent of the positive impact of the reforms in the banking sector has been curtailed. In 1995, the banking system's financial performance suffered, reflected in lower operating and post-tax profits, lower margins, higher non-interest expenses, and higher capital and interest-rate risk.[5] Competition had squeezed spreads and lowered margins, as banks competed for deposits. Additionally, the government banks had to clean up their loan portfolios to remain competitive with the better-managed private Pakistani banks.

At the same time, a number of external factors also combined to have an impact on banks' operating performance, and on the extent to which the sector supported economic development. The statutory reserve requirements for banks had been reduced between 1991–5, while ceilings on loans had been eliminated. But the government moved away from explicit prudential guidelines to implicit 'recommendations' and moral suasion. The latter has been a weapon in the armour of all central banks, but was used to the extreme by the State Bank of Pakistan throughout 1995-6, primarily to avoid IMF criticism over the use of excessive quantitative controls to regulate credit. As a result, banks curtailed asset expansion under an implicit threat of sanctions. This not only reduced their most profitable area of business but supported a widely-held view in the financial market, that given the government's inability to control the deficit, the first casualty would be credit availability to the private sector.

5. THE NON-BANK FINANCIAL SECTOR

Historically, banks shied away from providing term finance, either because of the mismatch of the maturities of assets and liabilities, or because their business was concentrated in short-term commercial loans. Term finance would have been risky, and therefore, expensive. Consequently, two alternatives were available: the development of a bond or corporate debt market, which took time and required considerable structural and institutional support; or the creation of specialized banks to provide long-term funds to sectors ranked by importance on the scale of development objectives. Pakistan followed the second route. Together with conventional forms of finance and new institutional investors, the specialized banks in Pakistan, called the development finance institutions (DFIs), played a critical role in economic development, especially since they permitted a new source of public sector borrowing.

A. DEVELOPMENT FINANCE INSTITUTIONS (DFIS)
The DFIs were set up in the early 1960s with the objective of providing large quantities of term finance at rates which were affordable, and to assist that segment of the corporate sector which did not have access to the regular banking system due to the quality of its collateral. The DFIs were encouraged to

mobilize resources by taking deposits and to act as a catalyst for the capital market by issuing suitable savings instruments which would attract fresh funds from the general public. Since the majority of DFIs were government-owned, or had a government equity stake, they were also easily integrated in macroeconomic policy. By 1995, there were fifteen DFIs in the country, three of which were also designated as banking companies. However, an evaluation of their performance reveals mixed results, both in terms of operations and their impact on the economy.

First, political influence, inherent in the structures of ownership, encouraged poor asset-liability management. This was reflected in a concentration of loan portfolios to a narrow enclave of borrowers whose poor credit worthiness eventually had an adverse impact on loan quality and added to operating costs. Second, the DFIs' own financing was usually so heavily subsidized that it was the effective equivalent of equity. This acted as a disincentive to them in establishing an independent deposit base, contributed to undercapitalization, and made them vulnerable when they lost their automatic access to foreign lines of credit in 1992. Third, in the critical area of the market for term finance, the DFIs failed to effect a transformation. They preferred to act as conduits for funds rather than financial intermediaries, irrespective of the fact that they did mobilize funds through attractive savings schemes. Fourth, there was a tendency to create a new DFI whenever the need for a new specialized financial activity was realized. This led to an 'overbanked' and fragmented system with a multiplicity of functions and rates, which overlapped the niches carved out by the government for DFI activities.

B. Institutional Investors

The role of institutional investors in Pakistan remained restricted both by managerial inhibitions and by the regulatory climate prevailing in the financial sector. Even after the 1990s liberalization of the financial services industry institutional investors in Pakistan were underdeveloped and unsophisticated, often duplicating each other in the limited scope of their operations, and contributing little to the growth of the debt market, to underwriting, to market making, or to other areas of corporate finance. For example, the investment banks, which entered the market in the late 1980s, often acted as the financial 'arm' of their respective sponsors. Otherwise, their emphasis was on brokerage services and money market accounts. In the past two years, some investment banks have made a conscious effort to develop corporate debt issues; a crucial component of term finance in more developed financial systems. Other traditional institutional investors included life insurance companies and mutual funds.[6] The former were dominated by the state-owned State Life Insurance Corporation, which was unable to create a viable mechanism for savings or have an impact on the capital market due to the lack of sophistication of its products and services, and the government's 'control' of its reserves. The entry of private life insurers in 1991 may force the industry to create products which provide a serious alternative investment, although their own investment portfolios still remain conservative. This is also true of the state-owned mutual funds, National Investment Trust and Insurance Corporation of Pakistan. Their survival is largely the result of the monopolization of their relative market niches. Indeed, some of their capital market activities, such as the preferential right to new issues, or 'buy and hold' portfolio management strategies, have done more harm than good: they distorted issue prices and reduced the available float for the public.

Specific local institutional investors are the National Savings Organization (NSO) and the *modarabas* (Islamic equity funds). The NSO, by offering high deposit rates, contributed to deposit mobilization in the country, although this probably involved a transfer from the commercial banks, where nominal rates were lower. Additionally, throughout the 1980s, government borrowing was increasingly derived from non-bank financial sources, which was at substantially higher cost and contributed to the country's future repayment problems. The *modarabas* emerged as a direct consequence of the transition to an Islamic financial system in 1985. However, their capital market impact was limited because the amount of capital raised was relatively small, and the incentives which allowed them to grow (lower taxes, less disclosure, flexibility in funds use) have gradually been withdrawn. On the other hand, leasing, which also emerged as a result of its acceptability under Islamic economic laws, may become an important avenue for industrial investment, given an environment of capital scarcity.

C. Informal and Quasi-formal Finance

The key financial institutions in this area include the co-operatives and investment finance companies. The former grew primarily for political reasons; the latter, as a direct result of remittances pouring in from Pakistani migrant workers in the Gulf. Co-operatives were used by successive governments as a means of distributing patronage on a personal and provincial level. The investment finance companies' main attraction were the phenomenal deposit rates offered: 70 to 80 per cent a year. Additionally, excessive regulations elsewhere also contributed to the growth of this sector. Consequently, informal and quasi-formal finance often substituted for the absence of capital formation and accessibility in the formal sector, although at a cost. The capital formation in this sector was the result of disintermediation from the formal sector, which had a negative impact on the volume of financial savings available for official investment. Also, since the sector was outside the jurisdiction of the regulatory authorities, it created problems in controlling liquidity and contributed to financial crises through spillover risks, as in the co-operatives scam of 1990–91. This not only affected the value of deposits in the country, but added to the volatility of the equities market.

During the late 1980s, there was a negative impact on the overall growth of time deposits in Pakistan. The State Bank of Pakistan statistics reveal that time and savings deposits, as a proportion of GDP, declined in absolute terms in the period 1988–90. While the negative real interest rates were a major factor in this trend, the investment finance companies scandal of 1988 and the co-operatives scam also contributed to a general mistrust of all financial institutions, particularly their solvency and their ability to guarantee deposits. At the same time, the withdrawal of funds from both formal and informal financial institutions due to this crisis in public confidence directly contributed to the growth of the equities market from 1991. A substantial influx of surplus funds seeking alternative investments with high rates of returns encouraged stock prices to hit record levels over the next two years. However, the technical adjustment of the Karachi Stock Exchange in 1992, with prices being revised downwards, is reflective of the volatility contributed by these funds. Experience would suggest that these newcomers have remained as investors on the exchange. If they follow the rule of seeking only high return investments, then their contribution to price volatility becomes long-term. However since these investors appear to have remained in the stock market, they have not contributed to market instability.

6. THE EMERGENCE OF SECURITY MARKETS IN PAKISTAN

In most countries, securities markets have become important sources of term finance for long-gestation industrial projects and corporate capital expansion. Amongst the emerging markets, the dynamic economies of the Far East have been particularly successful in accessing international markets through bond issues, hence raising billions of dollars since the late 1980s for economic development.[7] Well-functioning securities markets provide access to risk capital, create liquidity, allow risk diversification, and broaden the ownership of assets in the economy. However, a number of LDCs, including Pakistan, have fallen into the trap of a premature and hasty deregulation of the equities or stock market, without corresponding effort to develop securities market institutions, techniques, and the regulatory and legal framework. This change has come at the expense of the bond market and illustrates the limited ability of the stock market to compensate for controls on bank liquidity in LDCs.

A. Financial Reforms in Pakistan

The changes in the securities markets in Pakistan during the early 1990s were broadly similar to those in other emerging markets. The focus of the reforms included contextual changes in the rubric of companies law and specific policy initiatives by the government aimed at supporting disinvestment and deregulation. The latter included changes in the system of monetary management, incentives for foreign portfolio investment, the launching of country funds, an expansion in the range of financial intermediation, structural and technical changes, improvements in the system of underwriting and pricing of initial public offers (IPOs), and attempts to eliminate corporate malpractice.

The impact of these reforms was that the Karachi Stock Exchange (KSE) became one of the best performing markets in Asia in the early 1990s. Between 1990–95 alone, the number of companies listed on the KSE increased by over 50 per cent, with market capitalization close to Rs 400 billion. During 1994, the stock exchange index recorded new highs for turnover and price appreciation of listed stocks. This boom in secondary market activity also encouraged primary (new issues) market activity, which generated fresh funds from public subscriptions. These peaked in 1994 at around Rs 34 billion. Such phenomenal growth and the daily focus on the movement of the market index suggested the existence of a deep, well-regulated, liquid, and transparent market structure, providing a serious investment alternative for the public and the financing of the future for the corporate sector. However, such an assessment would be premature, given the decline of the stock market in 1994, and because of the factors described below.

B. The Limited Impact of Stock Markets

The country's stock markets lagged behind both the banking system and the non-bank financial system in terms of their contribution to capital mobilization. On average, between 1980–90, only 5 to 6 per cent of private funds have been mobilized through the stock markets, and even in the 1990s, the average amount raised through new issues was only Rs 7 to 9 billion, compared to Rs 75 to 80 billion from deposit mobilization by the commercial banking system alone. Hence, impressive statistics on new enlistments, turnover, and the price index notwithstanding, the stock markets made a minimal contribution to capital formation in the country. This could be attributed to a number of factors. For example, past policy (deficit financing) had acted against the development of debt securities, so institutions, techniques, and awareness in securities as a whole, were lacking. Of far greater importance are the structural constraints.

Pakistan's stock markets are 'thin' i.e. characterized by low turnover and limited liquidity. Thinness results from the structure of equity ownership in the country as well as the passive investment strategies of institutional investors; from the trading malpractices of brokers, which acts as a serious barrier to attracting investors; and from the inefficacy of the regulatory authorities and the exchanges to police corporate malpractice. The result is that stock is often unavailable for buyers and that liquid stocks trade at premium prices (the blue chips). As far as the investor is concerned, even if the stock is available, stock prices are fairly volatile and due to manipulation, the technical re-adjustments can often wipe out substantial values. Additionally, the investor has to cope with insider-dealing by the brokers and an abysmal record on dividend payments by the listed companies.[8] Given this situation, it is not surprising that the number of investors is probably less than one per cent of the country's population. This means that the extent of fresh capital mobilization is also very limited.

C. THE BOND MARKET

The bond market in Pakistan remains underdeveloped, despite attempts in the 1990s to introduce both corporate debt (Packages' Term Finance Certificates) and access international markets to raise term finance (Dewan Salman Convertibles).[9] However, the impetus for growth in this market is largely the result of controls on bank-lending to the corporate sector.

Historically, companies could borrow long-term at rates lower than that which would have to be offered by a debt instrument which properly incorporated the various risk premiums. During the 1960s and 1970s, this had hampered the indigenous growth of the bond market. However, fiscal difficulties forced the government to encourage the utility company, WAPDA, to tap the local market through its bearer bonds in 1988. This was the first major bond issue by a non-financial institution in the country. Since then, WAPDA has made additional issues, and a small number of companies have taken the first step in this direction. This change has been supported by the entry of discount houses, to buy and sell bonds, and by a credit rating agency.

However, a number of factors continue to work against the bond market in this country. First, the tax structure does not encourage companies to access debt markets. Second, the term structure of interest rates means that companies prefer to arrange revolving finance, or concessional loans through overseas donors. Third, company owners are concerned about the creation of a new class of agents, namely bondholders, who would have preference in the case of bankruptcy. Fourth, the poor disclosure record of listed companies means that investors find it difficult to assess the viability of debt issues. Fifth, the focus of public sector debt issues has been to tap the informal sector, and the preponderance of bearer (unregistered) certificates hampers overseas interest and the ability to tap international markets which have more rigorous reporting standards. Finally, the level of understanding of bond pricing and techniques is limited; as reflected by the mispricing in both the Dewan Salman and Sapphire Bonds cases.[10] In the former case, the investment bank concerned had to bear the losses incurred as a result of an adverse movement in prices. In the latter case, the same investment bank seriously miscalculated the rate of return being offered by the instrument. The end result is that the market is still in its early stages of growth, and the focus of investors and policy makers remains on the stock markets.

D. GOVERNMENT POLICY AND THE SECURITIES MARKET

Given the universally accepted position that stock markets are at best a complement to the development of universal banking and the bond market, the policy of successive governments in this direction has been of considerable interest. Since 1990, governments in Pakistan have gone out of their way to encourage portfolio investment, especially by foreign institutional investors. The deregulation in the stock markets is unprecedented even in this age of liberalization, making Pakistan one of the most 'open' financial sectors (generally) and stock markets (in particular) in the world. Several explanations can be forwarded for such a position by the policy makers. First, stock markets are very visible examples of financial market growth, and deregulated markets symbolize a country's commitment to reform. Second, it is easier to follow a policy of stock market liberalization than to tackle the structural problems necessary for consolidating the efficiency improvements gained by the banking system during the last five years. Third, the results-oriented strategies of donor agencies, such as the IMF, are particularly myopic with regard to the financial sector, and the focus on the stock market often satisfies even the most demanding donors.

CONCLUSION

The history of Pakistan's experience with financial market development is a history of government intervention in the financial market to sustain public sector borrowing. It was this intervention, initially justifiable, which encouraged the growth of bank branches, of bank lending and deposits, of specialized banks, and of new intermediaries. The same intervention also encouraged the introduction of interest rate and exchange controls, credit controls, and limits on asset expansion. The absence of complementary institutional and structural changes in the public sector in terms of the quality of regulation, the sophistication of financial tools and techniques, and the advancement of modern securities market legislation contributed to the relatively unsatisfactory record of savings mobilization and allocation, and in enhancing investor participation in the financial markets. This, in turn, forced liberalization and reform; which, in turn, was put on hold because the government again failed to make the necessary structural changes.

In this circle of cause and effect, it is possible to identify certain features of financial market development in the country and its impact on the real economy. First, the efficiency gains in the banking system, as a result of greater competition and the move to prudential rules and regulations, should not be eliminated by a return to the archaic and *ad hoc* system of administered controls. Second, the stock market is a side-show to the main thrust of financial and economic development, and the belief that foreign portfolio investment is a panacea for Pakistan's perennial problems with the resource gap is self-deluding. Third, for financial markets to contribute to economic development they must be viewed as a level playing field by investors. This requires the government to regulate transparently and to be seen to regulate transparently.

REFERENCES

Klein, Michael U. (1992), 'Commercial banking in Pakistan', *Financing Pakistan's Development in the 1990s*, (ed. Anjum Nasim), Karachi: Lahore University of Management Sciences and Oxford University Press.

Mahmood, Amir and Khan, Bashir A. (1996), 'Industry structure and the conduct of the Pakistani banking industry', Working Paper, Lahore University of Management Sciences.

Mohammed, Azizali F. (1992), 'Monetary management in Pakistan', *Financing Pakistan's Development in the 1990s*, (ed. Anjum Nasim), Karachi: Lahore University of Management Sciences and Oxford University Press.

Wai, U. Tun and Patrick, Hugh T. (1973), 'Stock and bond issues and capital markets in less developed countries', IMF Staff Papers, 20, pp. 253–317.

NOTES

1. The data base examines bank performance and structure in Pakistan between 1965–95. Six return measures (interest margin, net margin, asset utilization, return on assets, leverage multiplier, and return on equity) and four risk measures (liquidity, interest rate, credit, and capital) are estimated for each bank during this period. An attempt has been made to look at proper risk-adjusted measures in each case; however, the data set remains incomplete due to the absence or poor quality of the financial information. *See* Mahmood and Khan (1996).

2. The leverage multiplier is defined as total assets over equity. It reflects the extent to which a bank's assets are covered by shareholders' capital. A high multiplier implies more debt (leverage) and higher risk.

3. Contrary to much of the literature, the most important outcome of nationalization was not in the change in ownership but in the process of consolidation which introduced the market for corporate control, albeit in an administered way.

4. This was true of the state-owned life insurance companies as well. The willingness of financial institutions to hold low-yield government debt was the result of several factors. First, the State Bank of Pakistan accepted government securities as collateral for lending, and this created an incentive for banks and insurance companies to hold these securities. Second, since the NCCC formulated the credit plan on historic ratios, banks were willing to hold government securities because they felt that: (a) they would be looked upon favourably in terms of credit shares, and (b) they would be asked to increase their holdings (if they were close to the statutory requirements) to assist government borrowing.

5. Capital risk is the opposite of the leverage multiplier and is measured by the capital-to-assets ratio. It essentially reflects the 'safety' of a bank, since a higher ratio means that the bank has a greater amount of capital to cover for any contingencies. Interest rate risk is measured by the gap between interest-sensitive assets and liabilities. It simultaneously shows the extent to which banks have matched the maturities of their assets and liabilities, and also adjusts these balance sheet items by the risk inherent in them due to interest rate fluctuations. Thus, interest-sensitive assets would include loans and fixed income securities but not fixed assets; interest-sensitive liabilities would include deposits. The ability of banks to manage this gap effectively allows them to: (a) hedge against unforeseen interest rate changes, and (b) maximize income.

6. We are mainly interested in life insurance due to its implications for term finance.

7. These capital flaw, as we now know, are risky if the financial sector is not well-regulated and hence over-exposed.

8. On average, fifty per cent of the companies listed on the stock exchanges have not paid dividends to shareholders over the past ten-year period.

9. Term Finance Certificates (TFCs) are securities with a stipulated time period and predetermined interest rates, based on prevailing market rates. TFCs are issued for fixed assets expansion. The Packages TFC's have a maturity period of five years and offer an interest (or mark-up) rate of 18.5 per cent. The Dewan Salman Convertible was a Eurobond which could be converted into equity at a stipulated conversion price. It was issued in Luxembourg.

10. Sapphire Fibre issued a bond in the form of a TFC, with a five-year maturity period and 19.5 per cent rate of return. However, the bond suffered from a lack of liquidity i.e. it could not be encashed easily due to the lack of a secondary market, and other negative attributes, together with the marketing effort of the investment bank concerned contributed to its failure. A major miscalculation was in the actual as opposed to quoted rate of return. The actual return was substantially lower, reflecting technical inadequacies in bond pricing in Pakistan. The Dewan Salman Convertible issue suffered from an adverse movement in US interest rates, which led to mis-pricing. The investment bank accepted the loss incurred due to its contractual commitments.

PART THREE

CONTEMPORARY CONCERNS

9

Poverty in Pakistan:
A Review

*Haris Gazdar**

1. INTRODUCTION

A. OUTLINE

The aim of this chapter is to provide an overview of issues, debates, and empirical work in the study of poverty in Pakistan. The study of poverty is a wide area which includes work on themes as diverse and disparate as the conceptualization of poverty, the methodology of its measurement, estimation of time trends, and debates on probable causes and possible cures. It would be a daunting task, indeed, to provide a comprehensive review of all these subjects, and that too within the confines of a chapter, for a large and diverse country like Pakistan for a period of half a century. To some extent, the job is made easier because the country is relatively under-researched. Even so, rather than pretend to be comprehensive, this chapter gives a selective treatment to four different (though at times overlapping) themes in poverty analysis in Pakistan.

Firstly, the remainder of this section provides a brief review of some conceptual issues as they concern Pakistan as well as

* The author is a researcher at the Asia Research Centre, London School of Economics, and a Visiting Fellow at the Sustainable Development Policy Institute. He is grateful to Terry Byres, Athar Hussain, Shahrukh Rafi Khan, Mozaffar Qizilbash, Asad Sayeed, and Akbar Zaidi for comments on earlier drafts, and to Zainab Latif for research assistance. He acknowledges the errors as his own.

other developing countries. Two distinct strands have emerged in the way scholars, policy makers, and activists think about poverty. On the one hand, there is a well-established statistical, some say economistic, approach with its precise categories and a focus on measurement. This, indeed, has been the dominant approach to the analysis of poverty in Pakistan. As such, this chapter reflects the concerns of existing literature. On the other hand, a more institutional or 'process-based' approach is becoming increasingly popular and powerful. This approach, as it might be applied to Pakistan, is discussed in section 1B. The scope and the limitations of this study's approach to poverty in Pakistan is delineated in section 1C.

Secondly, section 2 provides a brief chronology of Pakistan's development experience, with a particular focus on issues relating to poverty and economic inequality in the evolution of the country's political economy over the last five decades. Changes in economic structure, policy regime, and external political and economic factors are discussed with reference to their probable impact on poverty and inequality. The perception of economic injustice has been a potent source of political mobilization, and by extension, of policy changes in Pakistan. Some of the important changes in the country's political economy are interpreted in the light of this two-way relationship between policy regime and public perceptions about poverty and inequality.

Thirdly, in section 3, methodological issues in conventional poverty measurement are discussed. This is done not merely as a prelude to the analysis of some survey data later in the chapter (section 4), but also because methodological issues have figured prominently in the literature on poverty in Pakistan. Methodological differences in poverty measurement are responsible for much of the discrepancy in estimates of poverty indicators produced by various researchers. It is hoped that the review provided here will be useful in assessing the comparability of various empirical findings. A number of important controversies in public debate are directly related to perceptions of changes in poverty under different policy regimes.

The analysis of poverty trends is hampered, however, by the non-availability of consistent time series. Recent trends in poverty indices, which are based on consistent methodologies, are also presented in section 3.

Fourthly, results of new work on rural poverty, based on the analysis of household survey data, are reported in section 4. Despite the political as well as policy importance of regional economic disparities, there is relatively little work on regional patterns of rural poverty. It is possible to explore some methodological issues in poverty measurement by examining regional differences in poverty indicators under different choices of measurement method. Regional analysis also presents the opportunity of examining the relationship between poverty and economic and social institutions. Institutional arrangements (including the working of markets) vary from region to region, and a regional analysis of poverty offers the opportunity of gaining some insights into this relationship.

B. APPROACHES TO POVERTY ANALYSIS

The conventional approach to understanding the problem of poverty has been based upon the concept of a poverty line in the income or consumption space. The poverty line is supposed to indicate a minimum acceptable level of income or consumption. Poverty, then, is the failure to attain some minimal level of income or consumption, and the poor are those who fail to attain that level. There is a large and sophisticated body of literature which deals mostly with measurement issues, not least, with questions about the demarkation of a poverty line, the ordering of the distribution, and the appropriateness of alternative methods of aggregation.[1]

While much of the economic literature on poverty is, indeed, about the identification of the poor, the design of anti-poverty schemes, and the measurement of poverty, there are, nevertheless, critical contributions that address more fundamental problems such as the normative ethical considerations that inform poverty measurement.[2] Partly as a result of this critique within development economics, and partly due to the growing recognition of social processes as legitimate development issues (as a result of the work of non-economists), development economics has been moving away from defining poverty exclusively in terms of income, consumption, or nutritional intake. This has been reflected in the wide range of indicators that are now commonly used for descriptions of the poverty situation.[3]

These wider approaches view poverty as the condition that restricts equal and unhindered participation in the economic, social, and political life of the community.[4] This definition of poverty is not, as a matter of fact, in contradiction to the established income- or consumption-based approach. The original argument behind income- and consumption-based approaches was that they are proxies for capturing precisely this ability of individuals to participate freely and with dignity in the affairs of the community, and to achieve objectives they might have reason to value.[5] In arriving at a participation-based definition of poverty we have, in some sense, come full circle. Participation-based approaches are important for at least three sets of reasons.

Firstly, because they allow insights into the process of poverty creation and therefore the possibilities of poverty eradication. This aspect of the participation-based approaches is quite well-understood and applied by development practitioners. For example, in the case of Pakistan, a number of successful anti-poverty initiatives have at their core a credit-saving-investment programme.[6] The idea is that the poor have restricted access to the formal credit market, and that the informal credit markets are dominated by local monopolists who charge extortionate interest rates. Poverty, in this respect, is the inability to participate freely and on equal terms in an economic institution, namely the market; in this case, the credit market.

Secondly, the participatory approach to poverty draws attention to forms of poverty that are extremely debilitating but may not be captured by consumption or income measures. Another example of poverty is the inability to participate in the market—in this case, the labour market. Labour and human rights organizations have been very active, and with significant success, in the emancipation of bonded labour. These interventions are not 'developmental' in the common usage of the term. Rather, they are more along the lines of fighting for basic legal rights. The ability to participate freely in the labour market, however, is a precondition for any escape from poverty. Likewise, a less extreme but more widespread form of poverty in Pakistan is the inability of people to read and write. Illiteracy can also be regarded as a condition that hinders free and equal participation in the affairs of the community. In fact, as all international and intra-regional comparisons have shown, Pakistan has lagged very seriously behind other developing countries, including its South Asian neighbours, in progressing towards universal basic education.[7] Perhaps one of the most debilitating constraints on social participation prevalent in Pakistan is the extremely limited agency of women. Income- and consumption-based approaches to poverty are practically useless in evaluating the social as well economic disadvantage faced by nearly one-half of the population.

Thirdly, emphasizing poverty as an inability to participate leads us to an enquiry into political questions, relationships, and processes. Poverty eradication can thus be viewed as the movement from formal citizenship to effective citizenship. Formal citizenship is based upon the equality of rights and duties of all members of the community. Effective citizenship is the positive ability to exercise these rights and to discharge these duties. Poverty eradication can thus be seen in the context of establishing a parity between the status of political and civil rights, and that of social and economic rights.[8] It is therefore, as much a process of making or facilitating specific interventions that assist the livelihoods of people with low incomes or consumption, as one of empowering people and changing the nature of the polity. Furthermore, economic development needs to be understood not only in terms of the usual yardsticks of economic growth or even income distribution, but also as a process of institutional change.

C. SCOPE AND LIMITATIONS

The participation-based approach does not undermine the value of doing a conventional poverty analysis but simply serves to place it in its proper perspective. Although income or consumption deprivation is not the 'be all and end all' of poverty, it is an important aspect of it.

Much of this chapter is an evaluation of the conventional approach to poverty and its study in Pakistan. This return to the conventional approach is useful for a number of reasons. Firstly, despite its many limitations as an adequate representation of poverty, it remains popular with academics and policy makers alike.[9] It is important, therefore, to evaluate the way this approach has been applied to the study of poverty in Pakistan. Secondly, a number of aspects that concern wider issues in poverty (such as health, demography, and education) have been addressed separately in subsequent contributions to this volume.

Another reason for the continued relevance of the conventional approach is that the results of poverty analysis, based on this approach, can themselves assume wider political importance. This has been the experience in India where (unlike Pakistan) poverty lines and poverty indices are published in official sources on a regular basis as relevant development indicators. By officially endorsing the poverty line, and by publishing poverty indicators, the Indian government implicitly accepts that poverty alleviation is an important policy objective. Likewise, the official poverty line is often used by anti-poverty activists and organizations as a means of influencing public debate.

The next section gives an account of Pakistan's development experience over the last five decades, with particular focus on issues relating to poverty and inequality. A more detailed review of poverty measurement in Pakistan is offered in section 3. In section 4, new approaches to the analysis of income- and consumption-poverty are explored with reference to regional poverty rankings, in the light of the review and discussion on methodology.

There are, of course, numerous issues relating to poverty that have been left out of the present study, and many areas where more work is required. Three broad areas, in particular, need to be mentioned here. Firstly, there is the need, of course, for the development of participation-based approaches in the Pakistani context. The agenda of research on poverty needs to be expanded to include the analysis of specific social, political, and economic institutions, and the power relations embedded in these institutions. Section 4 provides some glimpses of this research agenda, but a much more thorough appraisal is required. The issue of gender bias and women's agency in general, and that of intra-household allocations in particular have not been addressed at all in this chapter. Other crucial issues that receive peripheral attention in section 4D under the discussion of feudal patronage, but which demand more comprehensive treatment, are those concerning private power and unfree labour. More generally, any new research agenda on poverty needs to have a greater focus on problems of participation and exclusion and the content of 'effective' citizenship.

Secondly, a number of issues, such as basic education, health, and sanitation, that are now widely regarded as key aspects of poverty analysis, have been left largely untouched for the reasons listed above. Thirdly, within the conventional (income-based) approach to poverty, specific issues relating to urban poverty and rural-urban disparity do not receive any special attention here. Given the changing economic structure, rural-urban migration, and the prospects of job losses as a result of economic restructuring, issues in urban poverty need to receive much greater attention from researchers.[10]

2. HISTORICAL OVERVIEW

Decades happen to provide a useful periodization of phases in the development of Pakistan's political economy since 1947. The periodization suggested here corresponds roughly with major political and economic turning points. Although the periods suggested here do not correspond exactly with ten-year cycles, they come close enough. The purpose here is to point to some key features and developments in the political economy of Pakistan that are widely thought to have influenced the trends and patterns of poverty. The list of the features and developments that are discussed here is not exhaustive. They are issues, nevertheless, about which further insight could be gained by the analysis of poverty data.

A. CHALLENGES AND OPPORTUNITIES

The first decade, which can be thought of as stretching to around eleven years from 1947 to 1958, can quite naturally be regarded as a formative period in many senses. In terms of economic management, the task ahead of policy makers and the political leadership was no less than that of state-building. A rapid succession of crises and challenges presented themselves and were dealt with in varying degrees of success. The building of an administrative capacity, the settlement of refugees from India, the reorganization of the military and the coercive apparatus of the state, and the setting up of all the paraphernalia of a sovereign entity were carried out during the early years.

The emergence of new boundaries implied also a number of fundamental breaks from the past. The period witnessed a short war with India and the beginnings of the slide towards a severance of economic relations between the two national economies that had formerly been one. In West Pakistan, the very basis of the agrarian economy—namely the canal irrigation system—was up for fundamental reorganization following the partition of Punjab. A system of development planning in the shape of five-year plans was introduced in the early 1950s, and key economic institutions such as a central bank and a ministry of finance were initiated.

Some of the main political and economic developments that emerged from this formative decade and have remained relevant to our understanding of poverty in Pakistan today relate paradoxically, not to breaks from the past, but to the failure to make such breaks. In many ways, the first decade was one of both challenges as well as opportunities. While many of the challenges were successfully negotiated, some of the important development opportunities were missed. In terms of political change, the most conspicuous failure was the inability to evolve a representative constitutional form of government. This went hand in hand with the assumption of greater power by non-representative institutions of the state, including the military and the civil bureaucracy, and the eventual formal takeover of the state by the military in a *coup d'état* in 1958.

Alongside the failure in extending formal civil and political rights, it can also be argued that the opportunity was missed to initiate social and economic changes that have since come to be regarded as essential not only for economic development, but also for the effective exercise of civil and political rights. In particular, three areas of missed reform have, arguably, returned to frustrate the country's development process repeatedly. These areas are, respectively, education, agrarian reform, and decentralization. On the first two issues, the landmark *First Five Year Plan* document provides some useful insights into the priorities of policy makers (Government of Pakistan,1956). In a sixty page chapter on the educational sector, a mere eight pages are devoted to basic or primary education. The chapter on agriculture makes general references to the need for modern agriculture and land reform but no specific recommendations.[11] Far from instituting decentralization, the 1950s saw moves towards greater centralization of administration with the abolition of provinces in West Pakistan and their merger into a single administrative unit.

It is not being argued here that fundamental reforms of education, agrarian institutions, and administration could only be carried out in the first decade. There were other opportunities subsequently which also, with the benefit of hindsight, were squandered. The immediate aftermath of decolonization has provided the backdrop for significant social, political, and administrative reforms in other developing countries. The main point here is that such reforms were not forthcoming in Pakistan in its formative years. Many of the serious development crises faced by the country in its fifth decade could be traced back to missed opportunities early on, and to the failure to make subsequent corrections.

B. GROWTH AND INEQUALITY

The military *coup d'état* in October 1958 can be viewed as marking the end of the first decade of Pakistan. The new government promised political stability and development. Its economic programme was informed by the then state-of-the-art economic advice. The initial self-avowed strategy was to raise investment by enhancing domestic savings and foreign aid and to hasten the pace of industrialization. The economic indicators from this period are impressive enough. The economy grew at the rate 6.8 per cent per year compared with the virtual stagnation of the 1950s, with record growth in industry (Government of Pakistan, 1997). Glowing commendations from local as well as foreign experts attest to the general atmosphere of confidence and optimism that prevailed among policy makers during the 1960s.[12]

The 1960s also saw favourable developments in the agricultural sector. The Indus Basin Treaty governing the sharing of river waters was finally agreed between Pakistan and India, and this led to the setting up of large-scale irrigation development projects. The canal system of irrigation had been saved and, indeed, extended (Lieftinck et al., 1968). Private initiative was found to have been the main proponent of a large increase in groundwater development. There were also positive technological developments, particularly with respect to new seed varieties.[13] All of these developments took place within the context of the first ever land reforms in Pakistan, which came into force under a martial law regulation in 1959 (Khan, 1981).

These favourable conditions received a setback in 1965 when Pakistan and India went to war. The economic setback, moreover, was compounded by the loss of popular legitimacy on the part of the military government as a result of the war and its aftermath. By 1968, there were violent protests against the government in both East and West Pakistan, and in 1969, the government was replaced in another *coup d'état*. The 'development decade' had come to an end, but the end game was to be played out in 1970 with the secession of East Pakistan, and the coming into power of the first ever elected government in what remained of Pakistan.

It is now widely accepted that the events of the late 1960s, which put paid to the development decade, were due as much to a crisis of the development model as they were to political or constitutional crises. In particular, three related themes stand out. Firstly, there was the issue of regional disparity. Growth had occurred mainly in the agricultural sector in West Pakistan (primarily up to that point in Punjab). Industrial investment too, was concentrated in West Pakistan, mainly in Karachi and parts of Punjab. The political movement for regional representation, therefore, was strongly fuelled by a strong sense of economic deprivation among other regions.[14]

Secondly, as far as the industrial sector itself was concerned, the economic model that informed policy makers was one that involved growth in inequality alongside the growth of income. This was the era of the Lewis model which laid emphasis on raising the savings rate at the cost of current consumption. The economic model posited a trade-off between growth and equality, and the policy makers at the time were unambiguous about the part of the bargain they preferred. As it turned out, the trade-off which had been posited was not borne out by the experience of other growing economies, and in any case, even more devastatingly for the 1960s growth model, popular sentiment turned against the policy makers' perception that inequality was a price worth paying for growth.[15]

Finally, although there was fairly steady and rapid growth in the agricultural sector in West Pakistan, the 1960s also witnessed the beginnings of a major dislocation in economic institutions in the regions where growth was occurring the fastest. In particular, there was a marked decline in the incidence of share-tenancy in Punjab. In a region of relatively unequal land ownership, the leasing out of land by landowners to share tenant farmers was an important source of employment for landless households. The sharp reduction in the incidence of share tenancy has been described as 'eviction' by a number of observers. The main proximate causes of tenant eviction have been noted as the increasing use of tractors, as well as other technological changes in agriculture.[16] Whether the 'green revolution' was indeed responsible for eviction or not is a complex issue. It is not disputed, however, that agricultural growth in the 1960s did coincide with the large-scale removal of the landless from direct production. The perception of growing inequality and relative poverty was responsible for a great deal of popular discontent in parts of rural Punjab.[17]

Questions concerning poverty, income inequality, and other forms of economic disparities between regions, sectors, and classes assumed a great deal of political importance and played a significant part in the downfall of the government and its development model. Many of these questions are hypotheses that could, in principle, be tested empirically. Standard poverty and inequality analyses could also be used to sort out other relevant questions such as urban-rural disparities, regional poverty indices, and inequality trends.

Household budget survey data, notably the *Household Income and Expenditure Surveys* (HIES) from the 1960s, have indeed, been used to make assessments of changes in poverty and inequality over this period.[18] These results do not show evidence of a rise in inequality, contrary both to popular perception as well as to the implications of the development model being used. The HIES data from the 1960s, however, do indicate that poverty remained fairly stagnant.[19] There is a problem, however, in the interpretation of both the inequality and the poverty indices calculated on the basis of grouped published data. As discussed in greater detail in section 3D, these data group the sample by total household income categories. By not controlling for the size and the composition of households, the rankings obtained are very different from rankings that are used in standard poverty or inequality analyses.[20]

There are wage data series that can be used to shed some light on poverty trends. Here too, the evidence is inconclusive. Naseem (1977) reports two separate studies based on different surveys from the period, with contradictory results. His overall conclusion is that real wages in agriculture either declined or stagnated during the 1960s. Khan (1972) finds that real wages also declined in industry during this period. His estimates are based on published secondary data on nominal wages and prices. A recent study by Chaudhry and Chaudhry (1992) finds, however, that real wages in agriculture increased by around 5 per cent per year during this period.[21]

While the balance of the empirical evidence appears to be in line with popular opinion, that the 'development decade' of the 1960s delivered high growth at the expense of rising inequality and stagnant or even rising poverty, the evidence is far from conclusive. The perception of growing inequality, or perhaps more accurately, a growing sense of economic injustice, did nevertheless, play an important part in the political destabilization of the regime.

C. Populism and State Control

In 1971, Pakistan emerged from its multiple crises of political legitimacy, regional imbalances, and class disaffection with its first-ever elected civilian government in power, elected provincial governments, but with the loss of its largest province, East Pakistan. The transition from military rule to elected civilian government in the early 1970s can be regarded, with the benefit of hindsight, to have been an important watershed. Pakistan's first experiment with electoral representation at the national and provincial levels gave rise to, modified, or revived, institutions that continue to define the parameters of the political process. This might appear paradoxical, given that the elected government at the centre proceeded to dismiss elected provincial governments in two of the four provinces, and was then itself overthrown in a military coup merely four years after a constitution was promulgated in 1973. The 1973 Constitution and the institutions that it enshrines (including fundamental rights, universal adult franchise, representation at the national and provincial levels, and party-based politics) have remained the reference points for political and judicial development ever since. This is despite the fact the constitution and its institutions have frequently fallen prey to the ambitions of military rulers and civilian autocrats.

The political change in the early 1970s also signalled the arrival of overtly populist tendencies in Pakistan's economic governance. This was in large measure a reaction to the development strategies of the 1960s which almost made a virtue of their indifference to economic inequalities.[22] It is, of course, arguable whether the economic policies pursued in the 1960s were truly anti-egalitarian or whether the perception of social and economic injustice was more powerful than the reality. Similarly, it might be argued that the populism of the 1970s was less egalitarian than its public perception. These are empirical issues, and although we have some evidence on these matters, it falls far short of anything conclusive.

There are a number of ways, nevertheless, in which the populism of the early 1970s might have translated into actual redistribution in varying degrees. The most dramatic of these was an attack on sections of the small but wealthy industrial and financial elites. A large number of industrial and financial firms were taken over by the state in a wide-ranging programme of nationalization. The industrial-financial elite had come to be regarded as the main beneficiary of the 1960s regime and was the prime target of popular opposition to the military government of the time. In a related move, trade unions became a lot more powerful than they had been in the past. The large-scale takeover of private enterprises by the state implied a huge increase in the number of workers with secure employment and with access to union membership. In addition, new legislation on employment and industrial management enhanced the position of unions *vis-à-vis* employers at the work place.

In agriculture, there was another attempt at land reforms in 1972. The reforms of 1972, like the ones of 1959, have been dismissed as consisting mainly of cosmetic measures.[23] This perception is a fairly accurate one, judging by a number of criteria that might be used in assessing the effectiveness of such reform. In a country with a relatively high availability of land area, it is anomalous indeed, to find that a majority of rural households do not own any cultivable area. Neither the land reforms of 1959, nor those of 1972 were aimed at tackling the problem of landlessness. Likewise, while these reforms did lead to the breakup of some extremely large holdings, they did not fundamentally undermine the position of large landlords. Even the legally permitted ceilings (300 acres per person in 1959, and 150 acres in 1972 for irrigated land) allow landed families to retain relatively large holdings quite legally by division of the title deed and its transfer to family members.

Although the land reforms in Pakistan did not bring dramatic changes to agrarian relations, there is a sense in which the 1970s reforms improved the condition of a large number of the poorest in the rural areas of Punjab. The reforms included a scheme for the allotment of government land for residential plots to landless families. State land was made available for transfer to the landless.[24] This aspect of the land reform is well-known to administrators, lawyers and indeed, to the beneficiaries, but has not figured prominently in academic discussions of the 1970s land reforms. This is all the more surprising, given that the total number of beneficiary households of these residential plot schemes was more than double the number of beneficiaries of all other land reforms put together.[25]

The scheme for the allotment of residential property came at a time when landless tenants had already begun to be evicted in large numbers as landowners undertook self-cultivation. Quite often, the residential quarters of landless tenants belonged to the landowner whose land they farmed. Acquisition of property rights over their own homes would have led to the further weakening in the relationship between erstwhile clients and their patrons. If one of the conditions for a family's residence on the patron's land was that the members of the family provide labour to the patron, the acquisition of property rights are likely to have had some effect on the functioning of the rural labour market as well as on the mobility of workers.

Besides economic populism and its possible effects on poverty and inequality, the 1970s also witnessed the opening up of a new set of economic opportunities for Pakistan which have arguably caused fundamental changes in the labour market and in income distribution. Although the oil price shocks of 1973 and 1974 were costly for Pakistan, as they were for other oil-importing developing countries, they also led to a huge demand for labour in the oil-rich economies of the Gulf to which Pakistani labour responded in large numbers. Attracted by higher wages, a large number of workers invested their savings, and indeed borrowed, in order to ensure a place in this new and lucrative job market. The macroeconomic impact of this labour migration could be seen later in the early 1980s when workers' remittances became the largest single source of foreign exchange earnings for Pakistan.[26]

D. POLITICAL REPRESSION AND ECONOMIC LIBERALISM

The economic populism of the 1970s came to an abrupt end in 1977 when, following allegations of vote-rigging, the government was overthrown in a military coup. The change of government, and the imposition of a military regime, which was manifestly hostile to the erstwhile regime, marked a dramatic shift in the political environment.

There followed a period of severe political repression which resulted in a crackdown not only on overt political activity, but also on other forms of mobilization and organization, such as trades unions. Agrarian reforms, including further land redistribution and income tax on agricultural earnings proposed in the final months of the last regime, were shelved. The left-wing rhetoric of the previous civilian government was replaced by extremely conservative (even oppressive) social dictates along with liberal and pro-market expressions in the economic sphere. The military regime also entered into structural adjustment arrangements with the IMF, and undertook a number of measures such as limited privatization, devaluation, and loosening of exchange rate controls that were widely interpreted as commitment to market-orientation. A number of influential commentators have continued to regard this period as marking the shift from populist interventionism to economic liberalism (World Bank, 1995; Burki, 1992, 1993).

On the face of it, there was much to cheer the adherents of economic liberalism in Pakistan. The 1980s certainly did witness relatively rapid rates of economic growth, a steady diversification away from the agricultural sector, and rising standards of living for many. Real GDP grew at an average annual rate of 6.5 per cent through the 1980s compared to 4.8 per cent in the 1970s and 6.8 per cent in the 1960s. Compared to the 1970s, manufacturing output increased more than one and a half times as fast, and the rate of agricultural production more than doubled (*Economic Survey 1996–7*, Government of Pakistan, 1997).

It is tempting to interpret the growth in the 1980s as a continuation of the earlier experience of 'pro-market' growth in the 1960s 'development decade', following an interlude of interventionist populism in the 1970s.[27] Before giving in to such temptation, however, it is useful to take a closer look at Pakistan's economy in the 1980s, since this period holds the key to an understanding of current development problems and opportunities. There are three factors, in particular, that need more careful consideration.

Firstly, the 1980s growth coincided with a number of extremely fortuitous circumstances for Pakistan's economy that can be regarded as positive external shocks, since they had little to do with domestic policy. The migration of Pakistani workers to neighbouring oil-rich countries that had started in the mid-1970s increased further. Workers' remittances became the largest single source of foreign exchange earnings and in 1982–3 they peaked at over one-tenth of GDP. Another set of fortuitous external circumstances was provided by the war in Afghanistan and the decision of the military regime to play a frontline role. Large financial flows from abroad followed in the form of economic and military aid.[28]

Secondly, although the regime appeared to take a favourable view of economic liberalism, and though a number of measures were taken along these lines, the actual record of economic management in the 1980s was much less consistent. Though the military government introduced tight fiscal and monetary policies at the outset, this regime was abandoned within about three years. Thereafter, until the end of military rule in 1988 and Pakistan's entry into a new arrangement with the IMF, a period of fairly unhindered profligacy was to follow (World Bank, 1995; p. 11). It is perhaps no coincidence that stringent fiscal and monetary control was exercised only in the brief period when the government's external resource position was uncertain and its need of IMF assistance urgent. In a similar vein, other potential targets on the economic liberalist's agenda (e.g. producer subsidies, public ownership, financial indiscipline in state-owned banks) were untouched.

A more appropriate interpretation of the economic programme of the military regime is that there was no programme other than short-term economic management and political expediency.[29] As the crisis in the late 1960s had demonstrated, in spite of their considerable powers of coercion, unrepresentative governments remain vulnerable to political opposition in Pakistan. The military regime in the 1980s was also, despite appearances, politically vulnerable. The dereliction of economic strategy in favour of short-term management had the appearance of *laissez-faire* in some instances. This point is conceded by some of the economic liberals. An influential voice among these (Burki, 1988) however, argues that whether by design or by default, the withdrawal of the state from economic intervention was good for the economy and good for poverty alleviation.

Finally, whether such withdrawal was favourable or not in the 1980s, it is worth asking if the development achieved in that period was sustainable. Since much of the growth was built upon favourable but transient external circumstances, any question about sustainability is clearly a question about the deployment of the windfall gains of that period. As far as the remittances from abroad are concerned, there is a view that these were ploughed back as private investment into productive activities in agriculture as well as small-scale manufacturing (Burki, 1988). If so, the impact on poverty alleviation is likely to have been significant. The sustainability of the 1980s model of economic management, with the ending of high levels of resource inflow, however, was far less assured. At the end of the period, the macroeconomic situation appeared to be approaching crisis point. Macroeconomic management, stabilization, structural adjustment, and economic reform have come to dominate economic policy since about 1988.

E. Crisis and Reform

Pakistan's fifth decade began with a macroeconomic crisis that brought the country's problems of economic management into sharp focus. There is a growing realization however, that economic crises cannot be understood in purely management terms, but must be seen in their political economy context. Fiscal imbalances for instance, are directly related to the large demands of non-development expenditures such as military spending on the public exchequer, and the military's claim on the economy is based at least partly, on its political power. Similarly, the government's ability to raise adequate tax revenues in order to meet its expenditure requirements is frustrated by the need to manage various powerful economic lobbies.

Another set of crises that has received wide acknowledgement in the fifth decade is the one related to the extremely poor development record of the country in terms of improving the well-being of the population. Particularly stark is the lack of progress in education and health indicators, despite reasonable progress towards the alleviation of income poverty. In both sets of development crises—i.e. macroeconomic imbalances and the slow progress of well-being indicators—the failure and inability of the state to take effective action have been highlighted as an important causal factor. A popular characterization of Pakistan's development problems in the fifth decade is in terms of a 'crisis of governance'.

Debate in the 1990s, therefore, needs to address much more fundamental issues than the discussions in the earlier decades.

In particular, the focus of the debate needs to shift away from the rather narrow confines of the structural adjustment paradigm, or even the 'state versus market' debate, and move into the direction of fundamental issues in the country's political economy on the one hand and towards a deeper understanding of existing economic institutions on the other. The issue, for instance, is not simply that there might be chronic fiscal imbalances, or that the schooling system fails to perform, but that such failures are systematic and are related to problems of political power. Likewise, the relevant question is not whether or not markets ought to play an important role in allocating resources, but that the functioning of markets as well as non-market economic institutions needs to be understood within the overall political and social context.

The post-1988 period has also witnessed the unprecedented direct involvement of international economic organizations in policy dialogue and policy making in Pakistan. The general direction of economic reforms proposed by international organizations is similar to such reforms elsewhere; the emphasis is on trade liberalization, market orientation, and budgetary cutbacks. The distributional and poverty implications of the economic reforms advocated by international organizations are widely thought to be adverse (*see* for example, Sayeed and Ghaus, 1996). This view is supported, on the face of it, by the economic and poverty trends since 1988 (as reported in section 3E). Simple trend analysis, however, is not sufficient to evaluate the impact of the economic reforms undertaken under various structural adjustment programmes. It can be argued for instance, that given the economic crisis in 1988, the absence of reform would have led to even more adverse outcomes.[30]

While the relationship between the slowdown in economic growth and in poverty decline, and the rise in inequality in the 1990s and the structural adjustment programmes is not conclusive, it is interesting to note that proponents of the reform programme have ended up using similarly inconclusive evidence to argue for a positive link between structural adjustment and poverty alleviation. The poverty assessment report of the World

Bank (1995) is a good example of this. This document argues that structural adjustment and market orientation in Pakistan have been associated with rapid growth and poverty declines. Contrary to the usual interpretation of the history of economic reforms, the World Bank (1995) dates the start of structural adjustment to political transition in 1977. It is argued that the growth and poverty reduction in the 1980s, was a consequence partly of the economic reforms initiated in the late 1970s and early 1980s, in the aftermath of the populist and interventionist programme of the early and mid-1970s.[31] Without factoring in the contribution of extremely favourable windfall gains in the 1980s, it is difficult to arrive at authoritative assessments of the poverty impact of any market orientation that did occur.[32]

Besides structural adjustment, another consequence of this outside intervention has been that a number of issues that are at the forefront of development thinking internationally have found their way into policy dialogue in Pakistan. It can be argued, for instance, that the unprecedented (and long overdue) attention to themes such as 'poverty alleviation' and 'human development' in policy dialogue is at least partly a reflection of the concerns of the international 'development community' (of which Pakistani professionals and activists are also a part).[33] Similarly, innovative approaches to poverty, such as participatory development, the building of community organizations, the focus on women's rights and welfare, and attention to environmental problems, have, arguably been made possible because of the entry of non-state actors into policy dialogue.[34] This entry of 'outsiders' has been facilitated to a great extent by non-state (largely foreign) sources of finance for development.

The increasing importance of non-state interventions in policy dialogue, as well as in active intervention, needs to be seen however, against the backdrop of the overall policy prescriptions of international organizations. The 'state versus non-state' dichotomy in the debate on social policy is a natural corollary of the 'state versus market' dichotomy in economic policy. The latter framework has been used extensively to diagnose problems, evaluate the performance of economic institutions, as well as to suggest directions of change. While such diagnoses, evaluations, and policy advice do go some distance in clarifying the understanding of various economic crises, they typically fall short of explaining the endemic nature of these crises. While it is useful to know about the distortionary effects of particular subsidies or controls, the political factors that underlie the government's inability to make necessary changes do not figure in this analysis.

Similarly, in the case of state versus non-state solutions to poverty-related problems, there is a danger that political constraints that need to be overcome tend to get glossed over. Corruption in the delivery of public services or in the implementation of poverty alleviation schemes, for example, cannot be viewed simply, or even primarily, as an issue of administrative capacity. If what appears to be corruption is, in fact, part of an established system of patron-client relations, a policy reform that focuses exclusively on methods of delivery (i.e. state versus non-state) without addressing questions of political power at the local level is most likely to miss the point. There is a need for a clearer understanding of how social and economic institutions (including markets) work at the local and national levels. This is a broad research agenda within which poverty analysis might be more fruitfully pursued. Some of these questions are taken up in a tentative way in section 4.

3. METHODOLOGY, MEASUREMENT, AND TRENDS

There is a wide range of questions relevant to an empirical understanding of poverty as measured in terms of private incomes or consumption: what is the proportion of the population that lives in poverty? Where are they located? What is their socio-economic position? How has the position changed over time? A standard approach to the analysis of income or consumption poverty is the use of sample survey data on household budgets and economic characteristics. In Pakistan, such data have been available sporadically in the past, and on a more regular basis since around the mid-1980s. Consequently, standard poverty measurement has been restricted to the years for which comparable data are available.

The first set of nationally representative sample surveys, which included information that could be used for distributional analysis, were carried out in 1960–61 and 1961–2 under the National Sample Survey. This series was renamed the *Household Income and Expenditure Survey* (HIES) in 1963–4, and these surveys were conducted on a fairly regular basis till the early 1970s. Surveys were carried out in 1963–4, and 1966–7, and then for each consecutive year till 1971–2. After this, there was a gap of eight years and the next survey was conducted in 1979. This was followed by another gap of five years and HIES resumed on an annual basis for three consecutive years between 1984–5 and 1987–8. In 1990–91, the series was renamed yet again, as the *Household Integrated Economic Survey* (conveniently retaining its old acronym HIES), and there have been surveys in 1990–91, 1992–3, 1995–6, and in 1996–7. The 1992–3 survey is available only in aggregated form.

One of the first of these data sets to be made available in its raw computerized format to researchers was the 1979 HIES. The analysis of poverty based on data-sets before this date relies on published aggregated data. The 1979 HIES was not widely available and required a great deal of time and effort in data cleaning. The HIES series from 1984–5 onwards has been more accessible to researchers. It is really since the ready availability of the HIES series of mid-1980s onwards that the current literature on poverty in Pakistan dates.

Detailed reviews of these earlier studies are available elsewhere.[35] Here these studies are revisited with a view to examining two specific issues. Firstly, the use of large data sets for distributional analysis raises a number of pertinent methodological issues. Many of the results that are widely available and commonly accepted as stylized facts of poverty in Pakistan might be vulnerable to apparently inconsequential variations in methodology. Secondly, our own analysis of two of the available data-sets (section 4) involves choices about methodological issues. A review of these issues and of the literature on this in Pakistan is a useful starting point in clarifying the possible methodological choices.

The importance of the precise methodology used in arriving at poverty estimates can be illustrated with the help of an example. Table 1 shows the different head-count ratios which various authors have obtained all using the same data set, the 1984–5 HIES.[36] The head-counts derived for Pakistan as a whole range from 8 per cent to 45 per cent. Urban-rural breakdowns of poverty ratios are similarly diverse. The head-count ratio for rural areas varies from 20 per cent to 36 per cent, and for urban areas from 19 per cent to 49 per cent.

Table 1
Head-count ratios
HIES 1984–5

			Pakistan	Rural	Urban
Ahmad & Ludlow (1989), individuals		low	8 (126)		
		high	31 (174)		
Havinga et al. (1989), adult equivalents		low	31 (171)	20 (144)	23 (208)
		high	45 (199)	36 (171)	49 (250)
Malik, M.H. (1988), households		low		24 (159)	19 (185)
		high		29 (172)	26 (207)

Source: Gazdar, Howes, and Zaidi (1994).
Notes: Head-count ratios are the percentage of individuals, adult equivalents, or households below the poverty line. The description of the poverty line (low or high) refers to its designation by the author concerned. Figures in parenthesis refer to poverty line rupees per capita per month.

The most obvious source of discrepancy in these results is the use of different poverty lines. There are also other sources of variation. The 'high' rural poverty line used by Havinga (1989), for example, is close to the 'high' rural poverty line used by Malik (1988)—171 and 172 rupees respectively. Even so, the two studies report obtaining very different head-count ratios. Closer scrutiny of their respective methodologies reveals that while Havinga was counting the number of 'adult equivalents', Malik was counting the number of households falling below the poverty line.

In fact, poverty analysis using household budget survey data requires decisions and choices regarding a large number of issues including those related to data-cleaning; unit of analysis (households, individuals, or as in the case of Havinga, 1989, 'adult equivalents'); method of adjustment for cost of living differences and changes; welfare indicator to be used (income, expenditure, or consumption); and the choice of poverty line. As the above example illustrates, these decisions have non-trivial consequences for the interpretation of results of poverty measurement exercises.

A. CONSTRUCTION OF POVERTY LINE

Most empirical work on poverty in Pakistan has been carried out with reference to a poverty line or a set of poverty lines. One of the most popular approaches has been to define poverty in terms of the ability of a household or individual to attain a certain level of calorie intake. It will be argued in this chapter that although 'fixing' a unique poverty line may have some merit in the political economy of public policy,[37] it is of limited use as an analytical construct, and does not add very much to the conduct of poverty analysis. A more eclectic approach that involves using a range of poverty lines and focuses on relative poverty rankings of different population groups can be more informative of the nature of income- and consumption-poverty. Such an approach is, indeed, pursued in the applied poverty analysis in this chapter (section 4). Arguments about the construction of poverty lines cannot be ignored entirely, however, since much of the applied work on poverty analysis in Pakistan has been concerned first and foremost with these issues (*see* Table 1, and Gazdar, Howes, and Zaidi, 1994a). Moreover, barring a few exceptions, all applied poverty analysis takes caloric standards as the starting point.

The basic idea behind caloric approaches is that the poverty line (in the income or consumption spaces) needs to be set with reference to minimum recommended standards of calorie intake. It is assumed that there is a stable functional relationship between income or consumption and calorie intake. The recommended caloric requirements for healthy living are derived from clinical nutritional tests under controlled conditions.[38] The poverty line is simply that level of income or total consumption expenditure which is consistent with achieving the recommended daily intake of calories. The popularity of the calorie-based approach rests on its apparent scientificity, and the ease of interpretation. Neither of these two suppositions, however, turn out to be durable under scrutiny.

While it is true that clinical nutritional tests lie behind the recommended calorie standards, on which poverty lines are then based, the interpretation of these norms as immutable basic requirements is open to question.[39] Nutritional tests are carried out for controlled groups of subjects and under controlled conditions of physical exertion. There is a great deal of inter-personal variation in calorie requirements, as well a great deal of variation in the calorie requirements of a person under different circumstances. The poverty line, however, is a summary benchmark indicator, and poverty analysis is usually carried out using data sources that are unable to provide detailed information about a person's precise physiological condition or quantify her normal level of physical exertion. The possibility of wide inter-personal and inter-temporal variations in minimum caloric requirements is further complicated by the fact that there is no consensus among poverty analysts on which caloric norm to use for constructing poverty lines. Operationally, the norms that have been used vary between 2,000 to 2,550 kcal per day—a range of over 20 per cent. Even the apparently simple task of assigning minimum calorie norms on the basis of physiological testing rests to a great extent on the exercise of choice and judgement on the part of the analyst.

The mapping of caloric norms onto household incomes or consumption presents another set of problems. The most common method in this regard is based upon the estimation of a calorie-expenditure function. The relationship between total income or expenditure and caloric intake is estimated statistically using household budget survey data, which typically include information on the quantities of various food items consumed.[40] The poverty line is then set as that income or expenditure level at which the expected calorie consumption (based on parameter estimates) is just equal to the recommended caloric norm. Recent users of this approach in Pakistan have been Ercelawn (1991) and Malik (1991, 1994). A variation on this approach was suggested by Lanjouw (1994) where the consumption patterns of the poorest groups were used rather than those of the entire sample as in Ercelawn (1991) and Malik (1991, 1994). The basic idea here is that the consumption patterns in the sample itself are used to determine the level of total expenditure which is consistent with achieving the caloric norms.

Calorie consumption depends, however, on a whole range of variables and not simply on household purchasing power. For any given level of income, for example, a household whose members are involved in relatively arduous physical labour is likely have a higher consumption of calories compared to a similar household whose members have relatively sedentary work or leisure activities. A poverty line which is based upon the statistical relationship between calorie consumption and household expenditure is a rough average over households made of individuals of very differing physiologies and with very different rates of expending energy. To interpret such a poverty line as marking off potentially well-nourished individuals from potentially malnourished ones would require extremely stringent and untenable assumptions about the distribution of these other attributes.

Even seemingly 'objective' ways of arriving at poverty lines, therefore, are fraught with a large number of 'subjective' choices and decisions such as: which caloric norm to use? Whether to set the poverty lines according to the consumption pattern of the entire sample or a subset of it? And, how precisely to map calories to expenditure or income?

As noted above, there are few exceptions to calorie-based approaches to the construction of poverty lines. These exceptions (including Gazdar, Howes, and Zaidi, 1994a and Ahmad, 1993) are based on the argument that the poverty line could be interpreted as a 'minimum' or 'basic' needs consumption bundle. The precise composition and value of the basic needs bundle depends on the specific economic and social context under consideration. One way of thinking about the poverty line is that it represents the minimum level of income or consumption below which a person ought to be regarded as socially disadvantaged.[41] Ahmad (1993) arrives at this minimal bundle on the basis of a consultative exercise involving not only policy makers but also members of the public. His results were used by Gazdar, Howes, and Zaidi, 1994a.

These approaches have been criticized on the grounds that they are arbitrary and 'subjective' (Ali, 1995). This criticism reveals some confusion about the status of methods such as consultative exercises and opinion surveys. The main difference between such methods and statistical methods that estimate parameters from survey data is that the latter are based upon revealed behaviour while the former are based on express evaluations of social states. Surveys that collect data on opinions about social states are neither more nor less subjective than those which collect data on actual consumption. They are, in fact, attempting to answer different questions.[42]

Any particular method for the derivation of a poverty line involves a number of choices and judgements that need to be made by the analyst or the policy maker. The quest of a 'pure' scientific or 'objective' poverty line, therefore, is likely to remain unfulfilled. Rather than expend further intellectual resources in this quest, it would be better if researchers chose from existing poverty lines in order to take analysis further, or worked with a range of poverty lines without worrying too much about their pedigree.

The contrast between poverty analysis in India and Pakistan is quite interesting in this regard. The original rural poverty line in India was, indeed, referenced around a daily intake of 2,100 calories per person, while the urban line was based originally on 1,900 calories per day. This was done for 1960–61 in an influential study by Dandekar and Rath (1971). The difference between the rural and urban caloric norms was explained in terms of the higher energy needs of the rural population due to their more physically exacting work and lifestyles, but no reasons were given for the precise difference of 200 calories per day between the two groups.[43] In the subsequent updating and adjustment of the Indian poverty line, however, the reference to calorie standards was dropped and standard price indices were used. Although the poverty line in use currently is based on one that was first estimated with calorific standards in mind, no attempt has been made to refer the subsequent updating of this poverty line to calorific standards.

While in India much of the discussion has revolved around the methodology for updating an agreed benchmark poverty line over time and for regions, rather than on defining that benchmark, in Pakistan, a great deal of work in the measurement of poverty deals with the specification of the benchmark.[44] The most likely explanation for the general acceptance in India of one benchmark poverty line and the lack of consensus on this issue in Pakistan is that in India the government officially endorsed the poverty line. In Pakistan, despite a number of attempts by various bodies, no official poverty line has yet been endorsed.

For purposes of research into poverty, as well as for policy matters, the precise origin of a poverty line does not really matter, since any poverty line would be based at least partly on normative criteria, and thus there is some measure of arbitrariness in its choice. What is important is not how the initial poverty line was specified in the first place, but the methods which are used for updating it over time, across regions, and for rural and urban areas. For such analysis, in fact, it is better to use not one but a set of poverty lines.

B. INTER-REGIONAL AND INTER-TEMPORAL ADJUSTMENTS

The issue of adjusting a benchmark poverty line for different regions and over time—even a poverty line that might have been chosen completely arbitrarily in the first place—is an important one. There is a case, of course, for updating the initial bundle from time to time in order to reflect long-term changes in the economy and in consumption patterns. The poverty line is, after all, to a great extent, socially constructed. In other words, the socially acceptable minimum standard of living can and does change as economic conditions change. Updating the poverty line for medium- to long-term changes in economic conditions, individual preferences, and social norms, however, is not the same as adjusting the poverty line to account for changes in the cost of living over time, or to account for differences in the cost of living between different regions.

If the poverty line is regarded as the value of a minimum bundle, the appropriate method for adjusting it for different regions and for different time periods is the same as the method for making such adjustments for any other value that is expressed in money terms—i.e., a price index. The main issue is to find the appropriate adjustment factors for differences in the cost of living (or the cost of acquiring that bundle), and applying these adjustment factors to the benchmark poverty line.

While there is a fair degree of agreement over this method, some practitioners, particularly those who have favoured calorie-based approaches to the construction of the poverty line, have taken a different route. Ercelawn (1991), for example, estimated separate calorie-expenditure functions for each province and, indeed, for cities, towns, and rural areas respectively within each province. Malik (1991, 1994) conducted a similar exercise with the rural sample, and simply used the poverty line thus obtained for the entire sample. This method requires a brief comment, because it is popular among some poverty analysts and because its use is premised on the unfounded presumption of scientific objectivity.

The problems with interpreting any calorie-based poverty line as marking off actual or potential malnourished households or individuals from the rest were discussed above. Using estimates of separate calorie-consumption functions in order to make regional and temporal adjustments to the benchmark poverty line is fraught with even greater difficulties. One serious problem has been encountered in the separate estimation of calorie-consumption functions in rural and urban areas, and the use of a unique caloric norm for the type of area. If the rural sample includes a much higher concentration of workers involved in physically demanding labour (as is, indeed, plausible) and if the rural lifestyle, in general, requires a greater consumption of calories than the urban lifestyle (due to the need to walk longer distances to fetch water, for example), then for any given level of income, the rural households are likely to consume more calories, on average, than their urban counterparts. Estimating the poverty line from a calorie-expenditure function using a unique caloric standard for the urban and rural sub-samples would have the effect of over-estimating the urban poverty line in comparison with the rural.[45]

One way around such estimation biases has been to designate different caloric standards for urban and rural areas.[46] It is not clear, however, as to what the precise difference between the caloric standards for urban and rural areas ought to be. Often the difference is based on a judgement on the part of the analyst in order to produce plausible rural and urban estimates of relative poverty. In the case of poverty line adjustments also, therefore, the calorific approach has the appearance of 'objectivity' while relying, ultimately, on reasonable but subjective judgement in order to arrive at results that are plausible.

C. Welfare Indicator: Income or Consumption?

Thus far, in the discussion of poverty lines and methods for making adjustments for regional and temporal variations, the indicator of welfare has not received attention. Income, expenditure and consumption have been mentioned interchangeably as possible welfare indicators. Household budget data do, typically, allow for choice between various definitions of income, expenditure and consumption.[47] Strictly speaking, however, choices need not be made. As has been argued above with respect to the choice of poverty line, analysis can and should be carried out with the use of alternative criteria. This is the approach taken throughout this chapter, particularly in section 4 where regional poverty rankings are analysed.

The implications of the choice of welfare indicator require attention for the sake of comparability with previous studies of poverty where choices of this nature have been made. There are, broadly speaking, two sets of choices that have been made in earlier work. Firstly, whether to use income or consumption as the relevant welfare indicator, and secondly, in the case of consumption, which heads of expenditure to include in ranking households for poverty analysis.

On the first issue, the preference in studies of poverty in Pakistan has been for consumption rather than income as the welfare indicator. This choice has been guided by a number of considerations. It has been argued, for example, that the real variable of interest is neither current income nor current consumption but some measure of permanent income, and since current consumption is more likely to reflect permanent income, it is considered preferable over current income which is more variable. In the event of a negative income shock, for example, households might be able to maintain their consumption levels in accordance with their realistic expectations about future flows of income by borrowing or by dissaving.[48] Another argument draws attention to the fact that in an economy like Pakistan's, where most of the economically active population are not on salaried remuneration but are either self-employed or work in family farms or other family businesses, the reporting of consumption expenditures is likely to be more reliable than that of incomes.

Further questions arise with respect to the precise definition of aggregate consumption. For many expenditure items (such as food and fuel), there is no doubt that they should count towards total consumption. But others are more controversial. For instance, should expenditure on taxes or on durable items be counted as part of consumption expenditure or not? The approach followed in the empirical analysis in section 4 falls in line with Gazdar, Howes, and Zaidi (1994a), in that taxes and durable items are excluded. In addition, housing expenditure is also excluded. This is done because a large proportion of rural households own their dwellings, and for these households, housing expenditure is imputed on the basis of a fairly thin sample.

D. Individuals, Households and Equivalence Scales

The final set of methodological issues discussed here refer to the unit of analysis and the method of obtaining rankings. There are, broadly speaking, two questions of interest here: who to count, and how to rank? On the first question of 'who to count', it can be stated from the outset that the relevant unit of interest is the individual and not the household or any other composite. This needs to be reiterated because a number of recent studies on Pakistan report their results in terms of the number or proportion of poor households (or even adult equivalents) rather than individuals in the population (Ercelawn, 1991; Malik, 1991, 1994; Kemal and Mahmood, 1997).

Since the basic unit of observation for many of the relevant variables in a household budget data-set is, indeed, the household, the main non-trivial issue is: what are the criteria that need to be used in order to rank households for the purposes of poverty analysis? The head-count ratio of poverty, for example, counts the number of individuals who reside in households whose income or consumption is below the poverty line. In order to do this, households need to be ranked by their income or consumption. Since households vary from one another not only in terms of their income or consumption, but also in terms of their size and composition, the precise ranking depends on the method by which household income or consumption are adjusted for size and composition. A common practice is to divide household income or consumption by the number of household members and rank households according to per capita income or expenditure.

Studies based on grouped aggregated data have relied on the rankings of households by income group published in tabular form.[49] Published tables for the HIES use household income rather than, say per capita income, for grouping households. This practice is not particularly helpful for the construction of poverty indices, and contrasts with the practice in other countries where published tables provide groupings on the basis of per capita income or expenditure.[50] Studies that rely on published income groupings in order to obtain household rankings fail to make any adjustment to household size or composition. A household with ten members and a per capita income of 1,000 rupees would appear in the same income class as a one-person household with an income of 10,000 rupees. The results of these studies ought, therefore, to be interpreted with caution since they do not correspond with any conventional method of ranking households for poverty analysis.[51]

A common way of accounting for differences in household demographics is to simply divide household income or consumption by the total number of household members (i.e. work in per capita terms). While this avoids some of the extreme distortions in ranking due to household size, it does not make any adjustment for household composition. Two households with the same total income or consumption and with the same number of members, for example, would be given equal welfare ranking, even if one of the households is dominated by adults and the other by children. The lower consumption requirements of children compared with adults are not taken into consideration. There is no agreement in the literature about the appropriate equivalence scales to be used in Pakistan. Some scales assign different weights to children of various ages, and to males and females. The scales used in this study have been used in some studies in the recent past, and have the virtue of being relatively simple. All persons aged eighteen or less are assigned a weight equivalent to 80 per cent of an adult. A household with two adults and three children under eighteen is counted as consisting of 4.4 adult equivalents.[52]

Finally, an issue that has received some attention in the analysis of household budget data is that of scale economies. It has been argued that there are scale economies to be realized in consumption or certain goods and services that are, in effect, public goods within the household (say, for example, a water connection). Furthermore, larger households might face lower per capita costs even for goods that are typically privately consumed goods (food, for example) because they might be able to obtain lower prices due to high volume purchases.[53]

E. Poverty Trends

The construction of poverty trends in Pakistan, using household budget data, has been dogged by problems of consistency in data series and estimation method. As pointed out in section 3D, the use of published aggregated data is problematic in the case of Pakistan since published data are ranked and grouped by total household income or expenditure rather than income or expenditure corrected for household size and composition. The poverty indices obtained from using such rankings cannot be interpreted in the same way as standard poverty indices.

For more recent years, however, it is possible to construct a series of poverty indices that is based on the analysis of raw data—or on household level observations. One of the first such attempts was made by Ahmad and Ludlow (1989). They assembled household budget data for three years (1976, 1979, and 1984–5) and applied a consistent method to arrive at poverty indicators. Two of the three data sets used belonged to the HIES series. Table 2 gives a summary of their results as well as an update for two more recent data sets (HIES, 1987–8, and PIHS, 1991). The Ahmad and Ludlow series was updated following their method: the authors arbitrarily selected four separate poverty lines (ranging from low to high), and updated these lines using the GDP deflator. For extending the series beyond 1984–5, the 'high' Ahmad and Ludlow poverty line was updated for 1987–8 and 1991 using the same method.

Table 2
Poverty trend, 1976–1991

Year (survey)	Rural	Urban
1976–7 (MNS)	0.41	0.38
1979 (HIES)	0.38	0.29
1984–5 (HIES)	0.31	0.25
1987–8 (HIES)	0.28	0.21
1991 (PIHS)	0.32	0.20

Sources: 1976–7 to 1984–5, from Ahmad and Ludlow (1989), 1987–8 and 1991 calculated by author using Ahmad and Ludlow's method.

While there are a number of unresolved methodological issues in the Ahmad and Ludlow approach, not least in their use of the GDP deflator for adjusting for changes in purchasing power, it is useful nevertheless to have a consistent series stretching back to the late 1970s. Table 2 indicates that according to the Ahmad and Ludlow series, the head-count ratio of poverty declined sharply through the 1980s for both urban and rural areas. The decline was the most dramatic between 1979 and 1984–5, and less so between 1984–5 and 1987–8. After 1987–8, the rural head-count ratio actually increased, and the urban head-count ratio declined only marginally.

Table 3 gives a different time series, based on a method with significant differences (Gazdar, Howes, and Zaidi, 1994a) from Ahmad and Ludlow.

Table 3
Poverty trends, 1984–85 to 1990–91

Year	Mean consumption	Gini	Head count	HC se	Poverty gap	Foster F=2
PAKISTAN						
1984–5	424.1	.284	46.0	0.5	.111	.038
1987–8	456.5	.270	37.4	0.5	0.77	.023
1990–91	484.9	.287	34.0	0.8	.071	.022
RURAL						
1984–5	399.1	.263	49.3	0.7	.119	.041
1987–8	424.1	.240	40.2	0.6	.083	.025
1990–91	456.4	.267	36.9	1.0	.078	.024
URBAN						
1984–5	486.0	.314	38.2	0.7	0.92	.031
1987–8	535.0	.316	30.7	0.7	.061	.018
1990–91	545.7	.316	28.0	1.2	.057	.017

Notes: HC se: standard error for the head-count ratio.
Foster F=2: Foster-Greer-Thorbeck distribution-sensitive poverty index.
From Gazdar, Howes, and Zaidi (1994) Tables 4.1 and 4.4, based on HIES data for 1984–5, 1987–8, and 1990–91. The poverty line used is Rs 342 per adult equivalent per month in 1991–2 prices. Mean consumption figures are in terms of per adult equivalent per month and are in terms of rural 1991–2 prices. All indices measure the number of individuals.

The main differences are in the position of the poverty line, in the use of equivalent scales when ranking households, in the precise definition of consumption used, and in the prices used for making inter-temporal adjustments. Furthermore, the difference in the GHZ approach between rural and urban poverty lines is based on estimates of actual purchasing power differences between the two types of areas.[54] In contrast with Table 2, the GHZ shows that poverty indices fell quite sharply between 1984–5 and 1987–8 and continued to fall between 1987–8 and 1990–91.[55] Table 3 does indicate, however, that poverty indices fell less sharply in the latter period than in the former. Table 4 gives the results for rural areas by province. Here too, the general pattern of sharp declines in poverty in the mid-1980s, followed by less prominent declines since the late 1980s is repeated for Sindh and the Punjab.

Table 4
Rural poverty (head-count ratio) by province
1984–5 to 1990–91

	1984–5	1987–8	1990–91
PAKISTAN	49.3	40.2	36.9
Punjab	50.4	42.1	38.5
Sindh	45.3	34.0	30.8
NWFP	46.2	38.3	40.6
Balochistan	55.4	44.6	20.9

Notes: From Table 4.5 of Gazdar, Howes, and Zaidi (1994a), based on HIES data-sets for successive years. The poverty line used for these estimates was 296 rupees per capital per month in 1990–91 rural prices.

While household budget data-sets are recognized as the standard method of constructing poverty trends, an important limitation is their infrequency. Wages provide another possible source of examining poverty trends. Households that rely on casual wage labour are disproportionately represented among the poorest (*see*, for example Gazdar, Howes, and Zaidi, 1994b). The casual wage rate, therefore, can be a useful summary index of the trend in the purchasing power of the poorest. Time series for wages of casual labourers in rural and urban areas are available for Pakistan since 1983 and 1976 respectively.

Figure 1 traces the daily wages of casual labourers in the two types of areas using two alternative price deflators: the general consumer price index and the food price index.[56] The actual adjustment factor is likely to lie between the two indices. Since casual labourer households are among the poorest section of the population, they are likely to spend a relatively higher proportion of their income on food than the average household. Since food prices have risen somewhat faster than the general price index, a CPI-adjusted wage is likely to over-estimate wage increases.

Figure 1 indicates that urban real wages rose sharply in the mid-1970s, then declined until around 1984. They started rising again in the mid-1980s and continued to rise till around 1989. Between 1989 and 1994 they were on a downward trend, and then they began to rise again. Rural wages experienced a steady but not spectacular rise through the 1980s. In 1994 they were not much higher than they had been when the series began in 1983. In Figure 2, real wage indices are traced alongside the index of GNP per capita. It is interesting to note that although GNP per capita grew throughout, the period of its most rapid growth (early 1980s) coincided with a downward trend in real urban wages.

Wage data appear to confirm the general picture emerging from the household budget data-sets that the early 1990s were a period of less rapid decline (or indeed, increase) in poverty, though in the mid-1990s wages did appear to stage a reversal.[57] It is quite likely that real wages declined in 1997 due to sharp rises in the prices of staple food items.

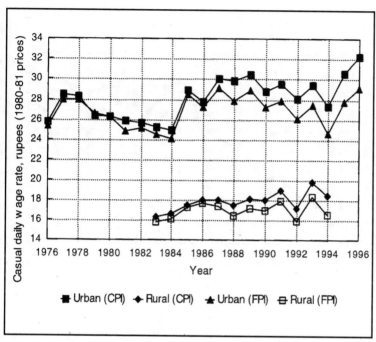

Figure 1: Real daily wage rates for casual labourers, urban and rural.

Notes: Wage rates deflated using general consumer price index (CPI) and food price index (FPI) respectively.

Sources: Calculated by author using *Economic Survey* 1996–97 for urban wages and CPI and FPI, and *Monthly Statistical Bulletin* (various) for rural wages.

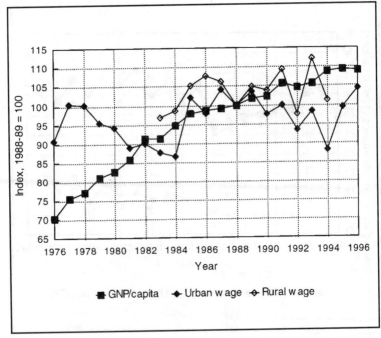

Figure 2: Trends in GNP per capita, urban and rural wages.

Notes: GNP per capita deflated using the GDP deflator, wage rates deflated using the
           food price index (FPI).

Sources: Calculated by author using *Economic Survey* 1996–97 for GNP per capita,
           urban wages, GDP deflator and FPI, and *Monthly Statistical Bulletin* (various)
           for rural wages.

4. REGIONAL RANKINGS OF RURAL POVERTY: THE INDUS BASIN

As thinking on economic development moves beyond the confines of the state-versus-market debate, the need for constructing a better understanding of institutional arrangements and changes in these arrangements is manifest. This need is nowhere more profound than in the analysis of poverty. Beyond the use of consistent methods for the identification of the poor through the distribution of income or consumption, poverty analysis is, after all, about understanding the processes behind the numbers.

The rural economy, in particular, has undergone a number of important changes over the past few decades not only in terms of technology of production but also in terms of the arrangements that govern economic relations between agents. Anti-poverty interventions are also based upon explicit or implicit ideas about the nature of economic and social institutions and their impact on poverty. One particular model of intervention, for example, is that of setting up credit and saving schemes. The case for such schemes as part of an anti-poverty strategy is based upon the premise that a credit constraint is an important cause of poverty. The analysis of poverty, therefore, needs to be placed within the context of such institutional (and technological) factors.

It is also possible to shed some light on larger themes and theses on poverty alleviation. For example, it is widely held that improvement in agricultural technology holds the key to poverty decline in rural areas. The experience of the 'green revolution' with high rates of farm mechanization, however, does not indicate a clear-cut relationship. Changes in land tenure patterns ensured that the landless poor did not participate directly in the benefits from technological advancement. It is worth asking if the areas that experienced the 'green revolution' did indeed end up with lower levels of poverty. Similarly, labour migration and workers' remittances have been thought to have had a decisive impact on poverty. The distribution of remittance payments from migrant workers can reveal something about both the impact of remittances on poverty as well as on the further prospects of remittances and labour migration playing a poverty-reducing role.

It is surprising, therefore, that in much of the empirical literature on poverty analysis in Pakistan, the focus is primarily (and often exclusively) on issues of measurement and the estimation of poverty indices. There are some notable exceptions, but these too, have not sought to address some of the concerns that have been raised widely about the relationship between economic growth, institutional persistence and change, and poverty. A number of studies have attempted analyses of these and other issues with the help of poverty profiles.[58] There are also some studies on the decomposition of income inequality using panel data from households in several districts (*see* Adams and Alderman, 1992, and Adams and He, 1995). None of these studies, however, have attempted to relate their findings to regional variations in institutional arrangements.

This section suggests lines of enquiry into rural economic and social institutions on the basis of the analysis of regional rankings of rural poverty obtained from representative household budget data. It is argued here that it is possible to account for variations in institutional arrangements governing key social and economic relationships by disaggregating the sample by region. Prior criteria, such as the history of agrarian institutions, the prevalence of landlordism, the potential for technological change, and patterns of labour market behaviour are used to make these disaggregations. Regional poverty rankings using variations of poverty indicators, poverty lines, and equivalence scales are constructed. These are interpreted in the light of prior information on the functioning of various rural markets as well as institutional arrangements that prevail in the various regions.

A. NOTE ON THE DATA

Two sources of household budget data are used in this chapter. The first is the *Household Income and Expenditure Survey* of 1987–8, and the second is the *Pakistan Integrated Household*

Survey of 1991. Both these data-sets are somewhat dated, particularly the HIES 1987–8. There have been a number of other national surveys since 1991 that can provide information about household composition, consumption, and income. The HIES series was renamed (*Household Integrated Economic Survey*) and has been updated in 1992–3 and 1995–6. Neither of the two latter instalments was available to the author in the raw data form at the time of writing. The PIHS has also been updated recently in 1995–6 and 1996–7. This most recent survey, too, was not available in a usable form at the time of writing.

Although the data sets used here are somewhat dated, this section is not primarily concerned with providing a detailed up-to-date poverty profile. The objectives here are more modest. Firstly, there is a methodological point. This is to check the robustness of regional poverty rankings to alternative and reasonable variations in poverty line, equivalence scale, and welfare indicator. Secondly, these rankings will be used in conjunction with other contemporaneous information on issues such as agricultural productivity, land tenure patterns, and the structure of the labour and credit markets, to say something about the relationship between social and economic institutions and poverty. Although these observations are, strictly speaking, based on the conditions that prevailed in the late 1980s, it is hoped that they will tell us something about these relationship after that period also.

Pakistan Household Integrated Survey (PIHS) was conducted in 1991 by the Federal Bureau of Statistics, Islamabad (FBS) and the Population and Human Resources Department of the World Bank. Based on a stratified national sample of over 4,500 households (of which around half were in rural areas), this survey collected data on the economic, demographic, and other characteristics of the sample households. While national household budget surveys have been available for quite some time in Pakistan—the main series being the FBS *Household Income and Expenditure Surveys* (HIES) most of which have been based, in fact, on much larger samples than the PIHS—the latter provides much greater detail on characteristics of household members, such as their employment and level of education, and on the ownership of economic assets. The HIES of 1987–8, by contrast, contains extremely detailed questions about household expenditure and consumption, less detailed but nevertheless useful information on income, but little else. The sample size, however, is around four times as large as the PIHS (over 18,000 households), and the rural sample numbers nearly 10,000 households. In interpreting the results presented below, it ought to be borne in mind that while the PIHS, due to its greater detail, might have better quality data as well as greater richness of detail in terms of the information available for households and their individual members, the HIES possesses some advantage in statistical representation, particularly at the regionally disaggregated level.

1. Sample Biases

One common complaint about large sample surveys is that they tend to underestimate inequality in the distribution due to sample selection bias. Both the upper and the lower tails of the distribution tend to be poorly captured in these surveys. There are straightforward institutional reasons for the lack of representation of the poorest. The sample is, after all, a sample of <u>settled households</u>. It purposely excludes some of the poorest, such as the homeless or nomadic people. At the other extreme, most such surveys also tend to under-represent the wealthiest households due to various sampling and non-sampling constraints.

Since the aim of the present exercise is to compare poverty and inequality across regions, the presence of sample biases that lead to underestimates of inequality is not of critical importance if this bias affects estimates for all regions in the same way. On the other hand, if there are regional biases in the sample, these can affect the validity of the results.

One way of checking for regional sample biases is to compare the regional profiles of indicators that are known to be highly correlated with income or consumption, and for which information is available from independent enumerations.

Comparison with census-based data, for example, can be informative.

Table 5 presents three sets of comparisons: literacy rate for females, literacy rate for males, and the incidence of land ownership. Since the surveys and the censuses are separated by a number of years, and because there might be differences in the precise definitions used and the way data are collected, it is quite reasonable to expect the percentages to vary. Regional rankings, however, are likely to be more robust to such variations.

Table 5
Sample cross-checks on HIES 1987–8 and PIHS 1991

	Upper Punjab	Middle Punjab	Lower Punjab	Sindh
Literacy rates (10+)				
Female Census 1981	13.5	10.4	6.4	5.2
HIES 1987–8	19.1	13.5	9.2	4.4
PIHS 1991	16.0	16.7	11.4	9.0
Male Census 1981	40.9	30.4	24.1	24.7
HIES 1987–8	55.7	40.6	38.2	43.7
PIHS 1991	57.1	46.4	32.5	44.9
Proportion of land–owning rural households				
Agricultural Census 1980	73.3	50.2	57.7	41.1
PIHS 1991	59.1	43.6	47.3	32.3

Source: Calculated by author from relevant sources.

The rankings obtained for female literacy between regions are quite similar for the census and the surveys. For male literacy, however, the 1987–8 HIES sample shows a better ranking for Sindh, and the 1991 PIHS sample again shows Sindh to be closer to the Middle Punjab literacy rate. In terms of land ownership, the regional rankings in the PIHS correspond exactly to those obtained using the agricultural census. Overall, the evidence for regional sample bias is not conclusive—of the three indicators, two give consistent rankings for census and survey data.

B. Agrarian Regions

Very few of the studies on poverty in Pakistan have paid attention to the regional dimension. Although some studies do report poverty indicators by province, they rarely go beyond simply describing the data.[59] This is a major shortcoming, since region is a crucial variable for both policy as well as wider political considerations. At an extremely simplistic level, the targeting of anti-poverty interventions would certainly require prior information about the regional distribution of the poor. Even in the allocation of other public resources, such as investment in infrastructure, a regional profile of poverty is likely to be an invaluable guide to the planner. On a wider political level also, regional disparities in income, or at least the perception of regional differences in poverty, have been potent factors for mobilization.[60]

There is another sense in which a regional analysis of rural poverty can be extremely insightful in Pakistan. Regions represent important variations not only in their resource endowments and infrastructure, but also in their distribution of resources, patterns of land tenure, class structure, and local power configurations (see, for example, Alavi, 1976). These institutional differences might themselves be partly due to differences in resource endowments, but are also due, at least partly, to other historical factors.

In this section, regional variations in two of the main agrarian provinces, viz. Punjab and Sindh, which together comprise over three-quarters of Pakistan's rural population, are considered. In operational terms, Punjab can be sub-divided into upper Punjab (Rawalpindi division, plus the district of Mianwali from Sargodha division), lower Punjab (comprising Multan, Bahawalpur, and Dera Ghazi Khan divisions), and middle Punjab (the rest, including Lahore, Gujranwala, and Sargodha divisions, minus Mianwali).[61] Sindh is treated as one region. The case for going down to lower levels of aggregation (say, districts) is strong on the grounds of institutional analysis, but weaker on those of statistical representation.

The use of administrative boundaries for the purposes of socio-economic disaggregation is not, of course, the best way to proceed. There are certain advantages in doing so, which do possibly mitigate the disadvantages. There is a geographical basis for focusing on regional variations within Punjab and Sindh. The areas comprising the two provinces closely approximate the Indus basin. This geographical unity of the Indus basin has been further enhanced by an integrated system of canal irrigation (Lieftinck et al., 1968). The Indus basin also represents a degree of cultural and linguistic continuity (Ahsan, 1997).

There are also important and interesting contrasts within the Indus basin that can provide useful variations in the analysis of poverty and local institutions. Punjab, which can be subdivided into another three zones, is in general considered to be more advanced in terms of the transition from pre-capitalist to capitalist agriculture than Sindh, where semi-feudal relations continue to prevail. Within Punjab, the northern districts of the Potohar plateau and surrounding highlands can be contrasted with the rest of the province in their agronomy. While these areas in upper Punjab rely mainly on *barani* rain-fed agriculture, the rest of the province is served by canal irrigation and tubewells. The 'canal-colony' areas can be further subdivided between middle and lower Punjab, with the latter having a higher concentration of land ownership, and a stronger political presence of powerful landowners. In this regard, lower Punjab shares some features of the agrarian economy of Sindh where rural economic and political life is dominated by large landlords.

For the remainder of this section, most of the results are presented for these four regions. Some of the salient features of economic and social development in the four regions are presented in Table 6.

Table 6
Agrarian regions in Indus basin:
selected indicators

	Upper Punjab	Middle Punjab	Lower Punjab	Sindh
Rural population 1981 Per cent of Pakistan's rural population	10.0	23.1	23.7	17.9
Agriculture Irrigated area as per cent of total cultivated area	30.0	84.3	91.4	79.8
Agricultural land area per rural person (acres per person), 1981 total cultivated	0.898	0.667	0.813	0.725
Irrigated equivalent	0.570	0.614	0.778	0.652
Proportion of rural households which own agricultural land, 1980 (per cent)	73.3	50.2	57.7	41.1
Proportion of cropped area in ownership of holdings > 150 acres (per cent)	14.4	8.6	15.2	22.2
Yield (tonnes/hectare) wheat, 1986.	1.32	2.04	2.11	2.11
Economic structure Per cent of rural workforce (1981) Agriculture Formal sector employment Other non-agriculture	54.1 22.8 23.2	51.6 18.1 30.4	64.2 15.1 20.8	74.1 15.0 11.0
Rural literacy rates (per cent) 1981 (age 10+) Total Male Female	27.3 40.9 13.5	21.0 30.4 10.4	15.9 24.1 6.4	15.6 24.7 5.2

Sources: Author's calculations based upon: *Population Census 1981* for population shares,
workforce, and literacy rates; *Agricultural Census 1980* for cultivated area, irrigated
area, land ownership, and land concentration; *National Commission on Agriculture
(1986)* for yield of wheat.

Upper Punjab is relatively poorly endowed with agricultural land. Although the cultivated area per person was the highest, little of it was irrigated. In terms of irrigated equivalent (counting each non-irrigated hectare as being equivalent to half an irrigated hectare), upper Punjab had the lowest land availability per person. It was also the region with the lowest yield per hectare for wheat. A relatively higher proportion of the workforce, however, was in non-agricultural activities, particularly in the formal sector. A high proportion of households owned some land, and literacy rates were relatively high.

Of all the regions, middle Punjab had the lowest proportion of its workforce in agriculture. Landlessness was relatively high, and certainly higher than in upper Punjab, but landlordism, as measured by the concentration of land ownership, was the least conspicuous of all the regions. Somewhat surprisingly, considering that middle Punjab is often thought of as the most progressive agricultural region, the yield of wheat in 1986 was lower than the yields obtained in lower Punjab and in Sindh.

Lower Punjab appears to have been located not only geographically, but in terms of land distribution and non-agricultural development, between middle Punjab and Sindh. Although landlessness was less severe than it was in middle Punjab, the concentration of ownership holdings was much higher. The proportion of the workforce in agriculture was higher than in either upper and middle Punjab, but lower than in Sindh.

The adult literacy rates in these sub-regions of the Indus basin were uniformly low, but the contrasts are noteworthy all the same. Upper Punjab had the highest rates of literacy, followed by middle Punjab, and lower Punjab and Sindh were at the bottom.

C. POVERTY RANKINGS

1. Mean and Distribution
The regional poverty rankings presented here are based on the HIES 1987–8 and PIHS 1991 data-sets. Table 7 gives mean income and consumption expenditure in each region for the two surveys.

Table 7
Income and consumption mean and distribution

	Upper Punjab	Middle Punjab	Lower Punjab	Sindh
HIEs 1987–8				
Income				
Mean Rs	4128	4568	3502	3403
Gini co-efficient	0.178	0.269	0.261	0.159
Consumption expenditure				
Mean Rs	3410	3589	2902	3132
Gini co-efficient	0.156	0.210	0.189	0.141
PIHS 1991				
Income				
Mean Rs	6575	7496	5661	5536
Gini co-efficient	0.425	0.565	0.531	0.446
Consumption				
Mean Rs	5588	5002	3682	4944
Gini co-efficient	0.148	0.235	0.234	0.205

Sources: HIES 1987–8 and PIHS 1991, calculated by author.
Note: Income and consumption expenditure are in annual per adult equivalent.

Both the variables are calculated in per adult equivalent terms, using the simple rule that each child aged eighteen or under is given the weight of 0.8 of an adult. The household's total income is divided by the total number of equivalent adults. The income variable includes all household income from wages, salaries, profits, and transfers, as well as the value of self-consumption of goods produced within the household. The consumption variable includes expenditure on all consumption items (non-durable) except for housing expenditure. The reason for the omission of housing expenditure is that the vast majority of the households in the two surveys own their dwellings. The reported value of imputed rent for the use of owned dwellings is not likely to be reliable, given that in many localities the rental market is not very active.

In terms of mean income and expenditure, middle Punjab was unambiguously the wealthiest region in 1987–8. It was also the region with the greatest inequality in both income and consumption in that year. In 1991 also, in terms of mean income, middle Punjab came out as the most well-off region. Its position in terms of consumption, however, was overtaken by upper

Punjab in that year. Sindh was the poorest region in terms of mean income in both years, but in each year its mean consumption was higher (in 1991 considerably higher) than lower Punjab. It was also the region, interestingly, with the lowest Gini co-efficients, both for income and consumption, in 1988–7 and the second lowest in 1991. Middle and lower Punjab samples showed, in general, greater inequality than upper Punjab and Sindh.

2. Relative Poverty Rankings

How these rankings in terms of mean income and consumption and in terms of overall distribution work out in terms of poverty indices is explored here with the help of dominance graphs. Instead of estimating head-count ratios and other poverty indices for the various regions with reference to any particular poverty line, the strategy adopted here is to construct these rankings for a range of possible poverty lines. The analysis of regional poverty rankings with reference to a range of poverty lines is useful for a number of reasons. Firstly, as discussed in section 3A, poverty lines are, by construction, somewhat arbitrary. Instead of relying on a unique poverty line, therefore, it makes more sense to conduct the analysis with respect to a number of possible poverty lines. Secondly, it is useful to know about poverty regional rankings and switches in regional ranks for different levels of poverty line.

A range of nine poverty lines ranging from very low (i.e. extreme poverty) to relatively high (i.e. moderate poverty) were chosen for this analysis. These were arrived at using the following method: taking the entire rural sample as a whole and then, the level of income or consumption that would have yielded national rural head-count ratios at 5 per cent intervals between 5 and 45 per cent were estimated. These nine poverty lines were then applied to the regional sub-samples in order to determine the regional rural head-count ratio for nine different levels of poverty. Figures 3 to 10 present the results of this exercise. Figure 3, for example, gives the head-count ratio for the four regions plotted on the y-axis, with the national rural head-count ratio on the x-axis. It shows, for example, that the poverty line at which the national rural head-count ratio was 20 per cent, the head-count ratio was around 11 per cent in upper Punjab, around 16 per cent in both middle Punjab and Sindh, and around 32 per cent in lower Punjab.

The figures above can be interpreted as dominance curves. If, for example, the curve for region A lies unambiguously below that of region B, it implies that region A had a lower head-count ratio of rural poverty than region B over the entire range of poverty lines. In Figure 3, for example, which presents the results for 1987–8 using income per adult equivalent as the welfare indicator, the curve for lower Punjab lies unambiguously above that for upper Punjab for the entire range. This means that lower Punjab had a higher headcount ratio than upper Punjab for a wide range of poverty lines, and their relative rankings are robust to the choice of poverty line. The same is not true in Figure 3 for the rankings of middle Punjab and Sindh. The curves for these two regions cross at the point where the national rural headcount ratio is 20 per cent. Below this poverty line, Sindh has a lower headcount ratio than middle Punjab, and above this line the rankings are reversed. In other words, for a relatively high poverty line, Sindh has a higher incidence of poverty compared to middle Punjab, whereas if concern was focused only on extreme deprivation, the proportion of the population in Sindh that is poor would be lower.

A similar analysis has been carried out with reference to consumption expenditure instead of income in Figure 4.

Here too, the rankings of lower Punjab and upper Punjab are unambiguous. Lower Punjab is consistently the poorest region, no matter what the poverty line, and upper Punjab comes across as the region with the lowest headcount ratio for the entire range. Sindh and middle Punjab switch ranks in this case too, but here the rank switch occurs at a higher poverty line than in the case of income poverty. Sindh turns out to be less poor than middle Punjab for all poverty lines up to the point where the national rural headcount ratio is around 37 per cent. For poverty lines higher than this, it has a higher headcount ratio than middle Punjab.

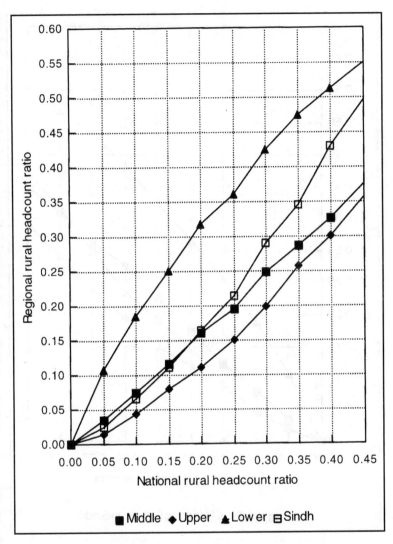

Figure 3: Regional poverty rankings, 1987–88. Income per adult equivalent, no scale economies.

Source: Calculated by author using HIES 1987–88.

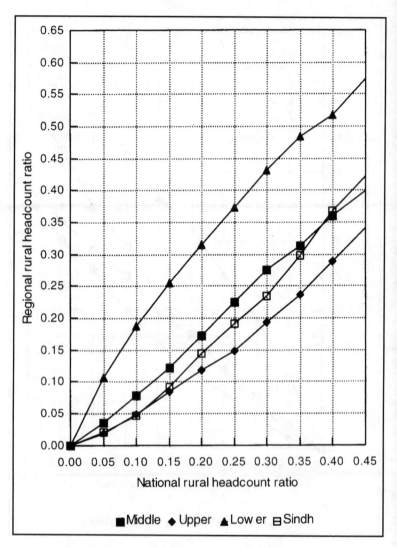

Figure 4: Regional poverty rankings, 1987–88, consumption expenditure per adult equivalent, no scale economies.

Source: Calculated by author using HIES 1987–88.

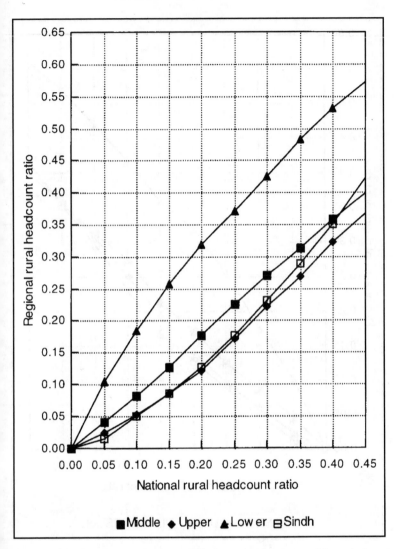

Figure 5: Regional poverty rankings, 1987–88, consumption per adult equivalent, moderate scale economies.

Source: Calculated by author using HIES 1987–88.

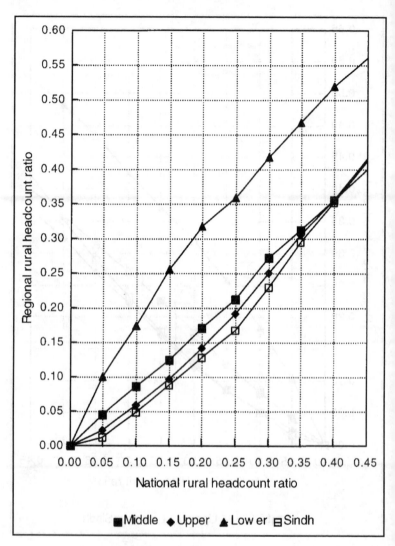

Figure 6: Regional poverty rankings, 1987–88, consumption per adult equivalent, high scale economies.

Source: Calculated by author using HIES 1987–88.

In Figures 5 and 6, headcount ratios are plotted with reference to consumption expenditure that is adjusted not only for adult equivalence, but also to allow for effects of scale economies. Larger households might benefit from economies of scale due to a number of factors. For example, the fuel costs of lighting a space or cooking a meal are likely not to rise linearly as the number of household members increase. It is also possible that a larger household allows for bulk purchasing of certain consumption items at lower per unit cost. In addition to adjusting total household consumption expenditure to household composition, therefore, it is useful to repeat the analysis for different assumptions about scale economies. Regional rankings might be affected by different assumptions concerning scale effects as there might be different social and economic constraints to household formation and size in different regions.

In the case of the regional sub-samples of the HIES 1987–8, the main impact of allowing the scale effects to vary is to alter the position of Sindh in the regional rankings. If moderate scale effects are assumed, Sindh comes across as less poor than middle Punjab for almost the entire range of poverty lines for which estimates have been obtained. If scale effects are assumed to be high, its rank improves further, and Sindh appears as the region with the lowest headcount ratio, lower even than upper Punjab, for nearly the entire range of poverty lines.

The same analysis was carried out using the PIHS 1991 and the results are reported in Figures 7 to 10.

No comparison is being made here in the level poverty estimates obtained from the two survey years. The only point at issue is the relative ranking of regions under different assumptions about the poverty lines (low national rural headcount ratio to high), welfare indicator (income or consumption expenditure), and household size and composition effects (adjustment by adult equivalence and effects of scale economies). The shape of the dominance curves over the range of poverty lines for 1991 is, as might be expected, somewhat different from those obtained in 1987–8. This difference is likely to be due as much to real economic changes between the two

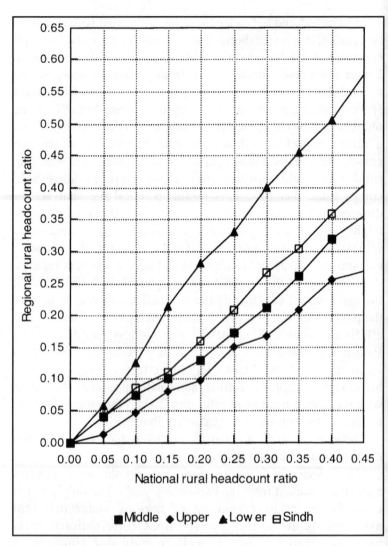

Figure 7: Regional poverty rankings, 1991, income per adult equivalent, no scale economies.

Source: Calculated by author using PIHS 1991.

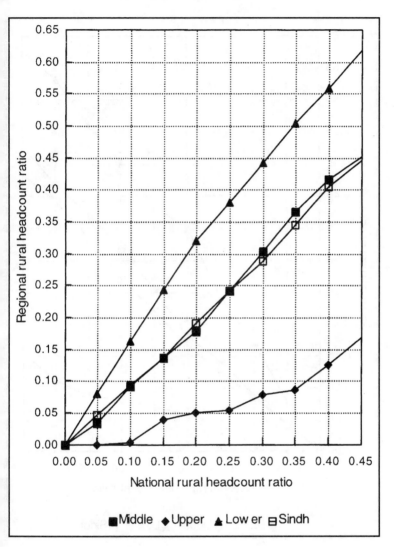

Figure 8: Regional poverty rankings, 1991, consumption expenditure per adult equivalent, no scale economies.

Source: Calculated by author using PIHS 1991.

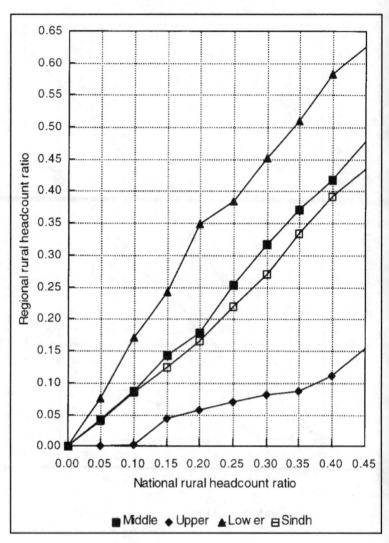

Figure 9: Regional poverty rankings, 1991, consumption expenditure per adult equivalent, moderate scale economies.

Source: Calculated by author using PIHS 1991.

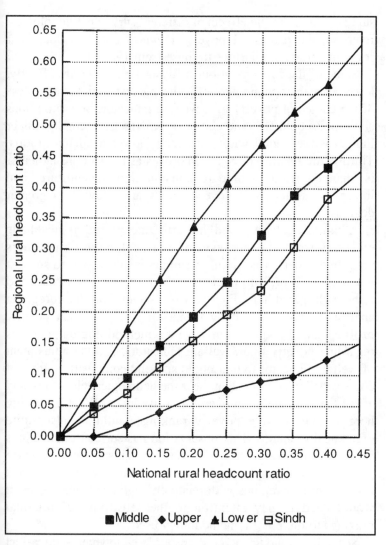

Figure 10: Regional poverty rankings, 1991, consumption expenditure per adult equivalent, high scale economies.

Source: Calculated by author using PIHS 1991.

survey years as to the effects of different survey methodologies. Even so, the pattern of poverty rankings obtained does bear some important similarities to those from 1987–8.

Some of the findings of our analysis are noteworthy. Firstly, lower Punjab is unambiguously the poorest region, regardless of the choice of poverty line, welfare indicator, or assumptions about household size and composition effects. Secondly, upper Punjab is the region with consistently lower headcount ratios. Thirdly, the ranking of Sindh improves as the welfare indicator is changed from income to consumption expenditure, and improves further as scale economies are allowed to greater degrees.

A number of new and hitherto unexplored issues have emerged from the analysis of regional poverty rankings presented above. It is useful to summarize these and to suggest potential areas of fruitful research. Two such sets of issues need to be highlighted here. Firstly, it is obvious from the foregoing analysis of household budget data for two years that poverty profiles can be quite sensitive to methodological choices regarding poverty lines, welfare indicators, and the adjustment of welfare indicator to household size and composition. It is, of course, well understood that these methodological choices would affect the estimate of an overall poverty index. What is striking here is that _relative_ poverty rankings could be also quite dramatically altered. This observation has serious implications for both further research into poverty in Pakistan, as well as for policy. If, for example, the federal government wanted to direct investment into regions with relatively high headcount ratios, it would need to pay attention to the sensitivity of regional rankings to the precise methodology used.

Secondly, although overall resource endowments do affect poverty outcomes, distributional and institutional factors play crucial intermediary roles. Lower Punjab, for example, appeared to have been the region with the most favourable agricultural resource endowments and upper Punjab the region with the least favourable (_see_ Table 6). In terms of rural poverty, however, lower Punjab turns out to be the basket case in Pakistan, whereas upper Punjab performs reasonably well. Furthermore, these distributional and institutional factors do not always appear to operate in the straightforward or expected way. Sindh, for example, which is known for its landlordism, is a region with relatively less inequality in income and consumption, and under certain conditions, low poverty. Middle Punjab, on the other hand, which is generally regarded as a progressive area in terms of its economic and social development, ranks below Sindh in terms of the headcount ratio under certain assumptions. This latter set of issues, i.e. the relationship between distributional and institutional factors and patterns of poverty is considered below.

D. INSTITUTIONS AND POVERTY

Differences between regions in their economic structure (noted in Table 6) are confirmed in the analysis of sources of income in household budget data.[62] Table 8 gives the breakdown of income by source for the four rural regions for 1987–8.

Table 8
Sources of Income (per cent of total income) by rural region, 1987–8

	Upper Punjab	Middle Punjab	Lower Punjab	Sindh
Wages (labour)	11.4	11.3	15.7	6.1
Salaries (white collar)	17.6	12.2	11.7	19.6
Agriculture (market)	14.9	20.7	29.0	42.0
Consumption of home produce	15.9	16.7	18.8	19.8
Non-agr. self-employment	10.0	10.7	8.7	7.0
Rent from property	2.5	2.5	2.4	0.8
Remittances	17.0	7.1	1.8	0.4
Other	10.5	18.8	12.0	4.3

Sources: Calculated by author from HIES 1987–8.

There are a number of striking features in this regional breakdown of income source which provide a useful entry point into the relationship between regional poverty and institutions. Firstly, though home-production (much of which was in the agricultural sector) was an important source of income in all regions, in lower Punjab and Sindh, it represented almost a fifth of total household income. At the same time, however, income from market-based agricultural activities varied a great deal between the regions. It accounted for nearly three times as high an income share in Sindh compared with upper Punjab. Secondly, remittances from family members living and working away from home also showed tremendous regional variation. They were negligible in lower Punjab and Sindh but extremely important in upper Punjab. The strong regional correlation of remittances has implications for their potential role in poverty alleviation. Thirdly, in Sindh and lower Punjab, two regions which were otherwise quite similar (in terms of the importance of agricultural income, home production, and the absence of remittances), wage labour played very different roles in the household economy. These issues are explored further by focusing separately on upper Punjab and Sindh respectively and on the contrast between these two regions and the core regions of middle and lower Punjab.

1. Upper Punjab: market responsiveness
Pair-wise comparison between upper Punjab and middle Punjab reveals the importance of distributional factors. Upper Punjab, with its less endowed and lower productivity agriculture, does consistently better than middle Punjab in poverty rankings as a result of a less unequal distribution. Both in 1987–8 and 1991, the mean income in upper Punjab was lower than in middle Punjab, and 1987–8 mean consumption was also lower. Yet in all the comparisons, the index for inequality was higher in middle Punjab. People in both these regions also rely relatively more on non-agricultural activities, but with different outcomes.

The greater equality in the distribution of income and consumption in upper Punjab is in line with the general pattern of land tenure in the region. Nearly three-quarters of the rural households own some land. The statistical results showing greater equality also accord with general impressions that economy and society in the rain-fed regions of upper Punjab are less polarized and fragmented than the situation in the canal colony settled areas in the plains of the Indus basin.[63]

Remittances play an important part in the economy of upper Punjab. As Table 9 shows, remittances and labour migration appear to be associated with upward income mobility. Wealthier households derive a greater share of their total income from remittances than poorer ones. Even the lowest quintile in upper Punjab, moreover, has a higher reliance on remittances than the wealthiest 20 per cent in middle Punjab. The comparison with lower Punjab and Sindh is not even worth the mention, given the marginal role that remittances play in those regions.

Table 9
Per cent share of remittances in income group
in upper and middle Punjab: 1987–8

Quintiles	Upper Punjab	Middle Punjab
Remittances		
Lowest	12.7	4.1
2nd lowest	15.7	5.7
3rd lowest	14.0	4.3
2nd highest	16.9	8.5
Highest	21.9	8.9

Source: Calculated by author form HIES 1987–8.
Notes: Observations from each region were subdivided into quintiles and ranked in ascending order by income per adult equivalent.

The factors that might account for the difference between the regions in their reliance on outside labour markets, or indeed, in their ability to participate in these markets are worth examining. Some of these are of a historical nature. There is a relatively long history, for instance, in the districts of upper Punjab of recruitment in the military. This outside link, it might be argued, has been further strengthened and diversified, as workers have taken advantage of other employment opportunities away from home. Labour migration to other parts of the country, and indeed overseas, has followed, arguably in continuity with an earlier pattern of extra-regional economic linkages. Furthermore, the higher spread of literacy in this region compared to others implies greater opportunity for migrant workers and other labour market entrants from this region.[64]

Wide participation in outside employment, be it in the military or in the labour market in general, and higher levels of education might be proximate determinants of less poverty but these factors themselves are, at least partly, determined by existing social and economic arrangements and individual choice. It is tempting to argue that the less than hospitable agricultural environment 'drove' people to seek employment outside. It is also worth pointing out, however, that 'feudal' relations were relatively weak in the region.[65]

The response to labour market opportunities, both historically as well as contemporaneous, ought to be viewed, therefore, in the light of pre-existing social and economic conditions. This contextualization is all the more important for a better understanding of conditions under which economic opportunities provided by the market might lead to poverty alleviation, and conditions where such a response may not be forthcoming.

2. Sindh: tenancy

One of the striking features in the regional rankings presented above was the relative position of Sindh, particularly in comparison with lower and middle Punjab. The relatively favourable poverty rankings of the region appear paradoxical given the extreme inequalities in land ownership, and the relatively low level of economic diversification away from agriculture. In terms of feudal relations also, Sindh would be at the opposite end of the spectrum from upper and middle Punjab, with a powerful landed gentry that dominates economic as well as political life.

The relatively better performance in terms of poverty indicators, of a region with manifestly unequal economic relations, is paradoxical. It is possible, of course, that there are serious non-sampling errors or other biases in the surveys on which these results are based. There is a sense in which data biases might result in an under-estimation of inequality. If the top tail of the distribution is responsible for a much larger proportion of total income or consumption in Sindh compared with other regions, and if, as argued in section 4D above, the tails of the distribution are universally under-represented, it is quite likely that the inequality indices for income and consumption in the region are biased downwards. Under-representation of the top tail of the distribution ought not, however, to affect the poverty rankings presented in Figures 3 to 10 which rely exclusively on the lower part of the distribution. Moreover, checks on the HIES and PIHS samples against information from other sources of secondary data do not suggest any obvious or systematic bias in the sample for Sindh.

Although the possibility of sample bias cannot be completely discounted, it is useful to look for other possible explanations for the observed paradox. A comparison between Sindh and lower and middle Punjab reveals three important differences. Firstly, for both the survey years, the poor appeared to be relatively better protected against consumption poverty than income poverty in Sindh. Secondly, in 1987–8, the poor appeared to be better protected against extreme deprivation in Sindh in comparison with the Punjab regions. Thirdly, household scale effects appeared to play a more prominent poverty-reducing role in Sindh.

Table 10 gives a summary of land distribution data for the four regions. These reveal that although Sindh was, indeed, the region with the highest rate of landlessness, it was also the region where the highest proportion of rural households operated land. Similarly, although the Gini co-efficient (inequality index) for land ownership was the highest in Sindh, the Gini for land operation was the lowest. In other words, the inequality of land endowments did not translate into inequality in access to land.

The high prevalence of tenant farming and share-cropping, particularly (*see* Table 10) in Sindh compared with the other regions, implied that a large proportion of the landless did have access to operational holdings.

Table 10
Distribution of land ownership and operation

	Upper Punjab	Middle Punjab	Lower Punjab	Sindh
Land Ownership				
Per cent households that own land	73	50	58	41
Mean size of holding (acres)	10.2	9.7	12.3	16.9
Gini co-efficient	0.729	0.786	0.769	0.827
Land Operation				
Per cent households that operate land	65	52	67	68
Mean size of holding (acres)	11.3	10.1	11.7	11.4
Gini co-efficient	0.705	0.714	0.661	0.634
Per cent of landless households which operate land	27	21	39	55

Source: Calculated by author using published data from *Agricultural Census* 1980.

It can be argued, quite justifiably, that access to operational holdings under conditions of unequal power relations between landlord and tenant ought to be regarded not as a positive economic opportunity but as a relationship of exploitation. A powerful landlord, after all, might be able to squeeze much of the surplus generated by the tenant and keep the tenant at his subsistence level. A landless tenant may not, according to this line of argument, be any better off than a casual labourer. These issues require more careful consideration.

Nevertheless, the decline of tenancy and share-cropping in the irrigated areas of Punjab from the 1960s onwards, and the rise in the number of casual labourers as a consequence, was universally regarded as being detrimental to the interests of the landless (*see*, for example, Hussein, 1980). This point can be further illustrated by the use of income shares from wage labour and self-employment in agriculture, respectively, for the regions (Table 11).

Table 11
Per cent share of wages and agriculture in income by income group, in middle and lower Punjab and Sindh, 1987–8

Quintiles	Middle Punjab	Lower Punjab	Sindh
Wages			
Lowest	25.9	34.5	8.3
2nd lowest	17.8	25.7	7.7
3rd lowest	14.8	18.8	6.7
2nd highest	10.0	11.4	4.7
Highest	4.1	6.1	4.2
Agriculture			
Lowest	12.9	20.0	38.8
2nd lowest	17.9	21.5	40.5
3rd lowest	21.4	24.7	46.5
2nd highest	23.0	32.9	41.3
Highest	22.4	35.0	42.3

Source: Calculated by author from HIES 1987–8.
Notes: Observations from each region were subdivided into quintiles and ranked in ascending order by income per adult equivalent.

While there is a strong positive association between income and the share of it that comes from agricultural self-employment in middle and lower Punjab, in Sindh the association is less conspicuous. The lack of access to agricultural resources (mainly land) is a close correlate of poverty, therefore, in the Punjab plains but not in Sindh. Likewise, reliance on casual wage labour, which in rural areas can be thought of also as a proxy for unavailability of self-employment opportunities in agriculture, is highly correlated with poverty in Punjab compared to Sindh.

3. Feudal patronage

A share-cropping transaction, moreover, can be regarded as part of a wider relationship between landlord and tenant. It is customary, for example, for the landlord to extend seasonal consumption advances to the tenant, which are then recovered at the time of the harvest. Credit transactions between parties that are engaged in other economic relationships are referred to as interlocking transactions. It has been widely argued that such transactions create a monopolistic situation for the lender and leave the borrower vulnerable to exploitation. As in the case of share-tenancy in the market for land however, interlocking credit arrangements might be the only form of credit available to the poor and assetless. If so, this relationship, even though it is exploitative, might be protective of the tenant's minimum consumption requirements. Table 12 provides some evidence on the prevalence of interlocking credit in Sindh. The figures based on the PIHS 1991 show that while a majority of loans in all the Punjab regions were taken from friends, relatives, or neighbours, the majority of the loans in Sindh were taken from landlords, employers, and shopkeepers, i.e., from sources with whom there were other economic transactions.

Table 12
Borrowings and sources of credit

	Upper Punjab	Middle Punjab	Lower Punjab	Sindh
Mean borrowings in previous year (rupees)				
All rural households	3,643	8,276	5,569	6,826
Landowning households	4,679	12,086	8,993	12,033
Landless households	2,340	5,619	2,346	4,482
Source of credit: landowning household (per cent of total borrowing)				
Formal institution	4	55	30	73
Trader/shopkeeper	1	4	7	14
Family /friend/neighbour	80	36	56	10
Landlord/employer	4	2	6	1
Professional moneylender	10	0	0	1
Other	0	3	1	1

Sources of credit: landless households (per cent of total borrowing)				
Formal institution	25	15	0	11
Trader/shopkeeper	0	10	18	23
Family/friend/neighbour	52	62	69	19
Landlord/employer	8	9	7	39
Professional moneylender	0	0	0	2
Other	15	4	6	6

Source: Calculated by author from PIHS 1991.

Table 12 also highlights the difference in access to formal credit between owners of land and the landless.[66] In the absence of formal credit markets for the poor in rural areas, informal sources of credit, particularly the seasonal interest-free consumption loans from landlords, are useful instruments for consumption smoothing. The prevalence of these credit arrangements might explain the observation that in Sindh, a given level of consumption appears to be sustained on the basis of relatively lower levels of income compared to other regions. While in Punjab, informal credit arrangements are mostly on the basis on social proximity between people who are likely to have similar asset positions, in Sindh, there appears to be much greater, and indeed systematic, prevalence of patron-client relations.

The idea that these various relationships, such as tenancy and credit, provide some level of consumption protection to the poorest is consistent with the pattern of poverty rankings obtained in Sindh. In particular, while for higher poverty lines its head-count ratio shows signs of converging with lower Punjab, it is in the case of extreme poverty that the advantage over lower Punjab, and indeed middle Punjab, is more apparent. The paradox of relative protection to the poorest in a region known for its extremely unequal feudal agrarian relations is also consistent with an interpretation of several relationships as those between patrons and clients. Feudal patronage, indeed, involves the co-existence of exploitation and protection.

As mentioned at the outset, much of the above discussion about the relationship between rural poverty and local institutions is of a speculative and exploratory nature, even if these speculations and explorations are somewhat guided by references to secondary data. A corollary to this discussion is the following question: what are the possible political and policy interventions to engender a transition from a patron-client type economy, which does nevertheless extend some measure of social protection, to one consisting of equal agents?

CONCLUSIONS

This chapter has attempted to provide selective reviews of four broad themes in the study of poverty in Pakistan. The reviews are not exhaustive, but it is hoped that they do convey the flavour of some of the important concerns in the literature. Since the areas covered have been quite broad, and because each of the sections is fairly self-contained, it is not necessary to go over all the conclusions again in any detail. Some important findings are recapitulated below.

The understanding of poverty has undergone many changes over the years. Conventional approaches were narrowly focused on income and consumption as the relevant criteria. More recent developments, both in the theoretical conceptualization of poverty as well as in operational responses to it, have been moving in the direction of defining poverty as a hindrance to full participation. These approaches lay greater stress on institutional processes and lead to political conceptions of poverty.

Much of the applied work on income or consumption poverty in Pakistan has been concerned with measurement and the estimation of poverty indices. Discrepant results obtained by different researchers, sometimes using the same data-sets, are due to differences in methodology. The estimation of poverty indices involves a large number of methodological choices and judgements. While some of these variations in method can be weeded out on the basis of economic argument, there is nevertheless, considerable scope for genuine and reasonable differences in methodology. Perhaps the best strategy is to estimate poverty indices for a range of possible methodological choices.

While there is much evidence of significant declines in poverty in Pakistan over the decades, trend analysis is made difficult by the paucity of consistent time series. This problem is compounded by the fact that earlier analyses of poverty have tended to use non-standard methodology, particularly with reference to obtaining rankings of households. Raw data from representative sample surveys have been available from the late 1970s onwards and these confirm steady declines in poverty ratios. The 1980s were a period of particularly rapid progress in this regard, but some of the evidence suggests that the process slowed down in the 1990s. Data on wage rates are also not conclusive with respect to specific time trends, but these, too, point to steady improvements over the decades.

Poverty alleviation has not figured as an explicit policy objective, or even a strategic goal in Pakistan until recently. Poverty and distributional issues have been significant political issues, however, and perceptions of economic injustice have played an important part in political mobilization at various junctures. The development model followed in the 1960s, for example, was associated with high rates of growth in industry as well as in agriculture. The almost deliberate disregard for distributional considerations during that period was to prove costly, as perceptions of increasing regional and class inequalities led to a build-up of popular discontent. This discontent and the political changes that followed were partly responsible for the subsequent greater invocation of poverty and the poor, at least in political rhetoric, in the 1970s.

The economic growth in the 1980s compared to the relative stagnation in the 1970s has been viewed by some as the favourable consequence of turning from an economic strategy of interventionism and state control to one of structural adjustment, deregulation, and market-orientation. The poverty declines in the 1980s, likewise, have been ascribed to this enlightened change. The issue of state intervention and market-orientation is a complex one in Pakistan. While the rhetoric in the 1980s was certainly more favourable to the private sector than that of the 1970s, the case for regarding this period as a turning point in the positive sense is weak. Any understanding of this period is incomplete without a proper recognition of the remarkably favourable external circumstances with large windfall gains to the government as well as to private individuals.

Economic crises in the 1990s are, in fact, quite substantially, the result of past errors and failures. Moreover, these crises, particularly the chronic fiscal crisis, can be viewed as arising directly out of the political economy of patronage and capture that flourished in the 1980s. The debate about structural adjustment in Pakistan is somewhat limited in its focus, as the prevailing framework is that of state-market dichotomy. Similarly, although the recent attention to poverty alleviation and social policy is very welcome, the 'state versus non-state' dichotomy that informs much of the dialogue and intervention is likely to prove quite inadequate for a proper understanding of Pakistan's development. Attention needs to be directed, instead, to the precise working of economic, social, and political institutions (including the state, markets, as well as other arrangements), and on the relations of power that are embedded in these institutions.

The regional analysis of relative poverty rankings provides an opportunity of probing into the impact of institutional variations on poverty. There are significant differences between regions in the incidence of poverty. Lower Punjab, in particular, stands out as a region of high poverty. This observation has implications for the interpretation of the routes out of poverty. Lower Punjab is a region of high agricultural potential and productivity which has benefitted from the technological developments under the 'green revolution'. It remains one of the poorest regions all the same. It is not clear whether significant poverty reduction could be achieved by simply banking on further growth in productivity.

At the other extreme, upper Punjab, which is an area of low agricultural potential, had consistently low poverty indices. This was also a region with a high degree of diversification away from agriculture, involvement in the labour market, and migration of workers to other parts of the country and abroad. Remittances from non-resident workers were an important source of upward mobility in this region. Workers' remittances were also important in middle Punjab, but not in lower Punjab and Sindh. The scope for migration and workers' remittances as channels of poverty alleviation needs to be understood within the specific context of access to labour markets and the history of participation in these markets in various regions.

Sindh stands out as a region of high inequality in land ownership, but relatively lower levels of extreme poverty. At higher poverty lines, its poverty ranking worsens. There is also smaller vulnerability to consumption poverty compared with income poverty in the region. The relatively protected consumption profile in a region of extreme land inequalities is due, possibly, to the protective role of otherwise exploitative patron-client relations.

Finally, the challenge of poverty alleviation in Pakistan needs to be taken up as a matter of political enterprise. If poverty is thought of as the inability to participate equally in the affairs of the community, then the agenda for poverty alleviation ought not to be confined to issues relating to income and consumption shortfalls alone. Issues such as the advancement of basic education, the provision of public health, and the protection of legal, civil, and political rights, all need to be addressed as integral parts of any anti-poverty agenda. Although this chapter has been focused, to a great extent, on income and consumption poverty, this focus is largely a response to the existing literature on poverty in Pakistan and not necessarily an indication of where the discussion should go. Ultimately, what really matters in terms of debate, policy, activism, as well as research on poverty, is that issues of vulnerability and power in economic and social institutions are addressed.

REFERENCES

Adams, R. H. Jr. and Alderman, H. (1992), 'Sources of income inequality in rural Pakistan: a decomposition analysis', *Oxford Bulletin of Economics and Statistics*, 54(4), pp. 591–608.

Adams, R. H. Jr. and Jane, J. (1995), 'Sources of income inequality and poverty in rural Pakistan', Research Report 102, International Food Policy Research Institute, Washington D.C.

Ahmad, E. and Alison, C. (1990), 'Poverty, growth and public policy in Pakistan', mimeo.

Ahmad, E. and Ludlow, S. (1988), 'On changes in inequality in Pakistan, 1979–84', DERP Discussion Paper No. 13, June 1988, STICERD, London School of Economics.

————. (1989), 'Poverty, inequality and growth in Pakistan', *Pakistan Development Review* 28(4), Winter 1989, pp. 831–50.

Ahmad, M. (1993), 'Choice of a norm of poverty threshold and extent of poverty in Pakistan', mimeo, Ministry of Finance, Islamabad.

Ahmed, V. and Amjad, R. (1984), *The Management of Pakistan's Economy, 1947–1982*, Oxford University Press, Karachi.

Ahsan, A. (1997), *Indus Saga: The Making of Pakistan*, Oxford University Press, Karachi.

Alavi, H. (1976), *Rural Elite and Agricultural Development in Pakistan*, (ed. Stevens et al.)

Alderman, H. and Garcia, M. (1992), 'Food security and health security: explaining the level of nutrition in Pakistan', The World Bank Working Paper WPS 865, Policy Research, Agriculture and Rural Development Department.

————. (1993), *Poverty, Household Food Security and Nutrition in Rural Pakistan: A Longitudinal Study*, International Food Policy Research Institute.

Ali, M. S. (1995), 'Poverty assessment: Pakistan's case', *Pakistan Development Review*, 34(1), Spring 1995, pp. 43–54.

Atkinson, A. B. (1993), 'The institution of an official poverty line and economic policy', Discussion Paper No. WSP/98, Welfare State Programme, STICERD, London School of Economics, December 1993.

Barbalet, J. M. (1988), *Citizenship, Rights, Struggle and Class Inequality*, Milton Keynes: Open University Press.

Beall, J. Kanji, Faruqi N., Hussain, F., C. M. and Mirani, M. (1993), *Social Safety Nets and Social Networks: Their Role in Poverty Alleviation in Pakistan*, 2 volumes, Development Policy Unit, University College London.

Bose, S. R. (1972), 'East-West contrast in Pakistan's agricultural development', in ed. Griffin and Khan, *Growth and Inequality in Pakistan*, Macmillan Press, London and Basingstoke.

Burki, S. J. (1976), 'The development of Pakistan's agriculture: an interdisciplinary explanation', in ed. Stevens et al.

———. (1988), 'Poverty in Pakistan: myth or reality?', in *Rural Poverty in South Asia,* (ed. P. Bardhan and T.N. Srinivasan), Columbia University Press, New York.

———. (1992), 'The management of crises', in *Foundations of Pakistan's Political Economy,* (ed. J. E. William and S. Roy), Sage, New Delhi.

———. (1993), 'Pakistan's economy in the year 2000: two possible scenarios', in *Contemporary Problems of Pakistan,* (ed. H. J. Korson), Westview Press, Boulder and Pak Book Corporation, Lahore.

Chaudhry, M. G. and Chaudhry, G. M. (1992), 'Trend in rural employment and wages in Pakistan', *Pakistan Development Review,* 31(4), Winter 1992, pp. 803–15.

Dandekar, V.M. and Rath, N. (1971), *Poverty in India,* Sameeksha Trust, Bombay.

Dasgupta, P. (1993), *An Enquiry into Well-being and Destitution,* Clarendon Press, Oxford.

Datt, G. and Ravallion, M. (1995), 'Why have some Indian states done better than others at reducing rural poverty?', mimeo, Policy Research Department, World Bank, Washington D.C.

Deaton, A. (1995), *Understanding Consumption,* Clarendon Press, Oxford.

Drèze, J. and Sen, A. (1989), *Hunger and Public Action,* Clarendon Press, Oxford.

———. (1995), *India: Social Opportunity, and Economic Development,* Clarendon Press, Oxford.

———. (eds.) (1997), *Indian Development: Selected Regional Perspectives,* Oxford University Press, Delhi.

Dutta, B. (1996), 'India: tradition for poverty research', in *Poverty Levels in India: Norms, Estimates and Trends,* pp. 1748–68, Economic and Political Weekly, August 21 1993, (ed. Øyen et al. EPW Research Foundation, 1993).

Ercelawn, A. (1991), 'Absolute poverty as risk of hunger', mimeo, Applied Economics Research Centre, University of Karachi.

Federal Bureau of Statistics. (1997), *Pakistan Integrated Household Survey, 1995–6,* Government of Pakistan, Islamabad.

Gazdar, H., Howes, S., and Zaidi, S. (1994b), 'A profile of poverty in Pakistan', mimeo, STICERD, London School of Economics and PRDPH, World Bank.

———. (1994a), 'Recent trends in poverty in Pakistan', mimeo, STICERD, London School of Economics and PRDPH, World Bank.

Glewwe, P. and Gaag, J. V. D. (1990), 'Identifying the poor in developing countries: do different definitions matter?', *World Development,* 18(6), pp. 803–14.

Government of India. (1993), 'Report of the experts group on estimation of the proportion and number of poor', Planning Commission, Government of India, New Delhi.

Government of Pakistan. (1956), *First Five Year Plan,* Government of Pakistan Planning Board.

———. (1986), Report of the National Commission on Agriculture, 1986.

———. (1988), *Agricultural Census of Pakistan 1980,* Agricultural Census Organization, Lahore.

———. (1997), *Economic Survey 1996–7,* Finance Division, Economic Advisor's Wing, Islamabad.

———. (various), *Monthly Statistical Bulletin,* Federal Bureau of Statistics, Islamabad.

Griffin, K. and Khan, A. R. (eds.) (1972), *Growth and Inequality in Pakistan,* Macmillan Press, London and Basingstoke.

Guisinger, S. and Scully, G. (1991), 'Pakistan', in *Liberalizing Foreign Trade: The Experience of Indonesia, Pakistan, and Sri Lanka,* (ed. Papageorgious, D., Michealy, M., and Armeane, M. C.), Basil Blackwell, for the World Bank, Oxford.

Haq, M. (1983), *The Poverty Curtain: Choices for the Third World,* Ferozsons, Lahore.

———. (1997), *Human Development in South Asia 1997,* The Human Development Centre, Oxford University Press, Karachi.

Havinga, I.C. et al. (1989), 'Poverty in Pakistan, 1984–5', *Pakistan Development Review,* vol. 28, pp. 851–69.

Howes, S. and Zaidi, S. (1994), 'Notes on some household surveys from Pakistan in the eighties and nineties', mimeo, STICERD, LSE.

Hussein, S. A. (1980), 'The impact of agricultural growth on the agrarian structure of Pakistan, with special reference to the Punjab Province: 1960 to 1978', unpublished Ph.D. thesis, University of Sussex.

Kaneda, H. (1972), *Economic Implications of the 'Green Revolution' and the Strategy of Agricultural Development in West Pakistan,* (eds. Griffin and Khan).

Kemal, A. R. and Mahmood, M. (1997), 'Poverty and policy in Pakistan', in *Just Development: Beyond Adjustment with a Human Face* (ed. Banuri et al.), Oxford University Press, Karachi.

Khan, A. R. (1972), 'What has been happening to real wages in Pakistan?', in ed. Griffin and Khan.

Khan, M. H. (1981), *Underdevelopment and Agrarian Structure in Pakistan,* Vanguard, Lahore.

———. (1994), 'The structural adjustment process and agricultural change in Pakistan in the 1980s and 1990s', *Pakistan Development Review,* 33(4), Winter 1994, pp. 533–91.

Lanjouw, P. (1994), 'Regional poverty in Pakistan: how robust are the conclusions?', mimeo, World Bank.

Lanjouw, P. and Ravallion, M. (1994), 'Poverty and household size', *Economic Journal;* 105(433), November 1995, pp. 1415–34.

Lieftinck, P., Sadgove, R. A. and Creyke, T. C. (1968), *Water and Power Resources of West Pakistan: A Study in Sector Planning,* 3 volumes, published for the World Bank, Baltimore: Johns Hopkins Press.

Lodhi, M. (1985), 'Bhutto, the Pakistan Peoples Party and political development in Pakistan 1967–1977', unpublished Ph.D. thesis, London School of Economics.

Mahmood, S., Sheikh, K. H. and Mahmood, T. (1991), 'Food poverty and its causes in Pakistan', *Pakistan Development Review,* 30(4).

Malik, M. H. (1988), 'Some new evidence on the incidence of poverty in Pakistan', *Pakistan Development Review,* 27(4).

Malik, S. J. (1991), 'Poverty in Pakistan, 1984–5 and 1987–8', in *Including the Poor,* (ed. M. Lipton and J. van der Gaag), Oxford University Press.

———. (1994), 'Poverty in Pakistan: 1984–85, 1987–88 and 1990–91', mimeo, IFPRI, Washington.

Minhas, B. S., Jain, L. R. and Tendulkar, S. D. (1991), 'Declining incidence of poverty in the 1980s: evidence versus artefacts', *Economic and Political Weekly,* 26 (27 and 28), 6–13 July 1991, pp. 1673–82.

Nabi, I., Hamid, N. and Zahid, S. (1986), *The Agrarian Economy of Pakistan: Issues and Policies,* Oxford University Press, Karachi.

Naseem, S. M. (1973), 'Mass poverty in Pakistan: some preliminary findings', *Pakistan Development Review,* 13(4), pp. 317–60.

———. (1977), 'Rural poverty and landlessness in Pakistan', ILO Report on Poverty and Landlessness in Asia, Geneva.

National Institute of Health (1988), *National Nutritional Survey, 1985–87, Final Report,* Nutrition Division, Government of Pakistan.

Novak, M. (1996), 'Concepts of poverty', in ed. Øyen et al., 1996.

Nulty, L. (1972), *The Green Revolution in West Pakistan: Implications of Technological Change,* Praeger Publishers, New York.

Osmani, S. R. (ed.) (1993), *Nutrition and Poverty,* University Press Ltd., Dhaka, first published in 1992 by Oxford University Press, Oxford.

Øyen, E., Miller, S. M. and Samad, S. A. (1996), *Poverty: A Global Review,* Scandinavian University Press, Oslo.

Papanek, G. F. (1967), *Pakistan's Development: Social Goals and Private Incentives,* Harvard University Press, Cambridge, Mass.

Parker, B. (1995), 'Pakistan poverty assessment—social analysis component: results of a qualitative survey', mimeo, The World Bank.

Pasha, H. A., Malik, S. and Jamal, H. (1990), 'The changing profile of regional development in Pakistan', in *Pakistan Journal of Applied Economics,* 9(1).

Qizilbash, M. (1997), 'Poverty: concept and measurement', paper presented at the Annual Conference of the Development Studies Association at the University of East Anglia, Norwich, 11–13 September 1997.

Ravallion, M. (1992), 'Poverty comparisons: a guide to concepts and methods', LSMS Working Paper No. 88, The World Bank, Washington D.C.

SAARC. (1992), 'Meeting the challenge', Report of the Independent South Asian Commission on Poverty Alleviation, South Asia Association for Regional Cooperation, November 1992, Sustainable Development Policy Institute, Islamabad.

Sayeed, A. U. (1995), 'Political alignments, the state and industrial policy in Pakistan: A Comparison of Performance in the 1960s and 1980s', unpublished Ph.D. thesis. Darwin College, University of Cambridge.

Sayeed, A. U. and Ghaus, A. F. A. (1996), 'Has poverty returned to Pakistan?', mimeo, July 1996, Social Policy and Development Centre, Karachi.

Sayeed, K. B. (1980), *Politics in Pakistan: The Nature and Direction of Change*, Praeger, New York.

Sen, A. (1984), *Resources, Values and Development*, Basil Blackwell, Oxford.

———. (1992), *Inequality Re-examined*, Russel Sage Foundation, New York and Clarendon Press, Oxford.

Singh, I. (1990), *The Great Ascent: The Rural Poor in South Asia*, The Johns Hopkins University Press, for the World Bank, Baltimore.

Stevens, R. D., Alavi, H. and Betrocci, P. J. (ed.) (1976), *Rural Development in Bangladesh and Pakistan*, University of Hawaii Press, Honolulu.

Subramanian, S. and Deaton, A. (1996), 'The demand for food and calories', *Journal of Political Economy*, 104(1), pp. 133–63.

UNDP. (various), *Human Development Report*.

World Bank. (1990), 'Pakistan: A Profile of Poverty', Report No. 8848-PAK.

———. (1995), 'Pakistan: poverty assessment', Report No. 14397-PAK, Country Operations Division, Country Department, South Asia Region, The World Bank, Washington D.C., September 1995.

Zaidi, S. A. (1989), 'Regional imbalances and national question in Pakistan: some indications', *Economic and Political Weekly*, 11 February 1989, pp. 300–14.

———. (1997). 'Politics, institutions, poverty: the case of Karachi', *Economic and Political Weekly*, 20 December 1997.

NOTES

1. *See* Ravallion (1992), for a useful practical review of this literature for problems of poverty analysis in developing countries.

2. The received framework of neoclassical welfare economics has been challenged from a number of standpoints in recent years. *See*, for example, Sen (1992) and Dasgupta (1993).

3. The World Bank's poverty assessment in Pakistan, for instance, adopts a broad approach which includes consideration of education and health indicators (see World Bank, 1995). The reporting of non-income

development indicators is standard practice, encouraged partly by publications such as the *Human Development Reports* (UNDP, various).

4. There are important differences within what are broadly defined as participation-based approaches that need not worry us for the purposes of this chapter. A number of these issues have been thrashed out in debates, notably between Sen and Townsend. For recent reviews of this literature, *see* Novak (1996), and Qizilbash (1997). For the evolution of one strand in the participation-based approach and its application, *see* Drèze and Sen (1989, 1995, 1997).

5. Sen (1992) traces the origins of these ideas to the classical economists, and indeed to Greek philosophy.

6. Notable credit interventions include among others, the Aga Khan Rural Support Programme and the Orangi Pilot Project. These models of micro-credit have been applied quite widely by other non-governmental organizations and rural support programmes, with varying degrees of success. *See* SAARC (1992) for case studies in Pakistan and other South Asian countries.

7. *See*, for example, inter-country comparisons in Drèze and Sen (1989), Haq (1997), and Federal Bureau of Statistics (1997).

8. Sen's (1992) notion of 'effective freedom' is interpreted here in the language of rights. This has the advantage of drawing the connection with the political processes. *See* Barbalet (1988) on post-Second World War theories of citizenship and the status of social rights in these theories.

9. Alternatives non-economics approaches that stress qualitative factors are receiving greater attention in policy research (*see* for instance Beall et al., 1993, and Parker, 1995) but are relatively neglected in the more academic work.

10. On some aspects of urban poverty, especially with respect to *katchi abadis*, *see* Zaidi (1998) and the literature cited there.

11. One of the main drafters of the First Five Year Plan resigned from the Planning Board soon after the publication of the plan in protest at the dilution of his already moderated proposals for land reforms.

12. *See*, for example Papanek (1967), who could barely contain his enthusiasm for the enlightened leaders and administrators at the helm of the 'development decade'. Unfortunately for the author, his book was published at a time when the magic had already worn off, and the same able leaders and administrators were beginning to be viewed in a rather different light (*see* Nulty, 1972, for example).

13. These technological developments, often labelled the 'Green Revolution', have been reviewed extensively. *See*, for example, Nulty (1972), Griffin and Khan (1972), Nabi et al. (1986), and Singh (1990).

14. On this, particularly on the issue of economic disparity between East and West Pakistan, *see* Bose (1972) and other contributions in Griffin and Khan (1972). Also *see* Sayeed (1995).

15. The most graphic illustration of the early enthusiasm among policy-makers of blazing through the supposed growth-inequality trade-off, and a dramatic change of mind subsequently, is offered by Mahbubul Haq (*see* Haq, 1983).

16. Though precise estimates of the number of tenants displaced per tractor vary, a number of writers have commented on the adverse distributional implications of the model of mechanization that came to be adopted in West Pakistan (*see* Kaneda, 1972, Alavi, 1976, and Hussein, 1980).

17. There is a well-known debate between Alavi (1976) and Burki (1976) on changes in the agrarian structure in Punjab in the 1960s. Burki on the one hand, argues that the power of the feudal aristocracy was broken and the middle peasant was the main initiator as well as the beneficiary of the 'Green Revolution'. In other words, the developments in the 1960s were associated with lowering inequality and not raising it. Alavi, on the other hand, argues that the hold of large landlords remained unbroken, and was, in fact strengthened. Even if Burki's view is correct (i.e. that middle peasants were the main beneficiaries in 1960s), it does not imply any relative improvement in the position of the land-poor and the landless, particularly those who relied on share-tenancy.

18. Details of the available data series, and critical assessments of methodology of earlier studies are provided in section 3.

19. Pioneering work on poverty assessment, using household budget survey data in Pakistan, was carried out by Naseem (1973). For the Federal Bureau of Statistics (FBS) time series on inequality measures since 1963–4, *see* Government of Pakistan (1997), Table 1.7.

20. While Naseem's (1973) poverty results for the 1960s certainly use rankings based on household rather than per capita income, the precise methodology of the FBS series is not known. It is likely that the results from 1979 onwards are based on rankings obtained using per capita income. Before 1979, however, it is likely that the FBS also used aggregated income groups based on household income. If so, the series is not consistent, and therefore, should not be used for trend analysis.

21. It is not clear, however, whether the data used by this study is from a different source as compared to the earlier studies. The authors simply report their source as ILO.

22. A definitive analysis of this period is provided in Lodhi (1985). Also *see* Sayeed (1995) for a later review.

23. *See* Khan (1981). Another, arguably more radical, attempt at land reforms in 1977 was thwarted when the civilian government was dismissed by the military.

24. This scheme came to be known as *ruhri ahata*. Plots of government-owned land on the outskirts of villages were assigned to landless (and land-poor) families for building homes. *See* Sayeed (1980) p. 93, for a brief description.

25. Sayeed (1980), p. 93, reports that the total number of beneficiaries of the residential plot scheme was 800,000. Beneficiaries of all other land reforms till 1976 numbered some 310,000 households.

26. According to Burki (1988), migration both within and outside Pakistan became a key avenue for the alleviation of poverty in Pakistan.

27. Even the 1960s growth experience cannot be interpreted simply as the response to pro-market policies. Two important factors that explain the high growth rates in the 1960s are the low initial base and the achievement of political stability in the early part of the decade. Stability was probably a key factor in inducing investment.

28. The full extent of financial flows to Pakistan as a result of its position in the Afghanistan conflict has not been documented. While some of the assistance the country received was in the form of direct transfers, other assistance in the form of easier borrowing conditions are not easily quantifiable.

29. *See* Sayeed (1995) for a recent statement of this view.

30. This is not to say that for particular segments of the population the reforms programme has not had and will not have direct negative effects. Large-scale retrenchment in the public sector, for example, will not only lead to rises in urban unemployment, but will also result in lowering the bargaining power of workers who remain in employment.

31. This dating of economic reform is quite surprising for a number of reasons. Firstly, as far as trade liberalization is concerned, an earlier World Bank study finds a steady programme of liberalization since the 1960s and all the way through the 'populist' experiment of the 1970s (*see* Guisinger and Scully, 1991). Secondly, as far as fiscal restraint is concerned, the 1980s was a period of considerable profligacy, supported by windfall gains in the shape of remittances and foreign aid transfers. It was only at the onset of a fiscal crisis in 1988 that a full-blown structural adjustment programme was agreed upon with the IMF.

32. In any case, as Sayeed (1995) points out, clientelism was actually rampant in the economic management of the 1980s.

33. It is interesting to note that an increase in the allocation of public resources to social sectors under the provisions of the Social Action Programme (SAP) is explicitly part of IMF's conditionality in Pakistan.

34. It is not being argued, of course, that innovative thinking on development comes from outside with international organizations; rather, that the presence of these international organizations in the policy arena makes it possible for new approaches and strategies by both local and foreign experts and activists. Home-grown interventions are too numerous to list here. *See*, for example, case studies in SAARC (1992).

35. Much of the discussion in this section draws upon earlier unpublished work, mainly Gazdar, Howes and Zaidi (1994a, 1994b). These papers are referred to, henceforth, as GHZ 1994a and HZ 1994b, respectively.

36. The head-count ratio is a widely used poverty statistic, and will be referred to extensively in the present study. It is the proportion of the total population with incomes less than a designated poverty.

37. *See* Atkinson (1993), for example, for a discussion of the possible impact of instituting a poverty line on public policy.

38. In the case of Pakistan, the caloric standards that have been in wide use are based on WHO norms. *See* Ercelawn (1991) for details.

39. For detailed arguments about the difficulties with such interpretation, *see* Osmani (1993). *See also* Subramanian and Deaton (1996) on the implausibility of a nutrition-based poverty indicator even in relatively poor countries.

40. Food quantities can be readily converted into caloric values using the relevant conversion tables.

41. This is in line with the participation-based approach to poverty discussed in section 1 above.

42. In fact, Ali (1995), who is also interested in the basic needs approach, but regards the Ahmad (1993) method as being 'subjective', uses household budget data to estimate linear expenditure systems. The use of linear expenditure systems, however, imposes unnecessary and untested extra conditions on the nature of the utility function, and is in itself open to the charge of 'subjectivism'.

43. *See* for example, EPW Research Foundation (1993) for a comprehensive summary of the Indian literature on the issue, and Government of India (1993) for the official view of the process. It should be noted that no attempt has been to update the poverty line whith reference to nutritional criteria.

44. *See* EPW Research Foundation (1993) and the literature cited there, in particular, Minhas et al. (1991).

45. This, indeed, has been the case for studies that make rural-urban adjustments on the basis of separate calorie-consumption functions for each type of area. *See* Ercelawn (1991).

46. This, indeed, was the strategy for the estimation of the original Indian poverty line (*see* EPW Research Foundation, 1993).

47. The identification of the poor, and poverty measurement are sensitive to the choice of indicator. *See*, for example, Glewwe and van der Gaag (1990).

48. These issues are reviewed in Deaton (1995).

49. *See* Naseem (1973, 1977) for studies where the ranking is the one based upon total household income. A more recent example is to be found in Kemal and Mahmood (1997).

50. Published data from the Indian National Sample Survey data is a case in point. These data can be, and have been, used for reconstructing the distribution of per capita expenditure (*see* Datt and Ravallion, 1995).

51. Both Naseem (1973) and Kemal and Mahmood (1997) who rely on published grouped data from various HIESs respectively, find that 'poorer' household are smaller than 'richer' ones. Given that the HIES income groups are based upon total household income regardless of household demographics, this result is more an artefact of the way observations have been grouped than an insight into a useful economic relationship.

52. Adult equivalence is used only for the purpose of ranking households, and not for counting the number of poor. The latter exercise assigns equal weight to each individual.

53. *See* Lanjouw and Ravallion (1995) for a review of the theory of household scale economies. The empirical basis of the study was, interestingly, household budget data from Pakistan.

54. Ahmed and Ludlow use poverty lines in urban areas that are higher than rural poverty lines but do not justify the precise difference in terms of cost of living differences.

55. The 1990–91 results are not, strictly speaking comparable between the two tables, since the update of the Ahmad and Ludlow series in Table 2 uses PIHS 1991 whereas the GHZ series used HIES 1990–91.

56. Urban wages are calculated as the simple average of wages in Karachi and Lahore.

57. These trends, estimated from published official data on wages and prices, appear to be at odds with the findings of Chaudhry and Chaudhry (1992), who report that agricultural wages grew at over 10 per cent per year in real terms in the 1980s. Since detailed information was not available on Chaudhry and Chaudhry's (1992) data source, it was not possible to account for this discrepancy.

58. *See*, for example, World Bank (1990), Gazdar, Howes, and Zaidi (1994b), and Kemal and Mahmood (1997). *See* also Pasha et al. (1990) for a ranking of districts using various secondary data.

59. *See* Table 1. Malik (1991) reports head-count ratios for agronomic sub-regions at lower levels of aggregation than provinces and obtains extremely interesting results. The same author drops this regional disaggregation in subsequent work and reverts to using provinces only.

60. The experience of the 1960s when perceptions of regional disparity played an important role in political mobilization remains a potent reminder of the importance of regional factors. *See*, for example, Zaidi (1989).

61. Provinces are divided into administrative divisions, and these are further divided into districts. The regions chosen for this study refer to district and division boundaries as they were in the early 1980s.

62. Observations about sources of income are based on HIES 1987–8 only due to inconsistencies encountered in PIHS income data.

63. Remnants of communal land ownership continued in parts of upper Punjab

until relatively recently, long after they had ceased to exist in the plains areas.

64. It is worth recalling (Table 6) that the male adult literacy rate was a third higher than in middle Punjab and over two-thirds higher than in lower Punjab and Sindh.

65. The weakness of feudal ties might itself have been a consequence of a relatively unproductive agriculture, with smaller possibilities of surpluses that would have sustained powerful landlords.

66. This result also provides some support for the high priority that a number of anti-poverty interventions have accorded to credit and saving schemes for the poor.

10

Population, Employment, and the State of Human Resources

Sohail Jehangir Malik* and Hina Nazli**

1. INTRODUCTION

In the past, development planning in Pakistan mostly emphasized physical capital accumulation. Thus, human capital accumulation remained sadly neglected. The full impact of this neglect has, however, not been felt as yet. Pakistan's economic growth record to this point of time has been quite reasonable; per capita income has more than doubled over the past three decades. Things could have been even better. There is considerable evidence to suggest that the lack of educated manpower and the poor quality of the work force has prevented the economy from attaining its true potential.

The poor quality of the workforce results from the rapidly increasing population and the low priority accorded to social sectors such as education and health. The poor standard of the social sectors also determines the overall quality of life of the people of the country, improving which is the goal of development. The performance of the social sectors in Pakistan has been highly unsatisfactory. This is evident from the low

* Vice President, John Mellor Associates, Washington D.C., USA.
** Research Economist, Pakistan Institute of Development Economics, Islamabad, Pakistan.

The authors are grateful to Dr Shahrukh Rafi Khan for providing background material and for being extremely patient. All errors of omission and commission are the responsibility of the authors.

literacy rates, lack of access to safe drinking water and sanitation facilities, high levels of malnutrition amongst vulnerable groups, low levels of labour productivity, and the high incidence of poverty. Driving all these, of course, are the high rates of population growth. The gender and regional imbalances in the provision of limited available social services, and the low allocation of public funds to education, health, and population welfare, places Pakistan in an unfavourable position even among the low income countries of the world.

This chapter focuses on human resources development in Pakistan since 1947. Human resource issues are examined in terms of the demographic trends affecting its burgeoning population. Human resource utilization is evaluated in terms of the productive employment of the available manpower in the country. The performance of key social sectors such as education and health and the equally important issues of nutrition are examined. International comparisons are made to highlight the shortfall in Pakistan's performance. The nature of the analysis is purely descriptive. Imbalances are highlighted and implications noted. No attempt is made to present remedial strategies apart from those that should be obvious from the presentation of the data. The remaining chapter is divided into five sections. An analysis of the state of population is presented in section 2. Section 3 looks at the situation of employment and unemployment. The performance of the education sector is described in section 4. Section 5 addresses the issues of health and nutrition. International comparisons of human development indicators are presented in section 6.

2. POPULATION GROWTH AND THE DEMOGRAPHIC SITUATION

Pakistan covers only 0.67 per cent of world's land area but contains 2 per cent of the world's population. Table 1 shows that at the time of independence, Pakistan's population was 32.5 million. This means that during the fifty years of its existence,

Pakistan's population has increased about four-fold. The annual growth rate of population was 1.8 per cent per annum in 1947. This increased to 3.1 per cent in 1981, which is one of the highest rates in the world. With this high growth rate, Pakistan will become the eighth most populous country in the world by the year 2010. This high population growth rate is brought about by the high fertility rate and the low mortality rate.

Table 1
Population and population growth rates

Years	Population (000)				% average growth rate of population per annum	Life expectancy at birth	
	Total	Urban	Rural	Share of urban population in total population (%)		Males	Females
1947	32500	5003	27497	15.4	1.8	–	–
1951	33707	6019	27798	17.9	1.8	32.9	34.4*
1961	42880	9655	33324	22.5	2.4	47.0	45.0
1972	65309	16594	48727	34.5	3.6	52.9	51.8
1981	84254	23841	60412	39.5	3.1	–	–
1991E	113791	35682	78110	31.4	3.1	59.3	60.7
1996E	131635	42650	88985	32.4	2.8	62.9	62.1

Sources: Rukanuddin and Farooqui (1988), NIPS (1987), *Economic Survey,* 1995–6.
Note*   Indicates only for Punjab for the year 1950–52
   E=   Estimated.

A. Fertility and Mortality Rates

Fertility and mortality rates are the two crucial factors affecting population growth. The mortality rate in Pakistan has declined significantly during recent years. The expansion of preventive medicines and public health services and the provision of safe drinking water and sanitation facilities from an almost non-existent base have led to significantly declining mortality rates. Table 2 presents information on the crude birth rate, total fertility rate, infant mortality rate, and crude death rates for different years. This table shows that the infant mortality rate, which was 122 per 1,000 live births in 1962, went down to 102.4 per 1,000

live births by 1991. On the other hand, the high total fertility
rate, at around 6 per woman, has remained almost constant.
Despite having a long history of officially sponsored family
planning programmes, surveys indicate that only 10 per cent of
married women use contraceptive methods and the desire to
have more than four children has not changed over the last
twenty years. Various reasons account for the slow progress in
reducing the fertility rate; for example, illiteracy, failure to raise
awareness about the problems of large families, inefficient and
unequal distribution of birth control facilities, the preference for
sons, lack of security in old age, etc. Similar trends can be seen
in the crude birth and crude death rates. The crude death rate
had declined to 9.8 per 1,000 live births by 1991 from 12 in
1962, while the crude birth rate had increased to 39.5 in 1991
from 37.1 in 1962.

Table 2
Important demographic variables

Years	Source	CBR per 1000 population	TFR per woman	IMR per 1000 live births	CDR per 1000 population
1951	Census	62.4	–	–	–
1961	Census	51.0	–	–	–
1962	PGE	37.1	6.5	122	12.0
1963	PGE	38.4	5.8	103	11.0
1964	PGE	42.0	6.5	115	13.0
1965	PGE	36.5	5.5	80	9.0
1968	PGE	36.4	5.7	124	12.0
1969	PGE	36.1	5.7	111	11.5
1971	PGE	36.9	6.3	106	10.6
1972	Census	52.2	–	–	–
1974	PFS	38.4	–	–	–
1976	PGS	42.8	7.1	87	11.5
1977	PGS	40.6	6.8	100	10.7
1978	PGS	40.9	6.8	95	10.0
1979	PGS	41.6	6.9	95	9.6
1980	PLM	38.4	6.5	–	–
1981	Census	37.1	6.5	–	–
1984	PDS	43.3	6.9	126.7	11.8
1985	PDS	43.3	7.0	115.9	11.5
1986	PDS	43.3	6.9	105.6	10.1

1987	PDS	43.3	6.9	103.9	10.5
1988	PDS	40.5	6.5	107.7	10.8
1989	PDS	40.9	6.4	106.7	10.1
1990	PDS	40.6	6.2	104.7	10.6
1991	PDS	39.5	6.0	102.4	9.8
1993	PDS	38.9	6.2	101.8	10.0

PGE = Population Growth Estimation.
PGS = Population Growth Survey.
PLM = Population Labour Force & Migration.
PFS = Pakistan Fertility Survey.
PDS = Pakistan Demographic Survey.

Significant differences in the rural and urban areas have been observed in the population growth patterns and other demographic indicators. According to the 1981 census, the inter-censal annual average population growth rate was 3.1 per cent per annum; 2.58 percent for rural areas and 4.38 per cent for urban areas. The crude birth rate, crude death rate, and infant mortality rates are all higher in the rural areas. The overall crude birth rate at 39.5 per 1,000 population in 1991 was made up of 34.4 for the urban areas and 41.9 for the rural areas. The overall crude death rate of 9.8 per 1,000 population was made up of 7.4 for the urban areas and 10.9 for the rural areas. The infant mortality rate, which shows a declining trend due to the Expanded Program of Immunization, was 102.4 per 1,000 live births in 1991; 68.9 in urban areas and 115.3 in rural areas. The high rates reflect the neglect of rural areas where a large proportion of the population is deprived of basic services and amenities such as potable water and sanitation facilities. In 1989, only 44 per cent of the rural population had access to potable water and only 19 per cent of the rural population had sanitation facilities. In rural areas, 95 per cent of population still obtains its water supplies from ground water. In Sindh, even in the cosmopolitan city of Karachi, 92 per cent of the urban population depends on highly polluted surface water. Furthermore, even the limited available health facilities are not fully utilized, especially in the rural areas. The lack of trained staff in the field of primary health care, such as traditional birth attendants and lady health visitors, the high incidence of waterborne diseases, and ignorance of family planning methods coupled with the non-availability of contraceptive devices are the major causes of the high infant and maternal mortality rates, crude death rates, and high fertility rates, particularly in the rural areas. The adequate provision of these services to the rural population is essential to reduce the imbalances between urban and rural areas.

Life expectancy at birth is regarded as the best indicator of mortality. It is also a good proxy for the prevailing health and nutrition conditions in the country. In Pakistan, this rate has increased since 1947. Life expectancy at birth in 1960 was only 43.11 years and it increased to 61.5 years in 1992. A high life expectancy contributes significantly to the achievement of a high rank on the human development index developed by the United Nations.

B. Dependency Rates

A high dependency ratio not only puts an extra burden on the working age population but also leads to the slowing down of the process of economic growth. As shown in Table 3, the share of the working age population (15 to 64 years) in the total population is around 52 per cent. Among them, a large proportion of females is not economically active, and this places an extra burden on the small proportion of the economically active population. According to the 1981 census, the youth dependency ratio in Pakistan is amongst the highest in the developing countries. The overall dependency ratio has increased from 89 per cent in 1951 to 95 per cent in 1981. This indicates that each person of working age has almost one dependent person to take care of. The decline in the fertility rate would help in reducing the number of the population under the age of fifteen years.

C. Urbanization

Urban settlements occupy less than 0.75 per cent of Pakistan's land and contain 30 per cent of its population. The figures from the 1981 census imply that the growth rate of urban population

(4.38 per cent) is higher than that of the rural population (2.58 per cent). In addition to the high fertility and low mortality rates, large-scale migration from rural to urban areas also contributes significantly to this high growth rate. The urban population was estimated to be five million in 1947 and forty-nine million in 1995; about a seven-fold increase in forty-five years (*see* Table 1). The share of urban population in total population has more than doubled. There are many reasons for rural-urban migration. Among these are modernization in agriculture and the resultant labour displacement, coupled with the rapid industrial development in the urban areas. Concentration of land in a few hands and lack of non-agricultural jobs in the rural areas also contributes to this migration. A large proportion of the jobless rural labour force tends to seek jobs in the urban informal sector and live in poor physical and economic conditions. The number of cities and towns has more than doubled since 1951. Most of the growth occurred in the major cities. For example, Karachi alone accounts for 21 per cent of the urban population. Lahore, Faisalabad, Rawalpindi, Gujranwala, Peshawer, Hyderabad, and Multan contain another 30 per cent of the urban population. Thus, more than half of the urban population lives in the eight major cities.

3. EMPLOYMENT AND THE LABOUR FORCE

Full utilization of human resources is based on effective and gainful employment. Employment and manpower planning are essential for adequate human resource development in Pakistan. According to the official classification, the labour force is divided into self-employed persons, employers and employees, and unpaid family helpers. Those involved in 'productive work', for which they receive wages and salaries, form part of the official classification. Housewives are not part of the labour force because they do not receive a wage and presumably do not engage in 'productive work'.

The size of the labour force, its distribution in various sectors, the levels of unemployment and underemployment, all have an important bearing on the human development as well as economic development of a country. In 1994–5, Pakistan's estimated population was 128 million and its estimated labour force was 35.68 million. Of this number, 33.99 million were employed; 10.45 million in urban areas and 25.23 million in rural areas. In Pakistan, the overall population and the working age population are both growing rapidly at more than 3 per cent per annum. This implies a need for creating more job opportunities to absorb the rapidly growing labour force. The low rate of employment generation coupled with the fast growth of the potential labour force has resulted in a high incidence of unemployment and underemployment. The labour force has increased from 16.40 millions in 1963–4 to 35.68 million in 1994–5. Table 3 shows a declining trend in the labour force participation rate; in 1963–4 it was 32.59 and it declined to 27.87 (45.2 per cent for males and 9.8 per cent for females) in 1994–5. This participation rate for females in the labour force is abysmally low in Pakistan even in comparison with other Islamic countries. The *Human Development Report 1995* notes that the economic activity rate among women in Pakistan during 1994 was only 14 per cent; while in India it was 28 per cent, in Sri Lanka 29 per cent, in Iran 19 per cent, and in Bangladesh 62 per cent.

Table 3
Labour force participation:
unemployment and underemployment rates

Year	Labour force (millions)	Employed labour force (millions)	Labour force participation rate (%)	Unemployment rate (%)	Underemployment rate (%)
1963–4	16.40	16.24	32.59	0.97	–
1964–5	16.65	16.47	32.17	1.08	–
1969–70	18.11	17.75	30.33	1.99	13.98
1970–71	18.70	18.37	30.41	1.76	8.31
1971–2	18.94	18.55	29.90	2.06	7.16
1972–3	19.61	19.29	29.76	1.88	–
1973–4	20.12	19.76	29.63	1.79	–

1974–5	20.64	20.30	29.49	1.65	8.39
1975–6	21.54	21.08	29.86	2.14	–
1976–7	22.48	21.89	30.24	2.65	–
1977–8	23.46	22.73	30.63	3.11	–
1978–9	24.49	23.62	31.02	3.55	4.79
1979–80	25.07	24.15	30.81	3.67	–
1980–81	25.65	24.70	30.59	3.70	–
1981–2	26.27	25.27	30.39	3.81	–
1982–3	26.91	25.85	30.19	3.94	13.00
1983–4	27.45	26.40	29.92	3.83	–
1984–5	28.00	26.96	28.67	3.71	13.96
1985–6	28.05	27.02	27.86	3.64	9.56
1986–7	29.60	28.70	29.40	3.05	9.75
1987–8	29.93	28.99	28.51	3.14	10.43
1988–9	30.87	29.90	28.83	3.14	–
1989–90	31.82	30.82	28.30	3.14	–
1990–91	31.83	29.83	27.97	6.28	11.01
1991–2	32.97	31.04	28.11	5.85	–
1992–3	33.97	32.08	27.87	4.71	–
1993–4	34.70	33.02	27.88	4.84	–
1994–5(E)	35.69	33.96	27.88	4.85	–
1995–6(E)	36.70	34.92	27.88	4.85	–

Sources: *Economic Survey* 1995–6, *Labour Force Survey*, various issues.
   E   = Estimated.

A. UNEMPLOYMENT AND UNDEREMPLOYMENT

Table 3 shows an increasing trend in the unemployment rate. According to the *Labour Force Survey*, this rate was 5.8 per cent in 1991–2; 5.4 per cent in rural areas and 7.0 per cent in the urban areas. There are a number of reasons for the increasing unemployment rates. These include the high rate of population growth, increasing levels of capital intensity in production through inappropriate choice of techniques, lack of technical education and training facilities, lack of education, and the mismatch of available jobs with the skills and education that the existing system is producing. The unemployment rate is higher in urban areas. The high rate of rural–urban migration adds to unemployment. Most of the industry is located in the urban areas. Pakistan has consistently moved towards more capital–intensive and labour-displacing technology. Therefore, industry does not keep up with the growing labour force. The lack of general education with an emphasis on financial and business management and service provision also restricts most of the potential labour force from jobs in the rapidly expanding service sector. The data

Table 4
Employment and labour productivity growth in various sectors

Sector	Employment growth				Employment elasticity				Labour productivity				% contribution in GDP growth	
	1971/72-1978/79	1978/79-1986/87	1986/87-1990/91	1974/75-1991/92	1971/72-1978/79	1978/79-1986/87	1986/87-1990/91	1974/75-1991/92	1971/72-1978/79	1978/79-1986/87	1986/87-1990/91	1974/75-1991/92	Employment	Labour productivity
Agriculture	2.2	1.6	0.44	1.0	0.92	0.41	0.02	0.34	0.2	2.3	4.34	2.7	27	73
Manufactuing	5.2	2.1	-2.41	0.1	0.99	0.21	-0.32	0.22	-1.1	7.16	9.16	7.5	1	99
Large scale	0.7	0.0	–	–	0.21	0.00	–	–	2.6	10.4	–	–	–	–
Small scale	6.1	2.4	–	–	0.80	0.28	–	–	1.0	5.9	–	–	–	–
Electricity, gas etc.	12.5	2.9	4.45	–	1.51	0.30	0.28	–	-3.7	6.6	8.91	–	–	–
Construction	9.0	5.2	3.58	3.9	0.84	0.16	0.89	0.51	1.6	3.0	0.37	1.0	79	21
Commerce	5.1	3.5	3.36	3.3	0.98	0.45	0.56	0.46	0.1	4.1	2.31	3.3	50	50
Transportation	3.2	3.8	0.81	3.0	0.45	0.48	0.20	0.49	3.7	3.9	2.96	3.2	49	51
Financing	3.1	1.1	4.26	–	0.28	0.14	0.05	–	7.8	6.7	2.04	–	–	–
Other services	3.4	4.2	4.25	3.8	0.43	0.61	0.63	0.87	4.3	2.5	2.17	2.6	58	42
All Sectors	3.4	2.5	0.97	1.7	0.66	0.36	0.16	0.41	1.7	4.3	4.14	4.1	30	70

Sources: Hyder (1994), *Workforce Situation Report 1993* (1995) and *Statistical Yearbook 1994* (1994).

indicate that the unemployment rate in the rural areas increases with the improvement in the educational level. Either the existing jobs in the rural areas are not sufficient to absorb the educated labour force or their education has imparted an urban bias to their expectations so that they prefer to stay unemployed in the rural areas as they wait for jobs in the urban areas.

Because of the existence of underemployment, especially in the wage sector, the unemployment rate may not accurately depict the unemployment situation. Persons working less than 35 hours per week are considered to be underemployed according to the official classification. The data for Pakistan shows fluctuations in the underemployment rate. It was 14 per cent in 1969–70, dropped to 4.79 in 1978–9, and increased to 13.9 per cent in 1984–5. It has fluctuated by about 10 per cent since then. While some of these fluctuations can be attributed to the changing definitions of key parameters in the labour force surveys, most can be explained by migration out of the country in the mid- to late 1970s. This created shortages locally and led to fuller employment. The return of the immigrants from the mid-1980s onwards resulted in a reversion to the higher levels of underemployment.

B. Trends in Employment

Employment patterns can be judged through the trends in the rates of growth of employment, employment elasticities, and labour productivity. These are reported in Table 4. Employment elasticity measures the relationship between employment (or quantity of labour) and output of a specific sector or economy and labour productivity explains the relationship between quality of labour and output. Labour productivity reflects the effects of improved education, higher technical knowledge, and technological advancement etc. It has a positive and significant effect on GDP, i.e., the more productive the labour force, the higher the GDP. This data in Table 4 implies that employment change causes 30 per cent change in the GDP whereas 70 per cent of the change in the GDP is due to the change in labour productivity.

According to data in this Table, employment grew at a slightly faster rate during the period 1971–2 to 1978–9. Its growth rate was 3.4 per cent per annum. The employment elasticity for this period was 0.66. This was mainly due to high demand for labour in the manufacturing, electricity and gas, and the construction sector. During this period, employment and the labour force grew at the same rate. High employment growth rates signify greater employment opportunities in specific sectors. The employment growth rate and employment elasticities dropped during the period 1978–9 to 1986–7. A further decline is observed during the 1986–7 to 1990–91 period.

Trends in both these periods indicate that employment in the commodity producing sector, i.e. in agriculture and manufacturing, has declined drastically. This is mainly due to the introduction of capital-intensive technology in both these sectors. The increasing employment opportunities in the services sector attract most of the labour force. This is evident from the declining employment elasticities in the commodity producing sector and increasing ones in construction, trade and commerce, and other services. The improvement in the quality of the labour force through education and training partly accounts for the labour productivity growth from 1.7 per cent during the 1971–2 to 1978–9 period to 4.14 per cent during 1986–7 to 1990–91 period. A large part of this productivity increase simply resulted from more capital-intensive technologies which produced higher output with lower levels of labour input. The low employment growth rates, low employment elasticities, and high labour productivity in the major sectors of the economy imply a need for improving the quality of labour through education and training and for creating more job opportunities, especially in the services sector.

During 1994–5, the employed labour force was estimated to be 33.99 million; 22.09 in the non-wage sector and 11.9 in the wage sector. In Pakistan, GDP grew at 5.65 per cent per annum and population is growing at 3.1 per cent per annum. This indicates the slow process of employment generation in the country. From Table 4, one can observe the situation of employment in various sectors. Agriculture was the largest labour absorbing sector in 1963–4. However, with the increase in employment opportunities in other sectors, its share declined steadily, although it still provides employment to nearly half of the labour force. Employment growth, employment elasticity, and growth in labour productivity are lower in this sector compared to others. This means that there is surplus labour in this sector and due to the existence of the law of diminishing returns, marginal productivity decreases with the increase in numbers employed. However, higher growth in average labour productivity than growth in employment implies that agricultural output can be increased by improving the quality of labour. According to Table 4, 73 per cent of the increase in agricultural output is due to the increase in labour productivity and only 23 per cent is due to increasing the numbers employed.

Employment growth in the manufacturing sector was recorded at only 0.1 percent during the period 1974–5 to 1991–2 while for the shorter period, 1986–7 to 1990–91, a negative growth rate has been recorded. Growth in labour productivity is, however, highest in this sector. Capital intensification is labour displacing but increases output per worker. The process of capital intensification in Pakistan's manufacturing sector is confirmed by the low employment elasticity in this sector. As data in this Table indicates, about 99 per cent of the change in the manufacturing output resulted from the change in labour productivity.

The growth rate of labour productivity is lowest (1.0 per cent) in the construction sector. By contrast, the employment growth rate and employment elasticity in this sector were quite high, i.e., 3.7 per cent and 0.51 per cent, respectively. However, the short term growth rate shows a declining trend. This implies that there is scope for creating more jobs in this sector.

In the commerce and trade sector, employment and labour productivity are growing at the same rate, i.e., 3.3 per cent. The employment elasticity is also high (0.49) and this indicates possibilities for increasing employment in this sector. The transport sector shows similar trends. Though labour productivity is higher than employment growth, a rather high employment elasticity suggests the potential for an increase in output by increasing employment. The 'other' services sector that includes public administration and utilities, has the highest employment elasticity (0.87), and the employment growth rate was the second highest, followed by the construction sector. However, labour productivity growth was only 2.6 per cent. In this sector, 58 per cent of output growth is caused by the growth in employment. The public sector has traditionally absorbed much labour, but with the onset of down-sizing it is unlikely to continue to play that role.

According to the *Statistical Yearbook 1993*, administrative workers account for only 1.2 per cent and professional workers for 4.9 per cent of total employment. Employment in these areas depends on high and professional education. However, there were only 6.7 per cent degree holders and 1.6 per cent postgraduates [*Labour Force Survey (1991–92)*]. These small percentages show the poor performance of our education sector. It is interesting to note that the share of female workers is considerably higher (20.2 per cent) among professionals. It is also interesting that female participation in higher education is relatively greater than that of males in both the urban and rural areas.

C. Informal Sector

Labour absorption has declined in many sectors due to the increasing reliance on capital-intensive techniques. The formal sector increasingly demands educated and skilled manpower. A large proportion of the population, consisting of the uneducated and the unskilled labour force, therefore seeks jobs in the informal sector. The informal sector is defined by the structure of the organization and the size of the establishment. This includes family enterprise, industrial establishment with less than ten workers, and non-industrial establishments with not more than twenty workers. In Pakistan, this sector accounted for 69 per cent of the urban employment in 1972–3 and 72.7 per cent in 1985–6 [*see* Guisinger and Irfan (1980) and Burki (1990)].

The informal sector serves as an important source of employment and income generation for the less educated and unskilled and semi-skilled labour force. Various studies, for example, Guisinger and Irfan (1980), Kazi (1987), Nadvi (1989), Chaudary, et al. (1989), Mehmood (1990), Ahmed and Arshad (1990), Burki (1990), Kemal and Mehmood (1993), and Sher (1995) have examined the structure of the informal sector by conducting surveys in different cities at different time periods. These studies highlight the main features of the informal sector and point to the growth constraints face by this sector. These studies categorize the informal sector workforce as consisting of self-employed, regular workers, family helpers, and *shagirds* (apprentices). A substantially low capital-labour ratio has been observed in the production process of the informal sector. Kemal and Mehmood (1993) estimated that the informal sector can create fourteen times the number of jobs that the rest of the economy can with the same level of investment. All the studies have consistently found lower wages prevailing in the informal sector as compared to the formal sector. The informal sector faces problems in obtaining raw material at low cost and in marketing its output. Easing some of these problems will significantly help the informal sector.

The Seventh Five Year Plan was the first instance in which explicit attention was paid to enhancing the productivity of the informal sector by expanding technical training institutions, improving the curriculum according to the needs of the rapidly changing technology, providing modern equipment and training materials in these institutions, and encouraging the *ustad* (master)-*shagird* training system.

A trade and location-specific credit policy would greatly help in the expansion of the informal sector. The government has introduced concessionary credit schemes to promote self-employment and employment in household and small-scale enterprises. Under the National Self-employment Scheme, 8,591 loans, amounting to Rupees 1,666 million, had been disbursed by February 1996. These loans are estimated to have generated employment for 26,877 persons. The Youth Investment

Promotion Society (YIPS) aims at providing opportunities for self-employment to unemployed youth through small projects in industry, mining, agriculture, trade, transport, health, education, and other service sectors. So far, this scheme has provided employment to 6,068 persons. In addition to these schemes, the government is taking special interest in improving the education and skills of women and in expanding their employment opportunities. For this purpose, programmes of vocational training in secretarial work, computers, communications, and commercial art have been introduced.

4. THE EDUCATION SECTOR

Education is considered to be the major form of investment in human capital and serves as a key input in human capital formation. It not only raises the productivity and efficiency of individuals but also improves the quality of their life by increasing earnings. Getting more education not only ensures higher paying jobs but also creates awareness about health, hygiene and nutrition. There is evidence to suggest that it also leads to small family size and greater female labour force participation. The importance of education is reflected in the fundamental teachings of Islam which places great emphasis on acquiring education for both males and females.

The education situation in Pakistan has been generally unsatisfactory. Low enrolment rates at the primary level, wide disparities between regions and genders, lack of trained teachers, deficiency of proper teaching materials, and poor infrastructure of schools reflect the substandard state of education in Pakistan. In the rural areas, the situation is more distressing.

Psacharopolous (1994) has reported the social and private rates of return for education in many countries. In the case of Pakistan, he observes that the social rates of return at primary level are higher than those at secondary and higher levels. The private rate of returns are, however, found to be highest at the tertiary level. Though these rates are lower than in other developing countries, they suggest that investment in education, especially at the primary level, is highly attractive from the social point of view.

Based on the Government of Pakistan's calculation, the overall literacy rate for 1995–6 was estimated at 37.9 per cent; 50 per cent for males and 25.3 per cent for females [*Economic Survey 1995–96*]. The *Human Development Report 1996,* which presents the Human Development Index for 174 countries, indicates that Pakistan falls in the category of 'Low Human Development Countries'. A number of countries in this category have per capita GDP lower than that of Pakistan, but significantly higher literacy rates as compared to Pakistan. For example, in 1992, Kenya registered a per capita GDP of $ 1400 (in purchasing power parity terms) and a literacy rate of 74.5 per cent. At that time, Pakistan showed a much higher GDP per capita, i.e $ 2890, but a much lower literacy rate, i.e., only 36 per cent. According to the *Human Development Report*, there are only seventeen countries with literacy rates of 37 per cent or lower, and Pakistan is one of them.

The literacy rates for Pakistan are presented in Table 5. Significant variations at the gender and regional level can be observed in this Table. In 1992, the literacy rate was 23 per cent in rural areas and 46 per cent in the urban areas. The urban bias in literacy in Pakistan is obvious. The literacy rate for females is less than half that for males. And among rural females it was abysmally low, i.e., just 12.4 per cent. Over time, the gap between the male and female literacy rates in the urban areas has narrowed, whereas in the rural areas, in absolute terms, it has actually widened!

Table 5
Literacy ratio (10 years and above)
by sex and urban-rural areas

	All areas			Urban areas			Rural areas		
	Both	Male	Female	Both	Male	Female	Both	Male	Female
1951	21.8	25.9	16.9	–	–	–	–	–	–
1961	18.4	26.9	8.2	36.7	46.8	23.3	12.2	19.8	3.6
1972	21.7	30.2	11.6	41.5	49.6	30.9	14.3	22.6	4.7
1981	26.2	35.1	16.0	47.1	55.3	37.3	17.3	26.2	7.3
1992	30.4	39.9	20.2	45.7	53.5	37.5	23.4	33.7	12.4
1996	37.9	50.0	25.3	58.3	–	28.3	–	–	–

Source: Malik et al., (1994); Government of Pakistan, (1994), *Workforce Statistical Yearbook* (1992), Government of Pakistan, *Economic Survey*, several years.

The performance of the education sector can also be measured by the enrolment ratios at different levels of schooling. This information is presented in Table 6. This Table shows that the enrolment ratio at each level and overall has more than doubled since 1951, i.e., from an overall rate of 14.6 in 1951 to 32.6 in 1981. Primary school enrolment ratios are higher than those of middle and high school levels. The enrolment ratio at the primary level was 20.1 per cent in 1951 and rose to 33.8 per cent in 1961. In 1972, it touched 40.5 per cent but declined to 40.2 per cent in 1981. An improvement in the female enrolment ratio at each level is obvious from this table, whereas male enrolment has remained stagnant at the middle and high school levels and declined at primary level during the period from 1972 to 1981. Due to various policies during recent years, however, enrolment ratios for both males and females have improved significantly at each level.

The availability of schools and qualified and trained teachers are the two major determinants of the quantity and quality of education. An increase in the number of educational institutions raises the literacy rate while an increase in the number of qualified and trained teachers improves the quality of education. Both of these have a direct effect on economic growth. Primary education provides a foundation for future manpower. The quality of education at the primary level in Pakistan can be

Table 6
School enrolment ratio by level and sex

	1951			1961			1972			1981			1993			1996		
	Both	Male	Female	Both	Male	Female	Both	Male	Female	Both	Male	Female	Both	Male	Female	Both	Male	Female
Primary School	20.1	32.5	5.8	38.8	49.8	15.3	40.5	55.9	22.9	40.2	51.7	27.5	68.9	84.8	53.7	73.0	89.0	57.0
Middle School	10.1	16.7	2.5	20.8	32.0	6.9	23.7	33.5	11.1	25.1	34.2	14.2	44.3	57.5	30.0	46.0	59.2	32.3
High School	4.6	7.4	1.3	11.5	17.4	4.3	14.6	21.2	6.4	15.3	21.2	8.4	28.1	37.0	18.4	32.0	41.6	22.0
All Schools	14.6	23.6	4.1	27.7	41.0	11.9	32.2	44.1	17.9	32.6	42.4	21.4	–	–	–	–	–	–

Sources: Malik et. al., (1994), *Economic Survey*, several years.

judged by the physical condition of the schools and the stated requirements for a teacher's job at this level. The physical condition of most of the schools in the rural areas, in particular, is quite poor. Open air schools, even in areas with harsh climatic conditions, are the norm rather than the exception. Electricity, water, latrine facilities, and sometimes even teachers, are missing. The low standard of the teachers at this level, depicted by the minimalist official requirements for this position, and the low salaries offered, signify the low priority accorded to this extremely important basic education level on which the human development edifice is constructed.

The resultant substandard levels of primary education in Pakistan are to be expected. Due to this low priority, around 48 per cent of the enrolled children drop out at the primary level. This is a major wastage of the already meagre resources invested in primary education.

During the Seventh Five Year Plan period, the enrolment at the primary level grew by 11.2 per cent. This growth rate was only 4.6 per cent during the Sixth Five Year Plan period. During the Eighth Five Year Plan, a high priority was given to the rapid spread of primary education. The year 1995–6 was declared as the year of 'Basic Education for All'. The enrolment rate at primary level for the year 1995–6 has been estimated at 73 per cent; 89 for males and 57 per cent for females. At the middle level this rate was 46 per cent; 59 per cent for males and 32 per cent for females. Likewise, for the high school level, the enrolment rate was estimated at 32 per cent; 42 per cent for males and 20 per cent for females [*Economic Survey 1995–96*].

The trend growth rates for educational institutions, enrolment in educational institutions, and the number of teachers in educational institutions at different levels, are all important indicators of the state of education in a country. These are reported in Tables 7, 8, and 9. During the period from 1959–60 to 1995–6, the educational institutions, enrolment ratios, and the number of teachers increased at rather high rates, particularly for females, reflecting in part the small, almost non-existent base from which these grew. The growth rate of the number of educational institutions, enrolment, and number of teachers for all categories were relatively high during the 1960s. The proportion of expenditure on education relative to the GDP was higher during the Second Five Year Plan as compared to the third, fourth, and fifth plans. Presumably during the second plan period, the government took a keener interest not only in opening up new schools but also in providing staff and increasing enrolment. Due to the official discouragement of the opening of private schools and colleges and the low levels of expenditure on education during the 1970s, the growth rates of all educational indicators fell drastically. During this period, most of the secondary vocational institutions were merged into high schools. Negative growth rates were observed for both the number of and enrolment in high schools. The period of the 1980s witnessed a rapid expansion in the education sector. The number and enrolment in secondary vocational institutions grew by 15.3 and 11.7 per cent respectively. During this period, female enrolment in all categories, except postgraduate universities, remained high. This may be due to the fact that the number of institutions for females and the number of female teachers both grew at rather high rates. Since the 1980s, enrolment at the primary level, especially for females, has been highly emphasized by each government. The growth rate of enrolment in technical and vocational colleges was 11.7 per cent during 1989–90. These colleges provide a large number of the teachers. Consequently, the number of teachers at the primary, middle, and high levels increased during this period. However, the numbers are still grossly inadequate. At present, the country has 116,000 primary, 33,000 middle, and 11,000 high schools. At existing rates, these require around 40,000 teachers annually. However, only 15,000 teachers are produced each year. To overcome this shortage, especially for female and rural teachers, the Allama Iqbal Open University has launched a federally assisted programmme through its 'Distance Education System'. There is a need to make an improvement in the teacher's training courses to enhance the quality of education.

Though Pakistan has achieved some success in increasing the

number of schools as well as the enrolment ratios, the drop-out rate has not declined. The high drop-out rate not only indicates the poor quality of education but is also the primary cause of poor human resource development. The high drop-out rate at the primary level causes low enrolment at the secondary and higher levels. Sarmad, Hussain, and Zahid (1988) found that during the period 1976 to 1985, the drop-out rate at the primary level was 48 per cent for males and 62 per cent for females. They explained this great discrepancy through a cultural constraint that works against girls. The relative lack of female teachers causes the removal of girls from schools when they get slightly older because parents do not want their daughters to receive instruction from male teachers. Poverty also compels parents to remove children from school and they generally remove the females first because of the cultural constraint mentioned above. For most families whose children drop out, expenditure on education is generally not considered to be an investment but a loss of income. Non-availability of schools, long distances between school and home, bad or no transport facility, lack of trained teachers, inappropriate physical facilities (such as proper school buildings, with running water and latrine facilities), high student-teacher ratios, harsh treatment of the students, and unsuitable curricula are the reasons most often cited in the literature for the high drop-out rates. As already stated, this drop-out rate is higher for females.

Non-formal education can play a significant role in bridging the literacy gap. Non-formal education programmes can quickly reach a significant proportion of the population through group discussion, practical demonstration, pictorial instructions, and the electronic media. In this regard, short-term adult literacy programmes, affordable home schools in low income areas, and mosque schools play a vital role. There are 25,200 mosque schools in the 47,000 villages of Pakistan. This number is sadly insufficient. Community participation is a significant factor in spreading education. Schemes based on community participation can provide a low cost alternative to the traditional government schools and also a means for lowering the drop-out rate.

Trend growth rates of the number of educational institutions

Period	Primary schools		Middle schools		High schools		Secondary vocational institutions		Arts & Science colleges		Professional colleges		Universities
	Total	Female	Total	Female	Total	Female	Total	Female	Total	Female	Total	Female	
Each Decade:													
1959–60 to 1969–70	7.51	11.02	6.83	11.86	6.16	9.67	6.58	8.61	8.94	11.03	4.00	0.00	5.28
1969–70 to 1979–80	2.94	4.30	3.72	4.78	5.65	6.41	-0.79	-4.04	4.17	3.82	4.81	4.21	9.06
1979–80 to 1989–90	7.14	4.79	4.56	7.96	7.67	7.48	15.34	18.20	3.06	6.68	-0.00	-1.01	2.79
1989–90 to 1995–96	0.35	1.50	4.61	3.98	4.38	2.81	-3.98	-3.62	3.19	3.35	9.51	2.10	1.71
Overall Period:													
1959–60 to 1995–6	4.83	5.47	4.64	6.81	6.05	6.81	5.68	6.09	4.27	5.32	3.37	1.84	5.31
Plan Periods:													
Second Plan: (1959–60 to 1964–5)	12.29	18.68	6.90	15.45	7.94	11.37	5.92	5.46	11.71	13.33	2.03	0.00	9.27
Third Plan: (1964–5 to 1969–70)	4.94	6.82	5.42	7.65	4.25	7.48	8.28	12.86	5.00	6.56	5.61	0.00	3.52
Non-plan Period: (1969–70 to 1977–8)	3.29	4.85	4.35	5.84	6.71	7.44	1.15	-2.55	4.95	4.10	5.78	5.75	9.50
Fifth Plan: (1977–8 to 1982–3)	4.97	4.49	1.21	0.97	2.74	3.69	3.45	4.89	0.79	1.05	0.59	5.10	7.25
Sixth Plan: (1982–3 to 1987–8)	8.20	4.08	4.72	7.31	7.52	8.49	15.84	23.93	3.58	8.26	0.00	-3.19	2.31
Seventh Plan: (1987–8 to 1992–3)	2.82	6.72	8.49	12.03	12.12	14.34	-0.51	-2.37	4.40	3.78	0.00	-0.00	1.02

Source: *Economic Survey*, various issues.

Table 8
Growth rate of enrolment in educational institutions

Period	Primary schools		Middle schools		High schools		Secondary vocational institutions		Arts & Science colleges		Professional colleges		Universities	
	Total	Female	Total	Female	Total	Female	Total	Female	Total	Female	Total	Female	Total	Female
Each Decade:														
1959–60 to 1969–70	7.61	10.71	8.18	11.68	8.00	9.86	6.08	5.49	9.75	14.11	9.78	9.78	12.55	13.43
1969–70 to 1979–80	3.24	5.36	4.84	7.29	4.38	7.86	-2.53	-5.57	3.13	5.64	8.12	8.12	11.26	7.43
1979–80 to 1989–90	6.36	6.58	6.27	8.04	6.01	7.31	11.71	18.56	6.15	6.70	2.27	2.27	5.76	4.79
1989–90 to 1995–6	0.45	4.69	2.80	6.71	5.35	5.31	-1.99	-4.77	8.57	9.02	12.66	4.92	-1.86	10.28
Overall Period:														
1959–60 to 1995–6	4.85	6.45	5.58	7.79	5.67	7.44	5.26	4.31	5.85	8.06	5.86	7.08	7.67	6.92
Plan Periods:														
Second Plan:														
(1959–60 to 1964–5)	9.58	11.81	7.90	15.31	9.05	17.28	10.66	11.22	12.52	15.42	7.65	9.86	22.47	24.21
Third Plan:														
(1964–5 to 1969–70)	5.49	8.71	7.09	5.51	7.64	5.14	6.00	10.20	5.83	12.21	14.01	7.73	2.65	2.23
Non-plan Period:														
(1969–70 to 1977–8)	4.37	6.36	5.59	8.38	6.06	9.00	-3.08	-3.97	2.73	5.13	7.97	12.16	11.59	10.47
Fifth Plan:														
(1977–8 to 1982–3)	7.08	4.75	3.17	4.53	3.17	2.79	13.20	3.05	6.07	7.08	-2.91	-5.82	4.32	5.24
Sixth Plan:														
(1982–3 to 1987–8)	4.65	5.52	5.90	8.73	5.06	7.62	10.50	26.38	3.89	5.37	4.89	12.16	6.11	4.97
Seventh Plan:														
(1987–8 to 1992–3)	11.20	9.76	10.43	13.24	10.84	15.35	-2.88	-3.36	6.08	10.09	0.77	3.40	5.27	2.67

Source: Economic Survey (various years)

Table 9

Growth rate of number of teachers in educational institutions

Period	Primary schools		Middle schools		High schools		Secondary vocational institutions		Arts & Science colleges		Professional colleges		Universities	
	Total	Female	Total	Female	Total	Female	Total	Female	Total	Female	Total	Female	Total	Female
Each Decade:														
1959–60 to 1969–70	6.97	10.29	8.45	14.44	6.89	10.25	0.00	0.00	0.00	0.00	0.00	0.00	12.72	12.71
1969–70 to 1979–80	4.35	6.50	4.71	6.39	6.82	7.69	2.05	3.39	4.71	3.98	8.01	10.16	9.39	11.72
1979–80 to 1989–90	5.78	7.99	3.78	5.30	7.50	7.30	11.52	16.63	4.32	6.13	3.27	7.14	3.35	6.40
1989–90 to 1995–6	2.05	5.63	2.55	4.39	4.58	5.64	-1.06	0.50	3.66	6.96	5.92	4.09	5.44	6.07
Overall Period:														
1959–60 to 1995–6	5.30	6.44	5.04	7.28	6.37	7.39	5.83	7.15	4.05	5.21	4.82	6.31	6.48	9.00
Plan Periods:														
Second Plan:														
(1959–60 to 1964–5)	10.82	13.58	10.55	18.62	8.03	10.31	0.00	0.00	0.00	0.00	0.00	0.00	24.10	16.42
Third Plan:														
(1964–5 to 1969–70)	4.26	8.26	7.05	9.20	5.37	8.98	7.08	7.40	8.48	9.92	6.66	5.73	2.94	9.51
Non-plan Period:														
(1969–70 to 1977–8)	5.09	8.20	5.33	7.96	7.69	9.09	1.71	4.19	5.22	3.97	9.04	12.45	10.77	15.08
Fifth Plan:														
(1977–8 to 1982–3)	4.66	-5.05	2.41	2.96	2.99	4.04	9.82	3.73	2.36	3.28	1.49	1.92	-0.18	4.80
Sixth Plan:														
(1982–3 to 1987–8)	2.80	4.16	1.64	1.88	6.47	7.09	12.04	22.50	6.79	8.63	5.04	9.47	3.75	5.92
Seventh Plan:														
(1987–8 to 1992–3)	11.70	6.48	7.48	11.12	11.27	7.60	-2.82	0.99	2.02	1.30	0.32	1.59	10.22	2.92

Source: *Economic Survey*, (various issues).

Affordable and accessible home schools with flexible timings
and duration suited to the needs of the children in the community
form part of this alternative. A large-scale non-formal primary
education project has recently been launched by the government
in collaboration with NGOs and the local communities. The
space for the schools under this program will be provided by
the latter and the government will arrange for the salaries of
teachers and their training. Under this scheme 10,000 schools
will be built by the end of 1996, 30,000 by 1997, and 200,000
by the year 2000. The NGO community in Pakistan is only now
providing this alternative. It will be a few years before the data
are available to evaluate them. In addition to these, the Allama
Iqbal Open University is also playing a crucial role in
disseminating education at different levels in various fields. It
enrollment in a variety of courses all over Pakistan, including
the remote Northern areas and Azad Kashmir, had increased to
4,29,630 in 1993–4 from only 976 in 1975–6.

A. TECHNICAL AND VOCATIONAL EDUCATION

Technical and vocational education produces skilled manpower
Unfortunately, in Pakistan, little attention has been given to this
type of education. So far, no effort has been made to co-ordinate
and standardize the curricula and the system of examination for
this type of education. Individual training institutions devise
their own courses depending upon the skills of the available
instructors. Examinations are not standardized. There is no
uniform criteria to evaluate the graduates of different institutions
In Pakistan, technical education and vocational training i
offered to the general public by private institutions and by
institutions under various ministries and departments at the
federal and provincial level. Informal training through the
traditional system of *ustad-shagird* (master-apprentice) also
provides training to a significant number who are engaged i
the informal sector as wage-earners or are self-employed.

The Ministry of Education, with the co-operation of the
education department, offers courses in wood-work, metal-work
electronics, and home economics as a part of the forma

education system for classes 6 to 8. Courses in agriculture are also offered at higher levels. Polytechnic, vocational, and commercial institutes offer courses in electrification, refrigeration, air-conditioning, engineering (including civil, electrical, electronic, and mechanical), computer software and hardware, typing, secretarial work, other office disciplines, tailoring, stitching, embroidery, textile designing, bio-medical, glass, wood and metal work, and ceramics etc. With the expanded agricultural and industrial activities and the development of transportation, banking, and commerce in both the public and private sectors, the requirement of technically trained clerical, managerial, and administrative personnel has however increased much more rapidly.

Vocational institutes offer certificate courses and commerce institutes award D.Com and C.Com degrees to their graduates while polytechnics offer diplomas to graduates. Table 10 presents data on the numbers enrolled in commerce, vocational, technical, and teacher's training institutes. These data are broken down by sex. In 1949, there were only five commerce and forty-one vocational institutes. The number and enrolment has increased considerably since then. In 1992 there were 237 commerce and 188 vocational institutes with 19,913 males and 1,493 females enrolled in the commerce institutes. The number of female students in vocational institutes is higher than that of males in each year. These institutes have, however, failed to fine-tune the skills of their graduates to the demands of the market. Consequently, males desirous of joining the work force prefer to obtain these skills on the job, while females generally attend these institutions in larger numbers because of the limited number of unskilled job opportunities in the market place for them.

On-the-job training is imparted in the informal sector through the *ustad-shagird* system of skill formation. The informal sector provides a variety of low cost goods and services and fulfills the needs of the low income group. Because the existing number of formal training institutions is not sufficient to cater to the demand for technical education and the skills that these institutions impart are not appropriate in fulfilling the existing demand, the *ustad-shagird* system of informal training plays an important role. It not only provides training but also ensures employment. This system works on a reciprocal basis and serves the interest of both parties. Chaudary, Azim, and Burki (1989) examined the role of the *ustad-shagird* system in skill development in twenty-four distinct activity groups by conducting a survey in the cities of Rawalpindi, Gujranwala, Sialkot, Deska, Lahore, Mian Channu, and Karachi.

They found a high demand for *shagirds* between the ages of 13 to 16 years, with an education level of primary or middle. In this system, the learning period varies from two to four years depending on the nature of the trade. Although the same period of time is required by the formal training institutions, the students there have to pay fees. In the *ustad-shagird* system, no fees are involved. Instead, a small but increasing stipend is generally paid to the *shagird* and the skills acquired are accompanied by the guarantee of employment.

In the formal sector, there were no polytechnic training institutions in Pakistan until 1960. During the 1960s, twenty-four polytechnics were established. In 1992, there were fifty-two polytechnics with 23,179 students; 21,503 males and 1,676 females. On average, these institutes produce 6,000 students every year. The skill concentration of these institutions however, does not seem to reflect the demands of the market place. This is why there is surplus skilled manpower in some trades and shortages in others. Due to this problem of mismatched supply and demand, the expansion of the polytechnics has slowed down. Butt (1991) found that due to the lack of communication between these institutions and industrial establishments, only 37 per cent of the graduates were able to obtain employment. Of these 37 per cent, many complained that their jobs did not match the skills that they had acquired at these institutes.

A number of vocational options are available to females, generally in the urban sector. The Department of Social Welfare provides training in skills like stitching, embroidery, knitting, block printing, dress-making, flower-making, and wood work in

Table 10
Number of technical training institutes and enrolment levels

Years	Commercial institutes			Industrial/vocational institutes			Polytechnic/technical colleges			Teachers' training institutes		
	No.	Enrolment		No.	Enrolment		No.	Enrolment		No.	Enrolment	
		Male	Female		Male	Female		Male	Female		Male	Female
1949–50	5	260	46	41	1735	1420	–	–	–	36	2729	1005
1959–60	11	581	–	48	2556	4786	–	–	–	55	4705	1501
1970–71	35	3352	53	81	499	6918	24	10755	–	66	9881	3030
1979–80	53	5522	8	88	3162	6343	22	10328	286	77	2405	3150
1984–85	73	15184	120	103	2882	7655	24	11947	1127	110	8003	1928
1989–90	156	17988	150	180	2257	9361	48	21860	1681	543	32247	22101
1991–92	237	19913	1493	188	2267	8801	52	21503	1676	208	19844	13305

Source: *Statistical Year Book*, (various issues).

2,030 training centres. Provincial Health Departments offer paramedical, dietitian, X-ray, and nursing courses. Various government and semi-government departments offer on-the-job training courses to their staff. A large number of private institutions and NGOs also provide training facilities. However, most of these are based in the urban areas.

The National Training Bureau is another official attempt at reducing unemployment by regulating and promoting technical and vocational training programmes. The Bureau has initiated the National Vocational Training Project (NVTP), the Special Human Resource Development Programme, and the National Talent Pool. In 1981, the NVTP was started to impart training in both the formal and informal sector. Its objective was to construct the National Training Development Institute, provide furniture, equipment, other training material, and trained staff, in addition to disseminating theoretical and practical knowledge, developing skill standards, and establishing standardized examinations. In Phase I, the National Training Development Institute started its work to prepare the standard curricula according to the needs of job market. These curricula have been approved by the National Training Board and are being followed by thirty-seven technical training centres, government vocational institutes, and apprenticeship training centres in the different provinces of Pakistan. These training centres produce 12,584 students annually on a double shift basis. Under this project, twenty-three training centres in Punjab, six in Sindh, five in NWFP, three in Balochistan, and one in Islamabad have been established. In the second phase, the enrolment and teaching staff in these centres have been increased. The special Human Resource Development Programme aims to open the vocational training centres in the rural areas. The National Talent Pool imparts a high level of scientific and technical training.

The Eighth Five Year Plan aimed at increasing the enrolment in technical and vocational institutions in order to produce skilled manpower. In this plan, the private sector was given an incentive to open and operate technical training institutes. The Allama Iqbal Open University also offers teachers' training

Table 11
Budget allocations on education by level (federal plus provincial)

Years	Total expenditure	Education expenditure by level							Development expenditure	Non-development expenditure	Expenditure on education as % of total
		Primary education	Secondary education	College education	University education	Technical education	Special education	Other items			
	(1)	(2)	(3)	(4)	(5)	(6)	(7)	(8)	(9)	(10)	(11)
1947–48	30.4	11.0	5.4	(a)	1.9	(b)	8.0	4.1	–	–	–
1949–50	43.9	20.8	9.6	(a)	6.5	(b)	1.3	5.7	–	–	–
1959–60	163.8	60.2	34.4	17.7	15.2	4.0	7.1	25.2	48.0	115.8	1.21
1969–70	578.7	196.8	91.8	49.6	44.7	46.7	16.5	132.6	170.1	408.6	1.40
1979–80	4153.5	1604.4	820.4	387.5	426.2	518.7(c)	71.0(f)	325.3	1060.2	3093.3	2.20
1989–90	32088.9	8397.0	7262.0	2607.0	4874.0	2119.0(c)	386.4(f)	6443.5	8608.8	23480.1	

Source: *Statistical Year Book, 1995*

Note: 1. Expenditure incurred on health, education, agriculture, veterinary, forest, industries, etc. has been included in technical and professional education.

a. Expenditure on college education included in universities.
b. Expenditure on technical and professional education included in special education.
c. Expenditure includes the expenditure on teacher training colleges.
d. Expenditure on teacher training schools only; expenditure on teacher training colleges included in technical and professional education.
e. Other items include expenditure on scholarships, administration, other facilities, lump sum provision, grant-in-aid, general and miscellaneous work etc. However, expenditure on work from 1970–71 onward has been included under the relevant sectors' development expenditure.
f. Expenditure on teacher training also includes technical and professional education partially, a break-up of which is available from budget accounts.

programmes. Computer education has also been introduced in these institutions during this plan.

Teachers' training is crucial for improving the quality of education. Unfortunately, due attention has not been given to this important factor. As a result, the teachers' training programme suffers from serious problems, such as lack of laboratories, science equipment, libraries, old curricula, and insufficient teaching staff. The number of teachers' training institutes has grown but both the quantity and the quality remain insufficient. In 1950, only thirty-six training centres provided teacher's training. By 1992, this number had increased to 208. The number of students in these centres also shows an increasing trend over time. Interestingly, during the 1970s, female enrolment was higher than male enrolment. This may have been due to large-scale migration, mostly male, to the Middle East.

B. Expenditure on Education

Table 11 shows that the total expenditure on education as a percentage of GNP has remained extremely low since 1947. It was only 0.99 per cent of GNP in 1960–61. Since then, this proportion has been increasing, but slowly. Before 1984–5, this proportion was less than 2 per cent in each year. In 1990, it increased to 3.4 per cent. This percentage is comparable with that of other high Human Development Index countries. According to the data in Table 11, a large proportion of educational expenditure is devoted to primary education. However, the expenditure on teachers' training has declined continuously.

Table 12 presents the public expenditure during each five year plan period. This table shows that public expenditure on education and manpower development was only Rs 0.23 billion during the First Five Year Plan (1955–60). Public expenditure on education remained low during the first five five-year plans. There was a sharp increase during the 1983–8 period. Under the Prime Minister's five point programme in the late 1980s, this expenditure jumped to Rs 22.72 billion. During this period, the expenditure on education as a percentage of GNP increased to

2.4 per cent. Due to financial difficulties and with the dismissal of the government in 1988, the programme was abandoned and the expenditure on education dropped to 2.1 per cent in 1988–9. Thus, the Sixth Five Year Plan (1983–8) failed to achieve its targets for education. The new government that followed launched the People's Works Programme. However, before it could announce its education policy, this government was also dismissed. Consequently, most of the targets of the Seventh Five Year Plan (1988–93) were not met. In 1992–3, the pressure from multilateral donors to address the imbalances in the social sector led to the formulation of the Social Action Program (SAP).

This programme focuses on promoting productivity, reducing poverty, and encouraging smaller, healthier, and better educated families by emphasizing basic education, population welfare, rural development, health, and nutrition. In education, the SAP has stressed the need for primary education, particularly for females. Priority is given to improving the school environment by providing trained teachers, teaching aids, and quality textbooks. In this programme, emphasis is also given to minimizing the existing disparities in the distribution of social services across genders and regions. The federal government encourages the provincial governments, the private sector, and NGOs to come forward and contribute to enhancing education at each level in all the provinces of Pakistan. During this plan period, according to the policy of Universal Primary Education, the People's Party government was committed to increasing the literacy rate to 70 per cent and to raising the budgetary share for the education sector to 3 per cent of GNP by the year 2000. However, late in 1996, that government was dismissed amidst claims of widespread corruption. The interim government was charged with holding general elections in February 1997, and then left it up to the new PML government to maintain and realize these goals. However, the pressure from the international donor community has now reached such an intensity that it will be extremely difficult for any government to turn away from such commitments. The government elected in 1996 committed

Table 12
Public sector expenditure on human development

	1st Plan (1955–60)		2nd Plan 1960–65		3rd Plan (1965–70)		Non-plan Period (1970–78)		5th Plan (1978–83)		6th Plan 1983–88		7th Plan (1988–93)		8th Plan (1993–98)	
	Rs billion	% of Total Exp	Rs billion	% of Total Exp	Rs billion	% of Total Exp	Rs billion	% of Total Exp	Rs billion	% of Total Exp	Rs billion	% of Total Exp	Rs billion	% of Total Exp	Rs billion	% of Total Exp
Education and manpower	0.23	4.71	0.46	4.34	0.56	4.24	3.44	4.55	5.64	3.69	14.27	5.95	25.7	7.91	9.8	1.63
Health and nutrition	0.08	1.64	0.17	1.63	0.28	2.12	2.38	3.15	4.58	3.00	10.37	4.32	13.3	4.10	5.2	0.86
Population welfare and human development	0.0	0.00	0.01	0.09	0.14	1.06	0.82	1.08	0.60	0.39	1.69	0.70	3.5	1.07	12.2	2.03
Total expenditure	4.88	100.00	10.60	100.00	13.20	100.00	75.54	100.00	152.61	100.00	239.75	100.00	324.7	100.00	599.4	100.00

Source: *Economic Survey, (1994–5)*

Rs 214 billion to SAP II which is more than twice the amount committed by the government to SAP I.

It is very difficult to judge the trends in the demand for education in Pakistan. Judging by what people actually pay for education, the indications are dismal. There are no data available to judge what people would be prepared to pay. However, data in Table 13 presents the national survey-based household expenditures on food, education, medical care, and housing. Before 1979, on average, more than 50 per cent of income was spent on food. This resulted from the high levels of widespread poverty in those years. Over the years, the share of food expenditure has declined. However, the expenditure on education has remained almost stagnant and extremely low. This may imply that individual households do not value education highly or are caught at such low levels of subsistence that they have very little to spend on education. Alternatively these trends most likely indicate that the problem is supply related.

The government is the only significant supplier of education at the national level. There are very few alternatives. Most households either do not send their children to these schools, or, if they do, pay the low subsidized fees. The data in this table shows a sharp rise in the household income in 1979 and again between 1979 and 1984–5. The noticeable increase during the 1970s and early 1980s was due to the large-scale migration of workers to Middle Eastern countries. Earnings from the Middle East were remitted back to Pakistan in large volumes. The majority of migrants belonged to the lower income groups with little or no education. The Middle East bonanza increased their incomes and expenditures, including those on luxury goods. However, expenditures on education remained small.

Table 13
Average monthly income and household consumption patterns per household

Year	Average monthly income per household (Rs)	Average monthly consumption expenditure per household	Total exp. on food as % of total exp.	Total exp. on education as % of total exp.	Total exp. on housing as % of total exp.	Total exp. on medical care as % of total exp.
1968–9	215	214	58.7	1.08	14.0	1.87
1969–70	223	224	54.6	1.16	14.9	1.85
1970–71	235	235	54.6	1.14	14.3	2.03
1971–2	265	265	55.0	1.25	13.9	1.98
1979	1032	951	50.8	0.86	17.5	1.79
1984–5	1774	1653	48.61	2.08*	18.88	2.32
1985–6	1889	11770	48.13	1.96*	19.31	2.39
1986–7	2062	1976	46.34	1.30	19.79	2.51
1987–8	2131	2029	46.57	1.17	20.11	1.87
1990–91	3168	2826	48.75	1.53	21.55	2.88

Source: *Household Income and Expenditure Survey*, (various issues),
Note: * Indicates that expenditure on recreation and entertainment was also included in these figures for these years.

For a host of reasons, discussed above, Pakistan has not yet obtained the desired level of literacy. This means that the limited resources allocated for education are not properly utilized. There is an urgent need to realize the importance of education. Emphasis should not only be given to the expansion of educational institutions and to increasing the enrolment rates but also to improvement in the quality of education. The provision of trained teachers and good quality textbooks, particularly at the primary and middle level, are important for this purpose. Special efforts are needed to arrest the high drop-out rates.

5. HEALTH NUTRITION AND SOCIAL WELFARE

The productivity of the human resources of a country also depends upon its standards of health and nutrition. Society's ability to provide social safety nets is an important insurance against income risk for its vulnerable sections. Health and nutrition are also important indicators for measuring social well-being and the quality of life. The availability of health facilities increases the probability of access to both preventive and curative medicine and reduces death rates. Proper nutrition improves the welfare of the poorer members of the society and enhances productivity, efficiency, and the ability to learn and work, and thus contributes directly to economic growth.

A. HEALTH

The incidence of waterborne disease, like dysentery and diarrhoea, is extremely high in Pakistan, particularly in the rural areas. According to the *Population Growth Survey (1971)*, about 64 per cent of all deaths were due to ineffective and parasitic diseases which are spread by contaminated food and water. Malaria is another major cause of death. The high incidence of both types of disease indicates the poor status of hygiene and sanitation facilities. Chronic respiratory infections due to indoor pollution from smoky cooking stoves are also very common. In addition to these, viral hepatitis, respiratory diseases, such as influenza and pneumonia, are also common. All these diseases are spread by air and water pollution. The Eighth Five Year Plan has, as one of its objectives, the provision of clean water to an additional 31.5 per cent of the population by the end of 1997–8.

Health facilities consist of hospitals, dispensaries, basic health units, rural health centres, doctors, nurses, lady health visitors, and other para-medical staff. The data on population per doctor, hospital bed, and nurse are presented in Table 14. The declining trend in all of these indicators shows an improvement over time in the health facilities. At the time of independence, medical services in Pakistan were insufficient for catering to the needs of the population. In 1948 the country had only 300 hospitals,

Table 14

Health facilities and expenditure on health

Years	Hospitals	Dispensaries	Basic health units (BHUs)	Maternity & child health centres	Rural health centres (RHC)	Tuberculosis centres	Beds in hospitals & dispensaries	Registered doctors	Registered dentists	Registered nurses	Registered lady health visitors	Population per hospital bed	Population per doctor	Population per dentist	Expenditure (Rs million) Development	Expenditure (Rs million) Non-development	Expenditure on health (Rs million)
	(1)	(2)	(3)	(4)	(5)	(6)	(7)	(8)	(9)	(10)	(11)	(12)	(13)	(14)	(15)	(16)	(17)
1947	–	292	272	–	91	–	3	13769	–	–	–	–	–	–	–	–	–
1950	–	304	807	–	107	–	3	14524	–	–	–	–	2431	–	–	–	–
1960	–	342	1195	–	348	–	–	22394	477	–	–	–	2038	–	8.70	57.00	–
1970	411	1875	–	668	217	98	28976	3913	384	5336	547	2061	15256	155468	61.70	151.00	0.41
1980	602	3466	736	812	459	220	47412	10777	928	16948	3106	1716	7549	87672	942.00	794.82	0.55
1990	756	3795	4213	1050	459	220	72997	51883	2077	16948	3106	1535	2127	53134	2741.00	4997.00	0.90
1995b	823	4205	4925	856	498	260	85552	69694	2753	22531	4277	1503	1837	46498	5741.07	10613.75	0.68

Source: *Economic Survey* (various issues).

a   = Expenditure figures for respective financial years (1991=1991–92).

b   = Provisional.

741 dispensaries, and 96 maternity and child health centres. These facilities employed 1360 doctors, 204 nurses, and 37 lady health visitors. By 1995, there were 823 hospitals, 4,205 dispensaries, 4,925 Basic Health Units, 856 maternity and child health centres, 498 rural health centres, and 260 tuberculosis centres. At present, Pakistan has 69,694 doctors, 22,531 nurses, 4,277 lady health visitors, 19,759 midwives, and 2,753 dentists. This shows a considerable improvement in the number of health services and health manpower. The high population growth rate offsets the expansion of health services and therefore the overall coverage remains low.

The slow progress in the provision of health services in Pakistan is due mainly to the low allocation of public expenditure on health. Table 12 reports the expenditure on various sectors during each plan. This table shows that health expenditure increased or remained constant until the Seventh Five Year Plan (1988–93), when it was 4.1 per cent of total expenditure, but allocations declined drastically for the Eighth Five Year Plan to 0.86 of one per cent. This resulted from, and in turn caused, inappropriate health policies during this period. Despite having ambitious objectives for the health sector during the Fifth Five Year Plan, only 55 per cent of the financial allocation had actually been spent on this sector and most of the health-related targets of this Plan were not achieved.

During the Sixth Five Year Plan, the financial allocation for the health sector had been increased. This Plan encouraged the private sector to invest in health care facilities. As a result, by 1994–5, 2,000 clinics, 520 medium to small hospitals with 16,000 beds, over 300 maternal and child health care centres, 340 dispensaries, and 450 small laboratories were operating in the private sector. The Social Action Programme, currently underway, has the objective of improving the efficiency of service delivery as well as its quality, especially in the rural areas. Improvement and upgradation of the existing health units have been emphasized during the Eighth Five Year Plan. This involves the availability of skilled staff, adequate provision of medical equipment, medicines, and transport.

The immunization programme has shown great progress. Nearly 98 per cent of the funds allocated for this purpose were utilized in 1994–5. In addition to the Expanded Immunization Programme, control of diarrhoeal diseases, acute respiratory infections, and nutrition are top priority for SAP. The eradication of malaria, leprosy awareness, family planning and primary health care, cancer treatment, and AIDS prevention are also important goals of this programme. In addition to this, the government is taking strong measures to eradicate the use of narcotics. The impact of these measures in reducing the infant and maternal mortality rates and increasing life expectancy at birth should show up by the end of the Eighth Five Year Plan.

The high population growth rate has increased the pressure on existing housing. This has led to a rapid expansion of *katchi abadis* and slum areas. Studies find that 20 per cent of the urban population lives in *katchi abadis* on illegally acquired state land. An examination of facilities available in these slums would show the deplorable state of the housing sector.

The share of household expenditure on medical care, based on the *Household Income and Expenditure Surveys,* has been presented in Table 13. The increase in this expenditure over time reflects in part the increasing consulting fees of doctors and the prices of medicines.

B. NUTRITION

Food is essential for the survival of human beings. Inadequate intake causes malnutrition, which further aggravates health problems. The incidence of malnutrition in Pakistan continues to be serious. This not only increases infant and maternal mortality but also has negative effects on human capital formation through reduced productivity and efficiency. There are various reasons for malnutrition. Low household income, non-availability of essential food items, individual tastes and preferences, and lack of nutrition education are all contributory factors. The high population growth rates, low levels of education, and poor sanitation and health facilities further exacerbate the situation. Despite the high growth in per capita income and the decline in levels of poverty, the level of malnutrition, especially among the vulnerable groups and particularly children under five, is still very high. Nearly 25 per cent of children in this age group were malnourished during 1994–5. In Pakistan, 65 per cent of the children, 45 per cent of the women of childbearing age, and almost 90 per cent of lactating and expectant mothers suffer from anaemia due to iron deficiency. About fifteen to twenty million people are at risk of iodine deficiency disorders. The Social Action Programme has the stated objective of improving the nutrition situation by establishing nutrition clinics in basic health units. This programme also has the aim of reducing micronutrient deficiencies, such as those resulting from the deficiencies of iodine, iron, and vitamin A. These deficiencies severely affect individual health, particularly in vulnerable areas of the country.

To reduce the incidence of malnutrition, there is a need for increasing food production at a faster rate than the growth rate of population, stabilizing food supplies and their prices, and improving access to food for the poor. In addition to this, further reduction in poverty and improvement in income distribution is also needed. The government has instituted specific policies to address chronic poverty. However, the experience with these schemes has been mixed.

C. Social Welfare Policies

During the Islamization process initiated in the 1980s, the system of Zakat and Ushr was introduced. The aim of this system was to eradicate poverty by transferring income from the non-poor to the poor. This system represents the formal enforcement by the government of the measures taken by the Prophet Mohammad (PBUH) to alleviate poverty. He encouraged his followers to give charity to the poor and the needy. *Zakat* and *ushr* funds are available for seven different purposes: subsistence allowances, rehabilitation grants, grants for marriage and dowry expenses, grants to schools of religious instruction, stipends through educational institutions, medical aid through hospitals and clinics, and grants to social welfare institutions. The first two are disbursed exclusively by local committees and therefore utilize both *zakat* and *ushr* receipts. The others, which utilize only *zakat* funds, are disbursed by the provincial councils. At present, due to mismanagement and various intrinsic faults in the system, it has failed to fulfil the subsistence needs of the vulnerable groups of the population. Actual *zakat* and *ushr* collections are below their potential. Usually payments are small and often erratic and do not always reach the targeted individuals.

Malik, Hussain, and Shirazi (1994) estimated the role of *infaq* (all Islamic transfers to the poor) in poverty alleviation. They observed a relatively higher level of poverty in the absence of *infaq* and concluded that *infaq* plays a significant role in reducing poverty.

The Pakistan Baitul Mal, established in 1992, provides financial relief to widows, disabled persons, orphans, and the destitute of any religion who are left out of the *zakat* and *ushr* system (*zakat* is collected from Muslims and distributed to Muslims only). With the help of the Baitul Mal, schools for rehabilitation of child labour, vocation training centres for young men, *dastkari* schools for women, and mobile dispensaries have been established. Plans for providing residential accommodation to the destitute and orphans are in the pipeline. Very little formal analysis is available to evaluate the performance of this scheme.

In addition to these schemes, the Social Welfare Department provides social services to the poor. Some of the prominent schemes in the area of social welfare programmes are: employees' old-age benefits scheme, social security for workers administered by provincial social security institutions, various skill enhancement schemes, and workers' welfare funds. The coverage of these programmes is low and programmes are being implemented only partially.

Despite achieving a reasonable growth rate of GDP and considerable reduction in poverty, Pakistan's performance in the social sector is not satisfactory. A high population growth rate, low literacy and enrolment rates, limited access to health facilities, and the low status of women place Pakistan among low human development countries.

6. HUMAN DEVELOPMENT INDEX AND CROSS-COUNTRY COMPARISONS

The Human Development Report of the United Nations presents the Human Development Index (HDI), which is an average of longevity, knowledge, and income. According to the *Human Development Report 1997*, the HDI for Pakistan was 0.445, which ranks it at 139 among the 175 countries on this list. This low rank indicates the unsatisfactory performance of the social sectors of Pakistan.

A comparison of the human development indicators for Pakistan with ten other countries is presented in Tables 15, 16 and 17. Table 15 shows that Pakistan's economy has been growing at the rate of 6.5 per cent per annum, which is higher than the other high HDI rank countries, for example, Malaysia, Iran, Sri Lanka, Indonesia, and Egypt. Real per capita GDP, that is an indicator of the standard of living, has increased more than three times since 1960 in Pakistan. The incidence of urban and rural poverty is lower than in India, Bangladesh, and Egypt. Table 16 presents a comparison of Pakistan's health sector with that of other countries. This table shows that longevity, which is measured by life expectancy at birth, has improved in Pakistan from forty-three years in 1960 to sixty-one years in 1990 and is comparable to several high HDI rank countries. This is mainly due to the decline in the infant mortality rate since 1960. The population growth rate, infant mortality rate, and maternal mortality rate in Pakistan are extremely high. The total fertility rate in Pakistan, of 6.2 per woman, is the highest among other developing countries. Only in thirty-two countries among the 174 in the United Nations HDI scale is the total fertility rate higher than 6.0, and Pakistan is one of these. In Korea this rate is 1.7; in China 2; in Sri Lanka 2.5, and in India the fertility rate is 3.8 per woman. The high fertility rate indicates that there is very little control on population increase. The high and uncontrolled population growth rate is the major obstacle to raising the standard of living despite the high economic growth rate. The poor condition of the health sector is evident from the

low levels of access of the population to health services, safe
drinking water, and sanitation facilities. Only 55 per cent of the
population has access to health facilities. In Korea, on the other
hand, 100 per cent of the population benefits from access to
health services. Access to safe water and sanitation facilities is
also extremely low in Pakistan in a comparative context.

Table 15
Human development indicators in international perspective: state of the economy and human development

Countries	GNP annual growth rate	Real GDP per capita		Food cons. as % of HH cons.	Population growth rate (%)	% Population in poverty (1990)		HDI Rank	
	1980–93	1960	1993			Urban	Rural	1994	1996
Pakistan	6.1	820	2160	37	3.0	20	31	132	134
India	5.0	617	1240	52	2.2	38	49	135	135
Sri Lanka	4.6	1389	3030	43	1.8	15	36	90	89
Bangladesh	4.5	621	1290	59	2.5	56	51	146	143
Egypt	4.6	557	3800	49	2.4	34	34	110	106
China	9.6	723	2330	61	1.9	–	12	94	108
Indonesia	6.0	490	3270	48	2.1	20	16	105	102
Iran	3.3	1985	5380	37	3.4	–	–	86	66
Korea	8.7	690	9710	35	1.8	5	4	32	29
Malaysia	6.4	1783	8360	23	2.6	8	23	57	53

Source: UNDP, (1994 and 1996).

Table 16
Human development indicators in international perspective: population demographics, health, and sanitation

Countries	Life expectancy at birth (years)		Total fertility rate (per woman)	Infant mortality rate per 1000 live births		Maternal mortality rate (per 10000 live births)	Population with access to:		
	1960	1993	1992	1960	1993	1992	Health services 1985–95	Safe water 1988–95	Sanitation facilities 1988–95
Pakistan	43.1	61.8	6.2	163	89	500	55	79	33
India	44.0	60.7	3.8	165	81	85	81	29	–
Sri Lanka	62.0	72.0	2.5	71	17	80	93	53	61
Bangladesh	39.6	55.9	4.4	156	106	600	45	97	34
Egypt	46.2	63.9	3.9	179	66	270	99	80	50
China	47.1	68.6	2.0	150	44	95	92	67	24
Indonesia	41.2	63.0	2.9	139	56	450	80	62	51
Iran	49.6	67.7	5.0	169	34	80	84	67	–
Korea	53.9	71.3	1.7	85	11	26	100	93	100
Malaysia	53.9	70.9	3.6	73	13	59	–	78	94

Source: UNDP, (1994 and 1996).

Why is it that despite the high GNP growth rate and the reasonable and comparable life expectancy at birth, Pakistan lies at the bottom of HDI ranking? The answer lies in large part in the extremely poor performance of the education sector. A comparison of Pakistan's education sector with other countries is presented in Table 17. Almost all the countries presented in this table started with similar economic and social conditions and most of them now show remarkable progress in the social sectors. These countries have made significant investment in the education sector. 'Knowledge' in HDI is the weighted average of the adult literacy rate (two-thirds weight) and mean years of schooling (one-third weight). The adult literacy rate in Pakistan was lowest (21 per cent) during 1970, and at 36 per cent, is still far behind other developing countries (India, 50 per cent; Sri Lanka, 89 per cent; and Korea, 97 per cent). Mean school years are also among the lowest in Pakistan, 2.9 years for males and 0.7 years for females. Hence the 'knowledge' component of the HDI really pulls down the overall rank.

The relative performance of the education sector can also be judged by comparing the gross enrolment ratio, drop-out rate, pupil-teacher ratio, and public spending on education in Pakistan with other developing countries. The gross enrolment ratio in Pakistan is lowest at each level as compared to the low income and low HDI rank countries such as India and Bangladesh. Per capita GDP in Sri Lanka and Indonesia (in PPP terms) is lower than in Pakistan but their literacy rate is higher than 80 per cent and the enrolment ratios exceed 100.

The quality of education can also be compared by the pupil-teacher ratio and drop-out rate. The pupil-teacher ratio in Pakistan is quite high; 43 at the primary level and 19 at the secondary level. This ratio is less than that of Iran and Korea at the secondary level and comparable to that of Malaysia and Egypt. Pakistan is facing a severe problem of extremely high drop-out rates at the primary level as compared to other countries. Only 48 per cent of the enrolled students in Pakistan complete the primary level. The completion rate in India is 62 per cent, in Sri Lanka 97 per cent, and in Korea 99 per cent.

The high drop-out rate, as already discussed before, is not only due to the high incidence of poverty but also due to the non-awareness of the value of education among parents. In addition, there are extremely low levels of investment by the government, especially in the early years of Pakistan's birth. Before 1984–5, public expenditure on education as a percentage of GDP was less than 2 per cent. The low levels of overall investment are compounded by the non-optimal sectoral allocation of these scarce resources i.e. higher education received much more investment than primary education. In a poor country like Pakistan, the concentration of public expenditure on higher education implies that the benefits of education accrue largely to the upper-middle or upper income class. Furthermore, the percentage of skilled manpower migrating abroad after graduating is higher than in most other countries. The majority of these migrants do not return to the country. The scarce public funds allocated for the higher education of these people is thus a large public loss. During 1987–8, 9 per cent of the graduates went abroad from Pakistan. This proportion was only 1 per cent in the case of India and Bangladesh. In contrast, Sri Lanka, China, and Iran invested heavily in basic education during the early years and show high literacy and impressive enrolment rates at each level.

The *Human Development Report* 1996 also presents the Gender Development Index (GDI) which reflects gender disparities in basic human capabilities. The GDI adjusts the HDI for gender equality in life expectancy, educational attainment, and female's income share in total income. A high GDI indicates the adoption of gender equality and women's empowerment as conscious national policies. Table 18 presents the information on GDI and its components for ten countries. The low rank for Pakistan in GDI indicates the existence of vast disparities between genders. The GDI for Pakistan is lower than even those countries that obtain a lower HDI rank, such as, India and Kenya. According to Table 18, life expectancy at birth for females is higher than that for males and is comparable with many other countries. However, the female literacy rate, the female labour force participation rate, and the share of earned income for females are extremely low in Pakistan. The Human Development record for Pakistan is therefore even more adverse when gender issues are considered.

Table 17
Human development indicators: gender related

Countries	GDI rank 1996	Female LFP rate (age 15+) 1990 (%)	Share of earned income 1993 (%)		Life expectancy in 1993 (Years)		Adult literacy rate in 1993 (%)	
			Female	Male	Female	Male	Female	Male
Pakistan	107	23	18.6	81.4	62.9	60.9	23.0	48.6
India	103	31	24.8	75.2	60.7	60.6	36.0	64.3
Sri Lanka	62	34	33.1	66.9	74.3	69.8	86.2	93.1
Bangladesh	116	41	22.8	77.2	55.9	55.9	25.0	48.3
Egypt	87	27	23.1	76.9	65.1	62.7	37.0	62.4
China	79	45	37.9	62.1	70.6	66.8	70.9	88.7
Indonesia	78	39	31.9	68.1	64.8	61.3	76.9	89.1
Iran	75	21	16.3	83.7	68.3	67.2	56.4	75.5
Korea	31	39	26.9	73.1	75.0	67.5	96.1	99.1
Malaysia	43	36	29.4	70.6	73.1	68.8	76.3	88.2

Source: UNDP, (1996).

Sri Lanka, Indonesia, Malaysia, and Korea achieved high HDI and GDI through the emphasis on reducing the population growth rate, improving the quantity and quality of education, and decreasing gender disparities. The low expenditure on health and education during the 1960s produced a low quality labour force. The vicious circle of poverty, unemployment, and high population growth, coupled with the extremely inequitable distribution of assets and opportunities, has prevented the fruits of the high GNP growth rate from reaching the majority of the people. Emphasis on education and improving the quality of the human resource would have been one way to break out of this vicious circle and redress the initial inequity. Many other countries which started with similar social and economic conditions, are now reaping the benefit of the heavy investments they made during 1960s in the social sectors. For Pakistan, there is an urgent need to compensate for this lack.

REFERENCES

Amjad, R. (1987), *Human Resource Planning: The Asian Experience,* ILO, New Delhi.

Asian Development Bank (1990), *Human Resource Policy and Economic Development.*

Burney et al. (1992), *Human Development Report for Pakistan,* Pakistan Institute of Development Economics.

Butt, M. S. (1994), 'Prospects of Pakistan urbanization', Research Report No. 101, Applied Economic Research Centre, Karachi.

Butt, Rafiq M. (1993), 'Monitoring and Evaluation of Vocational and Technical Education in Pakistan', in Hyder, S. N., (ed.) (1993), *Towards an Integrated Human Resource Development Planning in Pakistan,* UNDP/ILO/PMI, Islamabad.

Chaudary, M. A., Azim, F. and Burki, A. A. (1989), *Skill Generation and Enterpreneurship Development Under Ustad-Shagird System in Pakistan,* National Manpower Commission and FES.

Ghafoor, A. (1984), *Development of Human Resources: Population, Manpower, and Employment Policies in Pakistan,* Academy of Educational Planning and Management, Islamabad.

Government of Pakistan, (1988), *Seventh Five Year Plan (1988–93),* Planning Commission, Islamabad.

———. (1994), *Eighth Five Year Plan (1993–98),* Part I, Part II, and Part III, Planning Commission, Islamabad.

———. (1995), *Statistical Yearbook 1994,* Federal Bureau of Statistics, Economic Affairs and Statistics Division, Islamabad.

———. (1995), *Workforce Situation Report and Statistical Yearbook 1993,* Manpower Wing, Ministry of Manpower and Overseas Pakistanis, Islamabad.

———. *Household Income and Expenditure Survey,* (various issues), Federal Bureau of Statistics, Islamabad.

———. *Pakistan Economic Survey,* (various issues), Economic Advisor's Wing, Ministry of Finance, Islamabad.

Guisinger, S. and Irfan, M. (1980), 'Pakistan's Informal Sector', *Journal of Development Studies,* Vol. 16, No. 4.

Hamdani, K. (1977), 'Education and the income differentials: an estimation for Rawalpindi city', The Pakistan Development Review, Vol. 16, No. 2.

Haq, K. and Kirdar, U. (ed) (1986), *Human Development: The Neglected Dimension,* North-South Roundtable, Islamabad, Pakistan.

Hyder, N. S. (1994), 'Employment, unemployment and underemployment in Pakistan: an overview of the situation', in Proceedings of the Pak-American Institute of Sciences, Lahore, Pakistan.

Hyder, S. N. (ed.). (1989), *The Regional Workshop on Development and Utilization of Human Resources: Issues and Policies*, Pakistan Manpower Institute, Islamabad.

———. (ed.). (1993), *Towards an Integrated Human Resource Development Planning in Pakistan*, UNDP/ILO/PMI, Islamabad.

Ilyas, M. (1993), 'Technical education in Pakistan: its problems, issues and challanges', in Hyder, S. N., (ed.) (1993), *Towards an Integrated Human Resource Development Planning in Pakistan*, UNDP/ILO/PMI, Islamabad.

Kemal, A. R. and Mehmood, Zafar. (1993), *Labour Absorption in the Informal Sector and Economic Growth in Pakistan*, Fredrich Ebert Stiftung, Islamabad

Khan, S.R., Mehmood, N. and Siddiqui, R. (1986), 'Priorities and efficiency of Pakistan's public sector educational expenditure', in Ijaz Nabi (ed.) *The Quality of Life in Pakistan*, Lahore: Vanguard Books.

Malik, N. and Malik, S. J. (1992), *Reporting on the World Nutrition Situation: A Case Study of Pakistan (1976–1991)*, a Report prepared for ACC/SCN of the United Nations.

Malik, S. J., Aftab, S., Sultana, N. (1994), *Pakistan's Economic Performance 1947 to 1993: A Descriptive Analysis*, Lahore: Sure Publishers.

Malik, S. J., Hussain, M. and Shirazi, N. (1994), 'Role of *infaq* in poverty alleviation in Pakistan', *The Pakistan Development Review*, Vol. 33, No. 4.

Nabi, I. (ed.) (1986), *The Quality of Life in Pakistan*, Lahore: Vanguard Books.

Naqvi, S. N. H., and Sarmad, K. (1984), *Pakistan's Economy Through the 1970s*, Pakistan Institute of Development Economics, Islamabad.

National Institute of Population Studies, 1987, *The State of Population in Pakistan*, Islamabad.

Pak-American Institute of Management Sciences (1994), *Proceedings of National Seminar on Human Resource Development*, Lahore, Pakistan.

Pasacharopolous, G. (1994), *Returns to Investment in Education: A Global Update. World Development*, Vol. 22, Issue 9, September.

Rukanuddin, A. R. and Farooqui, M. N. I. (1988), *The State of Population in Pakistan*, National Institute of Population Studies, Islamabad.

Sarmad, K., Hussain, F. and Zahid, G. M. (1989), 'Some issues in the development of Pakistan's education sector', in Hyder, S. N. (ed.) (1989), *The Regional Workshop on Development and Utilization of Human Resources: Issues and Policies*, Pakistan Manpower Institute, Islamabad.

United Nations Development Programme, (1997), *Human Development Report 1997*, New York: Oxford University Press, several years.

11

Gender Inequalities and Development in Pakistan

Shahnaz Kazi*

1. INTRODUCTION

Although Pakistan has experienced substantial gains in per capita income, indicators of women's status have shown very slow progress. Inequities by gender continue to be high in terms of access to health, education, and employment. Girls comprise only one-third of the students at the primary level and the corresponding proportion falls to one-fourth at the secondary level. Fertility rates persist at high levels of between 5.5 to 6 births. Excessive and early childbearing is the major cause of high maternal mortality which is estimated to be in the range of 200 to 400 deaths per 100,000 births, a level which is considered alarming even by the standard of developing countries. Women's participation in the modern high productivity sector continues to be limited; they comprise less than 5 per cent of federal civil servants while their representation in banks, large-scale industry, and other formal sector institutions is negligible. These national averages mask huge differentials by class and region—poor, rural women are the most disadvantaged section of the population.

The differential access of males and females to development resources is usually attributed to social and cultural constraints

* Shahnaz Kazi is a social sector economist at the Islamabad Office of the World Bank. The views expressed in this chapter are her own.

on women's mobility. A patriarchal system continues to prevail in Pakistan which institutionalizes the subordination of women and their dependency on men for economic and social support. The system is re-inforced by asymmetrical rules of inheritance: Islamic law entitles daughters to half the share of the sons' entitlement; however, most women do not claim such property, particularly land. Women, as economic dependents, are to be provided for in various stages of their life cycle by men—fathers, husbands, and sons. Women can earn status only through marriage and reproduction. The girl's honour or reputation for virtue is critical to arranging a suitable marriage. The overriding concern with women's honour is the basis of the rigid cultural precepts which separate the activities of men and women— outside the home for men and within the home for women. In this cultural milieu, employment, health care, and education of women, which involve stepping outside the home and possible contact with non-related men, are viewed with suspicion and reflect negatively on the honour of the family.

In practice, adherence to these norms varies by age, class, and ethnicity. Older women enjoy far greater freedom of movement. Women in poor households, whose economic survival often depends on their earnings, cannot afford the luxury of staying 'indoors'. In general, upper and middle class urban women have access to education, health facilities, and modern employment.

The differential situation of women is also a symptom of the failure of development policy to address structural barriers which constrain their participation in the benefits of growth. Government plans and policies have incorporated a special focus on women since the late 1970s; plan documents include a separate chapter on women's development and a special ministry is in place with a mandate to incorporate women's concerns in the development process. However, the strategy for women's development has been limited in scope and has continued to indicate a welfare perspective. Women from low income households have been largely bypassed by these government programmes and policies, which have failed to address critical constraints to raising their productivity and improving their access to education and health services.

This chapter examines the changes in the situation of women after five decades of development. It reviews the available evidence on gender inequalities in access to resources including health care, education, and employment opportunities. It explores the underlying causes of gender disparities at the household level as well as the conditioning influence of cultural norms, institutions, and development policies in shaping these trends.

2. GENDER DIFFERENCES IN ACCESS TO HEALTH, EDUCATION, AND EMPLOYMENT

A. HEALTH

Gender disparities in health status are indicated in mortality and fertility indicators and statistics on maternal care. Given the continued prevalence of high fertility, there has been little change in the health situation of women in recent years. There has, however, been some expansion of health care facilities and improvement in overall nutritional intake which has resulted in a general decline in mortality.

Women's health is closely linked to their reproductive behaviour. Though evidence from South Asia, Bangladesh, Sri Lanka, and South India suggests the beginning of a declining trend, fertility in Pakistan, despite higher rates of economic growth and a long established family planning programme, has persisted at high levels. The total fertility rates ranged between 6 and 6.9 in the 1980s while estimates for 1990–91 vary between 5.5 and 6.0 (Sathar, 1993). The contraceptive prevalence rate, which is the major indicator of whether women are making conscious decisions about regulating their fertility, has, in fact, not risen very much. Whereas 5 per cent of ever-married women between the ages of 15 to 49 were using contraception in 1975, the corresponding proportion in 1991 was about 12 per cent (NIPS/IRD, 1992). The majority of women who are effectively controlling their fertility are almost wholly residing in urban areas of Pakistan or are women who have more than a primary education (NIPS/IRD, 1992). Further, women who do adopt contraception, do so usually after they have had several children already.

The continued prevalence of high fertility is a major cause of the poor health of women. Frequent births, followed by an average breast feeding period of nineteen months, is one of the principal reasons for the high levels of morbidity, prevalence of anaemia, and substantial levels of maternal mortality faced by women in the reproductive years. These problems are particularly severe for rural women who are largely illiterate and whose access to health facilities is greatly restricted. Not only are medical facilities sparsely distributed in rural areas but the quality of these services is widely regarded as extremely inadequate.

Recent estimates of maternal deaths per 100,000 births based on the Maternal and Infant Mortality Survey (MIMS) vary from 286 for squatter settlements in Karachi to 442 in Hazara, and high rates of 673 and 756 in Khuzdar and Loralai in Balochistan (Fikree, 1994).[1] These rates are high even by the standards of developing countries. Significantly greater risks of maternal deaths were associated with indicators of poverty such as *kutcha* construction of houses and lack of access to potable water, and among the biological factors, with young age at delivery. On the supply side, the distance to a hospital of more than 40 kilometres markedly increased the chances of maternal death. These risk factors are likely to be much more prevalent in rural settings which are greatly disadvantaged in terms of access to water, sanitation, and health facilities.

A great majority of rural women experience very poor delivery conditions. In 1990–91, 94 per cent of deliveries in rural areas took place at home as compared to 50 per cent in large cities and 85 per cent in urban centres (NIPS/IRD, 1992). Medical and paramedical assistance was availed in only 8 per cent of the rural cases and 30 per cent in urban centres, while over 50 per cent of women living in cities were assisted by a doctor or lady health visitor during childbirth. The village midwife does not have the capacity to deal with infections and complications. In case of problems, it is easier to seek timely medical assistance in urban areas as compared to rural areas where access to health facilities is severely limited.

Infant mortality was estimated at between 115 and 140 per 1,000 live births in the 1970s (Alam and Cleland, 1984). Since then, it has declined and is estimated to have reached a level of about 90 per 1,000 in the early 1990s (NIPS/IRD, 1992). Due to biological disadvantages, more boys than girls die under the age of one year, but between age one to five years, girls experience lower chances of survival which are related to differences in nutrition and health care. Estimated female mortality rate between ages one to five was 66 per cent higher than the corresponding estimates for boys in 1991(NIPS/IRD, 1992). Earlier findings based on national level data indicate a negative relationship between gender differentials in child mortality and income which is more pronounced in the rural sample (Sathar, 1987b). Female children experience relatively higher mortality. In poor households, the differential is removed at the middle income level while at higher levels of income there is evidence of relatively better chances of survival of girl children as compared to boys.

It is interesting to note that for both rural and urban households, the chances of a girl child surviving are lower if she is born after a girl rather than after a boy, providing further evidence of differential behaviour towards girls (Sathar, 1987b). A similar pattern has also been noted for India, a country with a common tradition of strong son preference (Dasgupta, 1987). The gender differences in child mortality in India have been attributed to deliberate discrimination against girls in food intake and health care (Dasgupta, 1987; Basu, 1989). The limited evidence for Pakistan also suggests a similar bias to the disadvantage of girls. Research on the determinants of the nutritional status of children across several rural and urban areas of Pakistan shows that the gender of the child is significantly related to nutritional status; female children are more likely to suffer from nutritional deficiencies (Bouis and Mahmood, 1993). The incidence of malnutrition is substantially lower in children from better-off households and those with educated mothers (Garcia and Alderman, 1990; Bouis and Mahmood, 1993).

Male-female differences in health care are also notable. The findings of the *Pakistan Integrated Household Survey (PIHS)*, undertaken in 1990–91, indicate that the reported incidence of diarrhoea and administration of oral rehydration therapy are about the same for boys and girls, but a higher proportion of boys than girls are taken for consultation for the illness and also for immunization (Behrman,1995). The gap in health care between boys and girls is greater in low income households. These findings are based on national level data and are therefore likely to understate male-female differences in access to health care in rural households, which face additional constraints in bringing children to health facilities, including transport costs and problems of mobility for girls.

Some further evidence that males and females have unequal access to health facilities is based on the admissions records at hospitals in the cities of Islamabad, Peshawar, and Chakwal and at rural health centres in the surrounding villages (Ahmed, 1990; Akhter, 1990). As compared to boys, a lower proportion of female children is noted across all the health facilities surveyed, which varied from 43 per cent in Islamabad to 37 per cent in the less developed region of Chakwal. The utilization of rural health outlets by girl patients is largely dependent on the presence of a female health provider. In rural health centres, where lady doctors or paramedics are in attendance, the proportion of female patients is considerably higher. Some of these patients come from distant villages.

The combined female disadvantage of relatively high mortality in childhood and during the childbearing years led, in the past, to much greater overall life expectancies for males than for females. At the present time, however, the trend seems to be changing, and the expectation of life of women is slightly higher than of men. Though this reflects an improvement over the past few decades, it should be noted that in the majority of countries women outlive men by several years.

B. EDUCATION

Despite some progress in the past two decades, literacy and school enrolment rates for Pakistan are among the lowest in South Asia. Between 1972 and 1981, the proportion of males who were literate rose from 30.2 to 35.1 per cent and the proportion of females increased from 11.6 to 16.0 per cent (Population Census Organization, 1981). In the urban areas, female literacy went up from 30.9 to 37.3 per cent during the period, while in the rural areas it rose from 4.7 to 7.3 per cent. The literacy levels are significantly higher and male-female differences less pronounced among the younger generation. For example, in 1972, a rural woman between 15 and 19 years of age was more than twice as likely as her mother to be literate, whereas by 1981 she was three times as likely to have this advantage.

The gap between males and females in the proportion of the school-aged population actually attending school has declined since the mid-1960s, although substantial inequalities remain. Over nearly three decades, the primary school enrolment rate for boys rose gradually from 59 per cent in 1965 to 73 per cent in 1991, while the rate for girls increased from 20 to 50 per cent (World Bank, 1988; World Bank, 1992). The secondary school enrolment rate for girls registered only a modest increase, from 5 to 12 per cent, over the same period. The continued prevalence of sex differentials in education is largely due to substantially lower enrolment of girls, at all levels, in rural areas while male-female differences in urban areas are relatively smaller. The gender gap in schooling in rural areas rises at each level and is very high at the secondary stage. Even at the primary level, only 40 per cent of rural girls are attending school as compared to 71 per cent of the boys in the relevant age group. At the secondary level, the enrolment rate for rural girls falls to only 6 per cent while the comparable rate for boys is 31 per cent (World Bank, 1992).

The large gender gap in schooling has been attributed to the existing differences in education facilities for boys and girls in rural areas (Sabot, 1992). Given the cultural restrictions that hold in varying degrees across all regions, segregated schools with female teachers are an important prerequisite to making female education more acceptable. Despite some progress in availability of schools, significant gender disparities remain in access to school facilities which are particularly marked in rural areas. The PIHS data for the early 1990s indicate a significant gender gap in access to public schools in both rural and urban areas. More than one-fifth of rural girls between the ages of 7 to 14 did not have access to a primary school within a distance of 1 kilometre as compared to only 9.1 per cent of rural boys while the corresponding proportions in urban areas were 18 per cent and 5 per cent respectively (World Bank, 1992). Whereas proximity to a school may not be such a problem for boys, access to a school within the village is, in most cases, a basic prerequisite to school attendance of rural girls.

While supply side influences are important, school attendance is also constrained by the lack of effective demand among the poorer households, particularly in rural areas. Poverty is the overriding factor mitigating against more positive influences on girls' schooling. National level findings from the PIHS reveal that the gender disparities in schooling and literacy rates are most severe for low income families in rural areas (Gazdar et al., 1994). In 1991, only 23 per cent of girls between the ages of 6 to 14 years from families living below the poverty line were attending school while 54 per cent of the boys were enrolled. Even among poor households in urban areas, only half the girls in the relevant age group were in school as compared to nearly two-thirds of the boys. The gender gap in school enrolments is negligible in urban households above the poverty line.

Low income households cannot afford to bear the cost of schooling both sons and daughters. Even where fees are nominal, the additional costs of textbooks and uniforms make it difficult for the poorest strata to afford schooling of children. The average annual cost of attending a public school in rural areas is estimated to vary between Rs 370 to Rs 430 per child (Sathar and Lloyd, 1993). In a situation of limited financial resources, there are greater economic reasons for educating sons since this would lead to better employment prospects, whereas daughters are not expected to seek jobs but to stay at home. The anticipated economic returns are negligible while the opportunity costs of educating girls are high. Evidence from micro-studies indicate that daughters are actively involved in assisting their mothers in productive, domestic and household maintenance activities (Sathar and Kazi, 1988; Parker, 1994; CIRDAP 1995). The opportunity costs of girls' education are particularly high in rural settings where there are earning opportunities for girl children, such as carpet weaving, farm labour etc. Parents are willing to forego the income from boy labour in the anticipation of improved job prospects but, at the household level, there are little tangible benefits of educating girls. The increasing trend in school enrolment of rural boys is associated with greater reliance on girls' labour.

A recent study has analysed the relative importance of supply and demand influences on child schooling in rural Pakistan using the PIHS data (Sathar and Lloyd, 1993). While access to a single sex girls' school within the village is significantly related to girls' enrolment, the effect of household income and mother's education is found to be considerably stronger. The positive association between household income and child schooling is more pronounced in the case of rural girls. The predicted proportion of girls enrolled in the highest income brackets in rural areas is nearly three times the comparable rate for the poorest strata. However, mother's education is the most important predictor of school attendance, particularly of rural girls. Its effect is much stronger than of access to a primary school.

The supply and demand constraints to girls' schooling increase dramatically beyond primary schooling. Middle and higher schools are more sparsely distributed, hence not likely to be located in the village, while the restrictions on the mobility of adolescent girls are more stringent. There is also little incentive to incur the extra costs, since employment is rarely a consideration in decisions related to female schooling. A positive trend has been noted in intensive studies of some more developed villages in the Punjab, where female education is beginning to be viewed as a means to better employment opportunities. This is in contrast to the usual responses in most rural households, where girls' schooling is perceived as enhancing women's domestic roles as wives and mothers (Sathar and Kazi, 1990; CIRDAP, 1995). Parental aspirations for better jobs for their daughters were associated with high enrolment rates for girls in secondary school, even though the education facilities were located outside the village. Some low income households were also investing in the education of their daughters in the expectation of their finding government jobs which were highly valued in these rural settings. Interestingly, employment in formal sector jobs was associated with better marriage prospects while education by itself was not particularly valued in the marriage market.

C. EMPLOYMENT

It is now widely accepted that women make a very important contribution to the economy through their participation in agriculture, manufacturing, and the services sector. However, due to the cultural milieu and the nature of their productive activities, which is usually outside the formal labour market, their work goes largely recognized. The 'invisibility' of women's work is further exacerbated by the inadequacy of labour force statistics.

Most standard labour force data, including the population census and labour force surveys, are known to greatly underestimate the extent of female labour force participation. The limitations of these official sources of data have frequently been pointed out in research on women's employment. These include inappropriate definitions of what is considered economic activity and questions which lay stress on recording a single main activity, as well as unsuitable methods of data collection where usually both enumerators and respondents are males. In the Pakistani context, where women perform multiple tasks and where there are social inhibitions to admitting to women's work, these procedures lead to underenumeration of the female labour force. The analysis of women's work patterns in the most recent period is based on findings from the *Pakistan Integrated Household Survey (PIHS)* and the *Agricultural Census* which are considered more reliable sources: particularly in the PIHS, special efforts were made to capture female employment through a detailed time allocation module and the use of trained female enumerators. The coverage of the *Agricultural Census* is limited to agricultural households, including households which own only livestock, while the PIHS includes a larger sample of rural households. The *Labour Force Surveys*, however, remain the only available source for assessing national trends in women's employment.

1. Rural Women

The evidence on trends in female employment in the rural sector is mixed. A comparison of *Agricultural Census* data for 1980 and 1990 indicates a decline in female activity rates in agricultural households from 73 per cent to 56 per cent over the past decade. A contrary trend of rising labour force participation rates as well as an increasing share of women in the category of agricultural workers is found in *Labour Force Survey (LFS)* data. Even though the level of female participation is greatly understated in the LFS, however, due to comparable methodology, it is considered a relatively more reliable source of assessing trends in employment patterns.

The findings of an increasing involvement of women in agricultural work is in keeping with certain developments in the rural economy over the past decade, particularly the migration of males to the Gulf and urban areas as well as the result of men diversifying into other non-farm occupations in the rural areas. The rural non-farm sector has grown rapidly in the 1980s, particularly in construction and transport, largely due to the demand generated by the inflow of remittances from migrants to the Middle East, the large majority of whom belonged to the rural sector (Irfan, 1988). The growing importance of the off-farm work force and migration squeezed male labour supply. Agricultural growth of over 4 per cent per annum and the steady rise in agricultural wages over the 1980s indicate that demand for labour was growing (Bilquees, 1992). Further, the rapid increased in cotton production at an annual growth rate of 14 per cent in the latter half of the 1980s (Government of Pakistan, 1992) is likely to have caused a tremendous increase in the demand for female wage labour since cotton picking is entirely done by women.

A more detailed picture of rural women's work patterns in the early 1990s is provided in the *Pakistan Integrated Household Survey* and the *Agricultural Census*. The large majority of economically active rural women work on their own farms. Estimates of female participation rates in agricultural work on their own farms varied from between 36 and 38 per cent while involvement in paid employment was extremely limited. According to the census, only 5 per cent worked for others of which only 1 per cent were engaged in agricultural work. A significantly higher participation of women in wage work was noted in the PIHS, whose coverage extended to landless households. Nearly 9 per cent of rural women were wage workers and, of these, 7 per cent were employed in the farm sector.

Gender differences were most marked in access to non-farm employment; while rural women are largely excluded from these jobs, the corresponding male participation rates were fairly high (Sathar and Desai, 1994). The non-agricultural sector was the main source of employment for 23 per cent of the males and only 2 per cent of the females while the reverse was true for agricultural wage work where women's involvement was higher; 7 per cent of rural women, as compared to only 3 per cent of the males, worked as agricultural labourers. Paid work outside the home is considered socially undesirable and only the poorest women work as farm labourers. Agricultural labourers are amongst the lowest paid group in the rural sector while incomes in the non-farm sector are substantially higher (Gazdar et al., 1994). The virtual exclusion of women from the more remunerative non-farm employment illustrates the multiple constraints that circumscribe women's work options. Social mores condition the attitudes of employers and households regarding the suitability of particular occupations and greatly restrict the range of employment opportunities available to women. Work in the non-farm sector is likely to be located further away and may involve travelling to nearby urban centres which is not acceptable from the point of view of female seclusion and is less likely to be compatible with their child care and domestic responsibilities. The divergence in male and female work patterns is in keeping with the tendency noted across many countries of shutting women out of better paying jobs and relegating them to low paying, low status activities.

Recent research based on the PIHS data indicates that access to land and other assets is found to be the main determining influence on work participation and hours of work (Sathar and Desai, 1994). Contrary to the general view, women belonging to households that own land or livestock are more likely to be in the labour force than landless women. The latter are more likely to work as agricultural labourers. However, the demand for wage employment is seasonal, limited to a few activities and certain regions, while lack of assets to work with excludes any possibility of self-employment. The net effect of these countervailing influences is a lower labour force participation rate for women from landless households. However, when they find employment, they work longer hours. In general, female sharecroppers are found to work the longest hours both on their family farms as well as in wage employment.

Within landowning households, the expected inverse association between size of landholding and women's work participation is observed but only after a threshold which varies according to land productivity in certain regions. The decreasing trend is more noticeable in irrigated and cotton growing areas while in the *barani* region, a positive relationship is observed except for the largest size farms (Zaman and Khan, 1987). According to the findings of the IFPRI survey of five rural districts conducted in 1987, the relationship is effective after a threshold of 12.5 acres while evidence from four villages in Sheikhupura indicates that women's participation was highest for holdings of between 6 to 12.5 acres as compared to smaller and larger farms (Alderman and Chishti, 1991; Ijaz and Mirza, 1984).

There are significant variations by agro-ecological zones in opportunities for women's wage employment and the extent of participation on family farms. Demand for female labour, which is seasonal and limited to specific tasks, is mainly concentrated in the southern cotton belt and irrigated regions. Cotton picking is entirely done by women while other activities include transplanting, weeding of rice crops, and picking of chillies and vegetables. While *barani* agriculture, characterized by a wheat pulse cycle, offers limited options for wage work, female participation on family farms is higher (Sathar and Desai, 1994; Zaman and Khan, 1987). The tendency reflects the interdependence between the activity patterns of men and women. Men in rain-fed regions have traditionally sought employment in the non-farm sector since crop production in the *barani* region is not sufficient to meet subsistence needs. Consequently, women have to take over a substantial burden of the work in managing agricultural production. Education is consistently found to reduce rural women's labour force participation as well as their hours of work. The negative association has been noted in village studies as well as more recently in research based on IFPRI and PIHS data (Masood, 1988; Alderman and Chishti, 1991). A possible explanation for the relationship is that the limited number of educated women in rural areas are likely to belong to well-off families where women are not expected to work. On the demand side, opportunities for educated women in the rural market have been limited to teaching and some other government jobs which require a minimum of secondary education. It is interesting to note the findings of the PERI study of rural Punjab which indicated a significantly higher participation in non-farm activities for women who had completed at least eight years of schooling (Khan and Zaman, 1987).

2. Urban Women

The rates of female work participation in urban areas, derived from official labour force statistics, varied between 4 and 9 per cent during the period from 1971 to 1992. While these data indicate a rising trend in female employment, they greatly understate the extent of urban women's contribution to economic activity and are contrary to the findings of micro-studies of urban areas, which point to an increasing influx of women workers, particularly in the informal sector. The findings of a survey of 1,000 women in Karachi fielded in 1987 showed that the majority of employed women, regardless of economic class, belonged to families in which women had never worked before (Sathar and Kazi, 1988). Many engage in home-based piece rate employment (Shaheed and Mumtaz, 1981; Bilquees and Hameed, 1989). Much of the activity takes place in the informal sector, and because it involves such endeavours as income-earning work undertaken at home or work for a family enterprise, it is unlikely to be captured in official statistics.

The distinguishing features of formal and informal employment should be reviewed at this point. The formal sector is usually characterized by an organized and protected labour market in which working conditions are safeguarded by laws and regulations ensuring workers of a certain degree of protection. Informal sector activities, on the other hand, are not regulated by contractual agreement or labour legislation. Thus, the formal sector in Pakistan includes all public establishments and those private establishments in sectors like industry and banking, that employ ten or more persons. These establishments come under the purview of labour legislation. In general, the formal sector is considered the more privileged stratum of the labour market in terms of earnings, security of employment, and working conditions. Women's participation in the formal economy has been limited with the exception of the occupational category of professionals and related workers. The female share of this group has risen significantly from 15 per cent to 21 per cent between 1984 and 1993 (Kazi, 1995). Although they have made some inroads in non-traditional areas such as engineering, banking, and law, the numbers in those fields have nevertheless remained very limited. The increases have been largely confined to the teaching and medical professions. The representation of women in other areas of the formal sector is minimal. Hence, they comprise less than 5 per cent of the federal civil service, and the proportion of women in managerial and clerical jobs is still extremely low (Kazi, 1995). Cultural norms not only determine the general attitude to work for women, but also the suitability of particular tasks. These attitudes largely explain the overwhelming concentration of women in the respectable lines of teaching and medicine as well as the low social status of sales and secretarial jobs which involve contact with men at a personal level.

Findings from *Labour Force Survey* data and special surveys of industrial workers indicate that the expansion of women's employment in the manufacturing sector has taken place outside the regular industrial workforce. Thus, within the officially enumerated workforce, although the share of women in the category of production workers has risen from 4.5 per cent in the mid-1990s to 8.6 per cent in 1990–91, only one-sixth were classified as paid employees. The rest were either unpaid family helpers or self-employed and therefore outside the sphere of formal manufacturing. Special surveys of industrial workers also indicate that, even when women are categorized as employees, they typically do not belong to the regular factory workforce but consist mainly of temporary and contractual workers (Hafeez, 1983; Khan, 1986). The findings of a nationwide survey of 2,000 industrial establishments revealed that even in the more developed provinces of Punjab and Sindh, only 20 per cent of the female employees, as compared to 50 per cent of the male employees, were in the regular workforce (Hafeez, 1983). The tendency to relegate women to temporary, casual, or contract work has also been observed more recently in a survey of selected registered factories in the large industrial centres of Karachi, Lahore, Faisalabad, and Multan (Piler, 1990). This type of employment does not provide job security or benefits such as maternity leave. In addition, subcontracting not only allows firms to circumvent labour legislation but also offers overhead cost advantages and enables employers to take advantage of a cheap source of labour supply.

Evidence at the national level on the growing concentration of women in the informal sector is provided in the PIHS (Kazi and Sathar, 1993). The overwhelming majority of women workers, more than three-fourths of economically active women in urban areas, are employed in the informal sector. Nearly four-fifths of the women in the informal sector work at home as subcontracted labour on a piece rate basis, as unpaid family helpers or as self-employed workers. The majority of home-based workers are engaged in petty manufacturing and produce a variety of goods involving intensive labour inputs. Women who were employed outside the home, comprising nearly one-fifth of informal sector workers, were mainly engaged in domestic service as maids, sweepers, cooks, and washerwomen.

Distinct differences in educational attainment, earnings, and duration of work were observed between women working in the formal and informal sectors as well as within the informal sector between home-based workers and those working outside the home. As would be expected, women who worked in the formal sector were better educated and had completed more than eleven years of schooling on average, as compared to informal sector workers, 77 per cent of whom had received no education. Home-based workers were the poorest paid group; mean monthly earnings of home-based workers were less than one-third the average monthly income of factory workers—the lowest level employees of the formal sector—and less than half the income of informal workers outside the home. Wide variations were also noted in hours worked. Women working outside the home in the formal or informal sector, on average, worked longer and more regular hours than women engaged in home-based income earning activities.

Informal sector workers are often exploited (Shaheed and Mumtaz, 1981; Bilquees and Hameed, 1988). The findings of a Karachi study noted that factory workers earn considerably higher incomes than home-based workers performing similar tasks, even after taking into account longer working hours in factories (Kazi and Raza, 1989). These women are constrained to work at home, in most cases, due to cultural restrictions to outside work which is associated with a loss of social status. The lack of job options, the dispersed nature of work, and their pressing need for income limits their bargaining ability and makes this one of the lowest paying activities within the informal sector. Even though the earnings of women in domestic service are considerably higher than the remuneration of home-based workers, in terms of total household income, they belonged to the poorest strata (Sathar and Kazi, 1988). Their earnings were critical to household subsistence comprising, on average, more than half of total family income.

Factors which have worked towards the expansion of informal activities have, to a large extent, affected women more severely then men. In an environment of low levels of labour absorption in the modern sector such as in Pakistan, women find it very difficult to enter the structured organizations of the formal sector due to various barriers. These include discriminatory attitudes to female employment, the perception of males as primary breadwinners, lower educational and skill levels of women, limitation on the mobility of women due to cultural restrictions and the demands of their reproductive roles. Also, on the demand side, keeping women out of the regular workforce and thereby avoiding restrictions on wages, working conditions, and retrenchment is part of a common strategy followed by formal firms to lower costs and also to maintain flexibility in the size of the labour force.

On the supply side, the evidence indicates that the vast majority of women work in response to economic need (Hafeez, 1984; Sathar and Kazi, 1988). While the incidence of absolute poverty has indicated a declining trend over the past decade (Gazdar et al., 1994), rising expectations of a minimal quality of life may be pushing women into the labour market to supplement family income. These women, given their lack of education and skills, have limited options, such as low paying menial jobs on the lowest rungs of the informal sector, often as domestic servants, or a diverse range of low productivity economic activities at home. The informal sector is often essential for the economic survival of women, particularly of poor women.

3. POVERTY AND THE SITUATION OF WOMEN

Women in poor households are doubly disadvantaged due to class- and gender-based inequities in access to resources. Despite the recognition of gender-specific problems of access to social and productive resources, research and public policy on issues related to poverty continue to view the household as a basic unit, implicitly assuming that all members of a poor family are equally disadvantaged. The preceding discussion has emphasized the increasing evidence that women and girls in poor households bear a disproportionately high share of the burden of poverty. In a situation of limited resources, gender discrimination in access to food, health care, and education becomes more pronounced. The differential impact of poverty is reflected in the lower nutritional status, higher mortality, and lower levels of education of women and girls in poor households.

Ownership of land is an important indicator of economic status in rural settings. The incidence of poverty is highest among landless and tenant households and in families of small owner-cultivators. Women are vital contributors to the economic survival of poor households. However, due to class- and gender-based discrimination, their employment options are more restricted than those of men. Access to land and livestock provides rural women with the main means of generating income for themselves and their families in rural areas. The negative consequences of landlessness are more severe for women, since their only source of livelihood is agricultural wage work while a large proportion of men find employment in the non-agricultural sector.

In urban areas, the evidence points to the overwhelming concentration of women in the informal sector. The informal sector covers a diverse range of activities, including viable small enterprises which hire workers, as well as various casual and unskilled occupations. There are wide variations in income within the informal economy. While earnings of small entrepreneurs and self-employed skilled workers are significantly higher than those of employees on the lower rungs of the formal sector, the incomes of hired workers in the informal economy are usually below the official minimum wage (Kemal and Mahmood, 1993; Kazi, 1989). Women are rarely represented among the more remunerative occupations of heads of small enterprises or skilled workers but are concentrated in the lowest tiers of the informal economy, employed in casual, unskilled, and menial jobs in manufacturing, services, and the construction sector.

The disadvantaged position of women in the labour market is manifested in the economic vulnerability of female-headed households, which are solely dependent on women's earnings. National socio-economic surveys indicate a very low incidence of female-headed households, comprising less than 5 per cent of all households (Gazdar et al., 1994; Sathar and Kazi, 1987). This is likely to be an underestimate given biases of both enumerators and respondents and the definition of household headship which is likely to be ascribed to any male member. Female-headed households should, in principle, include households where the male is permanently absent or where the male has migrated or is unable to provide for his family due to unemployment, disability, or drug addiction. In the cultural context of Pakistan, except in cases where males are absent, it is unlikely that even where women are the sole source of economic support they will be recorded as household heads.

Contrary to the findings from national surveys, evidence from an intensive study carried out in Karachi in 1987 indicated that 10 per cent of the households were headed by women (Kazi and Raza, 1988). The subset of female-headed households comprised three distinct groups: wives of migrants, divorcees and widows, and wives of non-earning husbands. While the first group was relatively well off, the other two categories belonged to the poorest strata in Karachi. The mean monthly household income of female-headed households was only one-fourth the family income of households headed by men.

The poverty of female-headed households was the result of both demographic and economic factors. Although household size was smaller, the dependency burden of female-headed households as measured by the child to adult ratio was nearly double the corresponding estimate for households headed by men. The earning capacity of the female heads was limited due to lack of assets and low endowments of human capital. The largely illiterate women were engaged in domestic service or in home-based earning activities while the relatively better off worked as factory labour. Daughters of female heads of households were relatively more disadvantaged since they bore a larger share of the burden of domestic work with negative consequences for their schooling. Thus conditions of poverty are perpetuated across generations.

Female heads of households also experience greater risks of maternal deaths according to the recent findings of the Maternal and Infant Mortality Survey (MIMS) data covering 10,000 households in the squatter settlements of Karachi (Fikree et al., 1994). While socio-economic indicators such as household assets and facilities were not found to have a significant impact on chances of survival, however, significantly increased risks of maternal deaths were found in households in which women were employed and husbands unemployed. Even among low income localities with little variation in assets and other amenities, households, which due to unemployment or disabilities of the husband, are solely dependent on female earnings are among the most impoverished.

A. CONSEQUENCE FOR HOUSEHOLD WELFARE

The differential position of women has serious consequences for the health and education of children in poor households. At the societal level, this results in difficulties for the attainment of development objectives of raising the quality of human resources, controlling population growth, and alleviating poverty. The evidence for Pakistan clearly indicates that the low levels of female education and the growing concentration of urban women in the informal sector exert a negative influence, independent of household income, on fertility, child health, and the education of the children. The continued prevalence of gender inequities is intensifying the intergenerational disadvantage of poor households.

Several studies in Pakistan, as in other countries, have shown that women's schooling is associated with lower fertility and better chances of child survival (Sathar, 1984; Casterline, 1984; Khan and Sirageldin, 1979; Sathar, 1987a; Sathar, 1985). Evidence from all the major fertility surveys has consistently indicated the significance of even a few years of schooling, usually post-primary level, on reproductive behaviour and child mortality. Women's education has a strong and direct impact on fertility. It has been found to influence family size norms, to improve knowledge and use of contraceptives, and to raise age at marriage. Better chances of child survival of mothers with some minimal levels of schooling have been attributed to their greater likelihood of adopting suitable feeding practices, more hygienic conditions, as well as a greater ability to seek appropriate and timely health care (Sathar, 1985). The improved nutritional status of children of educated mothers has been documented in some recent studies (Garcia and Alderman, 1990; Bouis and Mahmood, 1993).

Mother's education is an important determinant of the likelihood of schooling for both sexes in the urban and rural areas. Findings based on PIHS data show that educated women are not only likely to have more children in school but are also less likely to discriminate against daughters (Sathar and Lloyd, 1993). In rural areas, the predicted proportion of daughters enrolled of mothers with some education is more than twice the proportion for girls whose mothers never attended school.

The beneficial effects attributed to female education could be due to other influences which are clearly correlated to the education of women. For instance, women who have more schooling are likely to belong to better off households and be married to educated husbands and the positive outcomes may be reflecting the effect of these factors. However, the statistical relationships remain strong even after controlling for these influences. Whereas economic status is a significant determinant of child welfare and child survival, the nutritional status of children and child schooling show that maternal education is the predominant influence. For instance, findings of a multivariate analysis of the determinants of the nutritional status of children based on the IFPRI data show that raising the mother's education to primary level would reduce child wasting by 8 per cent while a 20 per cent increase in per capita income would lead to a decline of 2 per cent in wasting (Garcia and Alderman, 1990). Child schooling is positively associated with income; however, the mother's education is the most important predictor of child schooling, particularly the enrolment of rural girls (Sathar and Lloyd, 1993). Earlier research had indicated that father's education was the stronger or at least as important a predictor of school attendance as mother's education (Burney and Irfan, 1991; King et al., 1986). The limited number with any education in rural areas, particularly in the earlier data sets, may be an important reason for the relatively insignificant effect of maternal education. The impact of father's education on aspects of child health and survival has been consistently found to be insignificant.

Evidence for Pakistan indicates that differences in type of women's employment, between formal and informal occupations and within the informal economy between home-based workers and women working outside the home, are associated with marked variations in reproductive behaviour and have very different implications for child welfare. Findings from micro-studies as well as national level data indicate that formal sector employment in higher status jobs as professional and white collar workers or even as factory workers in large establishments is associated with lower achieved fertility while informal sector employment is not (Kazi and Sathar, 1993; Sathar and Kazi 1988). In fact, women engaged in informal sector activity, inside or outside the home, have higher levels of fertility than do non-working women. The significant effect of employment on fertility persists, even after controlling for socio-economic status and education, although its impact is reduced.

Findings from the 1987 Karachi survey suggest, on the contrary, that among poor women, seeking employment in itself is often precipitated by high fertility. Women in the informal sector enter the labour market after they have had at least four children (Sathar and Kazi, 1988). Supplementing family income in these cases is a more overriding need than staying at home to look after the children. These women are forced to enter the labour market because of their additional household expenditure due in most occasions to a large family size.

Informal employment of women outside the home is also found to have adverse consequences for child survival. The available research based on the Karachi survey indicates deaths were significantly higher for informal sector workers employed outside the home even after controlling for income and education (Sathar and Kazi, 1989). Informal sector workers were most disadvantaged in terms of child survival while home-based workers, also belonging to poor households, indicated less of a disadvantage.

The mother's occupation is an important determinant of child schooling. In urban areas of Pakistan, the chances of currently attending school are much higher for children of mothers working in the formal sector (Kazi and Sathar, 1993). The mother's employment in the informal sector is associated with a much lower probability of children being in school and a greater likelihood of their dropping out as compared to women in the formal sector as well as for non-working women. Gender discrimination in sending children to school seemed lower for women working outside the home, both in the formal and informal sector, despite considerable differences in the levels of children's schooling across the two sectors. Whereas the multivariate exercise controlled for education of women, it did not include a variable for income, and given the earnings differential between formal and informal work for women, it is possible that the differences by employment are partly reflecting differences in the level of income rather than the independent influence of variations in occupations.

These findings have grave implications in the context of the evidence of the growing concentration of women in the informal sector in urban Pakistan. Informal work outside the home has distinctly different demographic and health outcomes from the expected beneficial effects of women's employment in terms of lower fertility and better care of children. Women's work in the informal sector outside the home, although essential for household subsistence, is associated with high levels of fertility and less likelihood of child survival and child schooling.

4. GENDER INEQUALITY IN SOCIAL AND DEVELOPMENT INSTITUTIONS

Gender inequality in the household and in the labour market, with its manifold negative impacts, is further perpetuated by inequities in other institutions. This section focuses on discrimination at the institutional level, particularly in the legal system, in financial institutions, and in the development planning establishment.

A. THE LEGAL SYSTEM

Although the present constitution of Pakistan, which was adopted in 1973, ensures equality of women as citizens and also empowers governments to take affirmative action in favour of women, however, legislation enacted since the late 1970s effectively curtailed women's legal rights. Discriminatory laws against women include the Hudood Ordinance, the Law of Evidence, and the Qisas and Diyat Ordinance.

The Law of Evidence promulgated in 1984 stated that in matters related to future or financial transactions, the testimony of two women is equal to that of one man. It further stated that, for all such transactions, there should be two male witnesses or in the absence of two male witnesses, one male and two female witnesses. The law of Qisas (retaliation) and Diyat (blood money) differentiates between financial compensation paid to male victims and that paid to female victims of murder, manslaughter and other bodily injuries; compensation for a women who has been injured or killed is half that for a male victim of a similar crime or accident.

For criminal offenses that come under the Hudood Ordinance of 1979, which covers rape, adultery, and theft, only the testimony of adult muslim males is admitted in case where Hadd (maximum punishment) applies. Female testimony is acceptable when lesser punishment applies. For women, however, the threat of damage in the Hudood Laws is in *Zina*, which covers adultery, fornication, rape, and prostitution. In cases where maximum punishment applies, the same degree of proof is required for both adultery and rape i.e., that there should be four male eyewitnesses of good reputation. So, in effect, a provision that was meant to protect women from charges of adultery is used to protect rapists and makes it nearly impossible to prove the crime of rape. Further, this ordinance confuses rape with adultery, and instances have been recorded where women who reported cases of rape were punished for adultery on the basis of their own evidence, while the rapists went free for lack of evidence.

The Family Law Ordinance relating to marriage, divorce, child custody, etc. was enacted in 1961. It regularized procedures for marriage and divorce, made registration of marriages mandatory, and discouraged second marriages on the part of men by making it necessary for them both to seek permission from the current wife and to provide justification to the local union counsellor. The legal age of marriage was raised from 14 to 16 years for girls and from 18 to 21 years for boys. Whereas this law was supposed to be just a first step towards improving the legal status of women, it has remained thus far the only one, revealing the strength of the resistance of orthodox forces.

Women have legal rights to own, administer, sell, or buy property separately. Under Islamic laws practised in this country, men and women have a fixed share in the property of family members according to an intricate formula based on their relationship with the deceased. The female share in property, according to Islamic Laws, is half the male entitlement. In practice, women seldom get their due share of property and these rights are severely curtailed by selective application of traditional, tribal, and local laws. Even where legal ownership is vested in women, in practice, they have little control of the property. All decisions related to the use, sale, or transfer of property are usually made by male members of the family. Ownership in the name of women, while males retain effective control, cannot be associated with empowerment and enhanced economic status of women.

At present, the detailed breakdown of ownership of land and property by gender is not available. Some idea of the enormous male-female differences in the ownership of property is provided in a 1994 survey of over 1,000 households in rural areas of the Punjab province. Only thirty-six women owned land in their own name while only nine of these could sell or trade land without permission from male household members (SWAF, 1995). In nearly two-thirds of the households, daughters did not inherit land either because it was customary for only sons to inherit land, or even where daughters had the right to inherit, they did not exercise it.

Labour legislation in Pakistan also provides for comprehensive benefits for female employees. Such laws are seldom enforced in practice. Examples include the entitlement of women workers to maternity leave with full wages, and factories that ordinarily employ more than fifty people are expected to provide a room for female workers' children under six years of age.

B. Financial Institutions

The poor strata in general are disadvantaged in terms of access to credit, but women's access is further constrained by limited mobility, illiteracy, and most importantly, since women rarely have legal ownership of land, they lack assets for collateral. Consequently, women have been virtually excluded from institutional sources of credit in the past. More recently, there have been some limited efforts to increase women's access to financial facilities through formal institutions. These include some initiatives by the Agricultural Development Bank of Pakistan (ADBP), the Co-operatives Departments, and the First Women's Bank Ltd. (FWBL). NGOs have also started credit schemes for women on a small scale.

The Agricultural Development Bank of Pakistan, which is the major source of agricultural credit and loans to cottage industries in rural areas, has recently initiated the Agricultural Credit Programme (ACP) which includes special provisions to extend the bank's outreach to poor farmers and to rural women. The programme has experimented with various pilot schemes to deliver credit to women through using female field staff as well as trying different forms of collateral. A male/female mobile credit officer team is supported by a female village assistant to identify potential clients. The design of the project also includes a system of group guarantees or the use of gold as substitutes for land collateral. The use of NGOs as intermediaries is also planned. Despite incorporating all the right principles in the planning stage, the implementation has been problematic and the programme launched in July 1992 has yet to make any significant progress. After more than three years of operation, only 4,700 women had been given loans under the scheme. The hindrances identified by bank officials in implementing the programme include the high operational costs, problems in recovery, and the limited number of skilled women in rural areas which restricted the Bank's programme of loan diversification. The most important impediment was viewed as the lack of assets or property owned by poor women to serve as collateral and their inability to find a personal guarantor (UNDPUNIFEM/SUNGI, 1994). An independent assessment has identified a lack of commitment by the management to extend outreach to the poor, particularly women, as the principal reason for the slow pace of progress (Bennet and Goldberg, 1993).

The co-operative structure in Pakistan is essentially oriented to the problems of rural indebtedness through a supply of credit. Out of a total of 61,000 co-operative societies in 1990, only 952 were for women. Women's co-operatives comprised mainly thrift societies and some industrial societies. The main objective of the thrift societies is to promote savings and to introduce women to normal banking facilities and hence it does not extend to the provision of loans in contrast to the credit orientation of other co-operative societies. The industrial societies are supposedly producer co-operatives, although, in fact, they are welfare-oriented organizations which provide training in traditional skills and are financed by donations from prosperous women of the community. At present, special women's co-operatives, given their limited scope of activities, are excluded from the facilities available to co-operatives in general, such as credit and training provided through the Federal Bank for Co-operatives and the Co-operative Departments.

Special schemes to extend credit to rural women's co-operatives were included in the Seventh Plan (1988–93) programme for women's development. Although funds were sanctioned, the schemes could not be implemented. The major obstacle to initiating these programmes has been the inability of the provincial departments to work out alternatives to land or asset-based collateral requirements for extending loans to landless poor women (Planning and Development, 1990). There has been a move to change the focus of the project from the provision of production loans to a scheme for imparting training to women. The shift from a credit scheme to a special skill training programme highlights a tendency not unique to Pakistan, whereby even where the project design is based on women's productive roles, in the implementation stage the scheme is transformed into a typical welfare-oriented women's project.

The First Women's Bank Ltd. (FWBL) established in 1989 is the only formal financial institution set up to cater to the needs of women. The FWBL operates on commercial banking principles, although it has made some efforts to extend credit to low income women. A system of group guarantees has been instituted for small loans and the bank has collaborated with some NGOs to reach low income women in urban areas. However, access of rural women is limited due to lack of field personnel and the location of the bank branches in urban centres. Of the total loans sanctioned by the FWBL until 1994, only 5 per cent have gone to rural women (Kamal, 1994). The implementation problems experienced in the recent ACP programme of the ADBP, the limited outreach of the FWBL and the total exclusion of women from credit provided by the co-operative system is in direct contrast to the experience of the South Asian countries with a common socio-cultural environment which suggests that well-designed and well-implemented financial services can be an effective way to reach poor women.

C. GENDER INEQUALITIES AND DEVELOPMENT PLANNING

Development planning in Pakistan from the 1950s to the mid-1970s maintained a welfare approach to women's development. Though women were covered in various 'income generation' schemes implemented through the Social Welfare Department, they were not viewed as productive workers. The majority of these skill training programmes simply taught them traditional skills such as sewing, embroidery, or knitting which were primarily aimed at enhancing their domestic roles and had little relation to market demand or employment prospects (Khan and Shaheed, 1984). Women were viewed primarily as recipients of social services and not as active participants in the development process. However, even within the narrow focus of providing social services to women, the Plans failed to achieve any significant success. Not only were initial allocations low, but when it became necessary to cut back on development expenditure, the highest spending cuts usually applied to the social sectors.

It was not until the late 1970s that government policy in Pakistan explicitly considered measures for integrating women in the development process, largely due to external pressures from the United Nations and other international agencies. The existence of wide gender disparities in access to resources was acknowledged in the Sixth Five Year Plan as a major constraint to development and was attributed largely to the fact that women had been bypassed by the planning process (Planning Commission 1983). Women were viewed as a valuable resource which had to be effectively mobilized for the nation's development. The Seventh Five Year Plan also called for a 'full integration of women into society and not their channelization into limited activities and roles', (Planning Commission, 1988). Initiatives were taken for the first time after three decades of planning to develop an institutional framework for mainstreaming women's concerns in the planning and development process. A special administrative unit, the Women's Division, later upgraded to the Ministry of Women Development (MWD), was set up to ensure effective representation of women's issues in development policy and a separate chapter on women's development was included in the *Sixth Five Year Plan* document.

The development and equity-based approach to women's concerns in the Sixth and Seventh Plans was significantly different from the welfare perspective of earlier policy documents. Closer examination of the development strategy adopted during the period indicates a large gap between stated objectives and the formulation of policy, a gap which was further exacerbated by lapses in implementation. The policies outlined in the Plan documents were too limited in scope to serve as the basis of a programme aimed at integration of women in development. To enhance employment opportunities for women, the strategy relied primarily on expansion and diversification of vocational training. Other interventions aimed at promoting women's economic participation included increased recruitment of women in the public sector, particularly in the fields of teaching and health, the provision of credit facilities for women through co-operatives, and the introduction of incentive schemes for hiring of women by public and private enterprises. Most of these measures were never implemented. The Plans entirely disregarded the question of raising women's productivity in agriculture, despite the fact that the overwhelming majority of women are employed in the farm sector and are likely to be there for the next decade. Whereas both the Plans emphasize an integrated approach to women's development, the Sectoral Plans for agriculture and industry did not address women's roles in these areas.

The lack of a productive orientation in government programmes and policies and the poor record of implementation demonstrates the failure of the Women's Division and later MWD, to live up to its mandate of mainstreaming women's concerns in the planning process. The primary function of the organization was to ensure that, in the formulation of policies, the relevant ministries were responsive to the needs of women and thereby to ensure that women's concerns were integrated into the overall development programme and not confined to some special programmes for women. Its role was that of a catalyst to push and prod other government agencies into action (Planning Commission, 1983). In practice, the ministry has done exactly the reverse; it has concentrated on financing mostly welfare-oriented special women's projects, while its original mandate of influencing policies and programmes across the entire government machinery has been completely disregarded.

The goal of integration of women in the development process, however, was beyond the organizational and financial capacity of the MWD. The ministry had neither the funds nor the power to fulfil such a mandate. The share of the ministry of Women's Development allocation was minuscule at 0.2 per cent in the Sixth Five Year Plan and marginally higher at 0.3 per cent during the Seventh Five Year Plan. The limited financial allocation was in keeping with the promotional nature of the ministry's functions which were primarily meant to initiate projects and policies in the various other government departments. However, the ministry never had the administrative clout to address the role of a catalyst effectively. No institutional mechanism was specified which would enable it to influence the policies and programmes of relevant ministries/departments.

Even within the narrow project approach adopted by the ministry, the priorities, design, and formulation of the programme did not live up to its potential of a different development-oriented approach to women's projects. A few isolated schemes were sponsored by the ministry and implemented by the agriculture and forestry departments in the area of poultry raising, livestock care, sericulture, and training and recruitment of female extension agents. Some of these were initiated as pilot projects nearly a decade ago, but have remained marginal to the programmes of these agencies. In most cases, these projects have not been successful because they were designed without a proper assessment of women's needs and constraints both as service providers and as beneficiaries (Khan and Shaheed, 1984; Planning and Development Department, 1990). There has been no effort to devise more effective designs where earlier projects have failed or to expand the coverage of the schemes which had the potential for wider replication. Consequently, the large majority of rural women, who are actively involved in agriculture and livestock production, are almost entirely excluded from training and extension programmes.

The overwhelming bulk of the MWD programme comprised what are considered typical 'women's projects'. The underlying objective of these schemes is to combine the provision of social services with some skill training, which is usually geared to women's domestic roles and has little earning potential. A large number of multi-purpose women's welfare centres were established which provided an adult education course along with training in 'feminine skills' such as sewing, knitting, and embroidery. Most of these projects failed due to poor response from the intended beneficiaries, since the training in 'feminine' skills had little relevance to women's main source of livelihood in the agriculture and livestock sectors (Planning and Development, 1990).

In general, MWD's programme was along the lines of earlier government schemes. To some extent this was to be expected, since the majority of projects were designed and implemented by the same line ministries which have traditionally been involved in government schemes for women such as the Departments of Social Welfare, Education, Local Government, and Health. The involvement of departments representing the key economic sectors was minimal. Although women's work in these sectors is well documented, no significant effort was made to enhance their productive potential in the areas of agriculture, livestock maintenance, and small-scale industry. The projects funded by the ministry continued to be compartmentalized and isolated from the mainstream development programme.

CONCLUSIONS

The preceding review clearly points to the differentiated impact of development on men and women and between women across class and region. Nearly five decades of development have not led to any significant diminution in gender inequalities at the level of the household, the factor markets, and in social institutions. Public policy has failed to address critical structural and institutional barriers which constrain women's participation in the benefits of development and consequently also limit their potential contribution to growth. The high development costs of the persistence of gender disparities are manifested in Pakistan's low ranking across a range of social indicators, even when compared to countries with a common socio-cultural tradition and equivalent or lower levels of income.

While the societal benefits of investment in women are well documented, they are not reflected in private incentives which influence household allocation of resources to nutrition, health care, and education. Given the culturally defined gender roles, the expenses incurred on girls' education yield few tangible benefits while investment in boys' schooling is associated with high economic returns in the future. However, there is growing evidence that the traditional division of labour is changing at both ends of the socio-economic spectrum. Growing numbers of middle class urban women are availing of higher education and entering professional occupations in the modern sector. In the poorest strata, economic compulsions are pushing women into the labour market. The pervasive influence of cultural norms is reflected in the overwhelming concentration of women in home-based income-earning activities.

Women's employment opportunities are also circumscribed by institutional barriers in the factor markets. The labour market is segmented in a way which bars women's entry into the more remunerative, mainstream sectors and relegates them to marginal, low paying activities. Gender- and class-based inequities constrain the access of low income women to the institutional sources of credit and technology necessary to raise their productivity. The restricted job options and low returns to female employment inhibit any parental motivation to invest in their education, particularly in households where resources are limited.

In this environment, easing the structural and institutional barriers which constrain women's earning opportunities is a powerful lever for weakening the influence of cultural norms and for creating strong economic incentives at the level of the household for investment in women. Recent evidence from some developed villages of the Punjab shows the importance of economic compulsions in reducing gender differentials in access to schooling. The availability of government jobs in these settings has caused greater familial interest in women's secondary education, even among low income households, and has also led to a strong preference for educated and earning women in the 'marriage market'. In this context, the use of village-based female para-professionals by community-based NGOs and by the Departments of Health and Population is a critical intervention which will serve a dual purpose, not only extending effective outreach to female clients but also widening the employment options of educated girls in rural areas.

However, much more needs to be done. The policy response to gender inequalities has to move away from a narrow, welfare perspective and needs to be located in the context of institutional and development issues such as distribution of land, control of productive assets, sectoral development, poverty alleviation, non-farm employment, and segmentation of labour markets. The role of women as producers has not been addressed with any degree of seriousness thus far. While the official discourse on women's issues has become more informed in recent times, it has not been accompanied by any significant change in programmes and policies which continue to indicate a welfare rather than productive orientation. Consequently, women's development concerns have remained peripheral to the planning process and have been largely excluded from the development programmes operated by mainstream economic agencies. An effective integration of women in the development programmes would necessitate substantially greater effort, resources, and technical expertise than the current welfare-oriented programmes. Successive governments have not shown the requisite level of political commitment to expend these resources. The experience of Pakistan has shown that whereas external pressure may lead to the 'token' inclusion of women in the development agenda, but in the absence of political support at home, it will not lead to a redistribution of the resources necessary to ensure effective action.

REFERENCES

Ahmed, A. (1990), *Gender Differentials in Access to Health Care for Pakistani Children*, Vol. 1, UNICEF, Islamabad.

Akhter, T. (1990), *Gender Differentials in Access to Health Care for Pakistani Children*, Vol. 2, UNICEF, Islamabad.

Alam, I., and Cleland, J. (1984), *Infant and Child Mortality: Trends and Determinants*.

Alam, I., and Dineson, B. (ed.) (1984), In *Fertility in Pakistan: A Review of Findings For the Pakistan Fertility Survey*, International Statistical Institute, Voorburg, Netherlands.

Alderman, H., and Chishti, S. (1991), 'Simultaneous determination of household- and market-oriented activities of women in rural Pakistan', in ed. T. Paul Schultz, *Research in Population Economics*, Vol. 7, Greenwich, Connecticut: Jai Press.

Basu, A.M. (1989), 'Is discrimination in food really necessary for explaining sex differentials in mortality?' in *Population Studies*, Vol. 43, No. 2.

Behrman, J. (1995), *Pakistan's Human Resource Development and Economic Growth: Next Century*, The World Bank, Washington, D.C.

Bennet, L. and Goldberg, M. (1993), *Providing Enterprise Development and Financial Services to Women: A Decade of Bank Experience in Asia*, The World Bank, Washington, D.C.

Bilquees, F. (1992), 'Trends in intersectoral wages in Pakistan 1977–90', *Pakistan Development Review*, Vol. 30, No. 4.

Bilquees, F., and Hamid, S. (1989), *A Socio-economic Profile of Poor Women in Katchi Abadis*, Islamabad: PIDE.

Bouis, H.E., and Mahmood, T. (1993), 'Determinants of preschooler heights and weights in Pakistan: does age under-reporting vary by gender?', *Pakistan Development Review*, Vol. 32, No. 4.

Burney, N., and Irfan, M. (1991), 'Parental characteristics, supply of school and child school enrolment in Pakistan', *Pakistan Development Review*, Vol. 30, No. 1.

Casterline, J. (1984), 'Fertility differentials', in Alam, I. and Dineson, B. (ed.), *Fertility in Pakistan: A Review of Findings for the Pakistan Fertility Survey*, International Statistical Institute, Voorburg, Netherlands.

CIRDAP. (1995), *Women in Development and Poverty Reduction Efforts in Bank Financed Projects: Review of Performance*, Dhaka.

Dasgupta, M. (1987), 'Selective discrimination against female children in rural Punjab, India', in *Population and Development Review*, Vol. 13, No. 13.

Fikree, F., Gray, R. H., Berendes, H. W., and Karim, M. S. (1994), 'A nested control analysis of maternal mortality in Karachi', unpublished report, Aga Khan University, Karachi.

Garcia, M., and H. Alderman, (1993), *Poverty, Household Food Security, and Nutrition in Rural Pakistan*, IFPRI.

Gazdar, H., Howes, S., and Zaidi, S. (1994), 'Poverty in Pakistan: measurement, trends and patterns', mimeographed paper prepared for the World Bank.

Government of Pakistan. (1992), *Agricultural Statistics of Pakistan, 1990–91*, Islamabad.

Hafeez, S. (1983), *Women in Industry*, Islamabad: Women's Division.

———. (1984), *Impact of Employment on Women and their Families*, Islamabad: Women's Division.

Ijaz, K., and Mirza, A. (1984), *An Assessment of the Problems of Health, Nutrition, and Education of Rural Mothers and Children*, University of Agriculture, Faisalabad.

Irfan, M. (1988), 'Economic development and labour use in Pakistan', Pakistan Institute of Development Economics, Islamabad, unpublished report.

Kamal, S. (1994), 'Inequalities in women's access to and participation in the definition of economic structures and policies and the productive process itself', unpublished paper.

Kazi, S. (1989), 'Employment and skill acquisition in the informal sector of Pindi and Lahore', in F. Fluitman (ed.), *Training for Work in the Informal Sector*, Geneva: ILO.

———. (1995), 'Women and the economy: country study Pakistan', paper prepared for the Ministry of Women Development, Islamabad.

Kazi, S., and Raza, B. (1989), 'Women in the informal sector: home-based workers in Karachi', *Pakistan Development Review*, Vol. 28, No. 4.

Kazi, S., and Sathar, Z. (1993), 'Women in the urban informal labour markets in Pakistan: some economic and demographic implications', in the *Proceedings of the XXII General Conference on Population,* Montreal: IUSSP.

Kazi, S., and Raza, B. (1988), 'Households headed by women: income, employment, and household organization', *Pakistan Development Review,* Vol. 27, No. 4.

Kemal, A. R., and Mahmood, Z. (1993), *Labour Absorption in the Informal Sector and Economic Growth in Pakistan,* Islamabad: Friedrich Ebert Stiftung.

Khan, M.A., and Sirageldin, I. (1979), 'Education, income and fertility in Pakistan', *Economic Development and Cultural Change,* Vol. 27, No. 3.

Khan, N.S. (1986), *Women's Involvement in the Industrial Sector in Punjab,* Lahore: Applied Social Economic Research.

Khan, N.S., and Shaheed, F. (1984), 'Women's skill development and income generating schemes and projects in the Punjab', report prepared for UNICEF.

King, E. et al. (1986), 'Change in the status of women across generations in Asia', report prepared for the Rockefeller Foundation, New York.

Masood, F. (1988), 'Women in traditional irrigated farming systems', in *Rural Women in Pakistan's Farming System's Research,* Islamabad: Pakistan Agricultural Research Council.

National Institute of Population Studies/IRD. (1992), *Pakistan Demographic and Health Survey, 1990–91.*

Parker, B. (1994), 'Human resource development: a social analysis of constraints', report prepared for the Poverty assessment study, the World Bank, Washington, D. C.

PILER. (1990), 'Women in the industrial labour force', Karachi, unpublished report.

Planning and Development Department. (1990), *Evaluation of the Ministry of Women's Development Projects in the Provinces,* Islamabad.

Planning Commission. (1983), *Sixth Five Year Plan,* Islamabad.

———. (1988), *Seventh Five Year Plan,* Islamabad.

Population Census Organization. (1981), *Population Census of Pakistan, 1981,* Islamabad.

Sabot, R. (1992), 'Human capital accumulation in post green revolution in rural Pakistan: a progress report', *Pakistan Development Review,* Vol. 31(4), Part I.

Sathar, Z. (1984), 'Does female education affect fertility behaviour in Pakistan?', *Pakistan Development Review,* Vol. 23, No. 4.

———. (1985), 'Infant and child mortality in Pakistan: some trends and differentials', *Journal of Biosocial Science,* Vol. 17, No. 3.

———. (1987a), 'Seeking explanations for high levels of infant mortality in Pakistan', *Pakistan Development Review,* Vol. 26, No. 1.

————. (1987b), 'Sex differentials in mortality: a corollary of son preference?', *Pakistan Development Review*, Vol. 26, No. 4.

————. (1993), 'The much awaited fertility decline in Pakistan: the most recent evidence', *International Family Planning Perspectives*, Vol. 19, No. 4.

Sathar, Z., and Desai, S. (1994), 'Work patterns in rural Pakistan: intersection between gender, family and class', paper presented at the Annual Meeting of the Population Association of America, Miami.

Sathar, Z. and Kazi, S. (1987), 'Variations in demographic behaviour by levels of living in Pakistan', *Genus*, Vol. XLIII, Nos. 3–4.

————. (1988), *Productive and Reproductive Choices of Metropolitan Women: Report of a Survey in Karachi*, PIDE: Islamabad.

————. (1989), 'Female employment and fertility: further investigations of an ambivalent relationship', *Pakistan Development Review*, Vol. 28, No. 3.

————. (1990), 'Access to and use of basic services by the rural poor in Pakistan', unpublished report, Islamabad.

Sathar, Z., and Lloyd, C. (1993), 'Who gets primary schooling in Pakistan: inequalities among and within families', working paper No. 52, Population Council, New York.

Shaheed, F., and Mumtaz, K. (1981), *Invisible Workers: Piecework Labour Amongst Women in Lahore*, Islamabad: Women's Division.

UNDP/UNIFEM/SUNGI. (1994), *Report of the Workshop on Access to Credit for Rural Women in Pakistan*, Islamabad.

World Bank. (1992). *Pakistan Integrated Household Survey, Final Results 1991*.

Zaman, K., and Khan, M. J. (1987), *Female Labour Participation in Rural Economy of Punjab*, Lahore: Punjab Economic Research Institute.

NOTES

1. The MIMS was undertaken between 1989 and 1992 by the Aga Khan University Hospital. They sampled selected clusters in Sindh, Balochistan, and the North West Frontier Province covering 10,500 households in Sindh, 20,480 in Balochistan, and 7,732 in NWFP.

12

Environment: Some Key Controversies

Shaheen Rafi Khan* and Shahrukh Rafi Khan**

1. INTRODUCTION

Unlike the other chapters in this book, this chapter is forward-looking, and so the subject matter is different. Also, since a number of good reviews of the state of the environment exist, we have opted instead to focus on issues that are controversial and in some ways, represent both a challenge and an opportunity for the future.[1] One intent is to stimulate policy dialogue around these issues, and in a manner which ensures that the dialogue is consultative (involving key stake-holders), integrative (across themes and sectors), and encourages ownership (by clearly defining national as opposed to global priorities). There tends to be an inertial and passive aspect to policy making which reflects the absence of participatory pre-policy consensus based on up-to-date information and analysis. In the various sections of this chapter, we have attempted to remedy the latter deficiency.

In electing to write this chapter, our first concern was to strike an appropriate balance between brown and green issues and, in this context, to focus on controversial topics. However, as we began to think about these topics, the similarities, interactions, and overlaps across sectors and across the north-

* Consultant to the IUCN Commission on Environmental, Economic, and Social Policy, South Asia (CEESP-SA).

** Executive Director, Sustainable Development Policy Institute.

south divide started to become apparent very quickly. For instance, the enforcement of environmental quality standards on manufactured products, and the more broad-based emission controls mandated under the climate change conventions have both national, north-south, and global implications. Northern consumers have certain 'environmentally dictated' preferences for manufactured goods that contribute to alleviating global warming and reducing national health risks also. This adds a new twist to the perceived dichotomy in positions adopted in north-south negotiations, in so far as the distinctions become somewhat blurred. Thus, the north need not cajole and bribe the south into adopting 'unpopular' measures—the pot of gold syndrome. Nor should the south worry about exploiting the situation to its advantage, as benefits of ownership of the measures potentially resides with it also.

The Bretton Woods institutions are rightly viewed as imposing conditions on developing countries. Unfortunately, meeting fiscal demands, often is at high cost to humans and the environment. This is the case with respect to fertilizers and pesticides where subsidy cuts on domestic production have coincided with trade liberalization in these products. There is an inter-sectoral dimension here as well. The Green Revolution technologies are highly water-intensive, an important factor supporting construction of the Kalabagh Dam. However, this would contribute to further fragmentation of the inland water and delta ecosystem with adverse consequences for bio-diversity, livelihoods, coastal protection, and ultimately, for food production.

Some of the above may at this point appear elliptical but it does serve to introduce and point to the interactions among the topics we cover in the five sections following this introduction. The next section focuses on industrial emissions in which we take up the issue of self-monitoring as opposed to government enforcement. In section 3, we take up the issue of the potentially high environmental cost of attaining higher agricultural productivity. In section 4, we question just how severe the problem of waterlogging and salinity is. In section 5, we discuss the dangers to the bio-diversity of the inland ecosystem resulting from the current and planned water management system in Pakistan. In section 6, the north-south controversy on climate change is discussed from Pakistan's vantage point and we focus on the national dimensions of the issue. As the last section, it is the most comprehensive and forward-looking and takes account of the impact of socio-economic factors on the environment and also indicates the likely future scenarios emerging for the water, agriculture, and forestry sectors.

2. INDUSTRIAL EMISSIONS ABATEMENT

Many fear that the focus on the 'environment' is simply a way of keeping more competitive goods from Southern countries out of Northern markets. The issue is more complex. Southern countries like Pakistan must distinguish between restrictions imposed by northern governments and those imposed by northern businesses. If northern governments imposed import restrictions because southern countries are not doing enough about child labour or cleaner production technologies, this constitutes a non-tariff barrier. However, this is not the big danger that faces southern exporters. Increasingly, businesses in the north are being required by their boards/shareholders to do business with firms that meet certain 'voluntary' environmental and quality standards. In some ways, a cleaner environment is a luxury good and the more prosperous northern consumers require it. This is thus a market-dictated standard and not, as such, a non-tariff barrier imposed by northern governments. This is a very important distinction. The only option southern exporters have is to conform or lose markets.

Pakistan is currently confronting an enormous challenge, the extent of which has not been absorbed by our political leaders. Initially, southern exporters were confronted with meeting ISO 9000 standards, which are aimed at meeting customer requirements via a rationalization of the production process and via the institution of continuous improvements.[2] The government has agreed to meet half of the ISO 9000 certification cost for export industries. About fifty Pakistani companies are certified and more will be soon. Government subsidies to the private sector are questionable. However, in any case, the government is barely keeping up because the ISO 14000 series is already operational. The ISO 14000 series moves beyond the ISO 9000 so that environmental issues are included in the managerial and organizational purview.

The ISO 14000 environmental standards are important because they have been endorsed under the GATT agreement on Technical Barriers to Trade (TBT). Thus, if a government sets standards not consistent with ISO standards, they may be challenged under TBT by foreign governments. In this regard, the ISO standards set a standard ceiling. ISO's recognition also stems from its provision of a technical support role in relationship to the new and expanding WTO programme.

The ISO 14001 is the standard in the ISO 14000 series for which companies can get certified.[3] It does not access environmental performance or improvement in such performance. Thus, it is no substitute for a legal framework such as a rigorous environmental protection bill. However, ISO 14001 certification does mean that a company has an environmental management system in place that would be expected to lead to better performance. It has provisions for self-audits and hence a framework for self-regulation. In this regard, widespread adoption of ISO 14001 could alleviate the need for a strong environmental auditing infrastructure. Another interesting feature of this standard is that since the focus is on management systems; a company could be ISO certified even if it produced radio-active materials.[4] However, ISO 14001 requires an environmental policy statement and an environmental management system in place for ensuring compliance with that statement. The policy statement requires a commitment to comply with applicable laws and to continual improvement in the environmental context and to the prevention of pollution. However, if the environmental laws are deficient and establish a low base standard, a company can be ISO 14001 certified while operating at a very low environmental standard.

Pakistan now has a rigorous environmental policy in place. The 1997 Environment Protection Ordinance, which emerged from a consultative process, has been enacted. One key feature of the Ordinance is that it requires manufacturing companies to conform to National Environment Quality Standards (NEQS), and those not conforming will be required to pay a pollution charge.

An important innovation suggested by the National Environmental Standards Committee (which includes government, business and NGO representatives) is that compliance with the NEQS be based on self-monitoring. How could that be possible? The answer is that businesses would be required to have environmental audits conducted. Those in violation of the NEQS would pay a pollution charge into a 'fund' managed by an independent government/business/NGO Board of Trustees. The fund could be used for bettering business environmental practices. The modalities of this fund have yet to be worked out. Also, just as taxes are randomly audited by the Income Tax Department, the environmental audits can be randomly inspected by the Federal and Provincial Environmental Protection Agencies (EPAs).

One major advantage of this procedure is that companies whose management practices result in avoiding a pollution charge are also likely to be in conformity with ISO 14001. The government needs to take the following steps. First, since certification could take several years, be valid for a limited time period, and cost between $100,000 to $200,000, the government must help in ensuring that there are national accreditation bodies to adopt standards for ISO 14001 certifiers. To become accredited, a register must have competent auditors as its employees and there needs to be a continuous evaluation of such firms. This would avoid shipping in expensive consultants. Linkage and follow-up with the ISO Office in Geneva will help by showing that the government supports the process and for getting international endorsement for domestic certification.

Second, with the assistance of bilateral and multilateral donors, it must immediately start building the capacity of the national and provincial EPAs to conduct random environmental audits. The capacity of the relevant agency in government must also be built up so they can register and monitor private sector registers to conduct the audits. A large number of management consultant firms will get into the business of environmental audits (as accounting firms now do expenditure audits) but quality control processes need to be in place.

In Pakistan, there could be a phased process in the move towards meeting environmental standards. In the first phase, the enforcement of the NEQS would involve the development of monitoring procedures, sampling, analysis, and documentation within industry. The pollution charge would be contingent on the establishment of these processes. Simultaneously, the certification of environmental laboratories and the enhancement of capabilities of the Environmental Protection Agencies could take place. With the ground work complete, in the second phase, companies who have established environmental management systems could certify for standards like the ISO 14001.

Progress towards sustainable industrial production is being made in Pakistan. The Environment Standard Committee (ESC) was constituted in March 1996 to prepare recommendations for the implementation of the NEQS. The ESC includes representatives of government, business, and civil society groups. In a meeting in March 1998, draft guidelines for 'Self-Monitoring and Reporting by Industry' and a draft proposal for the 'Determining of a Pollution Charge for Industry' were presented by the Pakistan Environment Protection Agency to the ESC and approved by the ESC. The Federal Chamber of Commerce and Industry, Pakistan has already agreed to a specific pollution charge and the schedule via which it will increase over time. In addition, work is also underway on proposals to provide fiscal incentives and credit for cleaner production.[5] All these proposals will be presented at the next meeting of the Pakistan Environmental Protection Council (PEPC), the highest policy making organ on environmental issues. Thus there is hope that a move to cleaner production will be underway soon in Pakistan and that firms will hence position themselves for ISO 14001 certification.

Having said this, it is important to point out that implementing ISO 14001 will not be easy. It requires a company to inventory and assess all environmental aspects of its operations, products, and services. Thus all employees need to be trained with regard to the environmental consequences of their work.[6] To implement such a cultural change in a developing country with a low literacy rate will be a major challenge. Even so, it is possible that many buyers in the north will be pushed by their shareholders and boards to require certification from suppliers. Southern countries, who do not rapidly position themselves to meet this challenge, may rapidly lose markets.[7]

Certification could thus be viewed as an opportunity. The most critical factor in determining whether the opportunity will be realized depends on the understanding of our elected representatives. There appears to be a misconception that somehow cleaning up the environment is a luxury we cannot afford or that preventing environmental damage imposes an economic cost. This is true only when viewed from a limited short-run perspective. Politicians and businesses need to realize that pollution from emissions cause an immense loss in productivity as our water, soil, and air become polluted. Much more important is the loss of quality of life and productivity resulting from the impairment of the health of current and future generations. Politicians always speak for the poor, but it is the poor who are least capable of defending themselves from environmental ravages.

If improving the health, productivity, and quality of life of the current and future generations is not a sufficient inducement to act quickly, the potential huge loss of export markets should be. Here no simple distinction between export and non-export industries is possible since, via supply networks, the whole production infrastructure is highly integrated. Thus the approach in dealing with the environmental challenge has to be holistic and not piecemeal.[8]

3. TRADE LIBERALIZATION AND THE ENVIRONMENT[9]

In the section above, it is apparent that trade liberalization has willy-nilly been adopted by signatories to the WTO agreements, including Pakistan. Also, we argue that such liberalizations can present opportunities for partially setting Pakistan's environmental house in order. However, Pakistan cannot be entirely passive about trade liberalization. Trade liberalization is viewed to be damaging to the environment for several reasons. First, trade is considered to be a magnifier, and if the correct environmental policies are not in place, the enhanced production that accompanies enhanced trade could exacerbate the pressure on natural resources and increase industrial pollution.[10] Second, the social cost of liberalization, that results in unrestricted import of dirty, second-hand manufacturing technologies and hazardous agricultural inputs, may outweigh the social benefits. In this section, our major concern, from a Pakistani perspective, is with the imports of environmentally unfriendly agricultural inputs. Since environmentalists are often accused by neo-liberal economists of being one-sided, we look at both sides of these issues. While we did not have data to do a rigorous cost-benefit analysis, we have engaged in a 'suggestive' cost-benefit analysis to inform policy. We also argue that, even while conforming to the WTO agreements, countries have the ability to block some imports and check others by influencing demand.

A. METHOD

To get consensus on an appropriate methodology for cost-benefit analysis would be virtually impossible. Quantifying the benefits side is, in principle, relatively straightforward. One approach could be magnifying the results of farm studies, using reasonable assumptions. Thus, using a production function approach, it should be possible to isolate the contribution of pesticides and fertilizers in enhancing the output of different crops in varying agro-ecological zones. While straightforward in principle, this approach still requires a large number of careful studies. An alternative approach, which we adopted, is to get a ballpark valuation based on estimates of crop saving due to pesticide and crop enhancement due to fertilizer use.

One method of quantifying the costs would be to identify the direct medical costs and the costs of foregone earnings due to losses in work, in labour, and in land productivity. However, many would object to such quantification since it is much too narrow an approach to measuring the decrease in the quality of life resulting from the negative effects of pesticide or fertilizer use and ignores many other damaging environmental effects.

We agree with the latter view, but had data been available on work and productivity loss and on the direct medical cost resulting from the adverse medical effects of pesticide or fertilizers, we would have proceeded with generating a cost estimate. We concede that this would represent an understatement of the true social cost, but none the less, such estimates can inform policy. One could argue that even one life is worth more than all the crop gain from synthetic pesticide and fertilizer use. However, crop gains reduce food prices which could avert malnutrition and famine and hence save lives.

B. Benefits and Costs of Agricultural Input Import[11]

1. Pesticide trade liberalization
Pakistan began to liberalize its trade policy in earnest in 1991–2.[12] Although maximum tariff rates have been on the decline since then, the tariff rate on pesticides actually doubled in 1993–4.[13] In spite of this increase in the tariff rate, there has been no substantial decrease in the imports of pesticides, or in the value of domestic production.[14]

The duty on pesticides increased in 1994–5, ostensibly bucking the liberalization trend. Also, the additional duty of 30 per cent applied to the imports of packaged brands of insecticide appears to have restricted imports. However, the former policy did not discourage pesticide consumption as this increase in tariff rate was preceded by the liberalization of imports of pesticides under generic names in 1992. The regulatory duty was also imposed to discourage the more expensive brand name packaged imports in favour of the cheaper, domestically packaged generics. Information made available by the Ministry of Food and Agriculture reveals that generics were between about 50 to 70 per cent cheaper than the brands. The immediate effect of this policy was a sharp increase in the total quantity of pesticide imports.[15] Local dealers took the opportunity to import pesticide chemicals in bulk for supply to the local markets in local packaging.

In March 1995 however, the import of generic pesticides by local companies was discontinued. Local importers claim that this trade policy change was instigated by multinational corporations who were in cahoots with the bureaucracy. Cotton experts argue that local importers were engaged in adulterating pesticides and that this was responsible for immunities that developed among pests which then became resistant to even much stronger doses of pesticides (*Dawn*, 'Pesticide importers perturbed over ban,' 14 March 1995).

Another trade policy decision that the government took to make pesticides more readily available was announced in the *1995–96 Trade Policy*. The government decided to discontinue its policy of the *1971 Pesticide Ordinance* which required pesticides to be registered and in use in the exporting country. Thus, despite the seemingly higher duty of 1994–5, the objective of trade policy has been to make pesticides more readily available at cheaper prices.

a. <u>Benefits</u>: Jabbar and Mallick (1994, p. 4) claim that crop saving due to pesticide use is estimated to be 15 to 25 per cent of the total value of the crop. No source was available for this claim and so we are unable to assess it critically. However, these numbers are consistent with those cited elsewhere. For example, Gianessi (1993) cites a University of Texas A & M study claiming that if currently available non-chemical methods were substituted for synthetic chemicals, the production of soybean would decrease by 37 per cent, wheat by 24 per cent, cotton by 39 per cent, rice by 57 per cent, peanuts by 78 per cent, and corn by 32 per cent. Assuming that crop saving due to the use of pesticides in Pakistan is 15 per cent of the total value of the crop, the value of crop saving for the four major crops was computed by Khan (1997, p. 260) to be around Rs 16 billion. Sandhu (1993, p. 22) reports that the crop losses have been estimated to be 35 per cent, and if so, the loss would translate to about Rs 37 billion. This in fact is a conservative estimate, given that, where applicable, we have used prices for the inferior varieties of the crops and have calculated losses for only the major crops.

b. Costs: The costs are by now well documented and hence not difficult to classify. Carson's *Silent Spring* (1962) started the questioning and concern and many writers have since written about the negative effects of pesticides, particularly concerning their use in developing countries.[16] Weir and Schapiro in The *Circle of Poison* (1981, p. 11) pointed out that pesticide poisoning in LDCs was thirteen times greater than in the USA, due to the lower level of education, despite the much greater use in the US. Drifting pesticide sprays, leaky applicators, lack of appropriate precautions, and overuse result in run-offs into water and soil.

Residues in soil and food and unsafe contact result in various medical problems for people, including enzyme imbalances, skin and allergic reactions, delayed neurotoxicity, behavioural changes, lesions, changes in the central nervous system, peripheral neurities, carcinogenic diseases, sterility, cataracts, lung perforation, memory loss, and damage to the immune system. Colborn (1994, p. 89) points out that most of the past testing focused on individuals directly exposed and not on the functionality of their offspring. He points out that studies reveal that 'as a result of [pesticide] exposure in the womb of mammals, including humans, the endocrine, immune, and nervous systems of embryos do not develop normally'.

Sadhu (1992, p. 23) cited an FAO study claiming that only 5 per cent of the insecticide falls on target plants; the rest pollutes the environment.[17] The adverse impact on the land base includes a reduction in the natural fertility of the soil, harm to the soil structure and soil aeration, reduction of the water-holding capacity of the soil making it more prone to soil erosion by water and wind, and lower drought tolerance of crops. Finally, pesticides are viewed as indiscriminately killing useful insects, micro-organisms, and insect predator species, breeding more virulent and resistant species of insects and vectors, and reducing the genetic diversity of plant species.[18] Jabbar and Mallick (1994) reviewed the scanty evidence on this issue in Pakistan and based on that, reported the existence of residues in water, soil, food, and people.[19] This evidence also indicated the existence of the above-mentioned maladies resulting from pesticides.

As things stand, what can we say about Pakistan's pesticide import policy? We have a rough quantification of the benefits but none of the costs, beyond a documentation of the nature of the costs. Given this gap in information, we recommend caution. Manifold suggestions of the potentially serious social costs of pesticides, and the lack of hard evidence disputing them, suggest that the government's trade liberalization policies are uncalled for. This is particularly so since knowledge about alternatives, often included as part of an integrated pest management (IPM) strategy, are now widespread.[20] As early as 1987, the Office of Technical Assessment estimated that 'this approach could reduce pesticide use in the USA by 75 per cent on some crops, reduce pre-harvest losses by 50 per cent, and result in significant pest control savings'.[21]

2. Fertilizer trade liberalization

Imports decreased from about two-fifths of total fertilizer consumption in 1990–91 to 35 per cent in 1993–4.[22] At the same time, fertilizer subsidies have declined steadily from 10.5 per cent of total subsidies to just 0.9 per cent in the 1994–5 budget estimates.[23] All of this subsidy is now for imported fertilizers.[24]

a. <u>Benefits</u>: Once again, the benefits are, in principle, easier to quantify than the costs. We have adopted a similar back of the envelope approach to quantifying the benefits of fertilizer use as in the case of pesticides. Estimates were available from a total of 435 farm experiments conducted from 1980–81 to 1982–3 in Saleem et al. (1989, p. 29) of the incremental yield from the use of a combination of nitrogen, phosphorus, and potassium fertilizers. Although, these estimates are not recent, we assume that they provide an approximate indication of the effects of fertilizer on yields of the major crops.[25] These yield figures were converted into production equivalent data using a four-step method, and the results showed that the benefits from the use of pesticides amount to approximately Rs 61 billion.[26]

b. <u>Costs</u>: Qutab (1994, p. 16) documents the costs of fertilizers to human health and the environment. Excess nitrate and nitrite in water and foods can result in methemoglobinemia in infants, are viewed as carcinogenic, and can result in respiratory illnesses.[27] Run-off can result in eutrophication via enhanced algae growth and hence hurt fish stocks and also humans via algae toxins. Soil erosion could result from volatilization and denitrification. Finally, nitrates contribute to 'soil-pan formation and nitrogeneous gases can contribute to the green house effect'.[28]

Fertilizer use in Pakistan has steadily increased from 20 kgs per hectacre in 1971–2 to 91 kgs per hectacre in 1991–2. This exceeds fertilizer use in India and, interestingly, the United States, where fertilizer use has declined and in 1991–2 was 71 kgs per hectacre. Use is much more intensive in Europe and Japan with the Netherlands applying the most (599 kgs per hectacre) in 1991–2.[29] Evidence on the negative environmental impact of fertilizers in Pakistan is once again very limited. Ali and Jabbar (1992, p. 92) tested soils in Faisalabad in a pilot study and concluded that nitrates are present in sub-surface soils in considerable quantities.

As in the case of pesticides, alternatives have started being explored. In an ESCAP document (1992, p. 9), Integrated Plant Nutrient Systems (INPS) is presented as a method which entails the judicious and efficient use of mineral fertilizers, organic matter, green manuring, biological nitrogen fixation, and other inoculants. Further, minor modifications of existing practices could lead to a cut in fertilizer use by about one-third (p. 53).[30]

4. WATERLOGGING AND SALINITY

Waterlogging and salinity are also viewed as serious environmental problems in the agricultural sector and they tend to occur in tandem. Waterlogging is caused by a high water table, resulting from its continuous recharge, without offsetting drainage or evaporation. The recharge is caused by seepage from surface water flows and precipitation. Waterlogging can also take the form of surface ponding, a consequence of high precipitation and flooding. As the ground water table rises, it brings dissolved salts to the surface through capillary action, which result in both sub-soil and surface salinity. Alternatively, surface salinity can result from evaporation of accumulated ground water, saline or otherwise, which is usually pumped up by tube-wells. Salinity can affect soils in two ways; it can make them saline or sodic. Of the two types, sodicity is the more harmful as it causes formation of an impermeable hard pan below the surface.

The common perception is that Pakistan will continue to face serious problems of waterlogging and salinity. However, there are mitigating factors which suggest that this concern is exaggerated. These relate to the overall hydrological balance, soil conditions, crop specificities, chemical characteristics, and water management. Evidence on these factors is presented in support of the counter-proposition.

The hydrological balance is perhaps the most important consideration in assessing the gravity of the twin problems. Vulnerability with respect to water resources reflects the divergence between present and projected demand for water and the supply likely to be available. Demand is driven by population growth and sectoral requirements while supply aimed at meeting such demand, has both quantitative and qualitative aspects. Quantitatively, the concern is with the amount of water available to meet the needs of agriculture, household consumption, energy, industry, and coastal fisheries. The qualitative concern relates to deteriorating ground water quality which primarily has human health implications.

We focus our attention on the Indus Basin System, as it is pivotal to Pakistan's agricultural as well as other sector needs. Our aim is to demonstrate that available water is being fully utilized and that the situation is and will remain one of excess demand. Water resources are being continuously mined, with uptakes exceeding recharge. As such, the problem of waterlogging and salinity acquires a seasonal as well as localized character.

A. THE WATER POTENTIAL OF THE INDUS BASIN SYSTEM

The mean value over sixty-four years of water availability at the rim stations (that is entering the Indus basin within Pakistan) is about 146 million acre-feet (MAF). Of this, approximately 104 MAF are diverted at the canal head. The 42 MAF or so that flows into the Arabian Sea, sustains Pakistan's delta ecosystem—its aquatic life and mangroves—and acts as a buffer against salt water intrusion. After accounting for losses in the canal system, in watercourses, and in field applications, about 31 MAF of surface flows are actually used by the crops. Ostensibly, the loss rate is high, suggesting that additional water can be made available through the rehabilitation and proper management of the canal irrigation system. However, a significant proportion of this loss constitutes ground water recharge. Of the estimated 46 MAF total annual recharge, 41 MAF are already being used for crop cultivation. Thus, about 5 MAF represents the lower limit of additional ground water that can be tapped. The upper limit is 15 MAF, as claimed by experts from the Ministry of Power and Water Resources. This includes the sweet water underlays in brackish water zones, which can be drawn up by using up-coning technologies. However, with no increase in surface water supplies since the construction of the Tarbela Dam and a maximum additional 15 MAF that can be tapped from ground water sources, the long-term prospects for increasing irrigation water is limited. Against such relatively static supply, future demand will begin to create unsustainable pressure on water resources.

B. The Implications for Waterlogging

The canal irrigation system has, over the past century, caused the water table in the Indus basin to rise by an average 50 feet. This has raised a concern about waterlogging, a condition in which the soil is saturated to the extent that common plants fail to grow or their growth and yields are adversely affected due to poor aeration of the root zone. Also, due to high intensity monsoon rains, low infiltration rate of soils, blockage of natural drainage by the transport and irrigation infrastructure (canal alignments, road and railway network), it is estimated that as much as 10 to 15 per cent of the irrigated areas in the Indus basin may suffer from excessive wetness and ponding even though the water table may not be high.

The real extent of waterlogging is difficult to determine, as there is no single yardstick that can be used. In the first instance, this yardstick will differ according to the crop grown; for instance, rice can thrive in water tables above one metre while for cotton, the water table needs to be much deeper. There are other criteria as well, such as water quality, soil type, and precipitation/evaporation ratios. Additionally, water tables rise with the monsoons and fall in the *rabi* season.

Table 1 shows water table depths over the Indus basin Canal Command Area (CCA).

Table 1
Water-table depths

Water-Table Depth (Metres)	Quality of water	Area affected (hectares)	Share of gross canal command area @ (Percentage)
1.0	Sweet	121,862	0.70
1.0	Sweet/Saline	321,862	1.95
1.5	Sweet/Saline	5,300,000	12.90
3.0	Sweet/Saline	8,866,397	53.70

Source: NCS secretariat estimates.
Note: @ represents the surveyed CCA (13.6 million ha.).

Abstracting from the above qualifications, we assume zero to one metre as being the lower limit of the critical range for waterlogging. The total area with the water table going up to this level lies just above 320,000 hectares, or 1.95 per cent of the CCA. In the case of approximately 120,000 hectares of this area, the water table is sweet. Hence, it can be used to grow high-delta crops or phytophreatic trees and grasses. The saline/disastrous water-table zone constitutes 200,000 hectares or just 1.2 per cent of the gross CCA. Sindh suffers the most from this form of land degradation, with 5.1 per cent of the area surveyed thus affected. WAPDA has adopted the higher figure of 1.5 metres as its criteria for vulnerability. By their reckoning, about 12.9 per cent (2.54 million hectares, 1979) of the Indus basin fell in this category. However, two-thirds of the surveyed area, with the water table within 6 feet depth, is that of strongly salt-affected soils which have never been cultivated and are outside the CCA. As such, only 480,000 ha of non-saline cultivated land in the CCA is moderately to severely waterlogged. Table 2 shows the secular trend in waterlogging.

Table 2
Area where water-table depth is less than five feet:
by province and over time

Province	1979 Area	%	1986 Area	%
Punjab	1.22	12	0.77	8
Sindh	1.19	21	1.27	22
NWFP	0.03	5	0.04	7
Balochistan (Pat Feeder)	0.05	34	0.06	36
Pakistan	2.49	15	2.14	13

Source: Government of Pakistan (1987).
Note: These figures represent the pre-monsoon situation.

By WAPDA's higher criteria (1.5 meters), the incidence of waterlogging in Sindh has increased while it has fallen in the Punjab. Overall, for all of Pakistan, the waterlogged area has declined. This supports the earlier contention that a balance has been achieved between ground water recharge and utilization. In fact, in areas underlain by sweet ground water, there is recent evidence of dropping water tables in fourteen out of the forty-five canal commands.

C. Impact on Salinity

Controversy also surrounds the related problem of salinity. The Indus basin system overlays large salt formations, to which some 10.8 million tons of salts are added each year. However, as long as these salts remain below the reach of crops and trees, they do little harm. They become a problem when they are mobilized, either through a rising water table or the pumping of saline or sweet ground water. In the absence of good drainage, surface evaporation occurs, resulting in salt deposition.[31]

The overall figures for salinity are high. In the 13.6 million hectares of the CCA surveyed, the total saline area is 3.2 million hectares, or 23.3 per cent of the total CCA. Across provinces, some 28.6 per cent of surveyed area in Sindh is affected compared to 20.4 per cent in Punjab (*see* Table 3). However, the salt-affected area of prime significance is only the 1.2 million hectares of land which is under cultivation. Table 3 provides information on the extent of salt affected land within and outside the CCA.

Table 3
Extent of salt-affected land within and outside CCA: by province (1000 hectares)

	NWFP	Punjab	Sindh	Total Indus Basin
Total CCA	320	7,891	5,351	13,562
Within CCA				
Salt-affected area	14	1,614	1,532	3,160
Percentage	4.3	20.4	28.6	23.3
Outside CCA				
Salt-affected area	502	1,129	1,019	2,650
Total:	516	2,743	2,551	5,810

Source: Government of Pakistan (1979).

It could be argued that salinity could become a problem in the future as a result of the increased use of ground water. Canal water is practically salt-free. By contrast, even fresh ground water contains up to 1,000 parts per million (PPM) of total dissolved solids (TDS). Since ground water is opportunely and easily available, there is a tendency to overuse it. However, salt tolerance is a function of soil structure and management; that is, under marginal conditions, with fine clayey soils, no land leveling, water shortages, and poor irrigation methods, only a TDS of 500 PPM can be tolerated. Under optimal conditions, with coarse soils and good drainage, leveled land, plentiful water, and good irrigation methods, water with 1,500 PPM can be safely applied. In addition, salinity/sodicity occurs either as patches, covering 20 to 30 per cent area of the affected fields, or as small acreages of partially reclaimed soils in a mixed pattern within large areas of normal, non-saline soils. In fact, as earlier stated, sodicity is perceived to be the more serious problem, which changes the soil structure by creating an impermeable salt pan and needs to be chemically treated with gypsum.

5. BIO-DIVERSITY OF INLAND (AQUATIC) WATER ECOSYSTEMS: OPTIONS FOR CONSERVATION AND SUSTAINABLE USE

A. Tread Lightly on the Land and Water

Just as we showed in section 3 that there are high environmental, social, and economic costs associated with agricultural productivity increases based on chemical inputs, similarly, large-scale water management systems come with a big price tag. There are several perspectives from which large-scale water management systems, including big dams, have been critiqued including human displacement and economic feasibility. A less frequently heard critique concerns the bio-diversity loss of inland water ecosystems that results from such large-scale water management systems.

'Bio-diversity deficit', 'pulse disturbance', 'paradox of malnutrition' are key themes which should guide our understanding and approach to inland water ecosystem management in Pakistan. They are meant to provoke reflection on the ill-considered interventions which disrupt nature's rhythms and exacerbate the very problems they are meant to redress. For instance, large dam construction remains firmly entrenched in the minds of Pakistani planners as the ideal flood prevention device. The evidence shows otherwise: that the fragmentation of the Indus basin ecosystem, thanks to its network of dams, barrages, canals, and waterways, has led to an increased incidence of floods and, at best merely created 'flood threat transfer mechanisms'.[32] Similarly, a popular perception is that new 'eco-equations' have emerged as a result of such fragmentation, with new habitats replacing the ones destroyed. In fact, a 'bio-diversity deficit' is in the making, with species and organisms either threatened or on the verge of extinction. Also, retakes on mono-culture—with its mix of high yielding varieties, chemical applications, and intensive water use—point to adverse impacts on crop genetic diversity, and the availability and quality of water essential for nurturing downstream flora, fauna, and aquatic life. If the long-term environmental implications of mono-cropping are weighed against the more obvious and immediate productivity gains, the sustainability of such benefits becomes questionable.

Anthropogenic activity, which degrades the Indus basin system's ecological integrity, is an on-going process and a culmination of many factors. It is instigated and sustained by development and demographic pressures. It reflects the imposed dominance of technology over nature. It is an outcome of weak institutions which succumb to vested interests. It represents a failure to exploit the traditional synergies, practices, and interactions between communities and their environment. In the final analysis, such degradation is a symptom of the piecemeal and extractive manner in which ecosystem resources are utilized, and it contrasts with the common sense embodied in Abramovitz's (1996, p.10) remark that:

> freshwater ecosystems are the critical link between land and sea, in effect forming the planet's circulatory system; virtually every human action is eventually reflected in them.

This holistic view, which integrates spatial, biophysical, and human dimensions, should form the core of all efforts to manage ecosystem resources sustainably.

B. THE STATUS AND TRENDS IN FRESHWATER BIO-DIVERSITY: A CRISIS IN THE MAKING?

1. The Indus delta ecosystem
Mangroves are the mainstay of the Indus delta ecosystem, sustaining its fisheries, acting as natural barriers against sea and storm surges, keeping bank erosion in check, a source of fuelwood, timber, fodder and forest products, a refuge for wildlife, and a potential source of tourism. Without mangroves and the nutrients they recycle and the protection they provide, other components of the ecosystem would not survive. Mangrove estuaries have been found to be five times more productive than tropical estuaries. Many fish species are dependant upon this

high productivity and as many as 90 per cent of all tropical marine species (including shrimps and prawns, which are the mainstay of Pakistan's fish exports) pass at least one stage of their life-cycle in mangrove estuaries. Satellite images provided by SUPARCO (1991) showed the Indus delta as being covered by 50,000 ha. of dense mangrove, 210,000 ha. of normal mangroves, 140,000 ha. of sparse or no vegetation and 40,000 ha. of sand.

Valuation of the economic benefits of mangroves is neither systematic, nor is it up to date. In 1978, Pakistan earned Rs 5.8 billion from fish exports, of which shrimps and prawns constituted 72 per cent. The collective imputed income from fuel-wood, fodder, and forest products was another Rs 200 million. Even where numbers are absent, the functions are, in themselves, indicative. For instance, substituting natural with physical barriers (dykes, walls, dredgers) would entail enormously high capital and maintenance costs. In addition, the wild life and tourism potential of the mangrove swamps has not been exploited yet and could prove a source of additional income.

A community of about 100,000 people resides in coastal villages on the northern side of the Indus delta. The mangroves are a vital source of livelihood for them; both directly (fuel, fodder, grazing) and indirectly (fish, amenity values). An unfortunate and contradictory tendency is to describe these communities in the same breath as 'underprivileged', and as 'agents of destruction of natural resources.' There is an inherent fallacy in this juxtaposition; why a poor community should endanger the basis of its own existence is a little difficult to fathom. The true explanation lies elsewhere. Essentially, community practices have not changed, but they seem pernicious because the resource base has begun to degrade. Communities are more often the victims as opposed to the instruments of such degradation. The real culprits are water diversion, biological and chemical water contamination, and large-scale commercial practices, compounded both by institutional ignorance and complicity in such practices.

2. Threats to the system

Degradation of the Indus delta ecosystem and loss of bio-diversity is already a highly visible phenomenon. The present level of silt discharge, estimated at 100 million tons per year, is a four-fold reduction from the original level before the dams were built. The combination of salt water intrusion (some reports show this as 30 kms inland), and reduced silt and nutrient flows have changed the geomorphology of the delta considerably. The area of active growth of the delta has reduced from an original estimate of 2,600 sq. kms (growing at 34 metres per year) to about 260 sq. kms. Freshwater reaches only a few of the creeks and others have become blocked. The delta is being transformed by strong wave erosion, an increasing dominance of sand at the delta front, and an increase in wind-blown sand deposits as a result of losses in vegetation.

The effects of reduced water and nutrients, and of pollution on the mangroves are insidious. While there are no visible effects on existing mangrove stands, new seedlings will not grow and those that do, will develop into stunted trees. There is evidence of this in the abundance of stunted growth, in the stands of mature trees with few young trees, the receding and barren segments where mangroves once flourished, the erosion of banks, and the collapse of mangrove stands.

The water used for irrigation and returned to the system is polluted with chemical additives. To this are added effluents from Karachi's industrial centres with direct outlets into water bodies, and indirect run-offs from homes and municipalities. One among the many life threatening after-effects is 'eutrophication'. Excess nutrients, especially nitrogen and phosphorus, coming from human and animal wastes and fertilizers overstimulate the growth of algae. As this overabundant organic material decomposes and dies, it robs the water of oxygen required for fish and other aquatic organisms. Another consequence is that chemicals tend to bio-accumulate or bio-magnify up the food chain. Fish consumed by humans contains substances which act as endocrine disruptors, mimicking the action of hormones and causing deformities.

The degradation of mangrove stands and water pollution is not only threatening to the fish species but to a number of other wildlife species as well, threatened species include marine dolphins, porpoises, jackal, wild boar, and reptiles like snakes and marine turtles. Habitat loss could also reduce avian life, especially the flights of migratory wildfowl using the Indus flyway.

3. Proposed additional water diversions

Releases below the Kotri Barrage average 34 MAF. Of this, about 20 MAF actually reaches the mangroves, and that, too, between the *kharif* months of July and September. The rest is lost due to evaporation or diversions. According to the Sindh Forestry Department, about 27 MAF is required to maintain the existing 260,000 ha. of mangroves in reasonably healthy condition. This is 7 MAF more than currently available, a situation which has contributed to ecosystem instability.

Within the framework of the Indus Water Accord, an additional 10 MAF is proposed to be diverted for upstream storage construction (e.g. Kalabagh), to meet agricultural and hydropower needs. Abstracting from efficiency gains in the delivery system, which could compensate to some extent for this diversion, there would, in effect, be a further reduction in already sub-optimal flows. It would aggravate an already critical situation leading to further threats to the mangroves and species diversity.

4. Solutions

The basis for integrated ecosystem management lies in recognition of the values of bio-diversity, and of all those to whom bio-diversity is of value. This reflects an important sea change in thinking—one that is long overdue. In functional terms it means that: a) the usufruct rights of communities, recreation, and bequest values be considered when extracting ecosystem services; b) as a logical extension, the communities be allowed decision-making roles in ecosystem planning and management; c) larger areas and longer time scales be considered to maintain all of a system's processes and components and; d) at the institutional level, co-ordination between implementing agencies be ensured, along with the participation of civil society representatives and the information media. Implicit in such an approach is a qualitative change in the nature of interventions, such as a focus on preventive measures and the elimination of perverse subsidies.

6. DOES CLIMATE CHANGE MATTER IN PAKISTAN?

A. The Global Context

The basic premise of the Kyoto Convention was that the north is primarily to blame for global warming and climate change. At the outset, southern and enlightened EEC countries aligned themselves against the high emitters in the north, namely the US and Japan, both hostage to their industrial lobbies or, as in the case of Australia, comfortable with its vast spaces. The negotiations were hectic. Numerical targets for emission reductions (of mostly CO_2) promoted by the south and the EEC were: reduce emissions by 15 to 20 per cent of 1990 levels by the year 2010 in order to stabilise CO_2 concentrations. The conservative bloc offered to keep emissions at 1990 levels. A breakdown in the talks was averted by last minute concessions, namely a 5.2 per cent reduction. There was talk of emissions trading, namely, the north buying rights from the south to pollute the global commons. On the whole, it was a small but important victory for global awareness.

The majority of scientific evidence does point towards global warming, though there are plenty of dissenters. More well established is the fact that the north is the primary culprit, although obstructionists tend to hold China, Mexico, and Thailand—among others—as being equally culpable. However, a report by UNEP (1997, p. 23) has shown that the top-ranking emitters among developing countries have achieved and will continue to achieve greater CO_2 savings than industrialized countries. A telling commentary in the UNEP report states that:

much of the growth in emissions in developing countries results from the provision of basic human needs for their growing populations, while that in industrialized countries contributes to growth in a standard of living that is already far above that of the average person worldwide.

B. THE NATIONAL CONTEXT

1. Energy consumption

While the debate has polarized the north and south into opposing camps, ultimately the impacts are global and this—the bickering notwithstanding—offers hope for concerted action. This section offers a national perspective. It addresses two questions: first, how much does Pakistan contribute to global warming; and second, how is it likely to be affected by climate change? The answers to these questions will also establish the pattern of mitigation (to pre-empt climate change) and adaptation (to respond to climate change) responses.

On the one hand, Pakistan does not contribute to global warming for the simple reason that it is 'energy deficient'. On the other hand, it is also 'energy profligate' which has adverse environmental implications nationally. The respective indices are per capita energy consumption and energy intensity, both defined in terms of final energy consumption and measured in tons of oil equivalent (TOE) as shown in Figures 1 and 2.[33]

With initial and end values of 0.26 TOE and 0.32 TOE, per capita energy consumption is low compared to the EEC countries where, by contrast, consumption rose from an average 3.5 TOE to 4.2 TOE over the same period. The low level of consumption in Pakistan and its flat time profile has a three-fold and related explanation. It reflects: a) the overall state of under-development; b) the absence of energy infrastructure in the rural areas, where the bulk of the population resides; and c) reliance on traditional fuels, which both substitutes for and defers investment in such infrastructure. The last point is of note, that with regard to point c) the contribution of combustion of bio-mass (use of wood as fuel) to global warming [via emissions] is

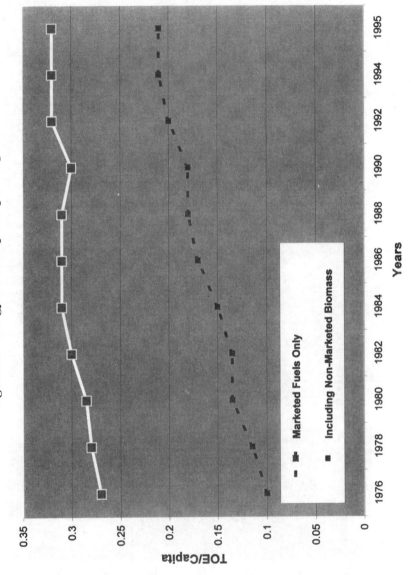

Figure 1: Energy Consumption per Capita

Figure 2: Final Energy Consumption
(Marketed Fuels Only)

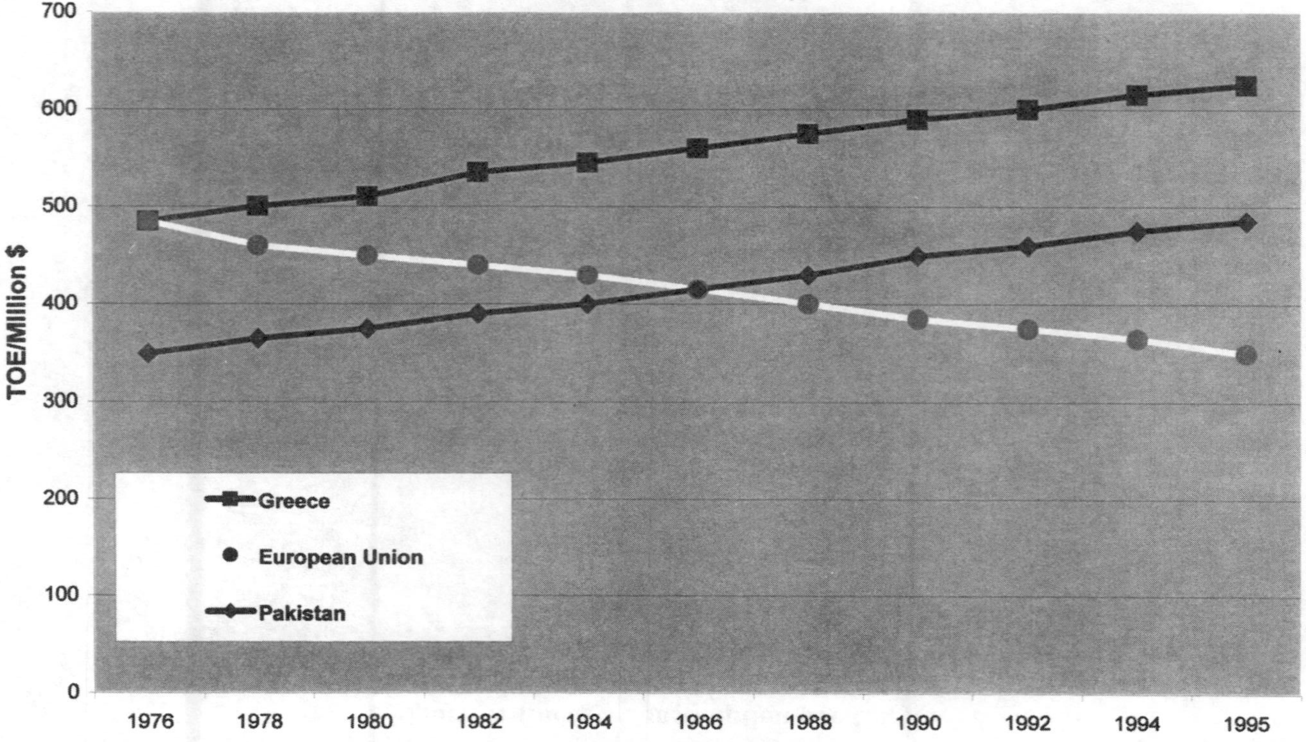
700
600
500
400
300
200
100
0
TOE/Million $
Greece
European Union
Pakistan
1976
1978
1980
1982
1984
1986
1988
1990
1992
1994
1995

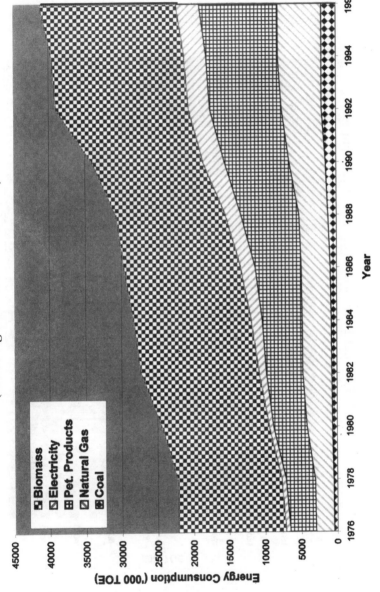

Figure 3: Final Energy Consumptio by Fuel Type
(including non-marketed biomass)

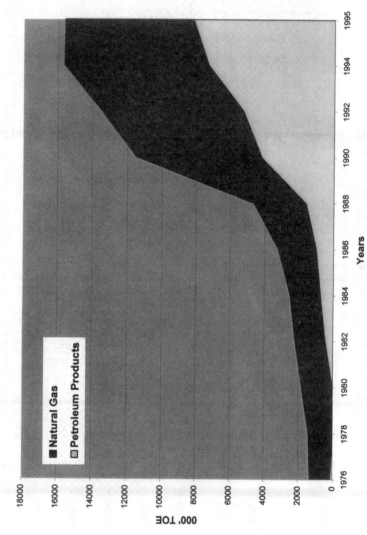

Figure 4: Thermal Power Generation by Fuel Source

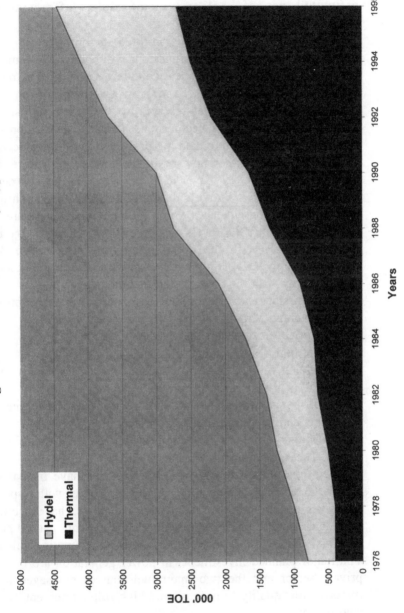

Figure 5: Power Generation by Type

estimated net of replacement of sinks (afforestation programmes).

There is a variant in the emission forecasts for the future—up to the year 2020. While such emissions will continue to remain low, both in absolute and in per capita terms, the growth trend is likely to be exponential. Such growth is premised on the substitution of depleting gas reserves by oil, increasing use of Thar coal as oil imports become unsustainable, expansion of rural energy infrastructure, and the proliferation of appliances.

Thus, Pakistan, either now or in the foreseeable future, is demonstrably not a key player in global warming. By contrast, its energy intensity levels have generated far-reaching environmental consequences within the country. As figure 2 shows, energy intensity levels converged to the EEC average in the year 1985, with the comparison becoming distinctly unfavourable in 1995. High energy intensity reflects inefficient use of energy with the contributing factors being:

- transmission and distribution losses in power distribution (an average 25 per cent over the past twenty years).
- fuel price subsidies on diesel.
- use of high lead content fuel.
- an ageing vehicle fleet (50 per cent over ten years old) and which is primarily diesel-powered (75 per cent).
- tariff concessions on imported second-hand machinery embedded in overall industrial protection.

Inefficiency impacts are compounded by fuel switching trends. These are shown in Figures 3 and 4.

Over time, the share of petroleum products have increased relative to bio-mass and natural gas. This is also true with respect to power generation: over time, thermal power has become dominant, with oil products becoming co-equal with natural gas as a fuel source. The future scenario is not encouraging either. The major planned investments in power generation are in the private sector and the two main fuel sources envisaged are imported low quality furnace oil and high-sulphur content Thar coal reserves.

2. Direct environmental impacts

The direct environmental impacts emanating from the energy sector activities and emissions are heterogeneous. They include land disturbance, displacement of people, habitat destruction, erosion and watershed disturbance, water pollution, loss of organic matter, and air pollution. Arguably, the most critical concern is urban air pollution and its resulting health impacts. As the following table shows, the combined emissions from different sectors are growing rapidly.

Table 4
Estimated air pollutants by sector over time

(thousand tonnes)

SECTOR	1977/78			1987/88			1997/98		
	CO_2	SO_2	NO_x	CO_2	SO_2	NO_x	CO_2	SO_2	NO_x
Industry	12,308	19	n/a	26,680	423	n/a	53,429	982	n/a
Transport	7,068	52	n/a	10,254	57	n/a	18,987	105	n/a
Power	3,640	4	3	11,216	95	10	53,062	996	76
Domestic	16,601	5	n/a	24,054	16	n/a	39,980	40	n/a
Agriculture	845	5	n/a	4,490	28	n/a	6,368	40	n/a
Commercial	1,726	11	n/a	2,587	13	n/a	4,261	25	n/a

Source: NCS Sector Paper on Energy.
Note: n/a: not applicable.

Furthermore, the truly dangerous pollutants to human health arise from non-stationary sources in urban areas. The National Conservation Strategy (n.d., 1991) cites some figures:

the average Pakistani vehicle emits 20 times as much hydrocarbons, 25 times as much carbon monoxide and 3.6 times as much nitrous oxides in grams per kilometre as the average vehicle in the US. Carbon monoxide levels in the range of 8–30 parts per million (ppm) and 6–40 ppm have been recorded for Lahore and Karachi, respectively. Ambient lead levels in Karachi have been measured at between 0.024 and 0.13 micrograms per cubic metre which far exceeds WHO/World Bank criteria.

The associated health effects are nervous system damage, respiratory problems, impaired eyesight, and brain damage, especially among children.

Thus, mitigation strategies aimed at curbing emissions, become a national rather than a global imperative. We will not elaborate on these as they can be found packaged in most climate change studies. Generically, they encompass fuel use efficiency and demand side management (DSM) interventions—either technology-based or economic.

3. The impacts of climate change[34]

It is tempting to subscribe to popular rhetoric that northern depredations, as manifested by its untrammelled emissions, will irrevocably harm Pakistan: that forests will shrink, water resources will be depleted, agriculture will fall victim to droughts and floods, people will be displaced, coastal areas will suffer salt water intrusion, and human health will suffer. None of this can be dismissed completely. But it is equally true that climate change impacts cannot be addressed in isolation from the underlying socio-economic conditions and changes. Pakistan, like many developing countries, is a society in transition from an agricultural to a modern industrial economy. The transition entails high population growth, rapid urbanization, infrastructure degradation, soil erosion, water and air pollution, and increased morbidity. Many of these processes create conditions very similar to those caused by climate change. For instance, sea level rise results in salt water intrusion but this can also be caused by diversion of freshwater outflows to meet the needs of agriculture, human consumption, and sanitation. Or climate change can erode watersheds and cause flooding but this can also be an effect of deforestation. When socio-economic factors and natural elements combine in this manner, existing vulnerabilities tend to be exacerbated. It also follows that adaptive responses need not necessarily be climate specific, and that climate change is likely to re-inforce them. Alternatively, foreseen climate change impacts can add force to lobbies against bad policies, as in the case of large dams.

Our aim then is to show—quantitatively where possible—that Pakistan's key resources, its economy, and society are at risk; that such socio-economic pressures and imbalances establish vulnerability to climate change; and that potential climate change impacts are likely to be incremental rather than substantive in character. By the same token, adaptations are not climate change specific but encapsulate its impacts. We focus on the three key sectors of water, agriculture, and forestry.

a. Water Resources:

In section 4, the divergence between present and projected demand for water and the supply likely to be available was described. Given the excess demand, additional surface storage has become central to current policy dialogue and planning, although it is surrounded by controversy as pointed out in section 5. The political concern is with equitable water sharing. The environmental and social concerns relate to displacement of communities, bio-diversity and species loss, and the disturbance of the coastal water balance.

While supply is fairly easy to forecast, demand scenarios are relatively more difficult to generate. However, Tables 5 and 6 make crude attempts to do this without and with climate change.

Table 5
Demand-supply balances without climate change

(MAF)

Year	2000	2010	2020	2050
Projected irrigation water demand (with Kalabagh)	104.87	110.04	110.04	110.04
Households & industry	5.90	8.70	12.00	20.00
Total projected demand	110.77	118.74	122.04	130.04
Projected supply	104.87	110.04	110.04	110.04
Projected deficit	5.90	8.70	12.00	20.00

Table 6
Demand-supply balances with climate change

(MAF)

Year	2000	2010	2020	2050
Projected irrigation water demand (with Kalabagh)	104.87	110.04	110.04	110.04
Households & industry	5.90	9.20	12.50	20.50
Total projected demand	110.77	119.24	122.54	130.54
Projected supply	104.87	110.04	108.85	106.98
Projected deficit	5.90	9.20	13.69	23.56

Source: SDPI in-house calculations and GOP/PSF (1997).

In the supply projections, we have factored in an additional 16 MAF over the projection horizon, due to the Kalabagh dam and additional ground water exploitation. Household and industry consumption reflects irrigation water re-use and vice versa. This is a fairly heroic assumption as it abstracts from deterioration in ground water quality and outflows to the sea from Karachi. The change in demand for irrigation water is synonymous with discreet additions to supply because, in the context of chronic under-irrigation, our concern is with demand that is actualized. Releases represent the continuous aspect of supply; the decline in these releases post climate change, and relative to supply, reflects the impact of climate change.

The relative orders of magnitude are illustrative. The deficit increases to 20 MAF, thanks to the growing needs of agriculture, households, industry, and energy. Supply, which is naturally constrained, is unable to meet this demand. The effect of climate change on this deficit is incremental—namely, an additional 4.37 MAF. The assumptions and abstractions notwithstanding, the message is clear. Climate change impacts are felt on the supply side and have a large stock-small flow character. Socio-economic pressures, on the other hand, are represented by a possible doubling of population, crop production, industry size, and energy production by the year 2050. As such, they are the key drivers with respect to the water resource situation. Furthermore, as pointed out earlier, it is not easy to differentiate the impacts of climate change, deforestation, and storage construction on the increased incidence of floods and salt water intrusion in coastal areas.

Regarding adaptations, climate change impacts re-inforce the case against large dams. Thus, the prospect of increased sea level rise (projected at 20 cms in 2020 and 30 cms in 2050) and reduced outflows in the increased warming and reduced precipitation scenario constitute an additional argument against constructing additional storage.

b. Agriculture

Constraints to growth in agricultural production fall into two categories: non-structural and structural. Non-structural constraints have traditionally been targeted by policies. The main problems are poor agronomic and post-harvest management practices, capital scarcity for small farmers, poor linkages between research and extension, and input-output price distortions. In recent years, structural constraints have become more evident which, essentially, inhibit production increases at the intensive and extensive margins. These include the following:

i. Land use limits: According to the NCS (IUCN/GOP, nd.), between 1947–52 and 1983–6, total cropped area, which includes area sown more than once, increased by 7.7 million hectares. Of this, 4.4 million hectares were due to the expansion of irrigated cropping areas and the rest due to an increase in double cropping. For the first twenty years, expansion was the main source of increase in cropped area (79 per cent). Since 1973–7, this ratio dropped to 33 per cent, with intensification accounting for the bulk of the increase.

ii. Unavailability of Water: Although limits to expansion at the extensive margin have been reached, production still remains well below its potential because of under-cropping. On the basis of just Class I and II irrigated soils, 12.2 million hectares of land are available for double cropping. This is almost three times the irrigated areas that actually grow two crops per year. However, this potential is unutilized because of a lack of water, a problem that we referred to earlier in section 5.

While slack in policies could be afforded previously because additional land and water were available, this is a fast diminishing luxury. In the supply projections below, we have made fairly heroic assumptions regarding policy implementation, which would result in both yield enhancements as well as product diversification.

Table 7
Projected demand-supply balances of major agricultural commodities

(Million tonnes)

	YEARS								
Commodities	1995			2020			2050		
	S	D	G	S	D	G	S	D	G
Wheat	17.0	17.9	-0.9	27.5	32.4	-4.9	35.7	43.0	-7.3
Rice	3.5	2.5	1.0	6.2	5.5	-0.70	7.9	10.0	-2.1
Sugarcane	47.2	41.6	5.60	50.0	75.3	-25.3	60.0	100.0	-40.0
Cotton (million bales)	8.7	10.6	-1.9	18.0	19.4	-1.4	25.00	25.9	-0.9
Fruits & vegetables	9.8	9.6	0.2	26.0	26.0	0.0	35.0	34.5	0.5
Meat	2.1	2.1	0.0	5.7	5.7	0.0	7.6	7.6	0.0
Milk	15.3	15.3	0.0	41.5	41.5	0.0	55.0	55.0	0.0

Source: SDPI in-house calculations.
Note: S = Supply, D = Demand, G = Gap.

Even dynamic policies may not be able to offset the deficits generated by additional demand. In the scenario presented above, the situation becomes critical by the year 2020, a milestone year— in the negative sense—as current surpluses of sugarcane and rice are converted into deficits. The wheat deficit increases seven-fold. Clearly, food security emerges as a key concern. Cotton holds its own, in as much as it is linked with agro-processing. Growth in the livestock sector is premised on higher yields per animal, as a result of breed and nutrition improvements.

Climate change impacts need to be viewed in the context of such deficits. In the modelled worst case scenario of increased warming and falling precipitation, growing season length reduces, especially in the arid areas where crops are already on the margin of stress. Increased heat and reduced soil moisture also causes accelerated growth early in the season and effects changes in the partitioning and quality of bio-mass. In combination, these factors are yield-reducing. This is offset by higher CO_2 levels which have yield-enhancing effects, especially on C3 and C4 crops like wheat, rice, and maize. The net impacts, therefore, are indeterminate. Crops like rice and sugarcane would be hard hit by water scarcity. Spatial shifts in production are also predicted, especially in the crop zones dominated by wheat, rice, cotton, and maize.

The most critical policy measures are those geared to enhancing yields but these also address climate change impacts, especially in the case of sugarcane and rice. Climate-exclusive adaptations involve research on heat-resistant cultivars. At the social level, alternative employment opportunities would need to be created for labour displaced by zonal shifts; women engaged in cotton picking and rice transplanting are an important target group.

c. Forestry

While climate change impacts were shown to be incremental with respect to water resources and agriculture, in the forestry sector such impacts are completely reversed when socio-economic factors are taken into account.

Nine forest types were identified by GOP/PFI (1997). The first order (bio-physical) impacts of increased atmospheric concentration, temperature, and precipitation were evaluated with the help of BIOME 3 model simulations. Of the nine biomes (forest types), three (alpine tundra, grassland/arid woodlands, and deserts, showed reduction in their area; five biomes (cold conifer/mixed woodland, cold conifer/mixed forests, temperate conifer/mixed forests, and steppe/arid shrub lands) increased in area. There was no change in the area of xerophrytic wood/scrubs in the simulations. Enhanced CO_2 concentration in the atmosphere appears to have a pronounced effect on a biome area's increase, even in the case of high temperature and low precipitation scenarios.

These results are completely at variance with the existing reality. In particular, it is a delusion to expect deserts to shrink or conifer dominated areas to increase. The reality is that Pakistan's forests are under severe pressure. As little as 4.5 per cent of its total area is under forest cover, whereas both economic and environmental considerations dictate a 25 to 30 per cent range. The annual rate of deforestation is about 8000 hectares representing, approximately, a 0.2 per cent decline in forest cover.

The two major reasons for forest depletion are logging for timber and cutting for fuel wood. Privately owned farmlands supply 50 per cent of the demand for timber, imports 36 per cent, and state forests only 14 per cent. On the basis of per capita income increases, the projected demand for timber in the year 2010 is 4.61 million cubic metres. State forests are expected to supply 1.2 million cubic metres and farm lands 2.1 million cubic metres, leaving a deficit of 1.31 million cubic metres. Since foreign exchange constraints are likely to become even more binding, this will put additional pressure on depleting forest stocks. Also, as a result of population increase, fuel wood demand is expected to rise by 55 per cent by the year 2020 and four-fold by 2050. This will intensify the depletion which is already excessive.

Deforestation also has adverse socio-economic impacts, which are likely to be exacerbated by climate change. Some of the critical problems are as follows:

i. Displacement of Communities: Land erosion and soil degradation caused by deforestation has displaced many rural communities in the Northern Areas, forcing them to migrate to crowded 'road towns' along the Karakoram Highway.

ii. Disruption of Communications, Energy Loss: Land slides in the Northern Areas, Azad Kashmir, and the Murree Hill tracts frequently disrupt communications. In general, land erosion results in siltation of reservoirs and reduces hydropower generation capacity. More frequent and torrential rains are a possible outcome of climate change. The resultant sheet erosion could cause further gullying and landslides in exposed locations, with both forms of degradation affecting standing forests and regeneration.

iii. Loss of Agricultural Land: The loss of forest cover in the riverain areas has created flooding problems and, through soil erosion, reduced agricultural potential. Growing demand for fuel-wood and continuing land use changes, thanks to population increase, will make the riverain areas even more vulnerable to the increased frequency of flooding.

iv. Damage to Coastal Infrastructure and Marine Habitat: As indicated in section 5, the clearing of mangroves in the coastal areas has resulted in sea encroachment and in loss of habitat for many marine species that are a source of livelihood for coastal communities. If unchecked, the loss of this natural barrier could expose coastal infrastructure to the increased frequency of storm flooding. Sea level rise could further damage marine habitats.

CONCLUSION: THE NEED FOR NEW APPROACHES

Our basic contention is that when the issues are so multi-faceted, involve so many actors, and have such potentially far-reaching consequences, there is a strong need for policy research and informed dialogue among all the actors. In its absence, misconceptions will persist and policy errors will continue to erode an already fast diminishing resource base.

Section 2 focuses on industrial emissions in which we take up the issue of self-monitoring as opposed to government enforcement. The premise is that environmental standards are not necessarily a non-tariff trade barrier being imposed by northern governments on southern countries. In fact, the impetus for such standards may primarily be coming from northern consumers demanding cleaner products and processes from companies they buy from or own stock in. We argue that the standards set by agencies like the ISO which have responded to such an impetus may be an opportunity. Governments could facilitate the establishment of environmental management systems and self-auditing by companies. This is an easier method of enforcement and would position Pakistan to retain, if not win, export markets. More important, it would contribute to ensuring a better quality of life for the most vulnerable.

In section 3, we take up the issue of the potentially high environmental cost of attaining higher agricultural productivity. Pakistan's trade policy is very much geared to the promotion of 'Green Revolution' input-intensive agriculture, even though this may have serious environmentally detrimental effects. Using back of the envelope calculations, we quantify the potential low end benefits from the use of pesticides and fertilizers. Even these are not negligible by any means (about Rs 100 billion). However, the list of the social costs to humans and the environment from the use of these chemicals and synthetic minerals seems endless. Given that the costs in Pakistan have not been quantified as yet, we recommend that as the first order of business. However, without awaiting results from these cost quantification exercises, we also recommend that the government use its extension service to start exploring and promoting strategies such as integrated pest management (IPM) and integrated plant nutrient systems (IPNS) to radically cut down use of these agricultural inputs. These alternatives are being demonstrated as not only environmentally friendly but also more productive.

In view of the above, Pakistan needs to reconsider its trade policy with regard to agricultural inputs. Succumbing to pressure from the Bretton Woods institutions, it fully discontinued subsidies to domestically produced fertilizers in 1994. It is still subsidizing fertilizer imports which are duty free. There is similarly an unusual recent history of a very liberal trade regime with regard to pesticides. In 1992, Pakistan allowed the import of generic pesticides to make them available at lower prices.

While allegations of adulteration and long-term damage via the development of pest resistance resulted in the discontinuation of this policy in March 1995, a more dangerous form of liberalization has been adopted. In June 1995, as part of its new Trade Policy, Pakistan has repealed the *1971 Agricultural Pesticide Ordinance*, and is now allowing the import of pesticides that are not registered and in use in the exporting country. Until results of cost quantification exercises become available, Pakistan should, at a minimum, re-introduce the repealed clause of the 1971 Pesticide Ordinance. Further, it should stop subsidizing fertilizer imports.

In section 4, we take an alternative and less sensational view of the problem of waterlogging and salinity. Waterlogging and salinity are viewed as important environmental problems in the agricultural sector. While this is true, there are certain other overlooked dimensions which reduce the intensity of the problem. Several points are noteworthy from our analysis. First, waterlogging is likely to stabilize and may even reduce with present rates of ground water exploitation. Second, there are multiple criteria which define waterlogging; in other words, there is no single critical level of waterlogging. Third, the perception is that salinity is widespread; in fact, it tends to occur in patches. Also, it needs to be linked with soil conditions and management practices. Fourth, the present balance between ground water recharge and use suggests that water table rise may not be the primary source of salinity in the future. Fifth, the critical problem is sodicity, as it forms an impermeable hard pan, and is both difficult and expensive to treat. Sixth, secondary salinization, caused by pumping ground water, will continue to be a problem in future, unless accompanied by effective drainage measures (surface and sub-surface tiled drainage). Finally, in general, saline water zones tend not to be cultivated but should be.

In section 5, we discuss the dangers to the bio-diversity of the inland water ecosystem resulting from the current and (mis)planned water management in Pakistan. The network of dams, barrages, canals, and waterways has fragmented the Indus basin ecosystem and poses a threat to the stability of the Indus delta ecosystem. The present silt discharge is about a fourth of the original level before the construction of large dams. This silt reduction, plus the salt water intrusion due to the reduced fresh water flow, has changed the morphology of the delta considerably. The active growth area of the delta is about one-tenth of what it used to be. The effects of the reduced water and the enhanced pollution on the mangroves and the species that thrived in them has been devastating. Currently the mangroves are getting seven million acre feet (MAF) water less than that required to maintain the mangroves in reasonably healthy condition. Implementation of the Indus Water Accord, 1991, would reduce outflows to the sea by another 10 MAF.

In section 6, the north-south controversy on climate change is discussed from Pakistan's vantage point and we focus on the national dimensions of the issue. As the last section, it is the most comprehensive and forward-looking and takes account of the impact of socio-economic factors on the environment and also indicates the likely future scenarios emerging for the water, agriculture, and forestry sectors.

On the one hand, Pakistan is not expected to be a player in global warming, although its energy-based emissions are a major source of pollution and environmental degradation within the country. On the other hand, Pakistan is vulnerable to climate change. The main contention in this section is that climate change impacts, which result from excess energy consumption, cannot be addressed in isolation from underlying socio-economic conditions and the expected changes in these conditions in Pakistan since they both generate similar impacts. In fact, the two re-inforce each other to enhance vulnerabilities.

The potential negative environmental impacts have been identified in the sectors of water, agriculture, and forestry. Such impacts are likely to be incremental and a function of the imbalances created by socio-economic pressures and structural constraints, as well as by climate change. It follows that planned adaptation strategies should be sourced in and re-inforce local efforts to address such imbalances. Another aspect of adaptations is that they tend to occur spontaneously and responsively, as in the case of the shift northwards of the lower Punjab cotton belt in the 1980s. Finally, many adaptions tend to respond to climate variability rather than to climate change *per se*, although the responses are applicable to the latter case.

Having overviewed the main findings of the various sections in the chapter, we want to address ourselves to the policy makers. All policy makers residing in Islamabad must put themselves through the following environmental lesson. On a clear day, they should drive to Pir Sohawa, which is about a ten kilometre scenic drive up and through the Margalla Hills. The road is now a good one since it was repaired when it was decided that Hilary Clinton would be driven there—a typical *ad hoc* 'development by dignitary visit' renovation, but that is another story. On arriving in Pir Sohawa, the policy makers should take a furlong walk to the 'Mount Happiness' peak. This will do much to whet the appetite for the delicious barbecue sold in the restaurant below, by the parking area.

Once on Mount Happiness, the policy maker should look south to Islamabad. Even ten years ago, they would have seen a spectacular vista of a growing city, once called 'Islamabad the Beautiful' and now 'The Capital City'. Now, more likely than not, the policy maker will get a hazy view of the city through the smog of the auto and industrial emissions. But the happiness should not dissipate. Indeed there is hope. For a vision of a possible future, the policy maker should turn a hundred and eighty degrees and face north. Facing north, they will be confronted with a crystal clear atmosphere through which they can behold the unspoiled and breathtaking beauty of the valley beyond the range they are on, and of ranges beyond into the far distance. Islamabad could once be viewed thus and could again represent a spectacular view from a far hill. For now, the view from Mount Happiness is as dull as the environmental consciousness of our policy makers.[35]

I mention Islamabad because it is close to home for most federal policy makers. To absorb real environmental lessons, one has to go beyond to the rest of the country where there are more than simply vehicular and some industrial emissions trapped by hills. Fifteen minutes of deep breathing in Lahore, Karachi, Peshawar, Quetta, and many other cities would be enough to cause most lungs to gasp, if they are not seized by an asthma attack. Of course, the lead poisoning and other ailments from which the children have started to suffer are less apparent.

Pakistani cities remind one of the irrational side of humanity. What we observe is individual welfare maximization resulting in collective suicide. All want the convenience of the automobile, but the incremental automobiles over the last fifty years have resulted in a urban environmental crisis in most of our cities. One can't point a finger at those using public transportation, but one can certainly blame governments that do not enforce existing laws requiring a reasonable level of emissions from private and public vehicles.

Most have acknowledged that there has been government failure in that existing laws have not been implemented. While one must always call for reform of government and hope for appropriate enforcement, this will take time. Inspectors will not do their job until the whole culture of civil and political administration has changed to one where the incentives are appropriate, merit is rewarded, and accountability is demanded. Realistically, political and public sector reform will take a long time, and it may be best to turn our attention elsewhere for the moment, such as instituting incentives for the right social decisions and for self-monitoring (*see* section 2).

Vehicular emissions is just one example of faulty private incentives and government paralysis or of neglect that has resulted in hugh environmental crises on many fronts over the last fifty years. Industrialists have not been required to pay for the social costs from industrial air and liquid emissions that have poisoned the air, water, and land. Timber merchants have engaged in cutting forests at will and have not had to pay for the social costs of soil erosion, flooding, and dam siltation. Pastoralists have not had to pay for the social costs of desertification. Large farmers have not had to pay for the social cost of waterlogging and salinity. Industrialists have not had to pay for the destruction of the mangroves and the consequent loss of species due to the unhindered flow of industrial poisons into the harbour, or for poisoning the air, water, and land in general.

Fortunately, the 1997 Pakistan Environment Bill has been enacted, even if fifty years after Pakistan came into existence. While this is not a perfect piece of legislation, it has done much to redress many of the shortcomings of the 1981 Pakistan Environment Bill. However, to be realistic, it will take a while for the enforcement machinery to be in place and perhaps much longer for enforcement to be effective, since that is part of a much broader institutional reform. In the meantime, the focus needs to be on giving the right signals via the pricing mechanism so that individuals and firms have to pay the price for the environmental destruction they cause.

We identify here several prescriptions for policy which, we think, apply across the board as do others that we have identified in the chapter. First, it often is more cost-effective to focus on 'policies' rather than 'projects' since the impact is much wider. Thus the pollution charge policy will affect all industry. Second, a focus on win-win policies and strategies is cost-effective. Thus, on a broader level, it is important to recognize that a cleaner environment means a healthier and more productive work force and a better quality of life for the poor. More narrowly, inducing energy efficiency and recycling would improve the environment and reduce the costs of production. Finally, a focus on the right incentives is cost-effective. Thus removing a subsidy on diesel would ameliorate urban air pollution, and tax incentives for clean public transportation could resolve the equity issue. Similarly, removing the subsidy for water would help in curbing excess water use and its negative environmental and social impact. Again, a more direct approach of assisting poor users would be preferable to a blanket subsidy benefiting the more powerful. Incentives are called for, for communities to preserve and sustainably harvest forest resources, and for forest managers to preserve forests rather than collude with those cutting them illegally.

REFERENCES

Abramovitz, J. M. (1996), *Imperiled Waters, Impoverished Future: The Decline of Freshwater Ecosystems.*

Ali, M., and Jabbar, A. (1992), *Effect of Pesticide and Fertilizer on Shallow Ground Water Quality*, Pakistan Council of Research in Water Resources, Islamabad.

Asian Development Bank. (1994), *Climate Change in Asia: Pakistan Country Report*, Asian Development Bank, Manila.

Avery, T. D. (1994), 'Do pesticides accumulate in the environment, posing a growing risk of cancer and other diseases?', *C. Q. Register,* Vol. 4, No. 4.

Birdsall, N., and Wheeler, D. (1992), 'Trade policy and industrial pollution in Latin America: where are the pollution havens?', ed. Patrick Low, International Trade and the Environment, World Bank Discussion Papers, No. 159.

Braga, C. A. (1992), 'Tropical forests and trade policy: the cases of Indonesia and Brazil', ed. Patrick Low, International Trade and the Environment, World Bank Discussion Papers, No. 159.

Brandon, C. (1995), 'Backgound paper for Pakistan 2010: valuing environmental costs in Pakistan—The economy-wide impact of environmental degradation', World Bank, Islamabad.

Carson, R. (1962), *Silent Spring*, Houghton Mifflin, Boston.

Casio, J., Woodside, G., and Mitchell, P. (1996), *ISO 14000 Guide: The New International Environmental Management Standards*, McGraw Hill, New York.

Colburn, T. (1994), 'Do pesticides accumulate in the environment, posing a growing risk of cancer and other diseases?', *C. Q. Register*, Vol. 4, No. 4.

Conway, G. R., and Pretty, J. N. (1991), *Unwelcome Harvest: Agriculture and Pollution,* Earthscan, London.

Cropper, M. L., and Oates, W. E. (1992), 'Environmental Economics: A Survey', *Journal of Economic Literature*, Vol. 30, No. 2.

Dean, J. M. (1992), 'Trade and the environment: a survey of the literature,' in ed. Patrick Low, *International Trade and the Environment*, World Bank Discussion Papers, No. 159, Washington, D. C.

Ericksen N.J., Chowdhury, A. R., Warrick, R. A. (1993), *Socioeconomic Implications of Climate Change for Bangladesh*, BUP/CEARS/CRU.

ESCAP. (1993), in *Regional FNDINAP Seminar on Fertilizers and the Environment,* Chiang Mai, Thailand, September 1992.

French, H. R. (1993), 'Costly trade-offs: reconciling trade and the environment', *World Watch Paper 113.*

GATT. (1992), 'Trade and the environment', in *GATT and International Trade 1990–91*, Vol. 1, Geneva.

————. (1994), 'Trade and the Environment', in *News and Views from GATT*, Symposium on Trade Environment and Sustainable Development, TE 008.

Gianessi, L. (1993), 'Why chemical free farming won't work', *Consumer Research*, Vol. 76, No. 12.

Government of Pakistan. (1979), Report of the national commission on agriculture, Ministry of Agriculture.

————. (1994), *Annual Fertilizer Review 1993–94*, Planning and Development Division, National Fertilizer Development Center, Islamabad.

————. (1995), *Agricultural Statistics of Pakistan 1993–94*, Ministry of Food Agriculture and Livestock, Economic Wing, Islamabad.

————. (1997), Bio-diversity action plan: Pakistan, (Draft), Ministry of Environment-IUCN-WWF.

————. *Economic Survey*, Finance Division, Economic Advisor's Wing, Islamabad, (several years).

Government of Pakistan/Pakistan Agriculture Research Council. (1997), draft report on climate change impacts and adaptation assessments in Pakistan: sectoral study on agriculture, Islamabad.

Government of Pakistan/Pakistan Forest Institute. (1997), draft report on climate change, impact assessment, and adaptation strategies for forestry sector in Pakistan, Islamabad.

Government of Pakistan/Pakistan Meteorological Department. (1997), draft report on climate change, impact assessment, and adaptation strategy in Pakistan: Climatology Group, Islamabad.

Government of Pakistan/Pakistan Science Foundation. (1997), draft report on climate change, impact assessment, and adaptation strategies: water sector, Islamabad.

Hadi, S. E. (1995), draft background paper for the Pakistan 2010 : project institutions, private sector participation, and infrastructure development in Pakistan, World Bank, Islamabad.

Harris, J. C., and Dudani, A. T. (1992), *Agriculture and People: Eco-health Hazards of Chemical Based Agriculture and Proposed Techniques for Sustainable Farming*, South-South Solidarity, New Delhi.

Harte, J., Holdren, C., Schneider, R., and Shirley, C. (1991), *Toxics A to Z: A Guide to Everyday Pollution Hazards*, University of California Press, Berkeley.

International Institute of Environment and Development (IIED). (1992), *Environmental Synopsis of Pakistan*, prepared for the Overseas Development Administration, UK.

International Organization of Standards. (1996), *Environment Management Systems-Specifications with Guidance for Use*, Geneva.

International Union for the Conservation of Nature-Pakistan (IUCN-P). (nd.), Environment and Urban Affairs Division, Government of Pakistan, The National Conservation Strategy, Karachi.

International Union for the Conservation of Nature. (1991), 'Possible effects of the Indus water accord on the Indus delta ecosystem', Korangi Ecosystem Project.

————. (1992), sector paper on energy, Ashfaq Mahmood, National Conservation Strategy.

————. (1998), 'Bio-diversity of Inland Waters', IUCN Policy Recommendations for COP 4.

————. (1998), workshop report: 'Preparing for CBD COP4', Ministry of Environment-IUCN, Bio-diversity Unit.

Jabbar, A., and Mallick, S. (1994), 'Pesticides and environment situation in Pakistan', SDPI Working Paper Series No. 18, Islamabad.

Jensen, J. K. (1987), 'Sustainable agricultural crop rotation through integrated pest management', *Development Environment and Agriculture*, Vol. 5, No. 1.

Khan, S. R. (1997), 'Trade liberalization and the environment: a view from the South,' in *Green Economics*, Sustainable Development Policy Institute, Islamabad/Heinrich Boll Foundation, Lahore.

Qureshi, S. A. (1995), draft background paper for Pakistan 2010: 'Governance issues', World Bank, Islamabad.

Qutab, S. A. (1994), 'The divergence between private and environmental costs and benefits: a case study of chemical and organic fertilizer in Pakistan', Tenth Annual General meeting of the Pakistan Society of Development Economists, Islamabad.

Saleem, M. T., David, J. G., Nabhan, H., and Hamid, A. (1989), 'Soil fertility and fertilizer use in Pakistan with special reference to potash', in *Potassium and Fertilizer Use Efficiency*, National Fertilizer Development Centre, Islamabad.

Sandhu, G. R. (1993), 'Sustainable Agriculture', a Pakistan national conservative strategy sector paper, IUCN and Environment and Urban Affairs Division, Karachi.

SDPI. (1995), *Nature, Power and People*, Citizens' Report on Sustainable Development, Sustainable Development Policy Institute, Islamabad.

SDPI. (1997), *Green Economics*, Sustainable Development Policy Institute, Islamabad.

UNCTAD. (1996), *ISO 14001: International Environmental Management System Standards*, United Nations, Geneva.

UNEP. (1996), *Handbook on Methods for Climate Change Impact Assessment and Adaptation Strategies*, United Nations Environment Programme.

UNEP. (1997), *Our Planet*, The UNEP Magazine for Environmentally Sustainable Development.

Von, Z. W. M. (1996), *Understanding the Environmental Standards*, Government Institutes, Inc., Rockville, Maryland.

Weir, D., and Schapiro, M. (1981), *Circle of Poison*, Institute of Food and Development Policy, San Francisco.

World Bank. (1994), *Pakistan Social Action Programme Project: Staff Appraisal Report*, Washington, D. C.

———. (1995), Pakistan 2010, preliminary draft report: 'Policy options for sustained growth into the next century—An overview and summary', Islamabad.

World Wild Life Fund. (1994), 'Agriculture in the Uruguay Round: Implications for Sustainable Development in Developing Countries'.

NOTES

1. The National Conservation Strategy itself is a good reference source. The International Institute of Environment and Development was commissioned to write a report by the IUCN on the State of the Environment (1994) which is currently (1999) being updated.

2. ISO stands for the UN International Organization of Standards. Literally, *iso* is a Greek word which means balance.

3. This paragraph is based on information drawn from Casia, Woodside, and Mitchell (1996), UNCTAD (1996), and von Zharen (1996) and from a reading of the primary documents, ISO 14000 (1996).

4. In this regard, the ISO 14001 is much less stringent than the British BS 7750 or the European EMAS standards which require action to protect the environment.

5. The Sustainable Development Policy Institute (SDPI) was the secretariat of the ESC and, in this capacity, provided technical assistance for the development of all these proposals.

6. Casio et al. (1996, p. ix).

7. UNCTAD (1996, p. 104) suggested at the time of writing their monograph on ISO 14001 that widespread adoption of the standard is uncertain. However, given that ISO 9000 became widely accepted and given that WTO has endorsed it, the probability of widespread adoption may be high. UNCTAD's recommendation was that the best course would be to explore the issue with buyers and to encourage the adoption of environment management systems (EMS) which would position firms to adopt specific standards if and when needed. There are already reports of companies losing business because of failure to conform to ISO 14001. ISO certification is being endorsed by trading blocks such as the EU and APEC. There are also reports that the US and Japanese governments may require certification as a condition for procurement. This information is reported in the March 1998 newsletter (*BRIDGES*, Vol. 2, No. 2, p. 11) of the International Centre for Trade and Sustainable Development (ICTSD).

8. UNCTAD (1996, p. 79) points out that generating a multiplier effect via supplier and contractor chains has always been the intention of the ISO series.

9. This section is based on Khan (1997).
10. GATT (1992, p. 20); (1994, p. 10).
11. Pesticides include insecticides, fungicides, herbicides/weedicides, acaricides, rodenticides, nematicides, and fumigants.
12. *See Economic Survey, 1991–92,* section on Economic Reforms.
13. There are some selective exemptions, e.g., the rate of duty on weedicides was still 10 per cent at the time this chapter was revised.
14. Domestic production here refers for the most part to domestic formulation by multinational corporations based on the import of the active ingredient and the other inputs. Information on tariff rates, imports, production, and total availability is based on *Agricultural Statistics of Pakistan 1993–94* (1995, p. 160). Since 1991, a regulatory duty of 30 per cent has been imposed on the import of insecticides in retail packaging.
15. We were told by a Ministry of Food and Agriculture official that the fall in the total availability from 1991–2 to 1992–3 represented the adjustment to excess imports due to the introduction of the generic scheme. Imports subsequently picked up again as is evident from the jump between 1992–3 and 1993–4.
16. Not all were persuaded by *Silent Spring* and the literature it spawned. Avery (1994, p. 89) argues that such argumentation stems from 'an almost mystical belief that man-made chemicals are more dangerous than natural chemicals. The latter, such as caffeic acid, limonene, and hydrazines are in various foods and ingested in much larger quantities than pesticide residue. Also, in rats 'natural' chemicals test out to be as dangerous as the synthetic variety. By implication, he argues, the human body is capable of handling the 'small carcinogenic insults' resulting from pest residues.
17. This is more likely to be the case for aereal spraying. Since 1981–2, the maximum aereal spraying has been 1.6 per cent of total cropped area in 1992–3. Ground plant protection in 1991–2, the latest year for which data were available, was about 20 per cent of total cropped area. *Agricultural Statistics of Pakistan 1993–94* (1995, pp. 154–8).
18. *See* Harris and Dudani (1992, p. 10, p. 14).
19. Most dramatic is an account of 194 cases of endrin poisoning in Talagang, Attock (p. 15). Seventy per cent of the cases were among minors between one and nine years and in all, nineteen people died. Harris and Dudani (1992, pp. 9–11) document pesticide poisoning cases in India and report 3,029 known deaths which occurred in 1990–91. Sadhu (1993, p. 22) cites a WHO study claiming that about half a million people in the world are poisoned each year and about 5,000 of these people die.
20. Harte et al. (1991, pp. 132–7) review alternatives to the use of chemical pesticides.
21. Jensen (1987, p. 17).
22. Data on imports, production, and subsidies are based on *Economic Survey 1994–95* (1995, pp. 74, 133, 167–8) and *Annual Fertilizer Review 1993–94* (1994, p. 48).

23. *Pakistan Economic Survey 1994–95*, Statistical section, p. 133.

24. The manufacture of urea in the country has suffered a severe loss since gas supply to the industry was diverted to producing electricity starting in January 1995 (Ikram Hoti, 'Fertilizer Industry Facing Crisis,' *The News*, 3 September 1995, p. 12.).

25. Saleem et al. (1989, p. 23) claim that the four major crops and maize account for 90 per cent of fertilizer use.

26. Khan (1997, p. 262).

27. Conway and Pretty (1991, pp. 232–57) cite evidence indicating that the link between nitrate up-take and the incidence of various kinds of cancers is not unambiguous.

28. For details on the human and environmental effects of fertilizer use, *see* Conway and Pretty (1991, pp. 157–271).

29. *Agricultural Statistics of Pakistan 1993–94* (1995, p. 142).

30. Also *see* Conway and Pretty (1991, pp. 581–612) for improved fertilizer application and alternatives.

31. Even sweet ground water has substantially more parts per million (ppm) of salts than surface water, and if continuous accumulation-evaporation takes place, deposition can occur.

32. Containing or blocking a river does not reduce the threat of floods, it merely changes their venue further downstream. As flood plains are destroyed by upstream storage construction, or by constricting the natural flow patterns of rivers, water absorptive capacity is reduced and the rate of flow of water dramatically increases. It is not surprising that the incidence of floods in Pakistan has increased in the past two decades, the Tarbela and Mangla Dams notwithstanding.

33. Energy consumption per capita is measured in tons of oil equivalent (TOE). This measure is usually referred to in the global climate change debates by proponents of the south to demonstrate how small a role it plays in global warming relative to the north. Energy intensity, defined as energy consumption per unit of GNP, is an indicator of energy efficiency. By this measure, the south is relatively worse off. However, the consequent environmental implications are more a national than a global concern.

34. This section draws on the four sectoral reports prepared for the UNEP Climate Change Study, which are listed in the bibliography but not referenced in the text. These are GOP/PARC (1997), GOP/PFI (1997), GOP/PMD (1997), and GOP/PSF (1997).

35. In all fairness, one needs to point out that, along with the construction of the capital, came the planting of thousands of trees for which the Capital Development Authority, Islamabad, deserves much credit. However, trees as a 'sink', are unable to keep pace with emissions, even in Islamabad.

The Economics Profession in Pakistan: A Historical Analysis[*]

*Nadeem ul Haque** and Mahmood Hasan Khan****

1. INTRODUCTION

Despite numerous domestic and foreign (multinational and bilateral) attempts to foster growth and development in many low-income countries, so that people in these countries could catch up with their richer brethren in high-income (industrialized) countries, growth has not been sustained at high rates in most such countries. The search for ways to make these countries achieve balanced and sustainable growth has preoccupied all serious social science and development policy making. To a large extent, many of the answers that are being derived relate to the failure of these countries to develop key 'institutions'. Most practitioners and thinkers are now in agreement on this issue, but remain perplexed at what is required to develop institutions. The attempts of the public sector (government) to develop institutions within its fold have not succeeded. The fostering of non-governmental institutions also remains fairly uneven in its results. Apparently, donor funding for institutional support too, has had very limited results in view of the extensive history of sectoral and institutional reform supported by substantial technical assistance and transfer of resources.

*   The views expressed in this paper are those of the authors alone and should not in any way be associated with the International Monetary Fund.
**   International Monetary Fund.
*** Simon Fraser University.

Among institutions in low-income countries, the structure and make-up of 'professions'—groupings of human capital engaged in education, training, and research—should be expected to play an important role in the development process. However, practitioners and thinkers in the area of institution-building have not paid much attention to the history of professions to see how they are developing, since most skills are developed in the fold of a profession. How does a profession acquire depth? How does it reach self-sustaining growth? These are important questions that may allow us to understand the difficulties with institution-building in low-income countries. It is with this in mind that we have approached the issue of development of the economics profession in Pakistan. This case study offers us a unique perspective to understand the issue of the development of a profession, because, at independence, Pakistan inherited very few trained economists. Since independence, numerous government and donor inspired efforts have been made to develop professional economists and the profession of economics. Our analysis focuses primarily on these efforts to see how a broad-based profession of economics can be developed in Pakistan. This study also has implications for governments, foreign donors, and other groups that seek to catalyze such developments in other low-income countries.

2. INDEPENDENCE TO DISMEMBERMENT OF PAKISTAN (1947–71)

It is common knowledge that at independence in 1947, we did not inherit a large stock of professionals in any field. While the number of professionals in several fields has increased quite significantly, we have not taken stock of professional development in Pakistan. There are no analyses available of any profession to see how we have developed from what we inherited. Such analyses are important to see whether or not the development of professions has been relatively healthy. It is in this spirit that we attempt to develop a history of the economics profession in Pakistan.[1]

At independence, there were hardly any economists in Pakistan. The most prominent of these were Anwar Iqbal Qureshi and M. L. Qureshi. The latter was, in fact, teaching chemistry in Delhi University at the time of partition. But he had obtained an MA in economics privately because of his passing interest in the subject. Independence offered him a new opportunity, and he became the first Chief Economist of the Planning Commission. In the education field, the only well-known economist was S. M. Akhtar who effectively acquired a monoply of the basic college and university textbook market in the 1950s and 1960s.[2] There was no institution involved in applied economics research, except for the Punjab Board of Economic Inquiry and the Agriculture College in Lyallpur. Academic economists (from East and West Pakistan) established the Pakistan Economic Association in 1950, which started to publish its journal, *Pakistan Economic Journal* (PEJ), in the same year and held annual meetings until 1968. Many of the contributors to PEJ were well-known international economists and others were Pakistani academics (mainly from East Pakistan).

A. THE FIRST PUSH

In the first five to six years after independence, two attempts were made to create economists to work mainly in the public sector. At the State Bank of Pakistan, the first governor, Zahid Husain, initiated a programme whereby economists were attracted to the Bank and offered a professional career. Some of them, such as A. S. Minai and Ziauddin Ahmed, were sent overseas for a Ph.D. in economics.[3] As Mahbubul Haq and Moin Baqai (1988) note, 'the first generation of economists in Pakistan was trained in the remarkable tradition of the State Bank of Pakistan'. At the same time, the government also established overseas training scholarships which were used by some economists. Moeen Qureshi and Aziz Ali Mohammed were among those who were trained abroad in this period.[4] However, both of them were attracted away by the International Monetary

Fund (IMF) and, as we all know, they had highly successful careers in the Bretton Woods institutions (IMF and the World Bank). The interesting point is that the country was not able to hold on to them or even attract them back. In fact, this has been a major problem of Pakistani institutions throughout the period.

B. The First Crop

The first main crop of economists was harvested with the advent, in the mid-1950s, of American aid and the involvement of the Harvard Advisory Group (HAG), from the Harvard University Centre for International Affairs, in Pakistan's economy.[5] As is well known, this group virtually designed our economic policy and vision in the Ayub era. They had the strong support of the international aid community. Their vision for Pakistan also included a large infrastructure for the development of economics and economists in Pakistan. Primed by the desire to promote and catalyze rapid economic growth in Pakistan, the HAG thinking (perspective) underlying these institutions was to quickly develop some policy analysis units that could be appended to the government. The framework of the time envisioned an activist government, to be led by the modernizing elite, which had altruistic sentiments and worked only for the good of the population. All that was needed was the economic expertise that could be grafted on to the policy making process.

In line with this thinking, they strengthened the Planning Commission and, with assistance from the Ford Foundation, established the Pakistan Institute of Development Economics (PIDE) in 1957. In the same year, PIDE started publishing its journal, *Economic Digest*, which was replaced by the *Pakistan Development Review* (PDR) in early 1961. The directors of PIDE and editors of *PDR* were Americans until the end of 1965. In early 1966, Nurul Islam became the first Pakistani director of *PIDE* and remained in that position until the PIDE ended its work in Dhaka in 1971. The Planning Commission, State Bank of Pakistan, and PIDE housed some of our most eminent economists in the 1950s and 1960s.

The HAG advisors also arranged to create some economists for the role that they had designed for them. They took back to Harvard several economists from these institutions to study for various degrees. They also arranged for several others to go to other prestigious places such as Princeton and Yale. This period saw many luminaries trained in the United States: Mahbubul Haq (Yale), Mohammed Yaqub (Princeton), Nawab Haider Naqvi (Princeton), and S.M. Naseem (Yale), followed by Jawaid Azfar (Harvard) and Sarfraz Khan Qureshi (Harvard) in the early 1970s. The country developed several visible economists who have continued to loom large in the economics profession in Pakistan.

C. DISTORTED DEVELOPMENT OF THE PROFESSION

The HAG vision was flawed in three major respects and it sowed the seeds of distorted development of the economics profession in Pakistan:

First, it did not attempt to develop an economics profession that was rooted in the country. The HAG economists left the universities and colleges in a state of neglect, using most of the domestic and foreign resources to build the largely non-academic, semi-bureaucratic institutions, and attempted to give these institutions the role of leadership in the profession. Without the seed of the pure profession being nurtured and jealously guarded in academia, the profession was bound to have distorted growth;

Second, the HAG-trained economists were very different from the mainstream economists of the time in the West. The HAG-sponsored training was development-oriented and specific to Pakistan. They were not encouraged to do any theoretical or pioneering research;

Third, given the importance of HAG and the new institutions, and the symbiotic relationship between these institutions and the bureaucratic and political structure of the time in Pakistan, the HAG-trained economists acquired a large and visible role in the economy. These visible economists have not only played an important role in Pakistan's history, but also, by and large, distorted the perception of an economist, the economics profession, and economic policy in Pakistan.

To drive all these ideas home, let us contrast these economists with the Indian economists of the time: first, all major Indian economists (Jagdish Bhagwati, Amartya Sen, T. N. Srinavasan, to name a few) are rooted in their academic institutions, having taught at home and in major universities overseas; second, they have engaged in theoretical and fundamental research, and not just development economics, and have published widely in major academic journals and not just on the Indian economy; and third, they have had limited visibility in the corridors of power in India, other than through their international prominence. Interestingly, the Indian economics profession matured in the 1970s, in the sense that the domestic teaching and research institutions reached a level of self-perpetuation such that its products are internationally recognized.

The implicit proposition here is that had the HAG vision been based on rooting the profession on sound academic lines in academic institutions in the country, perhaps Pakistan would have seen a wholesome development of the profession.

The academic economists in Pakistan started to appear in small number in the 1950s. However, the colleges and universities did not receive large-scale financial and institutional support to create a research-friendly environment. The internal administrative structure in the departments of economics was highly hierarchical, giving almost uncontested power to the senior faculty who had never been exposed to economics research or inquiry. A few who returned from abroad in the late 1950s to the mid-1960s did not survive (e.g., S. A. Abbas in Punjab University) and others resigned themselves to routine teaching.[6] Consequently, there was no economist engaged in serious research in academia. But that is not surprising, given that academia was ignored and its management structure was bureaucratic and, indeed, feudal. Perhaps the only exception to this model was the Department of Economics at the Quaid-i-Azam University which was established in the late 1960s and where a critical mass of foreign-trained economists collected.

But this too did not last long, thanks largely to the in-fighting among the faculty, and the department's progress came to a sad end towards the late 1970s. Since then, its record has not been much better than that of other departments of economics in the country.

D. Ideas Planted by the HAG-Trained Economists

By design, and due to the development thinking of the time, the HAG group was oriented towards intervention, planning, and budget allocation.[7] They mistrusted the market and had the arrogance of presuming to have more information than the market and the rest of society.[8] Because these people had no behavioural relationships in mind and no faith in markets, they did not merely push policy levers and study response lags and dynamics. Instead, they developed lengthy plans or wish lists and used the bureaucratic structures to control the environment to make these plans happen. This control-oriented and market-mistrusting civil service loved the HAG-inspired economic perspective.

This trend culminated in the establishment of the fields of development studies and public administration that, in any case, were closely associated with the generalist education offered to the civil servants in the civil service academy. Edward Mason at Harvard University, who had considerable influence on development studies and the US aid programme, encouraged young Pakistani civil servants and others to acquire training in Public Administration from US universities. The famous Edward Mason programme was set up in Harvard which awarded a Master's degree in Public Administration (MPA) to which promising mid-career bureaucrats were sent and who came back to dominate the economics profession. Because of their bureaucratic associations, Harvard education, and donor backing, these new MPAs were quite important in the economics profession in Pakistan. However, once again, this design inadvertently marginalized academia and universities.[9]

A second element in the thinking of the HAG economists was the increasing concern with poverty and inequality. Haq and Baqai (1986), two important economists of the HAG era, note with concern that 'early writing on economics in Pakistan surprisingly did not contain much reference to poverty-related themes'. It is interesting that most of the early econometric or behavioural research was done mainly by the HAG advisors, whereas the work on measuring poverty and productivity was done by the Pakistani economists. Before much about the economy was understood, poverty and regional inequality indices and the decline in real wages (when the wage data were barely available) were the main areas of concern for the Pakistani economists, as is reflected by articles in the *Pakistan Development Review*.

The manner in which these economists were trained itself created a certain perception among economists in Pakistan. They were trained to be policy-oriented development economists. A sharp distinction was made between such economists and those who studied more theoretical and academic economics. The erroneous impression was unintendedly cultivated that the study of theory or more rigorous economics was of limited use to the country. Such a pursuit was considered a luxury that the country could ill afford. This view has persisted and developed over time and re-inforced the perception that, to be a good economist for Pakistan, a grounding in economic theory is not required and perhaps may even be a hindrance. The result is that there is a tremendous disrespect for academic and theoretical economics. The term 'ivory tower intellectual' has been used to describe anyone who attempts to read and keep abreast of academic economics. Instead, an amalgam of general knowledge and mild development verbiage has been established as sound Pakistani development economics.

E. Fragmentation of the Profession

By the late 1960s and early 1970s, the HAG era was ending and fragmentation in the nascent economics profession was already visible. The lead in the academic field was being taken by Bengali economists whose major interest was to highlight inter-regional inequality and resource transfer. The West Pakistan economists were following the HAG design and were totally enmeshed with the civil service and the political scene in developing annual budgets and Five Year Plans. The Bengali economists were marginalized from this process and preoccupied themselves with laying the ideological and economic foundation for the emerging state of Bangladesh. The separate reports of the Bengali and West Pakistani economists for the *Fourth Five-Year Plan (1970–75)* remain perhaps the most important evidence of the contradictory visions of development in Pakistan.

The State Bank group was frustrated by the relative lack of importance of the Bank and monetary policy and the domination of the Bank by the civil service.[10] The possibility of an independent and professional Bank had apparently become more remote. Indeed, the State Bank of Pakistan never developed a core of economists given to serious research.

3. THE POST-BANGLADESH PERIOD (1972–97)

A. IMPACT OF THE BREAKUP

The academic and research environment for the economics profession in Pakistan started to change in the 1970s in several ways. First, Pakistan's dismemberment in 1971, splitting into what are Pakistan and Bangladesh now, had profound implications for the profession. The main institution for economic research, PIDE, was moved to Dhaka in 1969. Also, the main economists who were running it were Bangladeshis. The result was that the institute was virtually moribund. Second, even the Pakistani economists who remained were induced overseas by a combination of better incentives in international agencies and a feeling of devaluation of professional skills in the Bhutto period which was dominated by the rhetoric of 'Islamic' socialism and nationalization. The visibility that professional economists had acquired in the HAG-Ayub era was lost by now. They had little to contribute to public policy during the 1970s and the Planning Commission lost its earlier importance.

By the early 1970s, the HAG-trained economists had been marginalized by the political movement of Bhutto and the ideas of nationalization and socialism that it endorsed. Later, in the 1970s, the Zia revolution and its Islamization resulted in the civil service taking over and marginalizing the economists further. Pakistan's first crop of economists used their international development contacts to retreat to the international agencies where, as we all know, some of them had sterling careers.

At this stage, the first Pakistani academic economists also emerged and not through the government- or donor-inspired scholarship schemes but through individual career choices. Academics, like Aliuddin Khan, Mahmood Hasan Khan, and Mohsin Saeed Khan started publishing in overseas journals and occupied prestigious positions in universities and international organizations. However, given the dearth of academic institutions, incentives, and academic respectability in Pakistan, all of them have stayed abroad. Efforts to return were thwarted by the local academic bureaucracy which had entrenched itself in the educational and research institutions in the country.

B. INSTITUTIONAL PROLIFERATION

Attempts were made to compensate for these losses by means of some institution-building. The PIDE was re-established in Islamabad in mid-1972 through the efforts of M. L. Qureshi, Moin Baqai, and S. M. Naseem. Two years later, the Applied Economics Research Centre (AERC)—a 'centre of excellence'—was established in the University of Karachi. This eventually paved the way for the establishment of several institutions to ostensibly conduct economic research. These institutions, as they were formed, received substantial financial assistance from the federal government, USAID, and the Ford Foundation. A large number of young professionals from these institutions were sent overseas, particularly to the United States, for the Master's and Ph.D. degree programmes, with financial assistance from one or other donor agency. Some economists from universities were also sponsored to complete MA and Ph.D. degrees under different scholarship programmes.[11]

These institution-building efforts during the 1970s and 1980s have not borne fruit as they were plagued by four principal difficulties.

First, universities were not able to attract or keep the newly foreign-trained economists for lack of a favourable work environment—bureaucratic/feudal management structure, poor research infrastructure (books, journals, computing facilities, etc.)—and low material incentives. Some of these academics moved to public sector organizations, foreign universities, or international organizations.[12] There is not one department of economics in Pakistan today with a credible programme in economics. The academic quality of graduates at the MA level is, by and large, low and quite inferior to a middling BA in any international university. However, this reflects the larger national crisis in post-high school education in Pakistan.

Second, PIDE, which was the supposed leader and model of economic research, was also unable to attract and hold a core group of competent economists. The AERC too, which has made a significant reputation for itself largely through its entrepreneurial director, A. Hafiz Pasha, was unable to retain a significant grouping of economists. PIDE and AERC too, for more or less similar reasons, lost several well-trained economists to public sector institutions, international agencies, or foreign universities in the last decade.[13]

Third, interestingly enough, throughout this period, the fragmentation of the profession mentioned earlier has persisted, reflecting the poor institutional development in Pakistan. Whether the HAG-trained economists, who went overseas, took no interest or were not allowed to work does not matter since the result is the same. The new professionals attempted to contribute, but they were embroiled instead in internal institutional politics rather than professional or institutional development.

Fourth, fragmentation and institutional decline are also evident from the State Bank of Pakistan stopping virtually all its in-house research and publications since the mid-1970s. Moreover, all of the research centres and institutes, including

PIDE and AERC, have largely excluded from their programmes and studies the involvement of faculty from the departments of economics in universities in Karachi, Islamabad, Lahore, Peshawar, and Hyderabad. There is almost no formal joint study and research programme at any of these places. On the contrary, there is unhealthy competition for scarce resources and skills and even mutual resentment and hostility.

If we net out the migration of skilled economists to overseas positions, the supply of quality economists from Pakistan has remained, and continues to remain, quite limited. Notwithstanding the limited skilled resources, the push for creating new 'research' centres and institutes accelerated through the 1980s. During this period, several new centres (institutes) were established: e.g., the Centre for Applied Economics Studies in the University of Peshawar, the Economics Research Centre in the University of Sindh, the Punjab Economics Research Institute (formerly the Punjab Board of Economic Inquiry) in the Government of Punjab Planning Board, the Institute of Development Studies in the Agriculture University in Peshawar, and the Islamic Economics Research Centre in the International Islamic University in Islamabad. The available resources were spread too thin so that no core grouping of professionals has been formed anywhere.

There are several reasons for this mushroom-like growth. The most prominent of these is using new regional or specialized capabilities for economic research as institutional vehicles to attract projects and studies funded by governments and foreign donors. The case of the Islamic Economics Research Centre is somewhat special in that the establishment of the International Islamic University coincided with the policy of 'Islamization' in the Zia era. Several relatively young and promising professional economists were drawn into the teaching of and research on 'Islamic Economics' in the International Islamic University.[14] The other research centres and institutes have so far neither created a favourable environment for academic research nor published any research output.[15] The proliferation of these institutions was also accompanied by an increase in the number of universities in Pakistan. The traditional centres of learning in Pakistan, such as the Punjab University or Government College in Lahore, were meanwhile denuded of funding. The result of all this activity was to reinforce the notion established in the earlier period that the profession of economics was to be nurtured outside the university centres.

C. PROFESSIONAL ASSOCIATIONS: ATTEMPTS AT REDUCING FRAGMENTATION

At the meta-institutional level, an effort was made to revive the Pakistan Economic Association (PEA) in mid-1972, which held its sixteenth—and as it turns out, the last—annual meeting in Islamabad in early 1973. As stated earlier, PEA had held its annual conferences from 1950 to 1968 and maintained its quarterly journal, PEJ, to which papers were contributed by some well-known international scholars and academics. However, after its meeting in 1973, PEA went into a state of inaction from which it has not recovered to this day. The moribund state of PEA and its revival were discussed in several public fora in the late 1970s (University of Karachi) and early 1980s (University of Punjab), but without results. PEA was effectively controlled by senior academic economists, and its last president, Professor Rafiq Ahmed of Punjab University, did not hold the usual annual meeting for a number of years.

As an alternative to the defunct PEA, PIDE established the Pakistan Society of Development Economists (PSDE) in 1983. PSDE was established as an instrument of PIDE for its own purposes and not necessarily for the development of the profession. Its membership was not open. Professional associations normally select the president on the basis of intellectual stature and for a limited tenure, usually a year. An important function of the president is to conduct some key proceedings of the association to further his/her scholarly agenda. That is how a professional association remains alive and is invigorated. Contrary to this standard professional practice, the director of PIDE was also appointed the president of PSDE under its charter. PSDE activities have, therefore, highlighted the personal agenda of the director of PIDE. The annual meetings of PSDE have usually attracted some international economists (funded by foreign assistance from Germany and the PIDE Ford Foundation-established endowment fund) and some Pakistani economists from outside PIDE. But these PSDE meetings are perhaps more distinguished by the prominent Pakistanis that are often excluded from participation.

Considering the chequered life of the PEA and activities of PSDE, it is clear that Pakistani economists have been unable to create a forum that would disseminate economic thought and ideas and subject all to peer review and discussion. Indeed, this failure has been an important reason for the stunted development of the profession. The key challenge for the future is to lay the foundation of a professional association in an environment, where hierarchies and titles are less important than exchange of ideas through open debate, discussion, and critical scrutiny by professional peers.

D. RESEARCH AND JOURNALS

A detailed evaluation of research output from PIDE and AERC—the only major research institutions in the country—in the last fifteen years is hard to make, thanks to the lack of detailed information about their research programmes and research output. However, some meaningful comments can be made on the basis of published articles in PDR and PJAE and occasional papers and reports issued by PIDE and AERC.[16]

The PIDE research programme seems to cover a variety of issues or themes, driven mainly by their 'relevance' to Pakistan, availability of funds, and research staff. The research areas include demography (population and migration), industry (productivity and protection), agriculture (terms of trade, use of inputs, farm productivity), and monetary and fiscal economics (money demand, government spending, inflation). Articles published in the *PDR* are contributed both by the research staff of PIDE and outside contributors. Some of these articles are the products of project or programme-based reports prepared by the PIDE staff for the government and/or international donor organizations. Other articles are of some academic standing, based on doctoral dissertations of the PIDE staff and other contributors. A large volume of the papers published in PDR are presented at the annual meeting of PSDE, for which they are not even internally screened, much less refereed. It is worth noting that a high proportion of the PIDE papers are co-authored, reflecting 'team work', but usually carrying the name of a senior economist in PIDE. The PIDE research agenda does not apparently include many of the micro and macro aspects of the structural adjustment programmes, including distorted markets for products and resources (land, labour, and capital); effects of taxes and subsidies on private sector efficiency, consumption and savings; financial repression; trade liberalization; privatization; fiscal federalism; and regional resource transfer and disparities.

In 1982, AERC started its own biannual journal, *Pakistan Journal of Applied Economics* (PJAE), to publish the results of in-house research and contributions by outsiders. Looking at the issues of PJAE and AERC occasional reports, it seems that much of the in-house research has been driven by contractual project studies completed for governments, public sector agencies, and international donors. The contractual 'research' studies completed by the AERC staff reflect a limited number of areas: crop production, farm credit, local administration, urban growth, education, employment, and fiscal federalism.

Both PIDE and AERC seem to have very little to offer in terms of the topical issues of the day. For example, they have not examined or reviewed the structural adjustment programmes that Pakistan, like so many other low-income countries, has been slipping in or out of since the early 1980s. Also, there are very few examinations of the burning social and economic questions of the time: quality of governance and the declining quality of life in the country. Despite the exhibited vulnerability of the country to repeated supply shocks to its main export, cotton and its products, none of these two institutions has had anything to say on the issue. It seems that expensive projects with dubious payoffs or esoteric value, such as the much heralded 'macroeconomic model' of PIDE, have received extensive patronage without any input from external referees or peer review.

E. ACADEMIC MANAGEMENT AND INCENTIVE STRUCTURE
The major factors affecting the volume and quality of academic research in economics include: the internal management structure, work environment, and the reward system in academia and research institutes. Reflecting the pathology of the larger feudal-bureaucratic social order in Pakistan, the senior management generally follows the national model of centralized power without consultation and participation. A high proportion of the junior research and teaching staff finds itself in a patron-client relationship in which the patron has considerable power to punish and reward individuals. The personalized nature of power breeds mediocrity, since salary, scholarship, and promotion are rarely based on merit and personal achievement. Some of the senior research staff and faculty have achieved their positions through this system and suffer from insecurity.

One indicator of the lack of academic seriousness is that status and title are considered more worthy of merit than publications and the development of academic ideas. For example, a Ph.D. degree has been regarded by many senior academics and professionals as the end of their scholarship and research. They, therefore, set an example that young professionals are expected not to transgress if they want to build their careers.[17] Often, in the academic and teaching institutions, one finds that the volume and quality of research published by the senior research staff are indeed very limited. In addition, it is rare to see the names of Pakistani economists in local universities and research institutes as authors of paper in journals outside Pakistan.

It is worth noting that universities, including departments of economics and centres of excellence (like AERC), have enjoyed a large degree of autonomy in their management since they are not directly governed by federal or provincial governments. They receive their funding through the Universities Grants

Commission (UGC). This, however, does not mean that they are free from government interference, since public sector representatives carry substantial weight in the board of governors and the faculty are also subject to government service rules. As stated earlier, the internal management structures are, by and large, non-participatory and hierarchical. The reward system follows the national model of patronage. Finally, in the early 1970s, academics and professionals misguidedly fought for and received the national grade (and salary) structure followed in the civil service. However, they have not enjoyed the perks and rent-seeking opportunities available to civil servants. The salaries of most academic and professional economists are quite unrelated to their work and needs, leading to increased dependence on 'moonlighting' or the more lucrative private consultancy work.

In terms of management, the case of PIDE is special since it was established as an 'autonomous' entity in the federal government. Its board of directors is chaired by the federal Finance Minister and includes the secretaries of the Ministries of Finance, Economic Affairs, Planning, and Education. Other members of the board are the Governor of the State Bank, the Chairman of UGC, and five members of the Council of Senior Fellows of PIDE. The director of PIDE is ex-officio member of the board. The board chairman enjoys substantial power because of his/her official position. The Council of Senior Fellows, with fifteen members, includes representatives from regional universities and professionals selected by the director of PIDE. In theory, the Council supervises the research, training, publication, and professional functions of PIDE. In reality, the Council members act as 'friends' of PIDE and often rubber stamp the director's programme or agenda.

F. The Funding of 'Research'

There is little funding for economic research in the country. An academic has no way of finding funds for what he/she or his/her peer group might consider interesting or necessary for research. The only funding that is available is that which donors consider necessary for their operations. But then this funding is available to meet the priorities of lenders or donors and not to conform to the needs of the local economist community. The donor agenda in Pakistan, as in many other countries, has not been consistent over time, since it has changed according to the shifting development perspectives of the political elite in the donor countries and senior managers of donor agencies. Thus, donor funding has been unreliable and, dependent largely on the changing priorities and moods of those in power in the donor countries and agencies.

There is a new and somewhat ominous phenomenon retarding serious academic research. Careers in the consultancy industry started to emerge in the early 1980s and this has affected the economics profession in a disastrous way in Pakistan. Consulting on economic issues at the individual and institutional level is clearly associated with the growth of project- and programme-based foreign 'aid' from multilateral (e.g., World Bank and Asian Development Bank) and bilateral (e.g., United States, Japan, the European Union countries, Switzerland, and Canada) donors. Pakistan's dependence on foreign aid and its foreign debt liability have risen significantly in the last fifteen years or so and hence increased the involvement of the multilateral and bilateral donors. A major effect of this involvement of donors and inflow of resources for projects and programmes, mainly in the public sector, has been the growth of demand for local consultants (individual and institutional) as partners with foreign consultants or as independents to produce (feasibility and evaluation) reports on projects and programmes in a large number of sectors and for a large number of government and foreign agencies.

Consultancy has become a profitable industry for professional economists inside and outside universities and research institutes. Given the largely unfavourable environment for academic research in economics and the lucrative monetary gain and social status from consulting services, this industry has drawn the energy and time of almost every academic economist in the country. In fact, most of the so-called research agenda and output of academia and institutes is driven by the demand for studies and reports by donor agencies and government departments or organizations.

Coincidentally, there has been an impressive growth of Non-Governmental Organizations (NGOs) throughout the country, again based largely on foreign resources.[18] The NGOs, working in the economic and social sectors, have been able to attract many economists to work for them. Almost all of this work has no serious academic or research content—in fact, it is anti-intellectual since it wants immediate answers to self-serving propositions or questions—but its pecuniary benefits are generally much higher than in academia and it provides greater exposure to the wheels of power. The economists involved in consulting—and who is not?—have found a symbiotic relationship with the civil bureaucracy in Pakistan and officials of donor agencies. They need each other for their survival and growth. It seems that the economics profession is too well caught in this money-making but non-academic enterprise. Can it be saved from this malaise? It is hard to say at this stage.

CONCLUSION

Today there are very few Pakistani economists who have really seriously published and achieved a modicum of respectability in the academic world. They are to be contrasted with the HAG tradition in Pakistan of acquiring a doctorate and then writing high profile and catchy items for newspapers and magazines in Pakistan. Sadly enough, some younger economists are continuing the old tradition of decrying their own profession by asserting that 'much of it may not be applicable', and that 'theory is only for advanced societies'. Thus the old HAG divide continues!

To gauge the extent of the fragmentation in the profession, we recently conducted two simple investigations in Pakistan.

First, we surveyed the younger professionals to find out what sort of contact they had with their more senior counterparts, especially the first crop of Pakistani economists. The answer was uniformly 'no professional contact'. In addition, many of them also said that, if ever they met, the first crop either patronized them or found some innuendo to deride them (e.g., 'when are you going to get off your ivory tower and do some real work?'). None of them felt comfortable with the contact, noting that the first crop claimed hierarchical privilege and felt very uncomfortable with an equal debate of issues. Pakistani culture also does not help here, for age can often interpret a genuine difference of opinion as rudeness. Such expectations often prevent a dialogue.

Second, in looking at the development of professions and professionals in more advanced societies, we see that much skill transfer takes place through mentoring by senior professionals of junior professionals (apprentices). All the younger economists denied that they had received any mentoring from their more senior professionals. In fact, many of them found the first crop unapproachable. More interestingly, upon searching, we could not find any professionals that the first crop had mentored.

The avalanche of economics consultancy since the early 1980s has exacerbated the plight of the young professional in Pakistan. Pakistani economists, instead of attempting to create their own professional associations, develop peer review and evaluation, and set their own research and policy priorities, are investing their major efforts in finding ways to please donors and to compete, not often and only on the basis of professional competence, for the favour of the donor.

The building of an edifice on weak foundations is extremely difficult. Unfortunately, Pakistan did not inherit a tradition of learning and research. That in and of itself was a difficult obstacle to overcome. But this was capped by the advent of ideas from the donor development experts who did not root the academic profession in the cradle—the academic institutions— that would regenerate it. Instead, they created the visible development economist of Pakistan. These development economists have been seeking a political role and have contributed nothing to the development of the economics profession in Pakistan. They have always displayed an impatience for personal growth and development. It is not surprising that they have missed out on a fundamental truth of theoretical economics that economic development is not mere 'plan allocations' but human skill development. After all, they have no respect for the 'ivory tower' intellectual. The problem of the academic study of economics and the development of economic professionals in Pakistan has become even more serious in recent years in the light of the decline in the standard of education in academia and the growth of the consulting and NGO industries. If only all Pakistani professionals would seek to develop deep and broad professions in their own respective fields, meaningful development can and will occur. Economic development will be the sum total (and maybe even more) of the development of these professions.

REFERENCES

Haq, Mahbubul, and Baqai, Moinuddin (Editors). (1986), *Employment, Distribution and Basic Needs in Pakistan: Essays in Honour of Jawaid Azfar,* Lahore (Pakistan): Progressive Publishers.

Haque, Nadeem ul. (1992), 'Economists and the role of Government', *Pakistan and Gulf Economist.*

Hussain, Akmal. (1988), *Strategic Issues in Pakistan's Economic Policy,* Lahore (Pakistan): Progressive Publishers.

Islam, Nurul. (1981), *Foreign Trade and Economic Controls in Development: The Case of United Pakistan,* New Haven: Yale University Press.

Kardar, Shahid. (1987), *Political Economy of Pakistan,* Lahore (Pakistan): Progressive Publishers.

Naqvi, Zafar J. (1988), *Directory of Pakistani Economists and Demographers,* Islamabad: PIDE.

Pakistan Development Review, various issues.

Pakistan Institute of Development Economics. (1993), *Pakistan Institute of Development Economics: An Introduction,* Islamabad: PIDE.

———. (1993), *PIDE's Research Programme for 1993–1996,* Islamabad: PIDE.

Pakistan Journal of Applied Economics, various issues.

Samad, Abdus. (1993), *Governance, Economic Policy, and Reform in Pakistan,* Lahore (Pakistan): Vanguard Books.

Siddiqui, Akhtar H. *The Economy of Pakistan: A Select Bibliography,* PIDE: 1947–62; 1963–5; and 1973–85.

NOTES

1. The analytical framework that is developed here as well as some of the analysis presented are perhaps more broadly applicable to most professional development in Pakistan. It is the fervent hope of the authors that some effort will be put into the study of professions in Pakistan. Perhaps some donors might take an interest in this neglected area at some point.

2. Other academic economists of the time were Q.M. Farid (Karachi), Ahmed Mukhtar (Peshawar), and M. Rashid (Lahore).

3. Although for the sake of completeness we have cited names, we do not claim to be exhaustive. We apologize to any one to whom credit has not been duly extended. Also, we hasten to add that we have tried to use all resources available to us, but note that this project has been done purely for the love of inquiry. Considering the importance of this study (project), we would welcome all suggestions and help to complete the process.

4. The thinness of the profession is so evident from the fact that the economists of each period can be cited in a study such as this.

5. The term Harvard Advisory Group (HAG) has been used loosely in view of the fact that this group came to dominate economic policy and thinking in the country. In the early period, there were a number of U.S. universities and funding agencies (Ford Foundation in particular) working with Pakistan institutions.

6. For example, Ehsan Rashid, Ashfaq Kadri, and A. Sarwar Rizvi in Karachi; Mohammad Rafiq in Punjab; Elias Abro and Amjad Ali Beg in Sindh; and Abdul Mateen, Mian M. Nazeer, and Nurul Islam in Peshawar.

7. It is interesting to note that Haq and Baqai (1988) point to the 'widening in the choice of subjects in research' in the 1960s and 1970s. Their choices include: 'analysis of planning expertise'; 'powerful question of regional disparity'; 'question of dual exchange rate'; 'effective protection'; 'type of industrialization'; and the 'effect of the tube wells on agriculture'. They also note, somewhat disparagingly, that the 'focus of economic literature in the fifties was on monetary analysis, fiscal policy, deficit financing, and inflation'. These statements illustrate our point that the issues of concern to the development economist in the 1960s and 1970s were interventionist and distributional and not those dealing with macroeconomic stability backed by a market-oriented regime.

8. *See* Hussain (1988), who argues that 'the logic of planning is that the existing set of world prices is not an appropriate indicator of resource allocation', and concludes that the 'sixth five year plan constitutes an abandonment of...planning in the strictest sense of the term...since it adopts world prices and comparative advantage as a basis for the abandonment of national economic planning'.

9. Some of the prominent Edward Mason Fellows are Shahid Husain and Shahid Javed Burki.

10. In the opinion of Haq and Baqai (1988), the State Bank economist is indicative of the HAG's view presented earlier. In the 1970s and 1980s, an economist was supposed to be preoccupied with poverty and distribution and not with the macroeconomic policy necessary for the efficient working of the economy.

11. One difference from the earlier training programmes was that the trainees now were not guaranteed a place in a prestigious university but had to seek admission on their own merits.

12. For example, Rashid Amjad and Naved Hamid (Punjab University), S.M. Naseem, Ijaz Nabi, and Aly Arsalan (Quaid-i-Azam University), Shahid Alam, Farrukh Iqbal, Eshya Mujahid, Hanid Mukhtar, and Shahid Zahid (University of Karachi).

13. For example, Nadeem ul Haque, M. Zubair Khan,Shahrukh Rafi Khan, Abdul Salam, Mohammad Irfan, Nadeem Burney, and A.R. Kemal from PIDE, and Shahid Zahid, Hafiz Sheikh, Aly Arsalan, Eshya Mujahid, and Hanid Mukhtar from AERC. There are still about twelve economists in PIDE and four in AERC with a Ph.D. degree.

14. For example, these include M. Fahim Khan, Munawar Iqbal, Faiz Mohammad, Rauf Azhar, and Syed Tahir, all of whom had received their Ph.Ds. in Canada and the United States. The first three left the International Islamic University to work in the Islamic Development Bank, Saudi Arabia.

15. Samad (1993) argues that the underlying purpose of this proliferation of institutions is merely to satisfy rent-seeking demands. They are a means of allocating the donor and budgetary funds to political or other favourites of the day.

16. PJAE and PDR are the main economic journals in Pakistan. Like the proliferation of 'research' centres or institutes, a number of in-house journals, periodicals, and magazines of uneven quality are issued by small colleges and departments of economics. They usually reflect vanity publication efforts. Also, economic journalism in Pakistan has increased, but it is still weak and uneven in quality. Perhaps only one weekly magazine, *Pakistan and Gulf Economist*, has achieved a respectable status in recent years.

17. In fact, a larger social problem in Pakistan, especially among the 'intellectual' (technocratic) elite, is that a Ph.D. degree grants the individual the right to prefix 'Dr' to his/her name; which simply acts as a status symbol and confers membership to an exclusive club.

18. The question about whether an appropriate domestic research or policy agenda can be formulated when the local academics and professionals depend so much on donor funds is open to investigation. *See* Samad (1993).

INDEX

A

adhocism, 68, 69, 70
Adjustment with a Human Face, 7
AERC, 478, 479, 480, 482, 483
Afghan jihad, 71, 72
Agricultural Census, 386, 387
Agricultural Development Finance Corporation (ADFC), 113
Agriculture Credit Programme (ACP), 403, 405
Agriculture Development Bank of Pakistan (ADBP), 114, 115, 403, 405, 486
Agricultural Enquiry Commission, 137
Agriculture, investments, 11, 116, 117, 118, 119; inputs, 107; output, 98, 100, 101, 143; production, 97, 98, 99, 100, 101, 102, 103, 104, 105, 106, 107, 140, 388; problems, 11; public policies, 116, 117, 118, 119; sector growth, 76, 98, 99, 100, 143, 251, 252, 253; sources of growth, 107; stagnation, 63, 142; technical progress, 108, 112; transformation, 97, 98; value, 103
Agrarian regions, 286, 287, 288, 289
Agrarian structure, 97, 98, 109, 116, 121, 141
Aligarh, 55, 57, 62
Ali, Maulana Muhammad, 55
Annual credit budgeting, 67, 72, 74
Asian Development Bank (ADB), 135
Awami League, 67

B

Baghdad Pact, 63
Balochistan, 11, 109, 119, 131, 134, 135, 379
Bangladesh, 13, 82, 176, 177, 182, 183, 185, 334, 369, 371, 372, 378, 477
Banking, 219, 220; trends in, 220, 221, 222, 223, 224, 225, 226; nationalization of, 222, 223, 224; pre-nationalization, 221, 222; post-nationalization, 222, 223, 224

Basic Democracy System, 67
Bhutto, Benazir, 6, 72, 73, 214, 215
Bhutto, Zulfikar Ali, 6, 33, 68, 70
'Big Push' theory, 5
Black marketing, 65
Black economy, 81
'blue chips', 80
Bond market, 232, 233
Bretten Woods institutions, 10, 416, 456, 472
Budget deficit, 73, 74, 202

C

Capital accumulation, 54, 217, 327; investment, 5, 217, 218, 219; mobilization, 219, 231; productivity, 152
Central Board of Revenue, 202
China, 185, 372, 439
Citibank, 80
Climate, 439, 440
Colonial re-integration, 79, 80, 81
Consumption, 51
Cotton, 104, 105, 108, 143
Credit, 220, 221, 225, 234
Crops, major, 101, 103, 104, 105, 108; minor, 101; yield, 105
Currency management, 13

D

Dawat-e-Islami, 83
Deficit financing, 219
Defeminization, 81, 82
De-industrialization, 10, 74, 76, 77
Denationalization, 16, 218
Deregulation, 6
Devaluation, 80, 154, 186, 206
Development Finance Industries (DFI), 16, 71, 78, 79, 157, 226, 227